Capital, Power, and Inequality in Latin America and the Caribbean

New Edition

Edited by
Richard L. Harris and Jorge Nef

ROWMAN & LITTLEFIELD PUBLISHERS, INC.
Lanham • Boulder • New York • Toronto • Plymouth, UK

100555 2020

ROWMAN & LITTLEFIELD PUBLISHERS, INC.

Published in the United States of America
by Rowman & Littlefield Publishers, Inc.
A wholly owned subsidiary of The Rowman & Littlefield Publishing Group, Inc.
4501 Forbes Boulevard, Suite 200, Lanham, Maryland 20706
www.rowmanlittlefield.com

Estover Road, Plymouth PL6 7PY, United Kingdom

British Library Cataloguing in Publication Information Available

Library of Congress Cataloging-in-Publication Data
Capital, power, and inequality in Latin America and the Caribbean / edited by
Richard L. Harris and Jorge Nef. — New edition.
    p. cm. — (Critical currents in Latin American perspective)
  Includes bibliographical references and index.
  ISBN-13: 978-0-7425-5523-5 (cloth : alk. paper)
  ISBN-10: 0-7425-5523-2 (cloth : alk. paper)
  ISBN-13: 978-0-7425-5524-2 (pbk. : alk. paper)
  ISBN-10: 0-7425-5524-0 (pbk. : alk. paper)
  1. Latin America—Economic conditions—1982- 2. Latin America—Social
conditions—1982- 3. Latin America—Politics and government—1980- 4. Power
(Social sciences)—Latin America. 5. Equality—Latin America. I. Harris, Richard L.
(Richard Legé), 1939- II. Nef, Jorge.
  HC125.C32 2008
  330.98—dc22

                                                                      2007033030

Printed in the United States of America

♾™ The paper used in this publication meets the minimum requirements of
American National Standard for Information Sciences—Permanence of Paper
for Printed Library Materials, ANSI/NISO Z39.48-1992.

Capital, Power, and Inequality in Latin America and the Caribbean

Critical Currents in Latin American Perspective

Ronald H. Chilcote, Series Editor

The Catholic Church and Power Politics in Latin America: The Dominican Case in Comparative Perspective
Emelio Betances

The Prophet and Power: Jean-Bertrand Aristide, the International Community, and Haiti
Alex Dupuy

The Marxism of Che Guevara: Philosophy, Economics, Revolutionary Warfare,
Second Edition
Michael Löwy

Democracy: Government of the People or Government of the Politicians?
José Nun

Cardoso's Brazil: A Land for Sale
James Petras and Henry Veltmeyer

People's Power: Cuba's Experience with Representative Government, Updated
Edition
Peter Roman

Contents

Please see the book's website for additional materials:
http://www.rowmanlittlefield.com/isbn/0742555240

Acknowledgments

The editors wish to acknowledge Sandor Halebsky, the founding father of the first edition of this book. It was his vision, inspiration, and dedication that gave life to this collective endeavor in its original version. Without you, Sandy, this book would never have been published in its original version or this new edition. We also wish to express our deepest gratitude to Ronald Chilcote, the editor of the Critical Currents in Latin American Perspective Series for Rowman & Littlefield, as well as the editor of the series in which the first edition of this book was published in 1995. His support, guidance, editorial suggestions, and friendship over the years have been invaluable and were indispensable in bringing both the original and this new version of the book into print. In addition, we wish to thank Rowman & Littlefield's editorial and marketing staff, particularly associate editor Jessica Gribble, for their faith in this project, their support, and their assistance. Finally, we wish to acknowledge our deep and enduring reverence for the Americas (the people, flora, fauna, and physical geography of this magnificent region of the planet). This printed product of our collective intellectual labor was conceived, written, and edited with ineffable reverence for the Americas and the readers of this book.

Acknowledgment of Support

The publication of this collection of essays would not have been possible without the invaluable support of the Institute for the Study of Latin America and the Caribbean (ISLAC) at the University of South Florida. ISLAC provides support and encouragement for interdisciplinary research and teaching on Latin America and the Caribbean. Its support of this collection of essays reflects the mission of the institute, which is to foment and facilitate research and the dissemination of knowledge and dialogue about these two regions of the Americas among faculty, students, and interested publics at the state, national, and international levels. The focus of this collection, like that of ISLAC, is on Latin America and the Caribbean within the larger context of the Americas. This focus is based on the premise that Latin America and the Caribbean are interconnected with Canada and the United States and that they share multicultural societies composed of the descendants of the indigenous peoples of the Western Hemisphere and the Europeans, Africans, and Asians who have come to this hemisphere over the last five centuries. The editors wish to express their deep appreciation for the continuing encouragement and support they received for the publication of this volume from ISLAC and the University of South Florida.

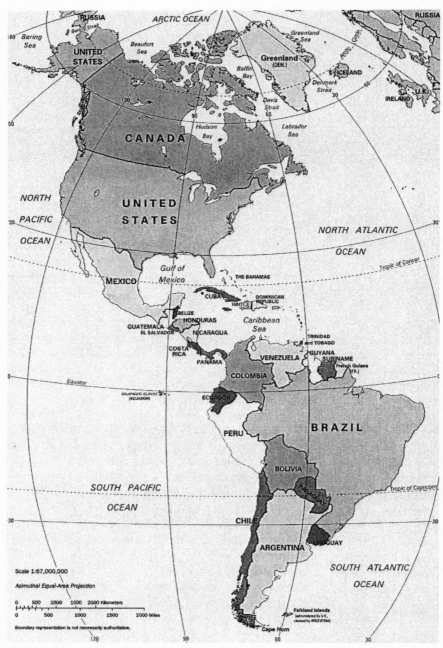

The Americas. *Source:* Central Intelligence Agency map, courtesy of the University of Texas Libraries, University of Texas, Austin.

Latin America and the Caribbean. *Source:* Central Intelligence Agency map, courtesy of the University of Texas Libraries, University of Texas, Austin.

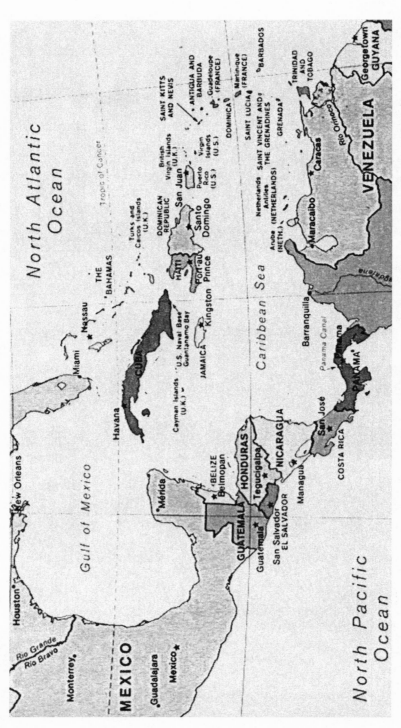

Central America and the Caribbean. *Source:* Central Intelligence Agency map, courtesy of the University of Texas Libraries, University of Texas, Austin.

Preface

Richard L. Harris and Jorge Nef

In eleven original, comparative essays, this volume offers the reader a comprehensive and integrated analysis of contemporary political, economic, and social conditions in Latin America and the Caribbean. Since the region has become increasingly integrated into the expanding global capitalist system, the focus of this book includes a critical examination not only of the major structures, processes, forces, and conditions in the countries of Latin America and the Caribbean basin but also the structures, processes, forces, and ideologies that have hemispheric and even global significance.

While the center of our interest is primarily contemporary Latin American and Caribbean affairs, the contextual scope of our analysis is much broader. The various chapters in this volume describe and analyze both the historical and international context of the contemporary transformations taking place in Latin America and the Caribbean basin. They examine the rural and urban areas, the economies and trading relations, the political structures and state policies, the social ecology, and the wide array of social movements that characterize the societies in this important region of the world. They also describe and analyze the major institutions and forces that have shaped, and are shaping, the course of economic, political, social, and cultural development in the region. There are chapters on the changing conditions of women, on the political and social influence of religion and religious organizations, on the indigenous peoples and their struggles, on contemporary health and environmental issues, on the hegemonic role played by the United States in the region's affairs, on the regional integration of the Americas, and on the region's role in the global capitalist system.

The various chapters identify and examine the relationships between basic structures and processes, past and current developments, the effects of historical legacies on contemporary realities, and the effects of international and transnational forces on national and local conditions. The critical perspectives provided by the authors do not examine contemporary conditions in the region with indifference and amoral detachment; they critically reveal the nature of the exploitative relationships, the environmental devastation, the extreme social inequalities, the elitist political regimes, the widespread poverty, and the relations of dominance and dependence that predominate throughout the Western Hemisphere. Their critical perspectives also enable readers to examine the contradictions, the dynamic forces of change in the region, and the extent to which individuals, organized groups, communities, and social movements have succeeded in transforming their immediate circumstances, as well as the surrounding political, economic, and social conditions. Thus, this volume offers the reader a critical inquiry into the forces of continuity and change in contemporary Latin America, the Caribbean, and the Americas as a whole. It also provides a vision of the prospects for progressive change and the elimination of the various forms of exploitation, domination, injustice, and discrimination that prevail in this region of the world.

Each chapter provides both an analysis and a synthesis of the most significant and distinct aspects of contemporary Latin American and Caribbean affairs. Some of the chapters also address certain basic conditions and patterns that, to varying degrees, are common to all of the countries of the Americas (i.e., North, Central, and South America, as well as the Caribbean islands). These common patterns include certain exploitative economic structures and relations of dominance; similar economic, political, and social inequalities; various types of cultural and ethnic discrimination; and unresponsive, authoritarian, and elite-dominated political structures.

Chapter 1 provides a general overview of the main themes examined throughout the volume and a comparative framework for comprehending the broader context and interrelationship of these themes. It provides a comparative, historical, and critical perspective on the major forces of continuity and change in the Americas. This introductory chapter highlights the historical context, major social structures, and economic processes that have shaped the past and current development of all the societies in the Western Hemisphere. It provides a broadly comparative analysis of the political economy of the countries in this important region of the world. This analysis reveals the basic relations and forces of production, the major power structures and processes, and the social forces that have shaped the development of the Latin American and Caribbean societies, as well as the social inequalities and injustices that mark them.

Chapter 2, by Cristóbal Kay, focuses on the rural sector of the contemporary societies of Latin America and the Caribbean. This important sector of the Latin American and Caribbean societies has historically been the foundational cornerstone of their economic, political, and social life. Therefore, it is appropriate that following the introductory overview of the region contained in the first chapter, the next chapter should focus on the rural domain and the rapid process of capitalist modernization that has taken place in this sector during recent decades. Chapter 3, by Richard L. Harris, complements Kay's analysis by exploring the structural characteristics of the larger political economy of dependency, underdevelopment, and globalization in the region. Taken together, these two chapters provide the reader with a broad analysis of the basic contours of contemporary economic and social life in the region, and they set the stage for the remaining chapters in the book.

Chapters 4 and 5 focus on contemporary political, economic, and social conditions that are touched upon or implied in the analyses contained in the first three chapters. Thus, chapter 4, by Viviana Patroni, examines the social and political conditions of the working classes in the region, concentrating its analysis on the effects of neoliberal government policies on the working class and on labor organizations in particular. It also discusses the future prospects of the working-class and labor organizations by exploring contemporary issues and trends that will have a direct impact on their destiny.

Chapter 5, by Jorge Nef, focuses on contemporary political conditions in Latin America. It provides a long-run and systemic perspective. This chapter concentrates especially on the demilitarization, normalization, and redemocratization of the political systems in the region and the transition from national security regimes to civilian rule that started in the 1980s and still continues in the region. Nef relates these political conditions to the surrounding economic and social context and discusses the prospects for greater political democratization in the region in view of recent developments and past experiences.

The next four chapters focus on social forces and popular responses to prevailing economic and social conditions in the region. Thus, chapter 6, by Judith Adler Hellman, provides a general overview and analysis of the wide variety of social movements that have appeared in the region, as well as the conditions that have given rise to these movements and their relations with other institutions and organizations. Chapter 7, by Francesca Miller, studies the changing social, political, and economic roles of women in Latin America and the Caribbean, giving particular emphasis to the development of women's organizations and movements.

Chapter 8, by Michael Kearney and Stefano Varese, examines Latin America's indigenous peoples and their historical and contemporary efforts to promote their economic, political, and social interests through their own movements and community organizations. Chapter 9, by Wilder Robles, offers a comparative analysis of the role of religion in the region and the relationship between religion and the popular social and political organizations that have been created by either the clergy or laity to address contemporary economic, social, and political conditions.

Chapter 10, by Guido Pascual Galafassi, addresses the social, economic, and political aspects of the growing ecological crisis in the region and the popular movements that have arisen around environmental issues.

Chapter 11, by Richard L. Harris and Jorge Nef, widens the focus to analyze the contemporary global context of the structures, conditions, and forces analyzed in the previous chapters. It examines inter-American relations and the integration of the Latin American and Caribbean countries into the larger global capitalist system and its evolving transnational economic, political, and social relations.

In addition to these chapters in the book, a chapter on health security and insecurity in the Americas has been placed on the book's website at www.rowmanlittlefield.com/isbn/0742555240. This chapter by Jorge Nef, Richard L. Harris, and Melinda Seid focuses on the health conditions and the various actors and interests in the health-care sector of the Latin American and Caribbean societies.

There is an intentional logical flow and sequence to the chapters, with the first and last chapters providing an integrative framework for the themes taken up in the other chapters of the collection. Throughout the book, the contributors analyze the most important aspects of contemporary Latin American and Caribbean affairs through the use of a comparative, historical, and critical approach. This perspective provides the reader with a comprehensive view of the region as a whole and reveals both the major similarities and the most important differences between the different societies in the region. The critical analytical perspective provided by all the authors reveals not only the prevailing conditions in these societies but their problems, dilemmas, injustices, failures, and social ills, as well as the aspirations of their peoples for a better life and the forces capable of bringing about socially progressive and ecologically sustainable improvements in these societies.

1

Capital, Power, and Inequality in Latin America and the Caribbean

Richard L. Harris and Jorge Nef

Almost three decades ago, two Latin American social scientists, Fernando Henrique Cardoso and Enzo Faletto, produced what has since become a classic analysis of the economic, political, and social development of Latin America. In the preface to the English edition of this much-acclaimed book, Cardoso and Faletto (1979) state their perspective quite eloquently:

> We seek a global and dynamic understanding of social structures instead of looking only at specific dimensions of the social process. We oppose the academic tradition which conceived of domination and socio-cultural relations as "dimensions," analytically independent of one another, and together independent of the economy, as if each one of these dimensions corresponded to separate spheres of reality. In that sense, we stress the socio-political nature of the economic relations of production, thus following the nineteenth-century tradition of treating economy as political economy. This methodological approach, which found its highest expression in Marx, assumes the hierarchy that exists in society is the result of established ways of organizing the production of material and spiritual life. This hierarchy also serves to assure the unequal appropriation of nature and of the results of human work by social classes and groups. (ix)

The present volume of comparative essays on contemporary Latin America and the Caribbean follows in the same intellectual tradition as that of Cardoso and Faletto. Over the last four decades, many other scholars have used a similar perspective to study the prevailing conditions and historical development of the region.

To analyze and make sense of the many complex and changing conditions shared in whole or in part by the societies that make up the Latin American and Caribbean region, we believe it is necessary to use a complex dependency perspective (Nef 1986) similar to the one used by Cardoso and Faletto. Moreover, we also think that this kind of analysis makes much more sense if we break away from the conventional "up here" versus "down there" perspective that conceives of two parallel and utterly different Americas: the normal, "functional," and developed North America and the anomalous, "dysfunctional," and underdeveloped Latin America to the south. We propose that the two realities are an integral part of an underlying whole. In this integrated system, development and underdevelopment are dialectically related, not as part of an abstract and mechanical system of international stratification but as concrete economic, social, and political structures of domination and resistance, exclusion and inclusion, and dependence and interdependence.

In order to provide an integrative framework that encompasses the various conditions analyzed by the contributors to this volume, we have selected three key organizing concepts that permit an integrated conceptualization of the underlying structures, processes, and relations responsible for the conditions that characterize the region. These three concepts are capital, power, and inequality.

These three concepts share in common certain important analytical qualities: they are multidimensional, multilevel, comprehensive, and integrative. They are theoretically powerful concepts that facilitate a comparative analysis of the many complex, dynamic, and interdependent societal structures, processes, and relations underlying contemporary inter-American affairs. They are also compatible with the tradition of comparative, structural, historical, interdisciplinary, and critical analysis that this volume takes as its inheritance.

In this regard, it is worth noting the justification that Cardoso and Faletto (1979) give for the importance they assign to the use of the key concept of capital in their analysis of Latin America's dependent development in the 1970s:

First of all, it is necessary to propose concepts able to explain trends of change. This implies the recognition of opposing forces which drag history ahead. Second, it is necessary to relate these forces in a global way, characterizing the basic sources of their existence, continuity and change, by determining forms of domination and the forces opposed to them. So, without the concept of capital as the result of the exploitation of one class by another, it is not possible to explain the movement of capitalist society. . . . It is through the elaboration of key concepts of that type that dialectical analyses explain historical movement in its "totality." That is to say: history becomes understandable when interpretations propose categories strong enough to render clear the fundamental relations that sustain and those that oppose a given structural situation in its globality. (xiii)

We use the concept of capital in a similar, classical manner as Cardoso and Faletto to draw attention to the inequitable manner in which wealth is accumulated in the Americas through exploitative relations of production and exchange that are particular to capitalism. Like Cardoso and Faletto, and the many others who have contributed to the intellectual tradition that this volume follows, we have chosen this powerful concept because it reveals the fundamental relations of exploitation underlying contemporary conditions in the region, as well as elsewhere in the world.

Power and inequality have the same conceptual and analytical properties that Cardoso and Faletto attribute to the concept of capital. These concepts focus the analysis on many of the fundamental relations, structures, and processes that underlie the contemporary conditions of human existence in the existing world order. Applied broadly to the study of social phenomena in Latin America and the Caribbean (and the Americas as a whole), the concept of power encompasses all those conditions and circumstances involving subordination and domination, force and coercion, and hegemony, empowerment, and emancipation. Thus, the application of the concept in this volume is not confined to what can be narrowly construed as merely "political" (state-centered) relations; rather, it encompasses all situations involving subordination and empowerment, as well as the use of force, ideology, and emancipation in the hemisphere. For example, it applies to the subordination of women within the paternalistic structures of Latin American society, the coercive influence that international organizations such as the International Monetary Fund (IMF) and the transnational corporations exercise over the national governments, the use of force by military and revolutionary organizations, and the empowerment of communities and social groups that organize themselves to promote their interests.

In a similar manner, the concept of inequality focuses attention on all the various forms of social inequity, injustice, and discrimination that exist in the region. Thus, at the microlevel, this concept applies to gender inequalities within the family unit; at the mid-level it encompasses racial and cultural discrimination, as well as the unequal access of different categories of the population to the basic necessities of human existence; and at the macro or global level, the concept encompasses the unequal terms of trade that exist between the Latin American and Caribbean countries and the United States. In fact, because social, economic, and political disparities are so ubiquitous, extreme, and widening throughout the Americas, it is possible to argue that inequality should be the main *explanandum* (i.e., focus of explanation) of any intellectual effort that seeks to account for the historical development and contemporary conditions of the Latin American and

Caribbean societies (Schuurman 1993, 30–31). It can shed some light in explaining similar circumstances in the North.

A serious attempt to explain, as well as understand, the extreme inequalities that characterize the societies in the Americas requires an examination of the relations of exploitation and power that foster and sustain these inequalities. Thus, an analysis of the conditions of inequality in the region inevitably requires a critical examination of the exploitative relations of capitalist production and distribution, the hierarchical structures of power and forms of coercion, and the networks of political and social influence that predominate in these societies. Cardoso and Faletto (1979) note the critical importance of the interdependent linkages between these social phenomena:

> Our approach of course assumes and demonstrates that in the kind of societies for which this mode of analysis is useful, the structures are based neither on egalitarian relationships nor on collaborative patterns of social organization. On the contrary, they are founded on social asymmetries and on exploitative types of social organization. Furthermore, it is assumed that an understanding of the strong inequalities characterizing these social structures, as well as an explanation of the exploitative process through which these structures are maintained, requires an analysis of the system of production and the institutions of appropriation, that is, the socio-economic base of society. Finally, in the approach here proposed, a central role is assigned to the analysis of the mechanisms and processes of domination through which existing structures are maintained. (x)

In analyzing "the system of production and institutions of appropriation" in Latin America, Cardoso and Faletto link "the strong inequalities" and "processes of domination" to the extremely exploitative and inequitable character of capitalist relations of production, distribution, and accumulation in the region. Thus, the interdependent linkages that exist between different types of social phenomena can only be revealed if the concepts of capital, power, and inequality are applied in unison.

The authors of the chapters in this volume use a wide variety of concepts to analyze and explain the specific conditions of contemporary Latin American affairs that fall within the focus of their comparative essays. The extensive variety of conditions and issues analyzed here require the use of numerous concepts and different approaches. However, the content of the analyses in all the chapters can be organized and integrated by using the concepts of capital, power, and inequality. These key concepts encompass all the conditions analyzed in this volume, focus attention on the linkages between these conditions, and reveal the underlying factors that tie them together.

HISTORICAL OVERVIEW OF THE
CAPITALIST DEVELOPMENT OF THE AMERICAS

The incorporation of the Americas into the world capitalist system has its origins in the European conquest and colonization of the Western Hemisphere during the sixteenth and seventeenth centuries. This aspect of the historical development of Latin America and the Caribbean has been discussed in the works of Chilcote and Edelstein (1986), Frank (1967), Bambirra (1972), Stein and Stein (1970), Marini (1974), Robinson (1996), and Cardoso and Faletto (1979).

It was during the germinal phase of capitalism that the embryonic development in Europe of mercantile capitalism, as well as the nation-state system and the expanding scope of the Roman Catholic Church (Robertson 1992, 57–60), gave impetus to the European conquest and colonization of the lands and indigenous inhabitants of the Western Hemisphere (as well as many other parts of the world). Thus, the inclusion of the Americas into the world capitalist system can be traced back to the sixteenth and seventeenth centuries when the Spanish, Portuguese, British, French, and Dutch set about bringing the so-called New World under their "civilizing" control (Stein and Stein 1970).

This phase of capitalism was largely propelled by European imperialism and was followed by what Robertson (1992) has called the "incipient phase" of globalization, which extended from the mid-eighteenth century to the 1870s. During this period, classical "liberal" thinking in Europe about capitalism, the nation-state, citizenship, nationalism, and "free trade" took hold in the Americas. Combined with the expansion of British imperialism and the industrial revolution, these developments gave rise to pressures upon and within the Spanish and Portuguese colonies for national independence and unrestricted trade with Great Britain and other trading states, contributing to the wars of independence that led to the disintegration of the Spanish colonial empire in the Americas, as well as British colonial rule in North America. These incipient forces of nationalism and capitalism led to the formation of the United States and the new states in Latin America and the Caribbean (see Cardoso and Faletto 1979; Frank 1967; Stein and Stein 1970; Chilcote and Edelstein 1986).

Between the 1870s and the mid-1920s, the globalizing forces that emerged in the earlier periods, such as industrial capitalism, imperialism, economic liberalism, and the conflicts between the major capitalist states for overseas markets and resources, gave rise to an unprecedented expansion of world trade and also to World War I. This period saw the inclusion of non-European states (e.g., Japan, China, and Turkey) in the evolving world capitalist system, the spread of international communications, and the formation of what Robertson (1992) has called a single "international society" (59). During the first part of this period, the development of the Latin American and Caribbean states was shaped by the hegemonic influence of Great Britain and, during the latter part, by the new hegemony of the United States as it extended its sphere of economic and political influence throughout the Western Hemisphere and the Pacific Rim (see Cardoso and Faletto 1979; Frank 1967; Stein and Stein 1970).

The neocolonial, export-oriented economies of the Latin American and Caribbean countries were integrated during this period (1870s–1920s) into the expanding world capitalist system to meet the needs of the major capitalist states at the center, or core, of this system, particularly their need for the natural resources and markets in the expanding periphery of the system. The landed oligarchy in most of the Latin American and Caribbean countries dominated the political regimes in these peripheral capitalist societies during most of this period. However, toward the end of this period, more "modernizing" capitalist elements within the urban upper and middle classes began to play an increasingly important role in the political and economic life of most of these countries. These elements were often closely associated with foreign investors, companies, and government officials—first, largely from Great Britain and other European powers, then increasingly from the United States.

From the late 1920s through the 1960s, the globalization of capitalism entered a new phase characterized by conflict between the competing centers of the world capitalist system over their respective spheres of influence, hegemony, and colonial domination. This period includes the Great Depression of the 1930s, World War II, and the Cold War. It involved confrontations between the Western liberal democracies and the fascist regimes of Germany, Italy, and Japan prior to and during World War II and between the Western capitalist states and the Soviet Union, People's Republic of China, and other state capitalist or self-proclaimed Socialist countries during the Cold War. The latter part of this period was also characterized by anti-imperialist struggles for national political and economic independence in the remaining European colonies and the neocolonial countries of the Third World (see Amin 1984).

Between the 1930s and 1960s, modernizing "national populist" regimes were established throughout Latin America and the Caribbean to promote the national industrial development of the societies in this region. These political regimes were based on a political alliance between the more urban sectors of the upper, middle, and working classes, often joined by foreign capital. This alliance supported state intervention in the economy to promote the industrial development of these countries (see Cardoso and Faletto 1979, 127–48). These regimes adopted a strategy of import-substitution industrialization with the goal of substituting locally manufactured goods for products imported from the major capitalist countries, which were preoccupied for most of this period with the Great Depression and World War II.

At the end of this period, the successful popular revolution in Cuba led to the installation of a revolutionary Socialist regime in that country. This regime subsequently nationalized most sectors of the Cuban economy (including U.S.-owned companies and agricultural estates), successfully resisted the efforts of the U.S. government and Cuban counterrevolutionary exiles to overthrow it, and entered into a close military, diplomatic, and economic alliance with the Soviet Union. The revolutionary and anti-imperialist example set by the self-proclaimed Socialist regime in Cuba inspired revolutionary Socialist movements throughout Latin America and other parts of the Third World during the 1960s and the 1970s (see Horowitz, de Castro, and Gerassi 1970).

The economic recovery after the end of World War II produced a great increase in world trade and an economic boom in the United States, Western Europe, and Japan. As a result, many of the larger corporations based in these countries expanded their investments in, and influence and control over, the more developed sectors of the Latin American and Caribbean economies. Toward the end of this period, these corporations also began to transform the structure of the world capitalist system in accordance with their new and expanding transnational interests (see Amin 1984; Evans 1979; Dos Santos 1970; Marini 1974).

During this period lasting from the late 1920s through the 1960s, the United States consolidated its hegemony over Latin America through various means (see Aguilar 1965; Pearce 1983). In the late 1920s and early 1930s, the United States used explicitly imperialist measures, or "gunboat diplomacy," particularly in the so-called banana republics of Central America and the Caribbean. This period of gunboat diplomacy was followed by the more informal hegemonic tactics of the Franklin D. Roosevelt administration's "Good Neighbor Policy" in the mid-1930s and 1940s. Thereafter, the U.S. government resorted to what became known as "dollar diplomacy" in the 1950s and the so-called Alliance for Progress in the 1960s (Nef and Nuñez 1994). In conjunction with the provision of foreign aid and economic assistance, the U.S. government used military interventions (e.g., the Dominican Republic in 1965) and more covert measures to topple populist governments (e.g., Guatemala in 1954 and Bolivia in 1964) and to suppress anti-imperialist and revolutionary nationalist movements throughout the 1960s in various countries.

The fifth and latest phase of capitalist globalization is the current phase of "uncertainty," which began in the late 1960s and started to display "crisis tendencies" in the 1990s (see Robertson 1992, 59–60). During the early years of this period, there was a significant increase of anti-imperialist consciousness throughout the region (as well as globally), particularly as a result of the so-called youth rebellion and antiwar movements of the late 1960s and early 1970s. This period was characterized by the Vietnam War, the international disarmament movement, the end of the Cold War, the dissolution of the Soviet Union, the breakup of the Soviet bloc of state capitalist countries, and the "trilateralization" or "tripolarization" of the world capitalist system (centered around the three poles of the United States, Japan, and Western Europe).

This last phase of capitalist globalization also encompasses the so-called revolution in information technology, the establishment of global telecommunications and transportation systems, the proliferation of a wide variety of transnational organizations and new social movements, and growing international concern about human rights and the protection of the global environment. In addition, this phase has included the formation of large trading blocs, such as the European Union (EU), the North American Free Trade Area (NAFTA), and the Organization of Petroleum Exporting Countries (OPEC). It has also included the spread of neoliberal ideologies and economic policies, the increasing indebtedness of most Third World countries, the "democratization" of many former dictatorial political regimes, and the development of ethnic, religious fundamentalist, and indigenous rights ("native peoples") movements.

In Latin America and the Caribbean, this period is characterized by the increasing "global integration" (denationalization) of the economies of all the countries in the region (except for Socialist Cuba) under the aegis of the IMF, the World Bank, the Inter-American Development Bank (IDB), the U.S. government, and U.S.-based transnational corporations (Harris 2000). This process of economic denationalization began in the late 1970s, when these international financial institutions (IFIs) and the major international commercial banks in the United States and Western Europe encouraged most of the Latin American and Caribbean countries to incur huge external debts. By the 1980s, they found it increasingly difficult to pay these debts and were, in essence, placed in receivership under the control of the IFIs.

Under dire financial circumstances, the Latin American and Caribbean governments were pressured by the U.S. government and the major IFIs in the region—the IMF, the World Bank, and the IDB—to scrap their state-subsidized national industrialization efforts and to give priority to servicing their external debts. These conditions led to the adoption throughout Latin America and the Caribbean of neoliberal economic policies that imposed harsh domestic austerity measures, drastic reductions in public expenditures, the privatization of state-owned utilities, and the elimination of the tariffs and economic regulations that protected local industries and agricultural producers from foreign imports. The IFIs and the U.S. government also insisted that the Latin American and Caribbean countries open their economies to the free flow, both in and out, of transnational capital (Harris 2000; Nef 1986).

In the political domain, most of the states in the region were taken over during the late 1960s and 1970s by repressive military regimes with an anti-Communist "national security" ideology (Nef 1991). With the support of the U.S. government, they launched a ruthless campaign to suppress not only all revolutionary movements and leftist political parties in their countries but nearly all forms of popular political expression and activity, as well as trade unions and other working-class organizations (Chilcote 2003, 90). These regimes imposed on the population the unpopular austerity measures mentioned above, as well as other neoliberal economic policies that held down the income of the popular classes and made them pay for the debts incurred by the upper classes and political elites.

Apart from the limited political democratization that took place in the region during the 1980s and the revolutionary regime established in Nicaragua (1979–1990), the 1980s represent a "lost decade" for Latin America (Schuurman 1993, 191). The highly indebted and extremely vulnerable export-oriented economies of many of the Latin American and Caribbean countries actually experienced "negative growth" during most of the 1980s (see chapter 3 in this volume). As a result, the economic gap between these dependent capitalist economies and the wealthier capitalist countries increased during this period as the incomes of the majority of the region's population and the region's share of world trade and economic output declined.

This period was also marked by Washington's efforts to reinforce U.S. hegemony over the region through a variety of political, military, and economic measures (see Petras and Morley 1992, 47–91). These measures included direct military interventions in Grenada (1983) and Panama (1989), the U.S.-financed and -equipped covert war that undermined the Sandinista revolutionary regime in Nicaragua (1982–1990), and support for repressive counterinsurgency efforts, such as the military and police "death squads" used to combat the revolutionary movements in countries like El Salvador, Guatemala, Argentina, and Chile during the 1980s and early 1990s. As indicated above, this final phase of capitalist globalization has also included the formation of NAFTA between the United States, Mexico, and Canada, the continued economic blockade of Socialist Cuba, and many other economic and political measures directed at keeping the Latin American and Caribbean countries firmly and securely under the control of U.S. economic and political interests.

As this brief historical sketch reveals, the contemporary "globalization" of the Americas has been largely the result of the worldwide or global expansion and evolution of capitalism. Today, most pro-capitalist and critical observers agree that the global expansion of capitalism has created a single global economic system. They disagree, however, about the manner in which this global process of capitalist expansion has taken place and about its effects. Marxist and neo-Marxist perspectives on this question are convincing. According to the basic propositions of Marxist theory, the motivating forces associated with the accumulation of, and competition for, wealth that underlie capitalism drive individual capitalists and capitalist enterprises to expand their operations and overcome all obstructing geographic, cultural, and political barriers (e.g., see Mandel 1978).

These same forces motivate individual capitalists and capitalist enterprises to concentrate and centralize their control over the various means whereby wealth is accumulated. As a result, individual capitalists and capitalist enterprises have extended their efforts to accumulate wealth to every corner of the planet. They have also increasingly integrated the world's national and subnational economies into a single, hierarchical global economic system as a result of their continuing attempts to expand, deepen, concentrate, and centralize their control over the accumulation process.

Certain social, cultural, and political institutions, as well as values, worldviews, and beliefs, have proven at different historical moments to be more compatible with the acquisitive drive of the forces of capitalism than others. As a result, these institutions, values, worldviews, and beliefs tend to have been combined with, and advanced by, capitalist forces and practices until they have outlived their usefulness. Thus, at one time or another, the nation-state, nationalism, representative democracy, imperialism, liberalism, individualism, militarism, fascism, certain forms of Christianity, and so forth, have been promoted by capitalists and capitalist enterprises because they have contributed to the private accumulation of wealth and the concentration of private ownership and control over land, other natural resources, labor, money, and so on.

While the expansion of capitalism went hand in hand with the development of nation-states and nationalism in Latin America and the Caribbean at one point, it has since undermined the development of national economic and political independence (see Torres-Rivas 1993). During the early period of the globalization of capitalism, the driving forces of capitalism promoted nationalism, economic and political liberalism, the formation of nation-states, and the dismantling of the Spanish and Portuguese colonial empires in Latin America (Cardoso and Faletto 1979, 66–67). However, with the Spanish and Portuguese empires out of the way, these same forces also fostered a new type of imperialism in the region as first British and then U.S. capitalists, both protected by their national governments, gained increasing control over the economic and political life of the new states formed out of the former Spanish and Portuguese colonial empires (see Chilcote and Edelstein 1986, 77).

It is important to note here that the role played by capitalism in the development of the Latin American and Caribbean states has taken on considerable local variation, and local conditions and forces have determined the concrete circumstances and specific course of events in each country and at each historical juncture in the evolution of the world capitalist system. In the historical development of these states, both "external" and "internal" forces have been closely linked in a dialectical and complex network of "coincident or reconciled interests" (Cardoso and Faletto 1979, xvi).

Consequently, local or internal conditions have been responsible for considerable variation between the Latin American and Caribbean countries in terms of their capitalist development. To quote Cardoso and Faletto (1979) on this important question:

> The expansion of capitalism in Bolivia and Venezuela, in Mexico and Peru, in Brazil and Argentina, in spite of having been submitted to the same global dynamic of international capitalism, did not have the same history or consequences. The differences are rooted not only in the diversity of natural resources, nor just in the different periods in which these economies have been incorporated into the international system (although these factors have played a role). Their explanation must also lie in the different moments at which sectors of local classes allied or clashed with foreign interests, organized different forms of state, sustained distinct ideologies, or tried to implement various policies or defined alternative strategies to cope with imperialist challenges in diverse moments of history. (xvii)

As Cardoso and Faletto note, the internal configuration of power between different classes and social forces has been an important factor in determining the manner in which international, transnational, and national actors and conditions have interacted and shaped the development of the individual Latin American and Caribbean societies (see Torres-Rivas 1993).

CONTEMPORARY CONDITIONS IN LATIN AMERICA

Many observers of Latin America in the early 1990s were quite optimistic about the then new conditions and course of events in the region. The bloody and repressive epoch of military rule that began in the late 1960s had come to an end. The scale of human rights abuses declined, elected civilian governments were established in most countries, and the worst forms of political violence declined greatly. The same observers also perceived that the neoliberal economic policies of many of the Latin American states increased trade and reduced inflation. In place of the dramatic flight of capital out of Latin America that characterized the late 1970s and 1980s, they observed that foreign investment was returning to the region. The financial crises of the 1980s—the so-called lost decade—brought on by the huge foreign debts of most of the Latin American countries also seemed to have subsided. In addition, diplomatic and economic relations in the region improved. Moreover, with the Cold War over, Latin America was no longer affected by the international conflict between the United States and the former Soviet Bloc. Thus, scarcely a decade ago, the future prospects for the region seemed to be considerably better at the end of the twentieth century than they had been for quite some time.

However, even in the midst of this optimism, it was possible to detect disturbing signs, especially if a more perceptive optic was applied. Even though one could point to a number of positive conditions in contemporary Latin America, on closer inspection the objective basis for optimism was clearly quite limited. The more optimistic observers ignored the major underlying political, economic, and social structures that adversely affect the day-to-day lives of the majority of Latin Americans and North Americans alike. The emphasis that they give to what are considered positive accomplishments do not offer any insight into the profoundly distressing reality hidden behind the superficial appearances of economic and political advances.

Among the many troubling features of the Americas today are profound social inequalities; extensive poverty; vast slums and shantytowns in the cities; precarious and illegitimate, and at times outright fraudulent, elected regimes; the increasing despoliation of the natural environment; continuing huge national debts; the prevalence and entrenchment of authoritarian state structures hidden behind a representative democratic facade; the continued presence of repressive internal security forces; the effective (as opposed to official) exclusion of the popular classes from political power; the reactionary influence of fundamentalist religious and economic ideologies; and the continuing destruction of indigenous cultural values and communities, as well as the fragile ecosystems upon which all life in the region depends. These are some of the more fundamental and enduring realities of the Americas, both North and South. They are responsible for the harsh, unjust, and repressive circumstances under which the large majority of people live out their daily lives. They also shape the circumstances that mold and determine the course of events in the region.

To understand its contemporary problems and the region's prospects for the future, a critical analysis of these circumstances is absolutely necessary. A critical, multidimensional, multilevel, and interdisciplinary examination of the "deep structures" of the contemporary societies in the Americas is required, one that includes the larger global context of political, economic, and sociocultural relations in which these societies exist.

The chapters in this volume provide this kind of critical, multidimensional, multilevel, and interdisciplinary examination of the contemporary societies of Latin America and the Caribbean in the larger context of the Americas. The comparative analyses provided by the authors of these chapters reveal the common structures and processes that exist throughout the region. They also unveil the underlying economic, political, and sociocultural factors that shape the various aspects of contemporary reality throughout the region.

The various chapters in this volume identify the fundamental structures, relations, contradictions, and processes responsible for the presence throughout the Americas of widespread economic exploitation, undemocratic politics, racial and cultural discrimination, subordination, and corruption. They also examine the extreme social inequalities, the impoverishment or precarious living standards of the popular classes, the increasing polarization of the population, the lack of political accountability and social responsibility, the degradation of the natural environment, and the powerful external (transnational) influences that undermine and thwart the balanced, equitable, and sustainable development of all the societies in the Americas, both South and North.

As several of the chapters in this book make clear, the region of human settlements known today as the Americas has its historical origins in military conquest, economic exploitation, political oppression, and religious, as well as cultural, domination. Contemporary conditions in the region are, to a large extent, the legacy of colonialism and slavery, the implantation of exploitive capitalist relations of production, the establishment of rigid class structures, the ideological dominance of exclusionary religions, and the institutionalization of various forms of racial and cultural discrimination. There is also a continuing legacy of militarism, authoritarianism, and the political exclusion and disenfranchisement of large sectors of the population, as well as a chronic pattern of political violence manifested in frequent military interventions, civil wars, popular revolts, military dictatorships, many forms of political repression, and the overwhelming presence of repressive national and international security apparatuses. The region suffers the consequences of this bitter legacy of the past in the form of persistent economic exploitation, authoritarian political structures, and extreme social inequality.

THE CONTEMPORARY NATURE
OF CAPITALISM IN THE AMERICAS

Over the last several decades, nearly every major aspect of contemporary economic, political, and social life in the Americas has been transformed as a result of the region's increasing integration into the global capitalist system. As the chapters by Cristóbal Kay, Richard L. Harris, Jorge Nef, and Viviana Patroni (chapters 2 to 5) reveal, the debt crisis and economic recession experienced by the Latin American countries during the 1980s and 1990s have made these societies extremely vulnerable to the pressures of the U.S. government and the international lending agencies, who have insisted that the Latin American and Caribbean governments adopt neoliberal economic policies that have had profound effects upon the economic, social, and political conditions in these societies.

These macroeconomic policies have been carried out under the mantle of the so-called Washington Consensus, the neoliberal agenda of the U.S. government and the IMF, World Bank, and IDB, which all have their headquarters in Washington (Harris 2005, 367–68). These policies have brought about a drastic reduction of government services, public subsidies, and public employment. In addition, they have involved the wholesale privatization and denationalization of state-owned utilities and enterprises, the deregulation of market relations and the human impact on the environment, and the abolition of protective tariffs and other forms of support for local industries. Currencies in Latin America and the Caribbean have also been devalued and/or dollarized, the growth of exports (particularly so-called nontraditional exports such as fruits, vegetables, and assembled manufactured goods) have been promoted in order to earn sufficient foreign exchange to pay the huge foreign debts of the Latin American countries, and previous efforts at import substitution have been largely abandoned.

A series of harsh "austerity measures" have been adopted by the governments of most of the countries in the region in order to reduce their expenditures so that they can make their debt payments. The South, as well as the North, has been dramatically affected by labor "flexibilization" policies whose net effect has been to destroy many of the hard-won gains of the working classes during the twentieth century. These measures have adversely affected the income and living standards of not only the lower classes but also the majority of the middle class. The consequences of these policies, in tandem with the effects of a major global economic recession during the 1980s and early 1990s, were graphically described by Juan de Dios Parra, head of the Latin American Association for Human Rights, at the beginning of the 1990s:

> In Latin America today there are 70 million more hungry, 30 million more illiterate, 10 million more families without homes and 40 million more unemployed persons than there were 20 years ago. . . . There are 240 million human beings who lack the necessities of life and this when the region is richer and more stable than ever, according to the way the world sees it. (Press 1993, E20)

In addition to causing human suffering and losses, these neoliberal economic measures have also jeopardized the advances toward political democracy and political democratization underway throughout the continent. Although these regressive policies were introduced mostly under military rule, the fact that the elected civilian governments that replaced the military dictatorships have continued these unpopular measures has undermined the legitimacy of these elected governments and tainted their democratic credentials.

As a result of both global and local conditions, the Latin American economies are increasingly being integrated into the U.S.-dominated hemispheric trading sphere and global capitalist economy. This has involved the expansion of the number and activities of transnational corporations throughout the region, both in the form of direct investments and through the external financing of local economic activities (MacEwan 1994). There is also an increased dependence on external trade as a result of the recent efforts of the Latin American countries to expand their exports and reduce their tariff barriers to foreign imports. Efforts at regional economic integration and interdependence have also increased, as evidenced by the growth of binational trade pacts, multinational free trade areas such as NAFTA, and the increased quantity of trade between the Latin American nations (Brooke 1994, 3). However, these developments are not strengthening the position of Latin America in world trade; instead, they are transforming the economies of many of the Latin American and Caribbean countries into captive markets for transnational corporations and U.S. investors.

Moreover, as Guido Pascual Galafassi reveals in chapter 10, the supposition that there is an unlimited supply of natural resources has resulted in a continuing, and in some cases increasingly deep, process of environmental deterioration. The high natural fertility of certain regions has hidden this deterioration process until recent times. The pattern of resource extraction that has been established in the region involves the unrestrained pillage of one area after another without any regard for resource renewal and conservation. The capitalist logic of minimizing costs and maximizing profits has resulted in the pillage to exhaustion of resources, and the geographic mobility of the transnational companies and foreign investors involved has made it possible to continuously repeat this pattern in new areas. Needless to say, the remaining virgin lands in Latin America are an incomparable natural treasure waiting to be pillaged.

The dominant style of development is characterized by what Galafassi describes as a unimodal approach in agriculture and resource extraction that assumes all regional ecosystems have the same stability and resistance. This assumption has led to the depletion of biodiversity and the destruction of the most fragile ecosystems. Contemporary productive practices have acquired a pattern of uniformity and homogeneity that has given rise not only to the depletion of biodiversity but also to the destruction of the cultural variability of the indigenous and peasant communities affected by these patterns of production.

THE CONTEMPORARY NATURE
OF INEQUALITY IN THE AMERICAS

As already mentioned, one of the most disturbing realities across the region is the extreme degree of economic and social inequality that characterizes most countries in the Americas, including the United States. The previous discussion has situated this inequality in the origins of these societies and their subsequent historical development. The extent of this inequality in the present moment is revealed by the disparity in income earned by the different sectors of the population, as revealed in Harris's chapter 3.

A concomitant of such income disparity is the fact that nearly 40 percent of Latin American households and about 14 percent of all North American households are below the poverty line, as defined in terms of the income required to satisfy needs for food, housing, and clothing. Moreover, rates of illiteracy and infant mortality, though they have improved steadily over the last thirty years, are still unacceptably high. Today, nearly 90 percent of Latin American and Caribbean adults can read and write, but these countries' relatively poor educational systems continue to produce new illiterates. According to the latest estimates made by the United Nations Educational, Scientific, and Cultural Organization (UNESCO), the region's illiteracy rate is 11 percent, compared to 40 percent in Africa and 45 percent in South Asia. However, UNESCO (2002) admits that the overall literacy rate "masks huge disparities within and between nations" in the region. While Argentina, Trinidad and Tobago, the Bahamas, Cuba, and Uruguay have illiteracy rates of less than 5 percent, 13 percent of Brazilians and almost one-third of adult Guatemalans cannot read or write.

Generally speaking, the rural population has rates of illiteracy that are 50 to 75 percent greater than the urban population. Moreover, for most of the population, access to doctors, medicine, and hospitals is severely limited, and there is an especially striking disparity in access between the rural and urban areas. But a health crisis is not only a Latin American phenomenon: the United States possesses a very costly health-care system with limited coverage and accessibility for a significant part of its population.

Another of the most striking conditions of inequality in most of Latin America is the sharp disparity in landholdings, which is deeply rooted in historical inequities and institutions and has been aggravated by the expansion of capitalist market relations, the widespread commercialization of agriculture, the development of agroindustries, and the concomitant displacement of large numbers of small farmers and poor peasants from the land. The general picture is one of a very small number of landholders who possess a very large proportion of the land. For example, in Brazil, less than 1 percent of the largest landholders owns approximately 78 percent of all agricultural land, while almost 70 percent of the total number of landholders possesses less than 6 percent of the land. Mexico, the second-largest nation, exhibits a similar pattern. Of the arable land in Mexico, 60 percent is owned by 1 percent of the landholders, whereas a little more than 60 percent of the total number of landholders owns only slightly more than 1 percent of the land. This situation reflects the fact that the majority of landholders cultivate an amount of land that is too small and insufficient for their subsistence. Most of these small landowners are thus forced to seek additional, often quite meager, sources of income. They add their labor to the growing pool of underemployed rural workers who have been displaced from their former plots of land by the expansion of commercial agriculture or who are the product of the rapid growth of the rural population.

At the root of rural poverty is the lack of sufficient land, the meager size of peasant farms, the poor quality of their land, the paucity of sources of financial and technical support for peasants and small farmers, low crop prices, the displacement of basic food crops by export crops, the limited sources of permanent employment in the countryside, and rapid population growth (which has not been offset by the large numbers of rural people who migrate to the cities or other countries in search of employment). Once again, while the characteristics of the rural poverty and inequity are striking in Latin America, a crisis in the rural sector is also looming in both Canada and the United States. The effects in terms of loss of livelihood and migration have been dramatic, as has the dramatic decline in farm incomes.

While many of the Latin American states have enacted some type of agricultural reform program, principally during the 1960s and 1970s, very few members of the rural population have benefited from them (Grindle 1986; Lindquist 1979; Thiesenhusen 1989). Even in those countries (such as Bolivia and Peru) where an extensive land reform took place, only a limited amount of land was distributed to poor and landless peasants, and the rural population's limited access to arable land remains a serious problem. Moreover, even those who did receive some land have in most cases received little or no government support (i.e., credit, technical assistance, the organization of cooperatives, etc.) to help them improve the cultivation and marketing of their crops.

THE CONTEMPORARY NATURE
OF POWER IN THE AMERICAS

Although considerable centralized state power and authoritarian civilian and military bureaucracy exist in all the Latin American countries, the role of the state in the economy has significantly declined as a result of the privatization of state assets, government deregulation of economic activities, and the drastic reduction of government social service expenditures and public employment. At the same time, the elected civilian governments, for the most part, merely represent the formal aspects of political democracy. Although the military remains a threatening and powerful force throughout the region, over the last decade they have by and large withdrawn from exercising direct control over the state. Nevertheless, they can always return to take control of the state. What has emerged is a peculiar form of civilian regime based on the exclusion of the popular classes from effective participation in the political system. Meanwhile, the armed forces and police are poised to combat what is now referred to as the "terrorist threat."

In general, Latin American political parties have gained a considerable degree of freedom in terms of their activities. There has been a notable decline in the level and extent of political violence, and governmental and political stability have begun to take hold, although deviations from this pattern have occurred with disturbing frequency. Guatemala, Haiti, and Colombia are cases in point. Nevertheless, one of the most disturbing features of the contemporary political scene throughout the Americas is the lack of governmental responsiveness to the needs of the majority of the population, even though the formal mechanisms of liberal democratic politics have been established.

The popular majority continues to be, for all intents and purposes, disenfranchised throughout the Americas since popular interests are not effectively represented in or by the state. In most countries, entire classes and class fractions are disenfranchised: the urban working class, traditional peasants, indigenous peoples, Afro-Latin Americans, rural workers, small farmers, landless former peasants, the lower sectors of the salaried middle class, and the large "lumpen proletariat" or "informal sector" composed of precariously placed participants in the economy, such as domestic servants, hired hands, and poor street vendors. Taken together, these various classes and sectors of the population represent anywhere from one- to three-quarters of the population, depending upon the demographic profile of each country.

Past efforts to organize and unite these sectors and classes for the purposes of representing their interests in the centers of state power have proved politically difficult and quite dangerous. In addition to the violent reaction of the military and right-wing paramilitary and vigilante groups, the political mobilization of these sectors of the population has been obstructed by traditional forms of political cooptation—such as clientelism and corporatism—which the political elite has used to subordinate and divide the members of these sectors.

What were formerly the more radical and progressive members of the intelligentsia in Latin America have in recent years tended to assume moderately complacent to utterly reactionary political positions. They have distanced themselves from the popular classes and sought to secure positions in the public and private sectors, often accommodating their views to the prevailing neoliberal orthodoxy (Petras and Morley 1992, 145–75). Many of the political parties and organizations (such as the unions) on the Left have assumed a low profile in the political scene (although there are notable exceptions, such as the Workers Party in Brazil), while others have fallen into considerable organizational and ideological disarray or have been co-opted. Revolutionary movements and insurgencies have largely disappeared, except in a few isolated cases. While the Socialist regime in Cuba has endured the collapse of the Socialist bloc and the continued economic and political embargo of the United States, it has been forced by the end of the Cold War and the "triumph" of Western capitalism to maintain an uneasy coexistence with the world capitalist system.

The militant working-class and radical peasant movements of the 1960s that were ruthlessly repressed by the military dictatorships during the 1970s have not returned to the contemporary political scene. On the other hand, the new grassroots social movements that arose in the 1970s and early 1980s, in spite of the repressive nature of the military dictatorships then in power, have continued to play an important role in contemporary social and political life, as indicated in chapter 6 by Judith Hellman. As Hellman notes, the hope for Socialist revolution in the region began to recede after the brutal military overthrow of the elected Socialist government in Chile in 1973, the U.S. military intervention in Grenada in 1983 and Panama in 1989, the electoral rejection of the Sandinista revolutionary regime in Nicaragua in 1990, and the defeat of revolutionary guerrilla movements in other parts of Latin America. As a result, people throughout the region began to view social movements in a different light, and once the expectations of full-scale revolutionary transformation diminished, there emerged a new interest in, and increasing emphasis on, small-scale, localized movements.

However, contrary to early optimism about these new social movements' potential to transform the fundamental nature of Latin American politics, most of them have not yet developed the linkages with each other or with national political organizations that they need in order to affect the direction of the region's political and social development significantly. As these social movements of all descriptions form links with independent trade unions and progressive political parties to defend their achievements and to push forward, there is hope that their goals and interests will be incorporated into national policies by progressive political regimes, such as those in Venezuela, Bolivia, and Ecuador, and by progressive political parties, such as the Workers Party in Brazil and the Democratic Revolutionary Party in Mexico.

Since the introduction of the first neoliberal and pro-globalization "reforms" in Latin America, there has been increasing popular resistance to these policies (Harris 2003). More often than not, this resistance has taken nonviolent and legal forms of expression, such as electoral opposition, lawsuits and court action, marches, mass rallies, picketing, work stoppages, strikes, and the formation of popular assemblies and parliaments as alternatives to the existing polyarchical political institutions. But there has also been an increasing incidence of extralegal, and at times violent, manifestations of popular resistance, ranging from the blockage of roads and highways to land occupations, urban riots, bombings, guerrilla warfare, and even popular insurrections.

Popular resistance to neoliberalism and capitalist globalization has also given rise to international forums, conferences, and networks that seek to coordinate and unify at the regional and international levels the resistance to neoliberalism and capitalist globalization shared in common by a growing multitude of national and subnational social movements and civil society organizations that have emerged throughout Latin America and the rest of the world (Harris 2003). These international forums, conferences, and networks provide important opportunities for these groups to exchange information about their ongoing efforts to develop popular alternatives to neoliberalism and corporate-dominated globalization. Examples of this form of resistance are the World Social Forum, the Pan-Amazon Social Forum, the Social Forum of the Americas, the International Conference against Neoliberalism and Exclusive Globalization, the assemblies of the Convergence of Movements of the Peoples of the Americas, and the Bolivarian Congress of Peoples (Harris 2003).

The wide variety of forms and increasing incidence of popular resistance reveal both the extensive and intensive nature of the opposition to neoliberalism and corporate-driven globalization throughout the region (and the world). The neoliberal regimes in Latin America have responded to the increasing popular resistance to their policies by relying on two types of measures: (1) tactical measures aimed at suppressing eruptions of popular resistance, and (2) more strategic measures aimed at preventing or containing within manageable limits the popular resistance to these neoliberal policies. It is important to note that the U.S. government and the IFIs have played a major role in both developing the second type of measures and assisting the neoliberal regimes in implementing them (Harris 2003).

Although some elements within the clergy of the Roman Catholic Church have supported the growing popular resistance to neoliberalism and globalization, as chapter 9 by Wilder Robles indicates, the conservative orientation of the religious hierarchy of the Roman Catholic Church has led to a crackdown on the progressive advocates of liberation theology within the clergy and the laity, severely diminishing the reformist potential of the grassroots ecclesiastical base communities set up by progressive priests, nuns, and lay members of the church during the late 1960s and 1970s. At one time, these were the most important of the new social movements, and some observers regarded them as the best hope for mobilizing the population to press for major political and social reforms. After more than two decades, this has not come to pass.

Nonetheless, these community-based organizations, as well as the many other new social movements created in the 1970s, 1980s, and 1990s, have contributed to the revitalization of civil society in Latin America. Furthermore, they continue to provide a potential reservoir of support for any progressive political movement capable of unifying and mobilizing these movements behind a program of major social, economic, and political reforms.

The direction the region will take in the coming decades of the twenty-first century is not clear. There are some indications that the region will continue to follow the course of development under the twin banners of neoliberal economics and moderately conservative civilian regimes. On the other hand, there has been a shift to the Left in Latin American politics, and there are many indications of growing discontent with the current pseudo-democratic regimes. This discontent can be found both among the popular classes, who have received few, if any, benefits from these regimes, as well as among the right wing in these countries and their allies in the armed forces, who fear that the democratization process has gone too far and radical forces are likely to take control.

The political Left and other progressive forces in the hemisphere have so far failed to develop an effective strategy for mobilizing the population around a viable alternative to the neoliberal economic project and neoconservative political agenda of the transnational elites that dominate most of the political regimes and economies in the Americas. With the shift toward the Left in recent elections in Latin America, a major change in the current course of development away from the neoliberal model of capitalist development in the direction of greater political, economic, and social democracy is possible.

However, for a real change of direction to take place, the progressive forces in the region must develop and pursue one or more successful alternative models of development. Alternatives do exist, and many civil society organizations and groups are actively trying to influence the future course of events. Lacking until recent times has been the appropriate correlation of political forces, conditions, and leadership to carry out an alternative project of development that inspires and mobilizes the support of the majority of the population for the construction of a more just, democratic, and environmentally sustainable order. Only the passage of time will reveal whether a genuinely progressive correlation of forces, conditions, and leadership will coalesce and give birth to a new social order in the Americas.

NOTE

The authors of this chapter have placed some suggested resources that you may wish to consult on the book's website at http://www.rowmanlittlefield.com/isbn/ 0742555240.

REFERENCES

Aguilar, Alonso. 1965. _Pan Americanism from Monroe to the Present: A View from the Other Side._ New York: Monthly Review Press.

Amin, Samir. 1984. _Transforming the World Economy._ London: Hodder and Stoughton.

Bambirra, Vania. 1972. _El capitalismo dependiente Latinoamericano._ Santiago: Prensa Latino-Americana.

Brooke, James. 1994. "The New South Americans: Friends and Partners." _New York Times,_ April 8, A3.

Burns, E. Bradford. 1991. "The Continuity of the National Period." In _Latin America: Its Problems and Its Promise,_ ed. Jans Kipper Black. Boulder, CO: Westview Press.

Cardoso, Fernando Henrique, and Enzo Faletto. 1979. _Dependency and Development in Latin America._ Berkeley: University of California Press.

Cardoso, Fliana, and Ann Helwege. 1992. _Latin America's Economy: Diversity, Trends, and Conflicts._ Cambridge, MA: MIT Press.

Chilcote, Ronald, ed. 2003. _Development in Theory and Practice: Latin American Perspectives._ Lanham, MD: Rowman & Littlefield.

Chilcote, Ronald, and Joel Edelstein, eds. 1986. _Latin America: Capitalist and Socialist Perspectives of Development and Underdevelopment._ Boulder, CO: Westview Press.

Dos Santos, Theotonio. 1970. "The Structure of Dependence." _American Economic Review_ 60, no. 2 (May): 231–36.

Evans, Peter. 1979. _Dependent Development: The Alliance of Multinational, State and Local Capital in Brazil._ Princeton, NJ: Princeton University Press.

Frank, Andre Gunder. 1967. _Capitalism and Underdevelopment in Latin America: Historical Studies of Chile and Brazil._ New York: Monthly Review Press.

Grindle, Merilee S. 1986. _State and Countryside: Development Policy and Agrarian Politics in Latin America._ Baltimore: Johns Hopkins University Press.

Harris, Richard L. 2000. "The Effects of Globalization and Neoliberalism in Latin America at the Beginning of the Millennium." In _Critical Perspectives on Globalization and Neoliberalism in the Developing Countries,_ ed. Richard Harris and Melinda Seid, 139–62. Leiden: Brill.

———. 2003. "Popular Resistance to Globalization and Neoliberalism in Latin America." _Journal of Developing Societies_ 19, nos. 2–3 (September): 365–426.

———, ed. 2005. *Globalization and Development in Latin America*. Oshawa, Ontario: de Sitter Publications.

Horowitz, Irving Louis, Josue de Castro, and John Gerassi, eds. 1970. *Latin American Radicalism: A Documentary Report on Left and Nationalist Movements*. New York: Random House.

Lindquist, Sven. 1979. *Land and Power in South America*. New York: Penguin Books.

MacEwan, Arthur. 1994. "Notes on U.S. Foreign Investment and Latin America." *Monthly Review* 45, no. 8 (January): 15–26.

Mandel, Ernest. 1978. *Late Capitalism*. London: Verso.

Marini, Ruy Mauro. 1974. *Dialectica de la dependencia*. Mexico City: Ediciones Era.

Nef, Jorge. 1986. "Crise politique et transnationalisation de l'etat en Amérique Latine: Une interprétation théorique." *Etudes Internacionales* 17, no. 2 (June): 279–306.

———. 1991. "Normalization, Popular Struggles and the Receiver State." In *Latin America: Its Problems and Its Promise*, ed. Jan Black, 197–216. 2nd ed. Boulder, CO: Westview Press.

Nef, Jorge, and Ximena Núñez. 1994. *Las relaciones interamericanas frente al siglo XXI*. Quito: Facultad Latinoamericana de Ciencias Sociales.

Nef, Jorge, and Francisco Rojas. 1984. "Dependencia compleja y transnacionalización del estado." *Relaciones Internacionales* 8–9 (December): 101–22.

Pearce, Jenny. 1983. *Under the Eagle: U.S. Intervention in Central America and the Caribbean*. Boston: South End Press.

Petras, James, and Morris Morley. 1992. *Latin America in the Time of Cholera*. New York: Routledge.

Press, Eyal. 1993. "Free-Market Misery for Latin America." *New York Times*, December 5, E20.

Robertson, Roland. 1992. *Globalization: Social Theory and Global Culture*. London: Sage Publications.

Robinson, William. 1996. *Promoting Polyarchy: Globalization, U.S. Intervention and Hegemony*. Cambridge: Cambridge University Press.

Schuurman, Frans. 1993. *Beyond the Impasse: New Directions in Development Theory*. London: Zed Books.

Stein, Stanley J., and Barbara H. Stein. 1970. *The Colonial History of Latin America*. New York: Oxford University Press.

Thiesenhusen, William C., ed. 1989. *Searching for Agrarian Reform in Latin America*. Boulder, CO: Westview Press.

Torres-Rivas, Edelberto. 1993. *History and Society in Central America*. Austin: University of Texas Press.

United Nations Educational, Scientific, and Cultural Organization (UNESCO). 2002. "Literacy in Latin America and the Caribbean." October 28. Available on the UNESCO website at http://portal.unesco.org/education/en/ev.php-URL_ID=8519&URL_DO=DO_TOPIC&URL_SECTION=201.html (accessed January 30, 2007).

2

Latin America's Rural Transformation

Unequal Development and Persistent Poverty

Cristóbal Kay

Latin America's rural economy and society have experienced two major waves of transformation since the middle of the twentieth century. The first transformative wave happened during the import-substitution-industrialization (ISI) period from roughly the late 1940s to the early 1980s, which was characterized by protectionism, relatively rapid industrialization, and high rates of urbanization. Priority in government policy shifted from the export of agricultural and other primary commodities to industrialization and production for the domestic market. This period also witnessed the emergence of peasant movements that, together with the implementation of agrarian reforms, challenged to a greater or lesser extent the traditional large-landlord system. The second transformative wave started with the shift to neoliberal policies in the 1980s (except in Chile, where this process started in the mid-1970s). These policies prioritized the integration of the national economies of the Latin American countries into the world economy by dismantling their protective measures, facilitating foreign investment, and liberalizing labor, capital, and land markets. The role of the state in the economy was substantially reduced as private capital, and increasingly international finance and corporate capital, gained even more power than previously in running these countries' economic affairs. However, since the turn of the century, these neoliberal policies have increasingly been challenged, especially by indigenous peoples and ecological and antiglobalization movements.

Today, rural economies and societies no longer play the primary role that they did in the past. While almost 60 percent of Latin America's population was rural in 1950, less than 25 percent was rural by 2000 (CEPAL 2005a, 146). However, these official data underestimate the importance of the rural sector. If the more realistic definition of "rural" used by the Organization for Economic Cooperation and Development (OECD) is applied to Latin America, then, by 2000, about 40 percent of Latin Americans lived in the countryside (de Ferranti et al. 2005). Over the same period, agriculture's share (including forestry and fisheries) in the total value of Latin American exports declined from approximately one-half to one-fifth of the value of all exports (CEPAL 2005b, 22–23), and agriculture's contribution to the gross domestic product (GDP) fell from approximately 25 percent to below 10 percent (IDB 1986, 397; CEPAL 2005b, 8). But if the value added by food-processing industries is included in agriculture's contribution to GDP, then the value of agriculture's contribution almost doubles (de Ferranti et al. 2005).

The once dominant, traditional *hacienda* or *latifundio* (large landed estate) has largely vanished today. Instead, modern capitalist farms and agroindustrial complexes, some owned by transnational corporations, hold sway over the Latin American countryside. As a result, the transformation of the social and technical relations of agrarian production has been profound. In the 1960s and 1970s, debate raged over whether to characterize the *hacienda* or *latifundio* as feudal or capitalist; the current debate focuses on whether the peasants' distinctive household economy will survive the ravages of the changes brought about by neoliberal economic policies. This debate raises an important question: can the peasantry thrive under neoliberal globalization and lead a process of capitalist development from below that is more inclusive and egalitarian than has been the case in the past, or will the rural transformations be dominated by capitalist farmers and agribusiness, which deepen exclusionary capitalism from above in the countryside?

Poverty continues to be the main problem in Latin America's rural sector. While the incidence of rural poverty reached 59.9 percent in 1980, it continued to be shockingly high after almost a quarter of a century of neoliberalism and still affected 58.1 percent of the rural population in 2004 (CEPAL 2005a, 55; CEPAL 2005c, 318). Rural poverty has remained much higher than urban poverty, due in part to the lower productivity of the agricultural labor force, which is only one-third as productive as nonagricultural labor. In the past, it was even worse. Agriculture's labor productivity was only one-fifth in 1970 (Dirven 2004, 24). Both agriculture and industry grew at a disappointing average annual rate of less than 2 percent during the period between 1980 and 2000, but in the period from 2000 to 2004, agriculture's performance improved at a rate of 3.1 percent compared to industry's 1.4 percent (World Bank 2006, 194–97). However, the benefits of agriculture's modernization were almost wholly reaped by the upper income groups, thereby deepening the unequal and exclusionary development pattern in the region (Spoor 2002). This unequal pattern of neoliberal modernization provides the basis for a major indictment of both the neoliberal policies pursued since the 1980s and the processes of economic globalization they have promoted.

Undoubtedly, the impact of these processes of neoliberal globalization on the rural economy and rural society has varied between countries. In certain instances, this chapter focuses on specific country examples, but in general this chapter focuses on the general processes of transformation throughout rural Latin America. The references at the end of this chapter will give interested readers greater insight into the experiences of specific countries, as well as expose them to perspectives different from those presented in this book.

GLOBALIZATION AND THE UNEVEN DEVELOPMENT OF AGRICULTURE

The relative position of Latin American agriculture in the world economy has undergone a striking decline since World War II. This deterioration can be partly attributed to the ISI strategy pursued by most Latin American countries until the 1980s. But the subsidies and protectionist measures maintained by the advanced industrial nations to safeguard their own agricultural sectors from agricultural imports are largely responsible for Latin America's declining share of international trade in agricultural commodities (Llambí 1994). Both the United States and the European Union (EU) heavily subsidize their agricultural sectors and their agricultural exports. It is estimated that 35 percent of the value of agricultural production in the OECD countries comes from subsidies (CEPAL 2005b, 42). As a result, the developed countries, particularly the United States and the EU, supply more than half of the world's internationally traded agricultural commodities. By comparison, Latin American agricultural exports provide only 13 percent of world agricultural exports (CEPAL 2005b, 21), although in the past agricultural exports from Latin America were two to three times this figure.

Latin American governments and industrialists were willing partners in encouraging the importation of cheap agricultural imports from the United States and the EU as this suited their interest in promoting cheap food for the rapidly rising population in their countries, particularly in the urban and newly industrialized sectors. Concessional U.S. food aid, together with the dumping of EU food surpluses on the world market, has enabled Latin American governments to maintain low food prices through cheap food imports. It has also helped governments to manipulate the exchange rate, which has overvalued the local currency, thereby favoring imports but penalizing exports by making them more expensive. Such measures have benefited urban consumers and the industrial bourgeoisie (owners and managers) because lower food costs have helped to keep industrial wages in check and support profits.

Since the late 1960s, there has been a shift toward the intensification of Latin American agriculture. Many governments encouraged the modernization of the *hacienda* system (large estates) through such measures as subsidized credits for the purchase of agricultural machinery, better-quality livestock, fertilizers, and seeds, as well as the provision of agricultural technical-assistance programs. Consequently, the less efficient *haciendas* were replaced by more productive large commercial farms that shifted to the cultivation of higher-value-added crops to meet the increasing demand of urban consumers. The large landowners also capitalized their enterprises through land improvements (for example, by increasing the area under irrigation), upgrading infrastructure, introducing mechanization, and so forth. This process of modernization has been characterized as the "landlord road" to agrarian capitalism, or "capitalism from above," since it is the large landlords who have transformed their large landed estates into profit-oriented capitalist farms (Kay 1974; Byres 1996).

In addition, what have been called "green revolution" technologies involving the use of high-yield seeds, tractors, and fertilizers were applied throughout Latin America and in other developing countries with the support of foreign aid and government assistance. For example, only 10.8 percent of Latin America's wheat-growing region was sown with high-yield varieties of seeds in 1970, but as the result of the spread of the so-called green revolution, this figure had risen to 82.5 percent by 1983 (IDB 1986, 111). The spread of the green revolution also entailed the use of more fertilizers and pesticides. Between 1950 and 1980, the use of pesticides and fertilizers multiplied by about fifteen, and the number of tractors increased by 600 percent (Ortega 1985, 97). Fixed capital formation also expanded considerably as the irrigated land surface grew by 77 percent, while the land under permanent crops (fruit trees, coffee, bananas, and vines) and semipermanent crops (such as sugar cane) grew by 72 percent. Moreover, livestock numbers increased 75 percent during this period.

Despite this extensive process of modernization prior to the more recent period of neoliberalism, the expansion of land under cultivation was more important than increases in land productivity as the factor responsible for 60 percent of agriculture's output growth (Ortega 1992, 123). Most of this expansion in cultivated land took place in Brazil due to the colonization of large areas in the Amazonian frontier (ECLAC 1993, 610). Furthermore, capitalization within agriculture has been largely confined to the commercial farm sector, leaving peasant agriculture relatively unaffected, as will be seen in more detail in the section on rural livelihoods and peasant prospects.

Since the 1980s, Latin America's shift away from a strategy of ISI toward a new, outward-oriented development strategy has integrated the region's agricultural sector into the world economy. Latin America's debt crisis of the 1980s and the subsequent adoption by most Latin American countries of the "Structural Adjustment Programs" promoted by the World Bank, the International Monetary Fund (IMF), and the international financial system have stimulated the production of agricultural exports in the hope that the income earned from these exports would alleviate Latin America's debt and foreign-exchange problems. As a result of this emphasis on exports, agricultural exports have been growing much faster than the production of agricultural goods for the domestic market.

However, even though the volume of agricultural exports has risen considerably, the amount of foreign exchange so earned has not kept pace accordingly because of falling international prices of agricultural exports on the world market (Weeks 1995). Nevertheless, over the last few years, the prices of some agricultural export commodities have significantly increased, which, together with their continuing expansion, has led to a rapid growth in agricultural export earnings.

A significant shift in the types of agricultural exports has also taken place. While in 1970 coffee and tea (38.9 percent) and meats and hides (15.5 percent) were the principal export products, by 2000 the principal export products were oilseeds and their derivatives (31.6 percent), largely vegetable oils and feedstuffs derived from soybeans, and fruit and vegetables (26.8 percent). Exports of forestry products, especially wood pulp for paper, and fish products have also made an increasing contribution to the total value of all agricultural exports. The main agricultural exporters in Latin America are Brazil and Argentina, which contributed 32.9 percent and 21.7 percent, respectively, to the total value of the region's agricultural exports in 2002. The case of Chile is noteworthy since it has increased dramatically its share in the region's agricultural exports from less than 1 percent in 1970 to almost 7 percent in 2002 (Long and Roberts 2005, 65–66).

Transnational corporations (TNCs) and agribusinesses have been key factors in shaping Latin American agriculture and linking it more closely to the economic requirements of the advanced industrial nations (Teubal 1987). The agricultural TNCs have developed global agrofood systems and spearheaded changes in consumption patterns, as well as changes in the production, processing, and marketing of Latin America's agricultural goods. Advances in biotechnology and genetic engineering have further enhanced the power that transnational agribusiness has over farmers and peasants (Goodman, Sorj, and Wilkinson 1987).

Land use has also been affected by the globalization of the production, processing, and marketing of agricultural products. Production has shifted away from staple foods grown for domestic consumption to the production of exports, particularly products such as soybeans, which are used mainly as animal feed in the industrial countries. In addition, technological developments in storage, processing, refrigerated transport, industrial organization, and communications have enabled the TNCs to take advantage of hemispheric seasonal differences by exporting vegetables, fruit, and flowers to the rich markets of the North, particularly during the winter months in the northern areas of the hemisphere. This trend is evident in the rapid growth of Mexico's exports of winter vegetables to the United States, in Colombia's emergence as one of the world's leading flower exporters, in the growth of Peru's exports of asparagus, in the explosive increase of Chilean fruit exports, and in Brazil's rapid expansion of soybean and soy oil exports, as well as its position as the world's largest exporter of concentrated orange juice.

The growth of the fast-food industry worldwide has meant that land previously dedicated to food crops for local consumption has been converted to pastures for livestock or for animal feeds used to produce meat products for the fast-food industry (Barkin, Batt, and DeWalt 1991). In addition, land recently colonized through the expansion of the agricultural frontier is being devoted to livestock rearing and soybean cultivation largely for export. These patterns of production are supported not only by international agencies, such as the World Bank, the IMF, and the Inter-American Development Bank (IDB), but also by the Latin American governments themselves as part of their export drive to repay foreign debts. Because such practices are detrimental to staple-food production, they have harmed the peasant economy and endangered food security in Latin America (Goodman and Watts 1997). The switch from food crops to livestock rearing and the expansion of soybean farming and the rise of forestry exports, much of the latter as a consequence of illegal logging, have also damaged the environment due to the destruction of tropical and native forests as farmers seek to create more arable land (Hall 1997).

These shifting production patterns have modified the rural social structure in Latin America. The capitalist farmers have been the main beneficiaries of the new opportunities inasmuch as the financial, organizational, and technological requirements of the new export products are beyond the reach of most peasants. Nevertheless, agribusiness contract farming has enabled some smallholders to produce agroindustrial products for export or for high-income domestic urban consumers. The integration of some peasants into the agrofood complex has accentuated socioeconomic differentiations.

Some peasants have been able to accumulate capital to expand production, evolving into "capitalized family farmers" (Llambí 1989) or "capitalist peasant farmers." Others have become wage-earning "proletarians in disguise" (i.e., they may be the formal owners of small landholdings but in effect depend for their survival mainly on wage-earning employment), or they may be "semiproletarians" as an important source of their income no longer derives from their small plot of land but from selling their labor for a wage (i.e., the defining characteristic of the "proletariat"). Furthermore, a significant proportion of peasants has been fully "proletarianized," that is, forced to depend totally on wage-earning employment by having lost their access to land. They have been displaced from the production of agricultural goods for their former markets through the shift in consumer tastes, cheap and subsidized food imports, competition (often unfair) from agribusiness, and technological obsolescence, among other factors (Burbach and Flynn 1980).

Latin America's agricultural resource base is increasingly directed toward satisfying the demands of local high-income urban consumers, as well as the consumers in foreign markets. The emphasis placed by TNCs on production for export and on crops for high-income consumers has created what can be called a "new world food regime" (Friedmann 1991). In this new food regime, the neglect of staple crops has resulted in an increasing dependence on food imports from the developed countries, particularly from the United States, thereby undermining Latin America's food security (Teubal 1995; Friedmann 2004). The importation of foodstuffs has soared since the 1970s and has increased Latin America's dependence on the international food markets and made the Latin American countries more vulnerable to fluctuations in these markets.

The attempts made by some Latin American governments to remedy this situation have all been short-lived, the most notable being the Mexican government's program called Sistema Alimentario Mexicano (Mexican Food System, or SAM) (Barkin 1987). During the 1990s, agricultural imports grew by 8.6 percent per year, while agricultural exports increased by 6.4 percent per year (ECLAC and IICA 2002, 115, 117). While most countries of the region have a positive trade balance in agricultural commodities, a few countries have a negative one. Mexico, which imports large quantities of meat, cereals, and oil seeds, has by far the largest negative trade balance, followed by Venezuela and Peru (ECLAC and IICA 2002, 133).

AGRARIAN REFORMS: UNFULFILLED
EXPECTATIONS, UNFINISHED TASKS

Haunted by the specter of socialism following the Cuban Revolution of 1959, the U.S. and Latin American governments launched the Alliance for Progress in the early 1960s. This was a development aid and cooperation program launched by the newly elected administration of John F. Kennedy in the United States. It was aimed at regaining the initiative in hemispheric relations after the Cuban Revolution of 1959. It promised aid to those countries that agreed to carry out an agrarian-reform program to defuse peasant uprisings and prevent more fundamental political and economic changes. The motivation behind these agrarian reforms was as much political as economic. In practice, the agrarian-reform policies sought to expropriate only those *haciendas* considered inefficient. Large estates, generally referred to as *latifundios*, dominated the agrarian structure in the 1950s and early 1960s. They constituted roughly 5 percent of all farm units but possessed about four-fifths of the arable land. Meanwhile, small farms, or *minifundios*, made up roughly four-fifths of the total farm units but controlled only 5 percent of the arable land (Barraclough 1973, 16). The *latifundios* underutilized land, investing only modest resources in extensive tracts of land, leaving a significant proportion uncultivated. The *minifundios*, by contrast, used too much labor on too little land. Not surprisingly, labor productivity was much higher on *latifundios* than on *minifundios*, while the reverse was true regarding land productivity.

The dominant social relations of production were those of unpaid household labor working on the *minifundio* and on various kinds of small-scale tenancies (e.g., sharecropping). Peasant landholdings occupied about half the agricultural labor force, of which four-fifths were unpaid family workers, while the large estates employed less than one-fifth of the agricultural labor force. An estimated one-quarter of all agricultural workers were tenant farmers or squatters, and a further one-third were either landless workers or proletarians totally dependent on wage-earning employment (Barraclough 1973, 19–23).

It was hoped that new reforms would increase agricultural productivity and production and improve access to land, rural income, and employment prospects, thus contributing to political stability. Urban consumers were also expected to benefit from lower food prices, and industrialists were to gain a wider market for their industrial goods. In the broadest sense, the agrarian reforms were regarded as a way of overcoming the domestic-market and foreign-exchange constraints that accompanied Latin America's efforts to industrialize.

The legacy of agrarian reforms has, however, diverged from the initial expectations. The reforms generally modernized the *hacienda*, transforming it into a capitalist farm rather than eliminating it altogether via the redistribution of *hacienda* lands to peasants. In this sense, many agrarian reforms merely accelerated the already well-established landlord path of development to agrarian capitalism (de Janvry 1981; Kay 1988). The agrarian reforms failed to fulfill their promises. In some cases, the political will or power to enforce them was lacking. Even though many Latin American governments presented land reform as a panacea, they failed to provide the needed financial, technical, and institutional support to make them a success. Mistakes in the design and implementation of the agrarian reforms also contributed to their unraveling. In some cases, an inadequate organizational model for the reform sector succeeded in alienating peasants by limiting their participation in the decision-making process or excluded them from the benefits of the reform altogether (Kay 1998).

The introduction of neoliberal policies further eroded most of the gains that the peasant beneficiaries had achieved from the agrarian reforms. At first sight, the shift in emphasis from collectivist forms of agrarian organization to individual peasant farms as a result of the introduction of neoliberal policies seemed to open the prospects for a peasant road to agrarian capitalism. However, in the neoliberal process of privatizing the reformed sector and communal lands, many peasants lost their access to land—as witnessed in Chile during the dictatorship of General Augusto Pinochet (Kay 2002) and in Nicaragua during the post-Sandinista period (Dore 2006). Furthermore, the withdrawal of government support, such as cheap credit and technical assistance, for the peasant sector, together with increased exposure to international competition and the emphasis on exports, have benefited farmers with access to capital, modern technology, and foreign markets. Only a minority of peasant farmers has been able to take advantage of the neoliberal policies, thereby furthering the process of social and economic differentiation among the peasantry (Thiesenhusen 1989; Barros 2000).

The breakup of the reformed sector under neoliberal regimes has led to a more complex agrarian structure. The development of the land market resulting from the neoliberal privatization process has enabled new types of entrepreneurs (often urban and foreign capitalists) to acquire land and invest in agriculture to a greater extent than in the past. Some capitalist farmers have acquired more land over time. However, talk of "neolatifundism" is inappropriate since the social and technical relations of production of these new large farms (often soy, livestock, and forestry farms) differ from those of the old *latifundios*. In short, the neoliberal policies have further strengthened the capitalist farmers and marginalized most peasant farmers.

Agrarian reform has therefore left a complex legacy. Certainly, the more radical agrarian reforms put an end to the dominance of the landed oligarchy in Latin America. In general, however, they contributed to capitalist development through institutional changes. By making land and labor markets more competitive and flexible, they enhanced agriculture's responsiveness to macroeconomic policy and market forces.

The increasing displacement of the peasantry from the land has moved the World Bank to put land reform back on the agenda by proposing a "market-friendly" or "negotiated" land reform whereby willing sellers of land (large farmers) offer land to willing buyers (smallholders or landless peasants), often through a land bank and overseen by a state agency (Deininger 1999). To facilitate the purchase of land by poor peasants, the World Bank, international development agencies, and government offer them subsidized credit. The record so far of this "willing-seller"/"willing-buyer" type of agrarian reform, which has been attempted mainly in Brazil and Colombia, has been dismal since few buyers and sellers have come forward. In particular, peasants fear that they may be unable to repay the debt they incur by purchasing the land and, thus, may end up in a worse situation than previously (Borras 2003).

These market-friendly land reforms have also been much contested by peasant organizations, especially by the Movimento dos Trabalhadores Rurais sem Terra (Landless Rural Workers Movement, or MST) in Brazil, which, through their policy of selective land occupation, have been the driving force for a peasant-led agrarian reform (Wright and Wolford 2003; Veltmeyer 2005). Furthermore, as argued by the doyen of agrarian-reform studies, Solon Barraclough (1999), "There was no evidence . . . that effective land reforms could result from 'market friendly' policies alone. Registering land titles and facilitating real estate transactions between willing sellers and willing buyers do not by themselves change power relationships in favor of the rural poor. In many situations, such policies are likely to reinforce agrarian structures by providing large landholders and speculators with additional legal protection, while leaving the bargaining power of the poor unchanged or diminished" (38).

NEW RELATIONS OF PRODUCTION

The quickening pace of the capitalist transformation of the countryside following neoliberal policies has restructured both technical and social relations of production. In addition, the spread and dominance of agroindustries and the growth of export agriculture have reshaped rural labor markets and production relations throughout Latin America. Macroeconomic policy, favoring the development and diffusion of capital-intensive technologies, and the bias of extension services in favor of commercial farmers have widened the technological gap between capitalist farmers and the peasant economy. It is difficult, if not impossible, for peasant farmers to adopt most of the new technologies. Besides being too risky and expensive, the new agricultural technologies are also not well suited to the small scale and inferior soils of peasant farming. In addition, the negative environmental consequences of fossil fuel–based technology are increasingly being called into question. The capital-intensive (and often import-intensive) nature of this technology is also held to be unsuitable for Latin American economies as it requires too many scarce capital resources (especially foreign exchange) and too few members of the abundant labor supply (Bebbington and Thiele 1993, 60–73). For these reasons, it would make sense to support peasant agriculture, but neoliberal policy has not changed course.

The modernization of the *latifundio* and its final transformation into a capitalist farm has had a major impact on rural labor. Unlike the old personalistic and clientelistic relations between landlords and peasants, relations between capitalist farmers and rural workers are increasingly mediated by impersonal market forces and characterized by new forms of exploitation and subordination. Four major changes in the composition of the labor force in the countryside can be highlighted: (1) the replacement of tenant labor by wage labor; (2) within wage labor, the growth of temporary and seasonal labor; (3) the increasing feminization of the agricultural labor force; and (4) the ruralization of urban workers and urbanization of rural workers.

First, tenant labor used to supply most of the *latifundios'* permanent and temporary labor needs. But as landlords modernized their estates by raising their productivity, tenant labor became increasingly more expensive for them than wage labor. The rental income received from tenants (sharecroppers, labor-service tenants, or others) became lower than the profit income landlords could earn by working the land directly with wage labor. Mechanization, which was attractive because of the often overvalued local currencies and the availability of government-subsidized credits, turned direct cultivation by landlords into a more profitable activity than tenancy. Thus, the higher opportunity costs of tenancies and tenant laborers resulted in the transformation of these workers into proletarians or their replacement by wage laborers. Landlords also reduced the number of tenants and permanent laborers they employed for political reasons. In the changing political climate of the land-reform period, landlords responded to pressure from rural labor, especially among tenants for land or reduced rent payments, by introducing labor-displacing technology.

Second, within the shift to wage labor, there has been a marked increase in the proportion of temporary, often seasonal, wage employment. In many countries, permanent wage labor has declined, even in absolute terms, although in almost all countries, temporary wage labor has greatly increased. This growth of temporary labor is related to the expansion of agroindustries that export seasonal fruit, vegetables, flowers, and the like, and is therefore particularly evident in those Latin American countries that export these products. While in the past about one-fifth to one-third of wageworkers were temporary, today this proportion has been reversed as only one-fifth to one-third of wageworkers are now permanent. The expansion of temporary employment has led to the increasingly precarious nature of rural wage labor. Temporary workers are generally paid a piece rate, are not usually entitled to social security benefits, and have no employment protection. This shift toward more casual and flexible labor has enabled employers to increase their control over labor by reducing workers' rights and bargaining power. They have been further aided by regressive changes in labor legislation, often introduced by the military governments but continued by their neoliberal civilian successors. The precariousness of rural employment has contributed to the fracturing of the peasant movement. Although seasonal laborers can be highly militant, they are notoriously difficult to organize due to their varied backgrounds and irregular residence. Thus, the shift from permanent to seasonal labor in the countryside has generally weakened peasant organizations and hampered efforts to negotiate improvements in their working conditions either directly with their employers or indirectly by pressuring the state. There are, of course, exceptions to this trend, as shown by the MST in Brazil.

Third, the marked increase in the participation of women in the labor market is associated with the expansion of temporary and/or seasonal wage employment. In the past, rural women worked as day laborers, milkmaids, cooks, or domestic servants on the landlord's estate. They also found seasonal wage employment during the labor-intensive harvests on coffee, cotton, and tobacco farms. With the increasing commercialization of agriculture and the crisis of peasant agriculture (as discussed in the next section), more and more rural women have joined the labor force, while at the same time continuing with their unpaid domestic work. The rapid expansion of new export crops (fruit, vegetables, flowers) has opened up wage-employment opportunities for women in agriculture (Collins 2003). Agroindustries largely employ female labor since women are held to be more readily available, more willing to work on a seasonal basis and to accept lower wages, less organized, and, according to employers, better suited for activities that require careful handling. Any permanent employment, however, tends to be the preserve of men. Although they are generally employed in low-skilled and low-paying jobs, for many young women, these jobs provide an opportunity to earn an independent income and to escape (at least partially and temporarily) from the constraints of a patriarchal peasant-family household. As a result of their incorporation into the formal labor market, they have begun to exercise increasing influence in the affairs of peasant organizations and, in some instances, have even established their own organizations.

Fourth, an additional dimension to the growth of temporary wage labor concerns the geographical origins of the workers so employed. An increasing proportion of temporary workers comes from urban areas. In some regions, especially near large cities, over half of the seasonal workers originate from urban areas. The improved road and transport infrastructure has facilitated this transformation. The growing presence of labor contractors, who hire gangs of laborers from small towns and cities for work in the fields, means that the farm owner or manager is often not the direct employer. Rural residents frequently have to compete with these urban laborers for agricultural work. The expulsion of tenant farmers, who used to reside on the estates, and the growth in temporary employment have often resulted in the creation of new rural villages or the expansion of old ones into rural towns. Without the basic physical and social infrastructure, these villages provide few, if any, social services like schools and medical centers. In the past, shantytowns were largely evident in the large cities of Latin America, but today they have spread to the smaller cities and even to rural towns (Davis 2006). This spread of shantytowns is explained not only by the demise of the traditional *hacienda* system and the changes in the agricultural labor market noted above but also by the peasant economy's inability to absorb the growing population, as will be seen in the next section. Thus, the increasing urbanization of the countryside is a mixed blessing.

RURAL LIVELIHOODS AND PEASANT PROSPECTS

The internationalization of Latin America's agriculture, the demise of the *hacienda* system, and the increasing dominance of capitalist agriculture are having a profound impact on the peasantry. As a result, the fate of Latin America's peasantry has been the subject of much debate. In the late 1970s, those who emphasized the resilience, vitality, and relative importance of the peasant economy challenged the dominant view that the landlord road to capitalism, or "capitalism from above," was steamrolling ahead. The ensuing debate between the *campesinistas* and the *descampesinistas* has continued (Feder 1977; Stavenhagen 1978; Warman 1980; Schejtman 1980; Esteva 1983; Bartra 1993, Otero 1999).

The *campesinistas* believe peasant farming, seen by some as superior to capitalist farming, will endure (Harris 1978; Heynig 1982; Astori 1984; Hewitt de Alcántara 1984). They reject the view that the wage relation is being generalized in the countryside and that the peasantry is disappearing, arguing that the peasantry is persisting and even being reinforced. Characterizing peasants mainly as petty commodity producers who are able to compete successfully with capitalist farmers, *campesinistas* have certain affinities with the neopopulist tradition of Alexander Chayanov (1966[1925]) and his contemporary followers like Teodor Shanin (1986).

By way of contrast, the *descampesinistas* argue that the peasant form of production is economically unviable in the long run and that peasants will eventually be eliminated as petty commodity producers. They argue that capitalist development increases differentiation among the peasantry and that, ultimately, most peasants will become proletarians and only a few will become capitalist farmers. The "depeasantization" approach (sometimes called "proletarianization") is influenced by classical Marxist writers on the agrarian question, such as Vladimir I. Lenin (1964[1899]) and Karl Kautsky (1988[1899]).

The debate over the future of Latin America's peasantry raises crucial issues about the characteristics of the process of capitalist development in the countryside (Llambí 1991). Although theoretical differences continue to feed the debate, the changing reality and the availability of new data also require an ongoing process of reinterpretation. The peasant economy will undoubtedly survive for some time to come in Latin America. The key question concerns the terms of this survival: prosperity or destitution?

It is estimated that peasant agriculture in the 1980s in Latin America comprised four-fifths of all farm units and accounted for one-fifth of total agricultural land, over one-third of cultivated land, and more than two-fifths of harvested area (López 1985, 26). The peasant economy accounted for almost two-thirds of the total agricultural labor force, the remaining third being employed by capitalist farms. Furthermore, peasant agriculture supplied two-fifths of production for the domestic market and one-third of the production for export. The contribution to food products for mass consumption is particularly important. At the beginning of the 1980s, the peasant economy provided an estimated 77 percent of the total production of beans, 61 percent of potatoes, and 51 percent of maize, as well as 41 percent of the share of such export products as coffee. In addition, the peasant economy owned an estimated 24 percent of the total number of cattle and 78 percent of pigs (López 1985, 28).

Although peasants are far from disappearing, they are not thriving. Their relative importance as agricultural producers has declined, particularly since the implementation of neoliberal policies. According to de Janvry, Sadoulet, and Young (1989, 396), the Latin American peasantry is experiencing a "double squeeze." First, they face a land squeeze. As they fail to acquire additional land to match their increased numbers, the average size of peasant farms has decreased. Furthermore, more than half of *minifundistas* lack property titles to the land they farm, which underlines the precariousness of their situation (Vogelgesang 1996). Second, peasants face an employment squeeze since employment opportunities have not kept pace with their population growth rate and they face increased competition from urban-based workers for rural employment. In many Latin American countries, more than one-quarter of the economically active agricultural population currently resides in urban areas. This double squeeze has led many peasants to migrate to urban areas and even abroad, feeding the continuing high, though declining, rate of rural out-migration.

Peasants have also responded to their livelihood crisis by seeking alternative off-farm sources of income (such as seasonal wage labor in agriculture) and/or nonfarm and nonagricultural sources of income (such as employment in small-scale rural enterprises and agroindustries). The proportion of the economically active rural population engaged in nonagricultural activities is rising. By the end of the 1990s, nonagricultural employment of rural residents contributed about one-third of total employment in rural areas and about 40 percent of incomes (Kjöllerström 2004, 7–8). This shift reinforces the trend in which an increasing proportion of total peasant household income originates from wages, whereas income from on-farm activities often comes to less than half the total (de Janvry et al. 1989, 60, 141).

The increasing importance of nonfarm and off-farm activities also furthers the process of peasant differentiation as those peasants with more capital and/or higher levels of education are able to engage in higher-value, more profitable, and better-paid activities, such as rural tourism, trade, money lending, agroprocessing, and skilled wage employment, whereas the more poorly endowed peasants rely largely on badly paid, casual wage employment, which has lower entry barriers (Reardon, Berdegué, and Escobar 2001).

In short, Latin America's peasantry is increasingly acquiring the characteristics of a semiproletariat. Off-farm sources of income, generally seasonal wage labor, enable peasants to cling to the land, thereby blocking their full proletarianization. This process favors rural capitalists as it eliminates small peasants as competitors in agricultural-commodity markets and transforms them into a source of cheap labor. Semiproletarianization is the most likely option open to those peasants who wish to retain access to land for reasons of security and survival because they cannot find safe enough, alternative, productive employment in either the rural or urban sector.

PERSISTENT RURAL POVERTY

Agricultural development in Latin America, with its emphasis on capital-intensive farming and the resource squeeze on the peasant economy, has made rural poverty a persistent and intractable problem. The neoliberal Structural Adjustment Programs of the 1980s have contributed to the rising incidence of poverty since government expenditures on social welfare, subsidies for basic foods, and other essential commodities and services were severely cut back. While the incidence of rural poverty increased from 59.9 percent of the rural population in 1980 to 65.4 percent in 1990, rural indigence or extreme rural poverty rose more sharply, from 32.7 to 40.4 percent (CEPAL 2005a, 55). Governments attempted to soften the negative impact by targeting welfare payments more closely, introducing poverty-alleviation programs, and gradually increasing social expenditures in the 1990s. However, these measures had only a minor impact.

While rural poverty declined gradually from its high point in 1990 to 61.6 percent in 2003, this was still higher than its level in 1980. According to the latest available data, the incidence of rural poverty had fallen in 2004 to 58.1 percent, which for the first time was below the 1980 level. However, rural indigence is still higher than in 1980, having reached 34.0 percent in 2004 (CEPAL 2005c, 318). The only country in Latin America where rural poverty has fallen significantly is Chile, where it had been reduced from 39.5 percent in 1990 to 20.0 percent in 2003, while rural indigence dropped from 15.2 percent to 6.2 percent (CEPAL 2005c, 317). This has been achieved by persistent high rates of agricultural growth, which have increased rural incomes, as well as by major investment and welfare programs targeting the rural poor (Kay 2006).

The main cause of rural poverty is structural due to the extreme unequal land distribution and the continuing exclusion of the peasantry and rural workers from access to credit, technical assistance, and fair markets. Poverty affects indigenous peoples and women to a greater extent due to centuries of discrimination and patriarchy. Tackling the root causes of poverty will require major land redistribution and rural investments, increased employment opportunities, and significant improvements in agricultural productivity, especially of smallholders (Akram Lodhi, Borras, and Kay 2007). Only by a generalized assault on various fronts will it be possible to reduce rural poverty substantially. Such an assault will depend on the organizational capacity of rural workers, as well as on their ability to forge alliances with other social groups so as to alter the balance of political power in their favor.

PATHS OF AGRARIAN CAPITALISM

The development path of Latin American agriculture has been the subject of extensive theoretical debate (Llambí 1990). In the early 1970s, I argued that the landlord road was the main route to agrarian capitalism in Latin America, a view largely shared by de Janvry (1981) and others (Kay 1974). Goodman and Redclift (1982), as well as the *campesinistas* in the debate mentioned earlier, criticized this view for underestimating the vitality of the peasantry. It was Lehmann (1982, 1986), however, whose work on Ecuador first clearly identified a viable peasant path to rural development. But this path was confined to a section of the peasantry that he conceptualized as "capitalized peasant farmers." Many other researchers subsequently discovered a "capitalized peasantry" in other areas of Latin America. I never denied the possibility that there might be a peasant path to agrarian capitalism, but I saw this course of development as either subordinated to the dominant landlord path or the possible result of a shift in the class struggle in favor of the peasantry, resulting in major redistributive land reforms and pro-peasant macroeconomic policies (Kay 1988).

In my view, the landlord road to agrarian capitalism was dominant in the past; however, a multiplicity of paths can be observed today. Compared with the previous bimodal structure of *latifundio-minifundio*, the Latin American countryside is now more heterogeneous (CEPAL and FAO 1986). A large proportion of former *haciendas* or *latifundios* have successfully been, or are being, converted into medium-sized or large modern capitalist enterprises that rely mainly on wage labor and advanced technology and are integrated into the domestic and international markets. In addition, in those countries where the reformed sector was subdivided into parcels and distributed to peasant beneficiaries (commonly known as *parceleros*), the peasant farm sector grew significantly.

A proportion of *parceleros* may eventually become capitalized-peasant farmers by exploiting new market opportunities, new products, improved links with agroindustries, pro-peasant government policies, the support of nongovernmental organizations (NGOs), and other possibilities. But the experience so far is not very encouraging (Murray 2002). Yet, at the same time, the modernization of the *latifundio* has led to the proletarianization of the peasantry, especially the tenant farmers. Meanwhile, the semiproletarianization of many small peasants is a significant and persistent trend (López 1985, 20–22), as is the increase of landless peasants (Barraclough 1991, 55). Consequently, today's agrarian structure is both more complex and fluid than it was in the pre-agrarian-reform period. New processes of concentration are taking shape, however, in which capital is gaining increasing importance over land.

In sum, the modernized capitalist farmers, often linked to agroindustrial and international capital, are undoubtedly setting the pace and controlling the direction of Latin America's rural developments. Agriculture is increasingly subordinated to the processes of trade liberalization and globalization.

Within this context, what then are the prospects for a peasant path to rural development? It is well known that access to capital, technology, and domestic and foreign markets, as well as knowledge and information systems, is becoming increasingly important relative to access to land in determining the success of an agricultural enterprise. Although in recent decades some peasants have managed to gain access to land through agrarian reforms, this by no means guarantees their success (Carter and Mesbah 1993). Indeed, peasants are in an increasingly disadvantageous position compared to capitalist farmers, and this does not augur well for their future prospects.

The widening technological gap between the capitalist and peasant farm sectors has prompted some scholars to urge international agencies, governments, and NGOs to adapt existing modern technologies to the needs of the peasant sector and to create more "peasant-friendly" technologies. While such technological developments are welcome, the sustainability of peasant agriculture depends on broader social and political conditions, particularly a favorable macroeconomic context (Figueroa 1993). A viable peasant road to rural development raises questions about development strategy and, ultimately, about the political power of the peasantry and its allies.

A successful peasant path to rural development requires a major shift in development strategy, land redistribution, and a major transfer of resources toward the peasant economy to ensure its capitalization on a scale broad and deep enough for it to compete both in domestic and international markets (Llambí 2000). The widespread adoption and intensification of liberalization policies in Latin America and the decline of the developmentalist state do not encourage such a possibility. But there are some areas scattered throughout Latin America where pockets of peasant farming have gained a certain dynamism by exploiting certain market niches (Long and Roberts 2005). Unfortunately, such examples have as yet not become more widespread.

Some scholars, activists, and NGOs became increasingly concerned about the adverse impact on the peasantry of the dark side of the neoliberal modernization process. As opposed to the concentrating and exclusionary nature of agricultural modernization, they call for a strategy that includes peasants in the modernization process (Calderón, Chiriboga, and Piñeiro 1992; Murmis 1994). Such an "inclusionary" strategy of modernization is seen as part of the democratization of rural society (Fox 1990); thus, they favor a "democratic modernization." They propose a development strategy that centers on the transformation of the productive structures and the widespread adoption of technological innovations so as to achieve genuine competitiveness based on higher productivity rather than on cheap labor. Such innovations, supported by appropriate state measures, are to be directed especially to small and medium-sized enterprises so as to ensure that they reap the benefits of higher productivity. Such a "reconversion" of the rural system based on social equity is viewed as the most sustainable way to meet the challenges of an increasingly internationalized and global world economy in the new millennium (ECLAC 1990, 1992). Forwarding these aims would require special government policies in favor of the peasantry to reverse the past bias in favor of landlords and rural capitalists. It is unlikely that in the current neoliberal climate, these kinds of policies will be adopted. On the contrary, the various free trade agreements that some Latin American countries have signed with the United States in recent years are likely to harm peasant farmers even further. It is generally acknowledged that the North American Free Trade Agreement (NAFTA), which entered into force in 1994, has had a negative impact on the Mexican peasantry (Wise, Salazar, and Carlsen 2003). But the neoliberal project has not gone unchallenged by peasants and indigenous peoples, as evidenced by the land occupations spearheaded by the MST in Brazil, the Zapatista rebellion in

Chiapas, Mexico, and the social movements in Ecuador and Bolivia, among others, as discussed in some of the chapters in this book (Petras and Veltmeyer 2002).

CONCLUSION

With the shift to neoliberal policies since the 1980s, Latin America's rural economy and society have become more fully and firmly integrated into the world economy. Agroindustrial modernization and globalization have extended and intensified the process of uneven capitalist transformation, thereby profoundly changing the technical and social relations of production in the countryside. The liberalization of markets, a less distorted foreign exchange rate, and the greater opening of the economy have favored those sectors producing tradable commodities, including agriculture. But this modernization has two faces. It is principally the capitalized producers who have been able to take advantage of the new opportunities, while the majority of the peasantry has been disadvantaged as the neoliberal policies have dismantled the various state institutions that previously provided some support, such as subsidized credit, technical assistance, and marketing facilities. Hence, this corporate-driven, export-oriented capitalist path of development "from above" is exclusionary as the vast majority of the peasantry is excluded from its benefits. It has furthered inequality and the concentration of capital. The beneficiaries are a heterogeneous group, including foreign transnational capitalists, agroindustrialists, capitalist farmers, some capitalized peasant households, and, in some instances, the more skilled workforce. The losers are the semi- and fully proletarianized peasants, who comprise the majority of rural laborers and whose vulnerability has increased as their employment conditions have become more temporary, precarious, and "flexible."

Smallholders have increasingly been driven to seek multiple sources of income as their household family farming no longer provides a subsistence income. In their quest to diversify their sources of income, they engage in off-farm activities by, for example, working as agricultural wage laborers on capitalist farms, as well as engaging in other nonfarm activities, such as rural tourism, petty trading, and wage employment in nonagricultural activities, for instance, in rural industries and construction. As local employment opportunities have become scarcer, a rising number of family household members have had to migrate to urban areas and, with increasing frequency, to foreign countries. Thus, remittances from migrant labor are becoming an increasing proportion of peasants' household incomes. In some countries, these remittances are beginning to exceed the total value of agricultural exports. Such a situation reveals the deep crisis facing the rural sector in many Latin American countries.

With the increasing linkages between the rural and urban sectors, the boundaries between them have become ambiguous. The massive rural out-migration has partly "ruralized" some urban areas, while the countryside is becoming increasingly urbanized. Urban and rural labor markets have become more closely interconnected. The land market has become more open and competitive, enabling urban investors and international capital to gain greater access to the region's natural resources. Competition among agricultural producers has intensified because of a more fluid situation in the land, capital, and labor markets. Peasant farmers find it increasingly difficult to survive in this more liberalized and globalized environment as they lack the resources to invest in innovations and adjust their production structures to changing international and domestic market conditions. It is paradoxical that as the economies liberalize and face greater competition (some of which is unfair due to subsidies received by farmers in the rich countries) and the peasantry's need for more financial, technical, and marketing support from the state increases, the state is reducing its commitments to the peasantry.

Although the rural economy and society is less important today than in the past, it still retains critical significance in most Latin American countries. Moreover, to ignore agrarian problems is ill advised. In several countries, the land-redistribution issue has not yet been fully addressed, while in many others, it remains unresolved. Rural poverty remains widespread, and discrimination against indigenous peoples and rural women is still pervasive. Last, but not least, ecological problems, such as desertification, the destruction of the rainforest, and the depletion of water resources, have become more acute.

The change from a state-centered and inward-directed development process to a neoliberal open-market and export-oriented model of development has weakened the peasantry and strengthened rural capitalists. Many social conflicts have erupted in the countryside due to the uneven and exclusionary character of the neoliberal capitalist development process. New grassroots organizations have emerged in the rural areas, particularly among indigenous groups, which have contested neoliberal policies from the privatization of water, land, and other natural resources to the free trade agreements with the United States and other rich countries. While these social movements have been able to modify aspects of neoliberal policies and have even managed to oust governments that pursued them, it remains to be seen whether a new development strategy will emerge in Latin America that is able to overcome the unequal and exclusionary development pattern, as well as the persistent poverty.

NOTE

The author of this chapter has placed some suggested resources that you may wish to consult on the book's website at http://www.rowmanlittlefield.com/isbn/0742555240.

REFERENCES

Akram Lodhi, Haroon, Saturnino Borras, and Cristóbal Kay, eds. 2007. *Land, Poverty and Livelihoods in the Era of Globalization: Perspectives from Developing and Transition Countries*. London: Routledge.

Astori, Danilo. 1984. *Controversias sobre el agro Latinoamericano: Un análisis crítico*. Buenos Aires: Consejo Latinoamericano de Ciencias Sociales (CLACSO).

Barkin, David. 1987. "The End to Food Self-sufficiency in Mexico." *Latin American Perspectives* 14, no. 3: 271–97.

Barkin, David, Rosemary L. Batt, and Billie R. DeWalt. 1991. "The Substitution among Grains in Latin America." In *Modernization and Stagnation: Latin American Agriculture into the 1990s*, ed. Michael J. Twomey and Ann Helwege, 13–53. New York: Greenwood Press.

Barraclough, Solon, ed. 1973. *Agrarian Structure in Latin America: A Resume of the CIDA Land Tenure Studies*. Lexington, MA: D. C. Heath.

———. 1991. "Migrations and Development in Rural Latin America." *Economic and Industrial Democracy* 12, no. 1: 43–63.

———. 1999. "Land Reform in Developing Countries." Discussion Paper 101. Geneva: United Nations Research Institute for Social Development (UNRISD).

Barros, Magdalena. 2000. "The Mexican Peasantry and the *Ejido* in the Neo-liberal Period." In *Disappearing Peasantries? Rural Labour in Africa, Asia and Latin America*, ed. Deborah Bryceson, Cristóbal Kay, and Jos Mooij, 159–75. London: ITDG Publishing.

Bartra, Roger. 1993. *Agrarian Structure and Political Power in Mexico*. Baltimore: Johns Hopkins University Press.

Bebbington, Anthony, and Graham Thiele. 1993. *Non-Governmental Organizations and the State in Latin America: Rethinking Roles in Sustainable Agricultural Development*. London: Routledge.

Borras, Saturnino M. 2003. "Questioning Market-led Agrarian Reform: Experiences from Brazil, Colombia and South Africa." *Journal of Agrarian Change* 3, no. 3: 367–94.

Burbach, Roger, and Patricia Flynn. 1980. *Agribusiness in the Americas*. New York: Monthly Review Press.

Byres, Terence J. 1996. *Capitalism from Above and Capitalism from Below: An Essay in Comparative Political Economy*. London: Macmillan.

Calderón, Fernando, Manuel Chiriboga, and Diego Piñeiro. 1992. *Modernización democrática e incluyente de la agricultura en América Latina y el Caribe*. San José: Instituto Interamericano de Cooperación para la Agricultura (IICA).

Carter, Michael R., and Dinah Mesbah. 1993. "Can Land Market Reform Mitigate the Exclusionary Aspects of Rapid Agro-export Growth?" *World Development* 21, no. 7: 1085–1100.

Chayanov, Alexander V. 1966[1925]. *The Theory of Peasant Economy*, ed. Daniel Thorner, Basil Kerblay, and R. E. F. Smith. Homewood, IL: Richard D. Irwin.

Collins, Jane I. 2003. "Transnational Labor Process and Gender Relations: Women in Fruit and Vegetable Production in Chile, Brazil and Mexico." In *Perspectives on Las Américas: A Reader in Culture, History, and Representation*, ed. Matthew C. Gutmann, Félix V. Matos Rodríguez, Lynn Stephen, and Patricia Zavella, 160–73. Malden, MA: Blackwell Publishing.

Comisión Económica de América Latina y el Caribe (CEPAL). 2005a. *Panorama social de América Latina 2004*. Santiago: Naciones Unidas, CEPAL.

———. 2005b. *Panorama 2005: El nuevo patrón de desarrollo de la agricultura en América Latina y el Caribe*. Santiago: CEPAL.

———. 2005c. *Panorama social de América Latina 2005*. Santiago: CEPAL.

Comisión Económica de América Latina y el Caribe (CEPAL) and Food and Agriculture Organization of the United Nations (FAO). 1986. *El crecimiento productivo y la heterogeneidad agraria*. Santiago: División Agrícola Conjunta CEPAL and FAO.

Davis, Mike. 2006. *Planet of Slums*. London: Verso.

De Ferranti, David, Guillermo E. Perry, William Foster, Daniel Lederman, and Alberto Valdés. 2005. *Beyond the City: The Rural Contribution to Development*. Washington, DC: World Bank.

De Janvry, Alain. 1981. *The Agrarian Question and Reformism in Latin America*. Baltimore: Johns Hopkins University Press.

De Janvry, Alain, Robin Marsh, David Runsten, Elisabeth Sadoulet, and Carol Zabin. 1989. *Rural Development in Latin America: An Evaluation and a Proposal*. San José: Inter-American Institute for Cooperation on Agriculture (IICA).

De Janvry, Alain, Elisabeth Sadoulet, and Linda Wilcox Young. 1989. "Land and Labour in Latin American Agriculture from the 1950s to the 1980s." *Journal of Peasant Studies* 16, no. 3: 396–424.

Deininger, Klaus. 1999. "Making Negotiated Land Reform Work: Initial Experience from Colombia, Brazil, and South Africa." *World Development* 14, no. 4: 493–522.

Dirven, Martine. 2004. *Alcanzando las metas del milenio: Una mirada hacia la pobreza rural y agrícola*. Serie Desarrollo Productivo 146. Santiago: CEPAL.

Dore, Elizabeth. 2006. *Myths of Modernity: Peonage and Patriarchy in Nicaragua*. Durham, NC: Duke University Press.

Economic Commission for Latin America and the Caribbean (ECLAC). 1990. *Changing Production Patterns with Social Equity*. Santiago: United Nations (UN) ECLAC.

———. 1992. *Social Equity and Changing Production Patterns: An Integrated Approach*. Santiago: UN ECLAC.

———. 1993. *Statistical Yearbook for Latin America and the Caribbean 1992*. Santiago: UN ECLAC.

Economic Commission for Latin America and the Caribbean (ECLAC) and Food and Agriculture Organization of the United Nations (FAO). 1985. "The Agriculture of Latin America: Changes, Trends and Outlines of Strategy." *CEPAL Review* 27:117–29.

Economic Commission for Latin America and the Caribbean (ECLAC) and Inter-American Institute for Cooperation on Agriculture (IICA). 2002. *Survey of Agriculture in Latin America and the Caribbean 1990–2000.* Santiago: UN ECLAC.

Esteva, Gustavo. 1983. *The Struggle for Rural Mexico.* South Handley, MA: Bergin and Garvey Publishers.

Feder, Ernest. 1977. "Agribusiness and the Elimination of Latin America's Rural Proletariat." *World Development* 5, nos. 5–7: 559–71.

Figueroa, Adolfo. 1993. "Agricultural Development in Latin America." In *Development from Within: Toward a Neostructuralist Approach for Latin America,* ed. Osvaldo Sunkel, 287–314. Boulder, CO: Lynne Rienner Publishers.

Fox, Jonathan, ed. 1990. *The Challenge of Rural Democratisation: Perspectives from Latin America and the Philippines.* London: Frank Cass.

Friedmann, Harriet. 1991. "Changes in the International Division of Labor: Agrifood Complexes and Export Agriculture." In *Towards a New Political Economy of Agriculture,* ed. William H. Friedland, Larry Busch, Frederick H. Buttel and A. P. Rudy, 65–93. Boulder, CO: Westview Press.

———. 2004. "Feeding the Empire: The Pathologies of Globalized Agriculture." In *Socialist Register 2005: The Empire Reloaded,* ed. Leo Panitch and Colin Leys, 124–43. London: Merlin Press.

Goodman, David, and Michael Redclift. 1982. *From Peasant to Proletarian: Capitalist Development and Agrarian Transitions.* Oxford: Basil Blackwell.

———, eds. 1991. *Environment and Development in Latin America: The Politics of Sustainability.* Manchester, UK: Manchester University Press.

Goodman, David, Bernardo Sorj, and John Wilkinson. 1987. *From Farming to Biotechnology: A Theory of Agro-industrial Development.* Oxford: Basil Blackwell.

Goodman, David, and Michael J. Watts, eds. 1997. *Globalising Food: Agrarian Questions and Global Restructuring.* London: Routledge.

Hall, Anthony. 1997. "Peopling the Environment: A New Agenda for Research, Policy and Action in Brazilian Amazonia." *European Review of Latin American and Caribbean Studies* 62:9–31.

Harris, Richard L. 1978. "Marxism and the Agrarian Question in Latin America." *Latin American Perspectives* 5, no. 4: 2–26.

Hewitt de Alcántara, Cynthia. 1984. *Anthropological Perspectives on Rural Mexico.* London: Routledge and Kegan Paul.

Heynig, Klaus. 1982. "The Principal Schools of Thought on the Peasant Economy." *CEPAL Review* 16:113–39.

Inter-American Development Bank (IDB). 1986. *Economic and Social Progress in Latin America: 1986 Report. Special Section: Agricultural Development.* Washington, DC: IDB.

Jansen, Kees, and Sietze Vellema, eds. 2004. *Agribusiness and Society: Corporate Responses to Environmentalism, Market Opportunities and Public Regulation.* London: Zed Books.

Kautsky, Karl. 1988[1899]. *The Agrarian Question.* 2 vols. London: Zwan Publications.

Kay, Cristóbal. 1974. "Comparative Development of the European Manorial System and the Latin American *Hacienda* System." *Journal of Peasant Studies* 2, no. 1: 69–98.

———. 1988. "The Landlord Road and the Subordinate Peasant Road to Capitalism in Latin America." *Etudes Rurales* 77:5–20.

———. 1998. "Latin America's Agrarian Reform: Lights and Shadows." *Land Reform, Settlement and Cooperatives* 2:8–31.

———. 2002. "Chile's Neoliberal Agrarian Transformation and the Peasantry." *Journal of Agrarian Change* 2, no. 4: 464–501.

———. 2006. "Rural Poverty and Development Strategies in Latin America." *Journal of Agrarian Change* 6, no. 4: 455–508.

Kjöllerström, Mónica. 2004. "Competitividad del sector agrícola y pobreza rural: El papel del gasto público en América Latina." Serie Desarrollo Productivo 155. Santiago: CEPAL.

Lehmann, David. 1982. "After Lenin and Chayanov: New Paths of Agrarian Capitalism." *Journal of Development Economics* 11, no. 2: 133–61.

———. 1986. "Two Paths of Agrarian Capitalism, or a Critique of Chayanovian Marxism." *Comparative Study of Society and History* 28, no. 4: 601–27.

Lenin, Vladimir I. 1964[1899]. *The Development of Capitalism in Russia*. Moscow: Progress Publishers.

Llambí, Luis. 1989. "Emergence of Capitalized Family Farms in Latin America." *Comparative Studies in Society and History* 31, no. 4: 745–74.

———. 1990. "Transitions to and within Capitalism: Agrarian Transitions in Latin America." *Sociologia Ruralis* 30, no. 2: 174–96.

———. 1991. "Latin American Peasantries and Regimes of Accumulation." *European Review of Latin American and Caribbean Studies* 51:27–50.

———. 1994. "Opening Economies and Closing Markets: Latin American Agriculture's Difficult Search for a Place in the Emerging Global Order." In *From Columbus to ConAgra: The Globalization of Agriculture and Food*, ed. Alessandro Bonanno, Lawrence Busch, William H. Friedland, and Lourdes Gouveia, 184–209. Lawrence: University Press of Kansas.

———. 2000. "Global-Local Links in Latin America's New Ruralities." In *Disappearing Peasantries? Rural Labour in Africa, Asia and Latin America*, ed. Deborah Bryceson, Cristóbal Kay, and Jos Mooij, 176–91. London: ITDG Publishing.

Long, Norman, and Bryan Roberts. 2005. "Changing Rural Scenarios and Research Agendas in Latin America in the New Century." In *New Directions in the Sociology of Global Development*, ed. Frederick H. Buttel and Philip McMichael, 57–90. Oxford: Elsevier.

López, Luis. 1985. "Transformaciones, tendencias y perspectivas." *Pensamiento Iberoamericano* 8:15–35.

Murmis, Miguel. 1994. "Incluidos y excluidos en la reestructuración del agro latinoamericano." *Debate Agrario* 18:101–33.

Murray, Warwick E. 2002. "The Neoliberal Inheritance: Agrarian Policy and Rural Differentiation in Democratic Chile." *Bulletin of Latin American Research* 21, no. 3: 425–41.

Ortega, Emiliano. 1985. "La opción campesina en las estrategias agrícolas." *Pensamiento Iberoamericano* 8:79–108.

———. 1992. "Evolution of the Rural Dimension in Latin America and the Caribbean." *CEPAL Review* 47:115–36.

Otero, Gerardo. 1999. *Farewell to the Peasantry? Political Class Formation in Rural Mexico*. Boulder, CO: Westview Press.

Petras, James, and Henry Veltmeyer. 2002. "The Peasantry and the State in Latin America: A Troubled Past and Uncertain Future." *Journal of Peasant Studies* 29, nos. 3–4: 41–82.

Reardon, Thomas, Julio A. Berdegué, and Germán Escobar. 2001. "Rural Nonfarm Employment and Incomes in Latin America: Overview and Policy Implications." *World Development* 29, no. 3: 395–409.

Schejtman, Alexander. 1980. "The Peasant Economy: Internal Logic, Articulation and Persistence." *CEPAL Review* 11:114–34.

Shanin, Teodor. 1986. "Chayanov's Message: Illuminations, Miscomprehensions, and the Contemporary 'Development Theory.'" In *A. V. Chayanov on the Theory of Peasant Economy*, ed. Daniel Thorner, Basil Kerblay, and R. E. F. Smith, 1–24. Madison: University of Wisconsin Press.

Spoor, Max. 2002. "Policy Regimes and Performance of the Agricultural Sector in Latin America and the Caribbean during the Last Three Decades." *Journal of Agrarian Change* 2, no. 3: 381–400.

Stavenhagen, Rodolfo. 1978. "Capitalism and the Peasantry in Mexico." *Latin American Perspectives* 5, no. 3: 27–37.

Teubal, Miguel. 1987. "Internationalization of Capital and Agroindustrial Complexes: Their Impact on Latin American Agriculture." *Latin American Perspectives* 14, no. 3: 316–64.

———. 1995. *Globalización y expansión agroindustrial. ¿Superación de la pobreza en América Latina?* Buenos Aires: Ediciones Corregidor.

Thiesenhusen, William C., ed. 1989. *Searching for Agrarian Reform in Latin America*. Winchester, MA: Unwin Hyman.

Veltmeyer, Henry. 2005. "The Dynamics of Land Occupations in Latin America." In *Reclaiming the Land: The Resurgence of Rural Movements in Africa, Asia and Latin America*, ed. Sam Moyo and Paris Yeros, 285–316. London: Zed Books, and Cape Town: David Philip.

Vogelgesang, Frank. 1996. "Property Rights and the Rural Land Market in Latin America." *CEPAL Review* 58:95–113.

Warman, Arturo. 1980. *Ensayos sobre el campesinado en México*. Mexico City: Nueva Imagen.

Weeks, John. 1995. "Macroeconomic Adjustment and Latin American Agriculture since 1980." In *Structural Adjustment in the Agricultural Sector in Latin America and the Caribbean*, ed. John Weeks, 61–91. London: Macmillan.

Wise, Timothy A., Hilda Salazar, and Laura Carlsen, eds. 2003. *Confronting Globalization: Economic Integration and Popular Resistance in Mexico*. Bloomfield, CT: Kumarian Press.

World Bank. 2006. *World Development Indicators 2006*. Washington, DC: World Bank.

Wright, Angus, and Wendy Wolford. 2003. *To Inherit the Earth: The Landless Movement and the Struggle for a New Brazil*. Oakland, CA: Food First Books.

3

Dependency, Underdevelopment, and Neoliberalism

Richard L. Harris

There is no single, homogenous pattern of characteristics that fits all the economies of Latin America and the Caribbean. In fact, there are considerable differences between these economies in terms of their size, industrialization, the diversity of their exports, their trading relations, the distribution of income, and other important variables. Nevertheless, they do share many similar characteristics and common conditions. In fact, the differences that exist between the Latin American and Caribbean economies do not detract from their commonalities. With the exception of Socialist Cuba (where most sectors of the economy were placed under state control in the early 1960s), all the Latin American and Caribbean countries have capitalist economies, and these economies all hold a subordinate status in the global economic order. In addition, their historical development has been "profoundly and continuously influenced" by the same "international economic and political forces" over the last five hundred years (Weaver 2000, 1–2).

In addition, the economies of the region have all undergone a common process of highly uneven, inequitable, and exploitative capitalist economic development. Over the last one hundred years, this form of economic development, which has been variously labeled "underdevelopment" or "dependent development," "uneven capitalist development," or "peripheral capitalist development," has produced a demonstrably slower rate of economic growth and more frequent and severe economic crises in Latin America and the Caribbean than in the advanced industrial countries (the United States, the members of the European Union, and Japan).

Like most other "underdeveloped" or "developing" economies[1] around the world, the most important sectors of the Latin American and Caribbean economies are dominated by transnational corporations and foreign investors that have their home bases in North America, Western Europe, and/or Japan. In addition, the contemporary economic policies of most of the Latin American and Caribbean governments are constrained by the regulatory dictates of the same powerful international financial institutions (IFIs)—the International Monetary Fund (IMF), the World Bank, and the Inter-American Development Bank (IDB)—and the World Trade Organization (WTO). All of these so-called multilateral intergovernmental institutions tend to promote the interests of the large transnational corporations and the governments of the Group of 7 countries (led by the United States). Most of the contemporary Latin American and Caribbean countries are also burdened by large external debts, which they owe to international private banks and one or more of the IFIs. Moreover, unfavorable terms of trade with the more advanced industrial economies at the apex or center of the global economic system have historically handicapped the economies of most of the Latin American and Caribbean countries.

Since the end of World War II, the increasingly powerful transnational corporations based in the advanced industrial countries have invested heavily in the Latin American and Caribbean economies to take advantage of their abundant supply of natural resources, cheap labor, lax environmental regulations, and consumer markets. These powerful corporations and the international financial institutions that support them have promoted the increasing "integration" of the Latin American and Caribbean economies into the global capitalist economic system, which is dominated by these very same corporations. Consequently, transnational corporations and foreign investment generally dominate the most developed sectors of the Latin American and Caribbean economies, which are export oriented and trade more with the advanced industrial economies than with other Latin American and Caribbean economies.

Along with these common economic traits, there are more distressing similarities between these economies. In most of these countries, a large percentage of the population lives in poverty, they have high levels of unemployment, and they have large informal workforces composed of precariously self-employed street peddlers, microentrepreneurs, domestic workers, and day laborers.[2] A large proportion of the workforce in these economies comprises generally low-skilled and semiskilled workers who receive much lower wages and fewer benefits than comparable workers in the advanced industrial economies.

Moreover, because a large percentage of the population is either unemployed, underemployed in temporary or part-time jobs, precariously employed in the informal sector, or engaged in subsistence or semisubsistence agriculture, an extremely unequal distribution of income also characterizes these economies. That is to say, the majority of the population receives a small fraction of the total income generated in these societies, while the wealthy elites receive a major proportion of the total income. This unequal distribution of income is coupled with the increasing concentration of other forms of wealth (land, personal property, stock ownership, etc.) in the hands of a relatively small percentage of the population, which forms the top layer of the steep pyramidal class structures that exist throughout Latin America and the Caribbean. Indeed, there is a growing income gap between the extremely wealthy upper classes at the top of these class structures and the middle and lower classes below them. As a result of this unequal distribution of income and wealth, there is extensive poverty, social exclusion, class discrimination, social injustice, and political inequality throughout Latin America.

GENERAL OVERVIEW OF THE LATIN AMERICAN ECONOMIES

Table 3.1 provides a set of basic indicators that provide a profile of the major economic dimensions of the Latin American countries (and the region as a whole) and how the economies of these countries (and the region) compare with those of the United States and Canada, which are the only two advanced industrial countries in the Americas (i.e., North America, Central America, and South America, as well as the island territories of the Caribbean basin). Except for Cuba, the Dominican Republic, and Haiti, this table does not include information on most of the island states of the Caribbean basin. The economies of these countries are in many ways similar to the economies of the smaller Latin American states, but data for most of these small economies are not included in the table. The primary focus here is on the countries included in table 3.1, but many of the observations and conclusions I make about the economic dimensions of these countries apply to the island states of the Caribbean basin that are not included.

At midyear 2005, the total population of the Americas was over 880 million, which represented almost 14 percent of the world's total human population of 6.4 billion (U.S. Census Bureau 2006). A little more than one-third of this total population of 880 million resides in the United States and Canada, while almost another third resides in Brazil and Mexico (the second- and third-largest countries after the United States in terms of population size). The remaining third of the total population of the Americas is scattered among the other countries and territories. The midyear estimate in 2005 of the total population of Latin America and the Caribbean was 555,432,455, and the total population of North America was 328,667,927 (U.S. Census Bureau 2006).

Table 3.1 reveals the wide range of differences among the Latin American countries in terms of the scale of their economies, represented in the table

Table 3.1. Latin American Economic and Social Indicators (compared with United States and Canada)

Country or Region	2005 Population[a] (millions)	2004 GDP (PPP)[b] ($ billions)	2004 GDP (PPP) per Capita[c] ($)	2004–2005 External Debt[d] ($ billions)	Ratio of Richest to Poorest 20 Percent[e]	2005 Main Export Destinations[f]	2002–2004 Trade-to-GDP Ratio[g] (%)
Argentina	38.7	533.7	14,109	118.6	17.6	EU, Br, US	43.2
Bolivia	9.2	25.6	2,817	4.8	42.3	Br, US, Ve	56.6
Brazil	186.4	1,576.7	8,584	191.3	23.7	EU, US, Ar	29.5
Chile	16.3	193.2	11,937	44.3	18.7	EU, US, Ja	71.7
Colombia	45.6	337.2	7,565	37.0	25.3	US, EU, Ve	40.4
Costa Rica	4.3	45.1	10,434	3.6	14.2	US, EU, Gu	98.7
Cuba	11.3	33.9	3,000	12.0	—	EU, RF, Ca	—
Dom. Rep.	8.9	65.0	7,203	6.4	14.4	US, EU, Ha	90.4
Ecuador	13.2	57.0	4,316	17.6	17.3	US, Pa, EU	55.7
El Salvador	6.9	31.0	4,511	4.9	20.9	Gu, US, Ho	70.2
Guatemala	12.6	57.0	4,155	3.7	20.3	US, ES, Ho	46.2
Haiti	8.5	14.9	1,783	1.3	26.6	US, EU, Ca	54.0
Honduras	7.2	21.7	3,009	5.6	17.2	US, EU, ES	99.8
Mexico	107.0	1,072.5	10,186	131.7	12.8	US, EU, Ca	60.1
Nicaragua	5.5	20.9	3,636	5.2	8.8	US, ES, EU	97.3
Panama	3.2	23.4	7,283	7.2	23.9	US, EU, CR	125.5
Paraguay	6.2	28.3	4,555	2.9	27.8	Ur, Br, Cl	95.0
Peru	28.2	167.7	5,983	30.1	18.6	US, EU, Chi	39.7
Uruguay	3.5	34.3	10,028	11.2	10.9	US, EU, Br	56.8
Venezuela	26.7	163.5	6,186	45.1	10.6	US, Co, EU	56.9
Latin America	**553.3**	**4,421.5**	**8,105**	**671.7**	**19.0**	**US, EU, LA**	**53**
United States	298.2	11,651.1	39,676	9,560.6	8.4	Ca, EU, Me	24.4
Canada	32.3	999.6	31,263	480.0	5.5	US, EU, Ja	72.9

a Population figures represent millions of inhabitants in the year 2005. *Source:* United Nations Population Fund, *The State of World Population* (2005).

b Gross domestic product (GDP) figures represent billions of international dollars measured at purchasing power parity (PPP). *Sources:* ECLAC, *Preliminary Overview of the Economies of Latin America and the Caribbean 2005,* and Central Intelligence Agency, *World Fact Book* (2006) for Cuba.

c GDP PPP per capita figures represent the gross domestic product (GDP) divided by population and expressed in international dollars measured at purchasing power parity (PPP). PPP takes into account differences in the relative prices of goods and services between countries and provides a better overall measure of the real value of the gross output (i.e., the GDP) produced by an economy when compared to other economies. *Sources:* same as above.

d Total gross external debt is defined as the total public and private debt owed to nonresidents and repayable in foreign currency, goods, or services. Figures represent billions of international dollars for latest year available, 2004 or 2005. *Sources:* same as above.

e Data in this column show the ratio of the income of the richest 20 percent to that of the poorest 20 percent of the population. *Source:* United Nations Development Program, *Human Development Report 2006.*

f Main export destinations are presented in order of percentage of total exports. Abbreviations are **Ar**gentina, **B**razil, **Ca**nada, Cayman **I**slands, **Ch**ina, **Co**lombia, **Cos**ta **R**ica, **El** Salvador, European Union, **Gua**temala, **Hai**ti, **Hon**duras, **Ja**pan, **Me**xico, **Ni**caragua, **Pa**nama, **R**ussian Federation, **United S**tates of America, **Ur**uguay, and **Ve**nezuela. *Source:* Central Intelligence Agency, *World Fact Book* (2006).

g Trade-to-GDP ratio is a measure of the total value of trade (exports plus imports) as a percentage of a country or region's GDP. *Source:* United Nations Development Program, *Human Development Report 2006.*

by the value of their gross domestic products (GDPs)—GDP is the total value of all the goods and services produced in a country—and their standards of living, represented in the table by the value of their per capita GDPs (which roughly indicate each country's average standard of living). A quick comparison of the GDP of the countries listed in table 3.1 reveals that Brazil, which had a GDP of $1,576.7 billion (all sums unless specified are in international dollars) in 2004, has the largest economy in the Americas after the United States. Brazil's economy is over one hundred times larger than the economy of Haiti, one of smallest economies in the region. Haiti had a GDP of only $14.9 billion in 2004. The combined GDPs of Brazil, Mexico, and Argentina, the three largest economies in the Latin American region, totaled $3,182.9 billion in 2004. Thus, these three countries accounted for almost three-quarters of the total GDP of the entire region, which was $4,421.5 billion in 2004. Moreover, the region's "Big Seven" economies (Brazil, Mexico, Argentina, Colombia, Chile, Venezuela, and Peru) accounted for almost 90 percent of the total GDP of the region in 2004.

By way of contrast, the combined regional GDP of all the countries in the Latin American region, $4,421.5 billion in 2004, represented only about one-third the value of the GDP of the United States, which was $11,651 billion in 2004. And the largest economy in the region (Brazil) was only about one-thirteenth the size of the U.S. economy in 2004. These comparisons indicate how much of a difference there is between the United States and the Latin American countries in terms of their relative economic wealth and the size of their economies. These comparisons also reveal that the economic wealth and power of all the Latin American countries combined cannot match the economic wealth and power of the United States, which has for this reason and others been called the "Colossus of the North."

In terms of their average standards of living, there is also a wide range of difference between the Latin American countries, on the one hand, and the United States and Canada, on the other. These differences are revealed in table 3.1 by the data on GDP per capita. This indicator is a rough measure for comparing the standard of living in different countries and regions. As table 3.1 reveals, Argentina has the highest GDP per capita, or average standard of living, in Latin America. In 2004, Argentina's GDP per capita of $14,109 was eight times greater than the GDP per capita of Haiti, which was only $1,783. Haiti's relatively low GDP per capita reflects the fact that it has one of the poorest standards of living in Latin America and ranks among the poorest countries in the world.

Table 3.1 also reveals that the largest Latin American economies do not have the highest GDP per capita (i.e., the highest standards of living) in the region. Thus, Brazil has the largest economy in the region, but its GDP per capita of $8,584 in 2004 was less than the GDP per capita of Costa Rica ($10,434 per capita) and Uruguay ($10,028 per capita). These are two of the smallest countries in the region in terms of their population size. Mexico has the second-largest economy in Latin America, but its GDP per capita of $10,186 in 2004 was approximately the same as the GDP per capita of Costa Rica and Uruguay. These differences in GDP per capita are in part due statistically to the difference in size of their populations, but they also reflect the fact that some of the smaller countries, such as Costa Rica and Uruguay, produce more wealth in proportion to their population size than the larger economies, such as Brazil and Mexico.

More importantly, the figures in table 3.1 reveal that even the countries with the highest GDP per capita in the region, such as Argentina and Chile, have standards of living substantially below the standards of living of the two most advanced industrial countries in the Americas, the United States and Canada. Thus, Argentina's GDP per capita of $14,109 in 2004 was less than half of Canada's GDP per capita of $31,263 in 2004 and only one-third the GDP per capita of the United States, which was $39,676 in 2004. And, of course, a much greater contrast exists between the GDP per capita of Latin America's poorest country, Haiti, and the GDP per capita of the United States and Canada. The average standard of living in these two "rich" countries was, respectively, twenty-two and seventeen times greater than Haiti's standard of living in 2004.

For the region as a whole, the average GDP per capita was $8,105 in 2004, which was approximately one-fifth the GDP per capita of the United States. This comparison reveals that the standard of living of the majority of the people living in United States is five times greater than the standard of living of the majority of people living in Latin America and the Caribbean. This quantum difference is hard to imagine unless one has seen the difference in material living conditions between these societies.

Table 3.1 does not reveal that the gap between the standard of living in the Latin American countries and the advanced industrial countries has been increasing over the last one hundred years. Historical data on the GDP per capita of the larger Latin American economies (Argentina, Brazil, Chile, Colombia, Mexico, Peru, and Venezuela) and the advanced industrial countries (the United States, the Western European countries, Japan, Australia, Canada, etc.) show that the gap in the standards of living between these countries has been widening over the last century or so (De Gregorio 2004, 1–2). As table 3.2 reveals, at the beginning of the 1900s, the GDP per capita for the larger Latin American states was 43 percent of the GDP per capita of the advanced industrial economies and 32 percent of the GDP per capita of the United States. However, by 2000, the GDP per capita of the Latin American states fell nine percentage points, to 34 percent of the GDP per capita of the advanced industrial countries, and dropped eight percentage points, to 24 percent (less than a quarter) of the GDP per capita of the United States.

Table 3.2. Gap between GDP per Capita in Latin America and Advanced Industrial Countries

GDP per Capita Comparisons	Year of Comparison	
	1900 (%)	2000 (%)
GDP per capita of Latin America as a percentage of GDP per capita of advanced industrial countries	43	34
GDP per capita of Latin America as a percentage of GDP per capita of the United States	32	24

Source: De Gregorio (2004).

There is a wide range of difference between the Latin American countries in terms not only of the size of their economies and their average standards of living but also their external indebtedness. The gross external debts of these countries consist of the total public and private debts owed to foreign residents and foreign organizations (international commercial banks, the IFIs, the U.S. government, etc.) by the residents and organizations in these countries.

The three largest economies (Argentina, Brazil, and Mexico) have the largest external debts in the region. In 2004, Argentina's total external debt was $118.6 billion, Brazil's was $191.3 billion, and Mexico's was $131.7 billion. In fact, the combined external debts of these three countries ($441.6 billion) represented almost two-thirds of the total external debt of the entire region, which equaled $671.7 billion in 2004 and 2005. These three countries are some of the most indebted countries in the world, especially in terms of the size of their external debts relative to the size of their economies.

Nevertheless, it should be noted that the external debts of these heavily indebted countries are smaller in amount than the external debts of Canada and the United States. In 2004, the total external debt of the United States ($9,560 billion) was fourteen times larger than the total, combined external debt of the entire Latin American region ($671.7 billion). And Canada's external debt ($480 billion) was larger than the combined external debts of Argentina, Brazil, and Mexico ($441.6 billion). However, the Latin American countries, for various reasons, find it more difficult to pay their external debts than the two richer North American countries.

Latin America is frequently referred to as "the world's most unequal region" (*International Herald Tribune* 2005). Table 3.1 provides an indicator of the extent of income inequality within each of the Latin American countries. In 2005, the country with the most income inequality was Bolivia. The income of the richest 20 percent of the population in Bolivia was some forty-two times greater than the income of the poorest 20 percent of the population (UNDP 2006, 335–37). Across the region, the ratio of income inequality between the richest and poorest 20 percent of the population ranged from a high of 42 in Bolivia to a low of 8.8 in Nicaragua in 2005.

For the region as a whole, the average ratio of income inequality in Latin America was 19 in 2005. In other words, the average income of the richest 20 percent of the inhabitants of the region was nineteen times greater than the income of the poorest 20 percent in 2005. This contrasts with an 8.4 ratio of income inequality in the United States, which has a fairly high ratio of income inequality for an advanced industrial country. Canada's ratio of income inequality in 2005 was only 5.5. In other words, the richest 20 percent of the population in Canada had an income that was only five and a half times that of the poorest 20 percent of the population in 2005. In contrast, the ratio of income inequality for the region of Latin America as a whole was almost four times greater than the ratio of income inequality in Canada and three times greater than the ratio of income inequality in the United States.

The fact that the ratio of income inequality in Nicaragua (8.8) is similar to that in the United States (8.4) does not mean that the poorest 20 percent of the population in both countries have the same standard of living. Nor does it mean that the poorest 20 percent of the Nicaraguan population is better off than the poorest 20 percent of the population in countries with a higher ratio of income inequality, such as Brazil (which had a ratio of income inequality of 23.7 in 2005) or Colombia (which had a income inequality ratio of 25.3 in 2005). In fact, because Nicaragua is one of the poorest countries in Latin America, with an average GDP per capita of only $3,636 in 2004, the poorest 20 percent of the population is as poor or poorer than the poorest 20 percent of the population in the rest of the Latin American countries. These people live in absolute poverty.[3] Their annual income is much less than the country's low average income of only $3,636 in 2004. Indeed, the poorest 20 percent of the population in all the countries of the region, with the exception of Cuba, live in absolute poverty.

As the following quote from a 2002 report on poverty by the United Nations Council for Trade and Development (UNCTAD) (2002) reveals, absolute poverty is generally defined by international agencies as an income of $2 per day or less.

> Poverty is understood in absolute terms as the inability to attain a minimally adequate standard of living. The standard of living is measured by the level of private consumption, and those who are poor are identified by adopting the $1-a-day and $2-a-day international poverty lines, which are now conventionally used to make internationally comparable estimates of global poverty. These international poverty lines specify the level below which private consumption is considered inadequate, and they are measured, again in line with current practice, using purchasing power parity (PPP) exchange rates, which seek to correct for differences in the cost of living between countries. (5)

However, this UNCTAD report argues convincingly that definitions of poverty cannot be confined to quantitative measures alone. In fact, this report acknowledges that "many now argue that poverty is multidimensional, constituted by an interlocking web of economic, political, human and socio-cultural deprivations, and characterized not simply by a lack of economic opportunity, but also by insecurity, vulnerability and powerlessness" (UNCTAD 2002, 5–6).

Thus, even though Cuba's GDP per capita is quite low by world standards (estimated by the U.S. Central Intelligence Agency to be approximately $3,000 per capita in 2004 and by the United Nations Development Program [UNDP] to be $5,400 per capita), Cuba has a relatively high quality-of-life ranking in the UNDP assessments. Cuba's well-developed social security system, the comprehensive social services provided by the government to the population, and the low-cost housing provided to the entire population give the Cuban people a relatively high quality of life by world standards (see Galbraith, Spagnolo, and Munevar 2006). Therefore, the quality of life in Cuba is relatively high, even though the GDP per capita and income per capita are relatively low by world standards. The explanation for this seeming inconsistency is that the country's wealth is much more equally distributed among the population than in the rest of Latin America, which also leads to considerable social equity in Cuba, in contrast to the rest of Latin America. This situation can be attributed to the Socialist character of the Cuban economy and the highly egalitarian norms that regulate Cuban society.

In the rest of Latin America, poverty and income inequality go hand in hand (as they do in most parts of the world). According to a 2006 World Bank report on poverty and income inequality in Latin America, the proportion of the population living in poverty throughout the region as a whole increased on average by about 1.5 percent per year during the 1990s. In 2005, this report indicated that at least one-fourth of the population in Latin America was living in poverty (Perry et al. 2006, 21). While a conservative estimate of poverty in the region, this still reveals that at least one out of every four Latin Americans lives on $2 or less a day ($2 is the poverty line used by the World Bank).

However, using different criteria for measuring poverty, the United Nations Economic Commission for Latin America and the Caribbean (ECLAC 2006a) reported that approximately 40 percent of the region's population was living in poverty in 2005 (see table 3.3), and over 15 percent was living in "extreme poverty" (Solimano 2005, 22). Since the World Bank tends to provide conservative estimates of poverty, its estimates can be considered low estimates of the number of people living in poverty throughout the region. The ECLAC estimates are probably much closer to the actual level of poverty in the region.

Table 3.3. Poverty and Extreme Poverty in Latin America and the Caribbean, 1981–2004

	Year of Estimate and Percentage of Population in Poverty			
Poverty Estimates	1981 (%)	1990 (%)	2001 (%)	2005 (%)
Poverty (ECLAC)	40.5	48.3	43.2	39.8
Poverty (World Bank)	27.4	29.0	24.7	24.6
Extreme poverty (ECLAC)	18.6	22.5	18.5	15.4
Extreme poverty (World Bank)	10.1	11.6	10.6	—

Source: Solimano (2005, 22).

As indicated by the 2006 World Bank study on poverty and inequality in Latin America, the standard indicators used by international organizations for measuring poverty "are very imperfect indicators of well-being" and quality of life (Perry et al. 2006, 21). Figure 3.1 reveals that the national estimates of poverty in Latin America, which are based on different definitions of poverty and different indicators, tend to be much higher than the estimates of poverty used by international organizations such as the World Bank. In fact, in some countries the national estimates of poverty are as much as two times higher than the poverty estimates of the World Bank (see figure 3.1). Even in the countries with the lowest percentage of the population living in poverty (Chile, Costa Rica, and Uruguay), the national estimates of poverty were considerably higher than the international estimates in 2004 and 2005 (see figure 3.1, next page).

During the 2004–2005 period, national estimates of poverty in Latin America (which are based on poverty lines that are generally higher than $2 per day) indicated that more than 40 percent of the population was living in poverty in Argentina, Bolivia, Colombia, El Salvador, Honduras, Mexico, Nicaragua, Paraguay, Peru, and Venezuela. The countries with the highest percentages of the population living in poverty, according to national estimates, were Colombia, Honduras, and Peru. In these countries, over half the population was estimated to be living in poverty in 2004 and 2005. Only in Chile and Costa Rica did both national and international estimates indicate that less than 10 percent of the population was living in poverty in 2004 and 2005 (see figure 3.1).

ECLAC estimates for 2005 and 2006 indicate that there was a modest decrease in poverty in Latin America and the Caribbean during the three-year period from 2004 to 2006, which appears to be related to the modest recovery of most of the Latin American economies during this time (ECLAC 2006a). According to ECLAC estimates, 39.8 percent of the population in

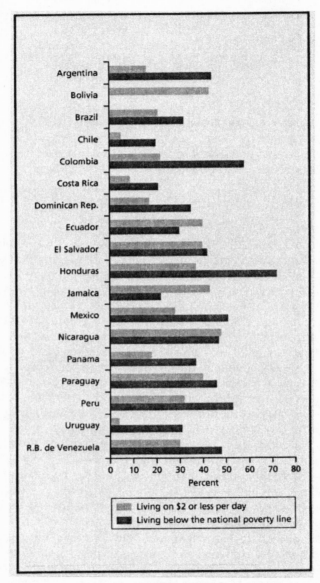

Figure 3.1. Nationally Defined Poverty Estimates. *Source:*
Cited in Perry et al. (2006, 22).

Latin America and the Caribbean (approximately 209 million people) was living in poverty in 2005 (see table 3.3), while 15.4 percent (81 million) was living in extreme poverty (sometimes referred to as indigence) (ECLAC 2006a). ECLAC projections for 2006 indicated that the number of people living in poverty in Latin America and the Caribbean had declined to 38.5 percent (205 million) by the end of 2006, and the number living in extreme poverty had declined to 14.7 percent (79 million). According to ECLAC (2006a), during the three-year period from 2003 to 2005, "the most significant improvements occurred in Argentina (26% poverty rate in 2003–05, compared to 45.4% in 2000–02), and Venezuela (37.1% in 2003–05, compared to 48.6% in 2000–02)."

A decline of "nearly 4 percentage points" in the number of people living in poverty was also projected by ECLAC for Colombia, Ecuador, Mexico, and Peru from 2003 to 2005 (ECLAC 2006a). However, despite these improvements in the number of people living in poverty during the 2003–2006 period, according to ECLAC (2006a), "poverty levels remain high and the region still faces a great task" in reducing these levels to meet "the first target of the UN Millennium Development Goals (MDG)," which is "to eradicate extreme poverty and hunger by the year 2015."

During the1980s and 1990s, both poverty and income inequality increased throughout the region. The "lost decade" of the 1980s erased the modest improvements that were made during the 1970s in reducing both poverty and income inequality throughout the region. As the 2006 World Bank study on poverty and inequality indicates, "Higher inequality, whether in income or other dimensions of well-being, means more poverty at any given point in time" (Perry et al. 2006, 6). Since the early 2000s, some progress has been made in lowering income inequality (and reducing poverty). The modest improvement in Brazil stands out (i.e., a 3 percent decline in income inequality between the early 1990s and the early 2000s) since it was historically the most unequal country in the region (Perry et al. 2006, 4). But throughout the region as a whole, "the more striking fact for the long term is the resilience of high inequality in the face of diverse economic and political regimes" (Perry et al. 2006, 5). Thus, in 2005, between 40 and 47 percent of the total income in most Latin American countries went to the richest 10 percent of the population, while the poorest 20 percent of the population received only 2 to 4 percent of the total income (Perry et al. 2006, 45).

To quote from the summary of the World Bank's report on poverty and inequality in the region, "Inequality is a pervasive feature of Latin American societies in terms of differences in income, access to services, power and influence and, in many countries, treatment by police and justice systems," and this study also notes that "the most distinctive attribute of Latin American income inequality is the unusually large concentration of income at the very top of the distribution" (Perry et al. 2006, 2–3). As this study and many other studies on the social and economic realities of the region indicate, inequality characterizes every aspect of social life in Latin America and the Caribbean. Some of the most important dimensions of this chronic problem include unequal access to critical public services, such as education and health care, as well as unequal access (or no access at all) to arable land, potable water, electricity, sanitation, and adequate housing or to credit, employment, insurance, pensions, and adequate political representation. According to the authors of the World Bank study on income inequality and poverty in the region, if Latin America had the same level of income inequality as most of the advanced industrial countries, the percentage of the population living in poverty would be closer to 5 percent of the region's population than to the actual rate of 25 percent (almost 40 percent according to ECLAC) (Perry et al. 2006, 45).

One of the reasons there is so much income inequality in Latin America is that the working classes have been subjected to frequent political repression and antilabor governmental policies and practices. Moreover, labor organizations, trade unions, and collective bargaining over wages and working conditions have not benefited from the market-liberalization, pro-business, and regional-integration policies implemented over the last twenty to thirty years under the aegis of neoliberal ideology. In most of the Latin American countries, neoliberal governments during the 1980s and 1990s (during the 1970s in Chile) introduced so-called labor-market reforms to deregulate the labor markets of their countries and make them more "flexible" (Weeks 1999, 4). While it is debatable whether the region's deregulated labor markets are any more flexible today than they were in the 1960s and 1970s, there is considerable evidence that the power and influence of organized labor declined significantly between the 1970s and 1990s, largely because the so-called neoliberal reforms carried out during this period weakened their bargaining power (Weeks 1999, 14–16). Therefore, in view of these so-called reforms and the history of political repression, it is not surprising that the distribution of income in the region does not favor the working classes.

By the end of the 1990s, due to antilabor and pro-business policies and practices, no more than one-third of the nonagricultural labor force belonged to trade unions anywhere in Latin America, and the average degree of trade union membership for the nonagricultural labor force was less than 15 percent for the region (Weeks 1999, 18). In fact, in several countries today, union membership is less than 10 percent of the nonagricultural labor force. To make matters worse, a large number of the unionized workers belong to "company unions" controlled by the employers of their workplaces rather than by the workers themselves (Weeks 1999, 25). Nevertheless, in spite of the low degree of unionization of the workforce and the erosion of such basic labor rights as the right to organize and bargain collectively for improved working conditions, trade unions still play an important role in many of the Latin American countries (e.g., Argentina and Brazil).

According to the international nongovernmental organization Human Rights Watch (HRW) (2002), workers "suffer myriad violations of internationally recognized labor rights" throughout Latin America and the Caribbean. In 2002, HRW reported that "workers' right to organize—the internationally sanctioned tool for demanding better working conditions and respect for labor rights—was obstructed or violated throughout the region." In this same report, HRW noted that "in Mexico, legitimate organizing activity was frequently hindered by collective bargaining agreements negotiated between management and pro-business, non-independent unions," while in other cases, "workers' right to organize was violated through direct anti-union discrimination, including the harassment, demotion, or dismissal of union members and sympathizers." In the worst cases, HRW (2002) noted that "union leaders and their supporters risked assassination" and reported that "Colombia led the world in such assassinations, with 112 trade unionists killed in 2000, and 125 killed in the first ten months of 2001." Moreover, HRW reported that Mexico, the United States, and Canada had failed to fulfill their obligations to protect labor rights under the labor-side accord of the North American Free Trade Agreement (NAFTA).

Turning now to the last two indicators in table 3.1, the data in the last two columns of this table reveal that all the economies of Latin America are heavily dependent on external trade and that the United States and the European Union (EU) are the primary destinations for the exports of most Latin American countries. The main export destination indicator in table 3.1 reveals how dependent most of the Latin American countries are on their trading relations with the United States and the EU. The data also reveal that intraregional trade (trade with other Latin American countries) is important but in most cases takes a backseat to trade with the United States and the EU.

The "trade-to-GDP ratio" is a frequently used indicator of the importance of international economic transactions relative to domestic economic transactions within an economy. This indicator compares the total value of each country's exports and imports to the total value of the country's GDP and expresses this ratio as a percentage (i.e., the percentage of the GDP's value represented by the value of the country's exports and imports combined). The trade-to-GDP ratio is often used as an indicator of an economy's "trade openness." The higher the percentage of the value of all exports and imports in relation to the total value of a country's GDP, the more an economy is said to be "open" to (or dependent upon) international trade. This indicator has also been used to indicate the extent to which a country's economy is "integrated" into the global economy. In this sense, the trade-to-GDP ratio can also be considered an indicator of the "globalization" of each economy. That is to say, it indicates the extent to which the economy is linked to the global economic system and the degree to which it is, therefore, influenced by (and vulnerable to) the global forces, conditions, and dynamics of this system.

However, the ratio of trade to GDP for some countries can be somewhat misleading. While countries with a high trade-to-GDP ratio (expressed as a high percentage in table 3.1) are generally more "open" to international trade and more "integrated" into the global economic system than countries with a low ratio of trade to GDP (expressed as a low percentage), this is not always the case for the larger countries (larger in terms of their population size) since the size of a country has an important influence on the ratio of trade to GDP. Generally speaking, trade is more important in the economies of countries that are small (in terms of population), and the trade-to-GDP ratio is generally lower for larger countries (larger in terms of population size and size of the economy), since larger countries tend to have more resources and are more self-sufficient than smaller countries (OECD 2003). However, larger countries can also be considered "open" to international trade and quite "integrated" into the global economy, even though their trade-to-GDP ratios are considerably lower than those of smaller countries.

For example, the two largest countries in the Western Hemisphere (both in terms of population size and the size of their economies) are the United States and Brazil, and these two countries have the lowest trade-to-GDP ratios in the hemisphere (see table 3.1). But trade is very important to both of their economies, and they are definitely "integrated" into the global economy. Indeed, the economy of the United States is at the core of the contemporary global economic system. Thus, for these larger countries, the trade-to-GDP ratio is not as accurate an indicator of their so-called globalization (integration into the global economy) and trade openness as it is for medium-sized and smaller countries.

The data on the trade-to-GDP ratio for the Latin American countries in table 3.1 reveal that the value of their exports and imports combined represents a significant share or percentage of the value of their GDP. In fact, on average, total trade represents more than 50 percent of the value of their GDP. Moreover, in the case of some of the smaller countries with export-oriented economies (Chile, Costa Rica, the Dominican Republic, El Salvador, Honduras, Nicaragua, Panama, and Paraguay), the value of their trade (exports plus imports) is almost equivalent to (or exceeds in the case of Panama) the total value of their GDP (see table 3.1).

It is not an exaggeration, therefore, to say that the fate of these economies depends upon their external trade, trade relations, and integration into the global economic system. Because trade is so important to the economies of all the Latin American countries, they are quite vulnerable to the frequent ups and downs of the world economy. Consequently, fluctuations in their external trade are one of the most important determinants of their economic (in)stability. And these fluctuations directly affect their people's standard of living. Consequently, because external trade is so important to the economic growth and stability of the Latin American countries, their trading relations with their main trading partners (i.e., the United States and the EU) have a tremendous influence on their domestic economic conditions and the standard of living of their people.

As table 3.1 indicates, the main trading partners for most Latin American countries are the United States and the EU. These two centers of global capitalism and global economic influence purchase the bulk of the region's exports and supply most of its imports. It most cases, trade with the EU involves trade with one or two of the more economically important EU member countries (Germany, Spain, France, the Netherlands, and the United Kingdom). Thus, in reality, the United States and one or two of these important EU countries dominate the trading relations of most of the Latin American countries.

Intraregional trade between the Latin American countries is low in comparison with intraregional trade in other regions (De Gregorio 2004, 3). Trade between the Latin American countries made up only 17 percent of the region's total trade between 2000 and 2003, whereas intraregional trade in North America during the same period comprised over 30 percent of its total trade, and intraregional trade in East Asia made up close to 50 percent of the total trade of the countries in this region (De Gregorio 2004, 3–4). Nevertheless, intraregional trade in Latin America has been increasing and is growing in importance.

In the 1960s, intraregional trade represented only 10 percent of the total trade of the region (De Gregorio 2004). Since the 1960s, it has slowly increased to its present share of 17 percent. Trade with other Latin American countries is particularly important for the land-locked countries that do not have their own seaports (i.e., Paraguay and Bolivia). It is also important for the economies of Argentina, Brazil, Venezuela, Ecuador, El Salvador, and Guatemala. As table 3.1 reveals, each of these countries has another Latin American country as one of its main trading partners. It is also important to note that some Latin American countries (Mexico, Cuba, and Haiti) have substantial trading relations with Canada (see table 3.1).

In the case of Cuba, trade with the Russian Federation is important and is a remnant of Cuba's close economic ties with the former Soviet Union and the other countries belonging to the Council for Mutual Economic Assistance (COMECON), the now defunct trade association that existed between Socialist countries. Since the breakup of the Soviet Union and the collapse of COMECON, however, Cuba's main trading partners have been the EU (Spain particularly), the Russian Federation, and Canada (World Trade Organization 2006). In recent years, Cuba's trade with China and Venezuela has also increased significantly.

In contrast to the other Latin American countries, since the early 1960s Cuba has not had normal trading relations with the United States. The U.S. government has tried to maintain an international economic blockade of Cuba since Cuba's revolutionary regime declared itself Socialist, entered into an alliance with the former Soviet Union, and nationalized the property and holdings of U.S. corporations and investors in Cuba. However, in spite of the U.S. economic blockade of the country, many countries have continued to trade with Cuba, including most of the United States' closest allies, and the U.S. government permits limited and highly regulated one-way sales (which have been increasing) of U.S. food and agricultural products to Cuba on a cash-only basis (CBSNews.com 2005).

As table 3.1 reveals, Chile has important trading relations with Japan, and Peru has important trading relations with China. In fact, in recent years, trade between Latin America and Asia, particularly Japan and China, has increased substantially, and Sino–Latin American trade reached $50 billion in 2005 (Malik 2006). China may soon become the region's third-largest trading partner, after the United States and the EU. In 2005, Argentina, Brazil, Uruguay, and Paraguay accounted for 85 percent of the total trade with China, according to data from the IDB (Malik 2006). Trade between China and Brazil has almost tripled since 2000, and one study by ECLAC contends that China has become the second most important destination for Brazil's exports since 2003 (Blázquez-Lidoy et al. 2006, 35).

THE COLONIAL ECONOMIC HISTORY
OF LATIN AMERICA AND THE CARIBBEAN

To understand the dependency of the Latin American and Caribbean economies on external trade, the gap between the Latin American and Caribbean countries and the advanced industrial countries in terms of their differences in standards of living, as well as other major aspects of the Latin American and Caribbean economies, it is necessary to review the economic history of Latin America and the Caribbean in the larger, global context of their historical development. An explanation for many of the region's contemporary problems and deficiencies can be found in the region's history over the last five hundred years. For example, the export orientation of the Latin American and Caribbean economies, which is one of their dominant characteristics, has its origins in the first two hundred years of Spanish and Portuguese conquest and colonization of the territories in which these economies now exist (Stein and Stein 1970). Between roughly 1500 and 1700, the Spanish and Portuguese conquerors and colonists established colonial economies in what is now Latin America and the Caribbean that were based on two important economic structures: mines and large agricultural estates (Stein and Stein 1970). The large estates either supported the mines with food, domesticated animals, and leather goods (e.g., the *haciendas* in Mexico), or they produced cash crops such as sugar, tobacco, cotton, and coffee for export to Europe (e.g., the plantations in the Caribbean and *fazendas* in Brazil). Both the mines (which were largely devoted to mining precious metals) and the large estates used oppressed workforces that were forcibly drafted from the indigenous population and/or acquired through the slave trade with Africa.

During the approximately three centuries of colonial rule that took place from the 1500s to the 1800s, these colonial enterprises—the mines and large agricultural estates—produced a tremendous amount of wealth, a large proportion of which was exported to Europe. The extreme forms of labor exploitation that they used drastically reduced the indigenous population (in some cases to total extinction). With time, they destroyed and replaced the indigenous economic structures that existed prior to the colonial conquest. In their place, they created a racially and ethnically stratified colonial society that subjected the majority of the population to more than three centuries of economic exploitation, political oppression, and cultural discrimination.

Despite their vast colonial empires, both Spain and Portugal were themselves "economic dependencies of Europe," and particularly of England, and "this anomalous status as colony and empire shaped the history of the Iberian countries and their colonial possessions" in Latin America, the Caribbean, and elsewhere in the world (Stein and Stein 1970, 4). In fact, by the early 1700s, the historical evidence suggests that "in a variety of ways the English, Iberian and Ibero-American economies were interlocked," and the raw materials and profitable markets that both the Spanish and Portuguese colonies provided for English products greatly contributed to England's economic growth and predominance in the 1700s and 1800s (Stein and Stein 1970, 7).

Genoese, French, Dutch, and English merchants, bankers, and shippers were the major beneficiaries of the wealth produced by the Spanish and Portuguese colonies in the Americas almost from the very beginning of the colonization of the region. This situation was due partly to the external debts incurred by Spain's and Portugal's monarchies and partly to both countries' dependence on imported goods from the more developed economic centers of Europe—in Holland, France, and England and on the Italian peninsula (Stein and Stein 1970, 17). Moreover, both Spain and Portugal "at the outset of their imperial experience, were imperfectly organized, export-oriented, and lacking a national bourgeoisie or a merchant capital- ist group capable of stimulating indigenous growth" (Stein and Stein 1970, 19). As a result, they passed on a legacy of what has been termed "under- development" and external "dependency" to their colonies, where in most respects they established the same kinds of economic structures as those that prevailed in Spain and Portugal during the 1500s and 1600s.

THE ECONOMIC LEGACY OF IBERIAN COLONIALISM

The legacy of Iberian colonialism from the 1500s to the 1800s, as well as the struggle for independence and civil wars that followed the breakup of the Spanish and Portuguese colonial empires in Latin America and the Caribbean during the 1800s, left the newly independent states formed out of these empires with largely neocolonial, export-oriented economies. These economies were, like those of the colonial mother countries, "imper- fectly organized" and "lacking a capable national bourgeoisie." In fact, the neocolonial economies of the new states of Latin America and the Caribbean were similar in certain respects to the plantation economies of the Southern states of the United States during the same period. As the his- torians Stein and Stein have observed, these economies "held the per capita income of the masses at a minimal level and inhibited capital formation in liquid assets"; as a result, they "reduced the possibility of sustained local de- mand for high cost products of infant industry" (Stein and Stein 1970, 134).

Moreover, the massive importation of British manufactured goods inhib- ited the development of local industries. Following their independence, the states of Latin America and the Caribbean, like the Southern states of the United States, inherited this type of economy and were forced to "search for export staples, traditional or new, to pay for imports" rather than develop new industries to produce local manufactures for domestic consumption (Stein and Stein 1970).

Thus, the export of minerals, raw materials, and cash crops remained the main characteristic of the economies of the new states of Latin America and the Caribbean throughout the remainder of the 1800s after their indepen- dence from colonial rule. After independence, they failed to create the bases of sustained, national economic growth through a balanced development and diversification of their agriculture and industry, and they remained de- pendent upon external demand for their agricultural exports and the sup- ply of manufactured imports (Stein and Stein 1970, 131). Along with their continued emphasis on the export of primary products (raw materials and agricultural goods), the neocolonial economies of the newly independent states of Latin America and the Caribbean continued to rely on large, agricultural estates and plantations as the primary units of agricultural production and on the continued use of coercive forms of labor exploitation.

Significantly, the major beneficiaries of the postcolonial period of export expansion in Latin America and the Caribbean were the British merchants, bankers, manufacturers, and shippers who profited richly from British domination of the trade and investments in the region. British dominance of the economic life of the region was unchallenged until the late 1800s and early 1900s, when U.S. economic interests backed by the U.S. government increasingly replaced the dominant influence of British interests, first in Mexico, Central America, and the Caribbean, then in South America.

By the end of the 1800s, British investments in railroads, port facilities, and public utilities built largely with machinery and technical expertise imported from Great Britain had contributed to a significant expansion in Latin American and Caribbean exports and the rapid growth of the major ports and capital cities throughout the region. The British also supplied the investment capital for port facilities and docks, street lighting, sewage and water systems, and urban transportation. Thus, British interests were a major factor in the destruction of the Iberian colonial empires since they encouraged and supported the independence movements in both the Spanish and Portuguese colonies, and it was British interests that established a new "informal imperialism of free trade" (Gallagher and Robinson 1953) and foreign investments in the newly independent states established on the ruins of these empires.

British historians have documented this informal "imperialism of free trade" (see Gallagher and Robinson 1953). They have shown convincingly that the British government and commercial interests supported the colonial rebellions against Spain during the early 1800s "to gain informal supremacy and the good will which would favor British commercial penetration" in the new states created out of the former Spanish colonies (Gallagher and Robinson 1953). As clear evidence of the British government's intentions, British foreign secretary George Canning stated in 1824, "Spanish America is free and if we do not mismanage our affairs badly, she is English" (quoted in Kaufmann 1951, 178).[4] During this critical period of Latin American and Caribbean history, the British government's "underlying objective was to clear the way for a prodigious British expansion by creating a new and informal empire" in Latin America and the Caribbean, while at the same time Great Britain extended its "formal empire" in Africa and Asia through the colonial annexation of large swaths of territory in both regions (Gallagher and Robinson 1953).

During the latter half of the 1800s and the early 1900s, what some scholars have called "the export age" occurred in Latin America and the Caribbean (Cárdenas, Ocampo, and Thorp 2000). Under British and then increasingly U.S. economic influence, the export-oriented economies of the new states of Latin America and the Caribbean greatly expanded their exports of primary goods to Europe and North America. The income from these expanded exports, as well as other conditions internal to these societies, gave rise to a small national bourgeoisie of merchant capitalists and a small commercial and professional middle class in most of the major ports and capital cities of Latin America and the Caribbean (Stein and Stein 1970, 190). Both members of the more traditional oligarchy of large landlords and these largely commercial capitalists and middle-class elements in the urban centers were influenced by, and became advocates of, the prevailing economic ideology of the times: economic liberalism. This capitalist economic ideology supported the expanded production and export of primary products in the Latin American and Caribbean countries on the grounds that this expansion of exports would increase per capita income, increase domestic consumption, lead to the introduction of new technology, attract more foreign investment, bring about rising standards of living, and, ultimately, lead to the development of modern industrial economies in Latin America and the Caribbean similar to those in Great Britain, Western Europe, and the United States.

THE INDUSTRIAL DEVELOPMENT
OF LATIN AMERICA AND THE CARIBBEAN

The expansion of Latin American and Caribbean exports during the late 1800s and early 1900s and the increased construction of railroads, ports, and public utilities, as well as the rapid growth of the major urban areas where trade and investment were centered, seemed to confirm the validity of this ideology (Stein and Stein 1970). Moreover, during this period, a limited number of local industries were established in the more prosperous countries (Argentina, Brazil, Chile, Colombia, and Mexico). However, this unparalleled period of international trade and export expansion came to an abrupt end during the late 1920s as a result of the worldwide economic depression—the Great Depression—and the associated trade crisis that took place between 1929 and the late 1930s. Prior to the Great Depression and the accompanying decline in world trade, the economies of the Latin American and Caribbean countries were largely "open" to foreign trade and specialized in exporting raw materials and cash crops to the industrialized economies of North America and Europe.

During the Great Depression, Latin American and Caribbean exports declined dramatically (e.g., from $5 billion to $1.5 billion between 1929 and 1933), and the industrial countries refused to extend any more credits and loans to the Latin American and Caribbean countries to finance the importation of goods manufactured in the industrial countries. Because there had been extensive borrowing of foreign credits and loans made during the preceding period of export expansion and so-called free trade, more than $5 billion in debt payments were collected by foreign creditors before most of the Latin American and Caribbean governments were forced to default on their remaining debts. Thus, the Great Depression of the 1930s brought about not only a collapse in the prices and volume of Latin American and Caribbean export commodities but also a debt crisis in most of these countries (Theberge 1999, 13–15).

Under these circumstances, the governments of most of the Latin American and Caribbean countries had to take extraordinary measures to address the serious economic and political consequences stemming from the drastic decline of their exports and their inability to pay their external debts. They also had to take special measures to address the increasing inability of their countries to pay for their imports as the foreign-currency holdings of these countries dwindled along with the decline in their export sales (Rojas 1993). In fact, the Latin American and Caribbean countries had no choice but to decrease drastically the importation of manufactured goods from the United States and Europe. Thus, they were forced to adopt a variety of measures to conserve and ration the use of their decreased supply of foreign exchange so that they could at least purchase their most essential imports. As might be expected, in this context of economic crisis and uncertainty, there was considerable political turmoil, and several governments were thrown out of office or overthrown.

During this period, most of the Latin American and Caribbean governments introduced a series of economic policies that increased or created new tariffs (taxes) on trade. They also established and enforced import quotas to restrict the types and quantity of imports. And they placed restrictions on the use of the dwindling supply of foreign currency that their countries earned from the reduced volume of, and prices paid for, their exports (Rojas 1993). In this environment of economic crisis and increased government intervention into the economy, Latin America's political leaders, the major economic groups, journalists, and intellectuals were forced to reassess the prevailing ideas about "free trade," export-oriented economic expansion, and the limited role of government in economic life previously upheld by the dominant ideology of economic liberalism (Rojas 1993, 191–92).

Moreover, the reduction in imports during this period created increased demand and opened up the market for locally produced manufactured goods (Rojas 1993). As a result, the political leaders and business elites in many of the Latin American and Caribbean countries began to promote what subsequently became known as "import-substitution industrialization" (ISI). This inward-oriented approach to economic development required government investment and subsidies to stimulate and support the creation and expansion of local industries and joint ventures with foreign firms in the establishment of local manufacturing and assembly plants.

In terms of the export-oriented and "free trade" economic liberalism that had prevailed during the latter half of the 1800s and the early 1900s, the Latin American and Caribbean economies ceased to be "free trade" economies in the 1930s and 1940s. Instead, they became increasingly "protected" economies focused on domestic economic considerations rather than export production and international trade. In these circumstances, the more progressive sectors of the business elite in Latin America, which Marxists often call the "national bourgeoisie," became increasingly involved in the development of local industries to fill the gap created by the scarcity of imported goods. They took advantage of the new "protective" trade barriers, the controls on imports, and the financial and regulatory incentives for producing, or increasing the domestic production of, local manufactured goods.

These more progressive sectors of Latin America's capitalist class joined with nationalist political leaders in the government, as well as the trade unions of blue- and white-collar workers, to promote the development of local industries, sometimes in partnership with foreign firms. In general, these groups tended to base their actions on the following assumptions and justifications (Rojas 1993): (1) the existing major industrial countries (especially the United States and Japan) industrialized their economies behind high protective tariffs on imports; (2) industrializing countries need to develop a mature, domestic industrial infrastructure behind high protective tariffs before they can engage in unprotected "free trade" with already industrialized countries; (3) in industrializing countries, protective government policies are needed to promote a wide range of domestic industries that produce domestic substitutes for previously imported manufactured goods; (4) these protective government policies will create new employment opportunities and rising incomes for the urban population; (5) the governments of industrializing countries need to follow monetary policies that keep local currencies overvalued in relation to the currencies of the major industrial countries so that imports from these countries will be expensive and less attractive to domestic consumers and the trade deficit with the industrial countries will be balanced by the earnings from the exports sold to these countries; and (6) if most industrial and essential consumer goods are produced locally, then the economies of these countries will be insulated against massive worldwide economic shocks, such as the Great Depression and the two world wars.

By the 1950s, these assumptions were formalized into a new economic ideology and a package of national economic policies aimed at promoting the national industrial development of most of the Latin American and Caribbean countries. The general approach identified with this ideology of national industrial development and the associated set of policies became known as "import-substitution industrialization," or ISI.

Under the leadership of a well-known Argentine economist named Raúl Prebisch, who had headed the central bank of Argentina, the ISI approach to the region's economic development was refined and promoted by the new United Nations Economic Commission for Latin America (Comisión Económica para América Latina, or CEPAL, in Spanish, it was later renamed the Economic Commission for Latin America and the Caribbean, or ECLAC). In 1950, Prebisch released a groundbreaking CEPAL study titled *The Economic Development of Latin America and Its Principal Problems*, which has often been referred to as the ISI "manifesto." It sparked a wave of critical thinking throughout Latin America about the causes of the region's economic "underdevelopment," its failure to catch up with the economic development of the major industrial countries, and the measures the Latin American and Caribbean countries should take to close the gap with them.

In this publication, Prebisch essentially argued that colonialism and international trade had not benefited the economic development of Latin America as most conventional economists in Europe and the United States maintained. He contended that the Latin American and Caribbean economies (like other colonial and ex-colonial economies in Africa, Asia, the Middle East, and the Pacific Islands) had been relegated by the colonizing countries to "the periphery" of the world economic system, where they were subordinated to producing cheap primary goods (raw materials, precious metals, agricultural products, etc.) for the richer, industrialized countries at "the center," or apex, of this system. He also argued that the Latin American and Caribbean countries had been maneuvered soon after their independence into continuing to produce relatively cheap export commodities for the industrialized countries and providing profitable markets for the manufactured exports and capital investments of these industrialized countries. Meanwhile, their own industrial development was arrested, while their economies became increasingly dependent upon (overspecialized in) the exportation of a limited number of agricultural commodities and raw materials with fluctuating demand and unstable prices in international markets.

Prebisch claimed international trade statistics clearly indicated the terms of trade between the Latin American and Caribbean countries and the United States and other industrialized countries had declined over time in favor of these industrialized countries at the center, or core, of the system. He contended that the prices of manufactured goods produced by the industrialized countries and purchased by the countries at the periphery had risen faster than the prices of the raw materials, cash crops, and foodstuffs produced and sold by the economies of the periphery to the industrialized economies. As a result of this deterioration in the terms of trade between the countries of the periphery and the center, the "peripheral countries" were continuously forced to export more of their primary products in order to obtain the same amount of manufactured exports from the industrial economies at the center of the international economic system. Prebisch and his associates at CEPAL claimed that this situation in effect resulted in the wholesale transfer of resources and capital from the periphery to the industrialized countries at the center of the international economic system. He and his associates argued that the unfair terms of trade allowed the industrialized countries in the center to grow richer at the expense of the continued underdevelopment of the economies in the periphery.

Social scientists, intellectuals, and political activists around the world since the 1950s have continued to use Prebisch's conceptual division of the world economy into two spheres, the "center" and the "periphery." Based on his analysis of the truncated development and unfavorable conditions confronted by the economies of the peripheral countries in the international trading system, Prebisch recommended that the governments of the Latin American and Caribbean (and other peripheral) countries adopt economic policies that favored the diversification of their exports and the promotion of ISI. He contended that ISI policies were needed to stimulate domestic manufacturing in the peripheral countries and to reduce their dependence on the importation of costly manufactured goods from the United States and other industrialized countries.

This import-substituting strategy was adopted in varying degrees by many of the Latin American and Caribbean countries, as well as other "underdeveloped" or "less developed" countries around the world. It involved government intervention into economic affairs through economic planning, the establishment of state enterprises, and the creation of state development agencies. Generally speaking, this import-substitution strategy in Latin America was implemented by a "triple alliance" of state-owned enterprises, national private enterprises, and transnational corporations, which often formed "joint partnerships" to finance and develop the selective industrialization of the countries involved (Evans 1979). The balance between these three elements in carrying out the import-substitution strategy varied from country to country and led to what Evans later called "dependent development" in Brazil (Evans 1979).

By following this industrial-development strategy during the 1950s and 1960s, most of the Latin American and Caribbean countries experienced moderate to strong economic growth (Weeks 1995). Even though the terms of trade for many Latin American and Caribbean countries declined after World War II, there was an increase in private and official capital investment in their economies for the purpose of promoting industrial development, and this investment tended to offset the effects of the unfavorable postwar

Table 3.4.   Per Capita GDP Growth in Latin America, 1951–1999

Period	Annual Rate of per Capita GDP growth (%)
1951–1959	2.1
1960–1969	3.0
1970–1979	2.9
1980–1989	–0.3
1990–1999	1.4
1951–1999 (average)	(1.5)

Source: Weisbrot and Rosnick (2003).

terms of trade. Moreover, most of the Latin American and Caribbean countries benefited from the relatively stable international trading and monetary system established after the end of World War II. As tables 3.4 and 3.5 reveal, the rate of economic growth (increase in GDP) and increase in the GDP per capita per annum during this period were higher than at any other period of the twentieth century, especially in the countries that followed a serious national industrial-development strategy (i.e., Argentina, Brazil, Chile, etc.).

This period of growth was facilitated by fixed exchange rates regulated and monitored by the new IMF after the end of World War II. The IMF was established along with the World Bank at the end of the war through a series of international agreements reached at the famous Bretton Woods (New Hampshire) conference on international monetary management. Over forty countries signed these agreements in July 1944.[5] The Latin American and Caribbean countries actively participated in this conference and also participated in the preferential trading agreements negotiated and entered into with the industrialized countries during the immediate postwar period (Weeks 1995).

The ISI approach succeeded in promoting the industrialization of the larger and more prosperous Latin American and Caribbean countries, but only up to a point, since it also created "severe imbalances" that threatened

Table 3.5.   Nine Latin American Countries' Aggregate Annual Rate of Growth in GDP

Period	Growth per Annum in Aggregate GDP (%)
1900–1913	2.1
1913–1929	2.8
1929–1954	3.5
1950–1960	5.4
1960–1970	5.5

Source: World Bank data cited in Rojas (1993).
Note: The nine countries are Argentina, Brazil, Chile, Colombia, Ecuador, Guatemala, Mexico, Peru, and Venezuela.

the continued growth and socioeconomic stability of these countries (Rojas 1993). These imbalances included large deficits in their current accounts caused by the importation of expensive capital and intermediate goods needed for the new industries established during this period, as well as increasing income inequality and, particularly, a growing gap between the incomes of the urban and rural populations (Rojas 1993). In addition, the ISI approach to national industrial development "did not diminish the domestic economy's external dependence, but merely changed its nature" by adding new forms of "technological and financial domination by foreign capital" in the new manufacturing sectors to "the classical domination of the mining and agribusiness sectors" by foreign investors and corporations (Rojas 1993). Moreover, the emphasis on manufacturing led to "a dramatic neglect of agriculture, and therefore a low rate of growth of agricultural products became the norm," which contributed to "shortages of food which added to the polarization of income and made social unrest a characteristic of Latin American and Caribbean political life in the 1950s to 1970s" (Rojas 1993).

As Weeks argued in his contribution to the first edition of this book (Weeks 1995), the economic growth of the Latin American and Caribbean countries during this period was so substantial that by the end of the 1960s, government policy makers and political leaders throughout Latin America were forced to concede that the gains from this growth should be shared with those sectors of the population still mired in poverty and largely excluded from the benefits of the growth of these economies. Indeed, equity considerations became an integral component of the definition of "economic development" in Latin America (and throughout the Third World) during the 1960s and 1970s.

However, proponents of what has been called "modernization theory" or "development theory," which was the dominant perspective held by foreign policy makers in the United States and Western Europe during the 1950s and 1960s, agreed with neither this emphasis on the equitable distribution of the benefits of the region's economic growth nor the basic assumptions of the ISI approach. United States and Western European proponents of this so-called theory of modernization or development propagated it as a prescriptive theory concerning capitalist economic development in general and the underdevelopment or "backwardness" of the Latin American, Caribbean, and other "underdeveloped" economies in particular.

CONFLICTING PERSPECTIVES ON
LATIN AMERICA'S ECONOMIC DEVELOPMENT

In order to understand the contemporary economic history of Latin America, it is important to review the conflicting perspectives on the region's economic development that held sway in the 1950s, 1960s, and 1970s, both in Latin America and outside the region. From the 1950s through the 1980s, the United States and its Western European allies were embroiled in the Cold War with the Soviet Union and its allies. Modernization theory or development theory became an important ideological weapon of the United States and its allies in the first decades of the postwar period of intense ideological and international conflict between the "Western Free World" (the "First World") and the "Socialist Bloc" (the "Second World"). The United States and its allies used this ideology in their struggle with the Soviet Union and the so-called international Communist movement. It was used to prevent the "Third World" of former colonial countries in Africa, Asia, the Middle East, Latin America, and the Caribbean from joining the so-called Socialist Bloc led by the Soviet Union and the People's Republic of China. Critics of this perspective have described it as "the ideological arm of U.S. expansion throughout the world for the supposed purpose of diffusing 'development' and 'democracy' to the Third World" (Berberoglu 1992, 7).

This Cold War economic ideology aimed at containing the international influence and expansion of the Soviet Union, the People's Republic of China, and the international Socialist movement. The international Socialist movement was inspired in varying and conflicting degrees by the ideologies, economic-development strategies, and achievements of the Soviet Union, the People's Republic of China, and the revolutionary regimes in Cuba and Vietnam. Modernization theory was developed as an alternative model of capitalist development in juxtaposition with the Socialist development models advocated by the Soviet Union, China, Cuba, and other Socialist movements and regimes around the world.

The most prominent U.S. contributor to modernization theory was Walt Rostow. He led the U.S. State Department's Policy Planning Council during the early 1960s and served as special assistant for national security affairs to U.S. President Lyndon Johnson from 1966 to 1969. In his widely distributed book, *The Stages of Economic Growth: A Non Communist Manifesto* (1960), Rostow put forward the major assumptions of this Cold War ideological perspective on economic development; that is, the "modernization" of the tradition-bound "backward societies" in Africa, Asia, Latin America, and the Middle East required the adoption of "modern" Western capitalist ideas, institutions, and methods and a prolonged multistaged transition from their traditional "backwardness" to the achievement of a "mature" capitalist economy and democratic political system. These assumptions were delivered as prescriptions to the government leaders, urban elites, and middle classes of Latin America and other "Third World" countries during the 1950s and 1960s by U.S. and Western European political leaders, foreign-assistance advisers, economic experts, international bankers, educators, diplomats, and journalists.

Modernization theory, or "development theory" as it was more often called during this period, provided the ideological justification for the Cold War policies and practices that the governments of the United States and its Western European allies followed in their dealings with the governments of the Latin American countries. The influence of this ideology became particularly strong in Latin America after the Cuban Revolution and the U.S. confrontation with the Soviet Union over its support of the revolutionary regime in Cuba at the outset of the 1960s. It provided the ideological justification for the trade policies, foreign-assistance programs, and political strategies followed by the U.S. and Western European governments in the region during the 1960s and early 1970s, until it was undermined by its own shortcomings, new circumstances that it could not adequately explain, and the appeal of opposing perspectives.

By the early 1970s, the Cepalistas, the more progressive proponents of the ISI approach to national development, and the more radical critics of modernization theory succeeded in undermining the legitimacy of this perspective. In particular, they succeeded in making the case that sustained economic growth required a more equitable distribution of income than modernization theory was willing to accommodate since this so-called theory was based on the assumption that rapid economic growth and increasing income inequality were both compatible and necessary during the transition from backward to mature capitalist economies. In the face of rising demands for greater income distribution and the eradication of widespread poverty in the Third World, even the World Bank adopted a "basic-needs" approach in the1970s and emphasized the "alleviation of poverty" in the conditions it set for its loan recipients in Latin America and other "developing" countries in Africa, Asia, and the Middle East (Ghosh 1984).

However, the radical critics of both modernization or development theory and the ISI approach (which was called *desarrollismo,* or "developmentalism,*" in some Latin American and Caribbean circles) attacked the superficial efforts made during this period to alleviate poverty and promote the "development" of the region with foreign capital and technical assistance. They argued that radical structural changes at both the international and domestic levels were needed to develop the Latin American and Caribbean economies and put an end to the poverty and inequality that characterized the region.

During the 1960s, both economists associated with CEPAL and other social scientists not associated with CEPAL developed a radical school of thought about the "underdevelopment" of Latin America and the Third World, which became known as "dependency theory." Some of the leading proponents of this perspective were the Brazilian social scientists Fernando Henrique Cardoso, Theotõnio dos Santos, Ruy Mauro Marini, and Vania Bambirra; the Argentine historian and sociologist Sergio Bagú; the Chilean social scientists Osvaldo Sunkel and Enzo Falleto; the Mexican social scientists González Casanova and Rodolfo Stavenhagen; the Peruvian sociologist Anibal Quijano; and the German-born, but U.S.-educated, radical economic historian André Gunder Frank.[6] Although there were considerable differences among the views of these social scientists and experts, they all criticized the prevailing approaches to economic development in the region and helped to create a critical awareness throughout Latin America and the rest of the world about the nature and conditions responsible for the inequitable and retarded development of the "underdeveloped" or "peripheral" economies in Latin America, the Caribbean, and other parts of the Third World.

These progressive scholars and experts criticized the prevailing ideas about economic development and the policies followed by the governments of most of the Latin American and Caribbean countries on the grounds that they failed to address adequately the continuing presence of widespread poverty and inequality in Latin America, as well as the growing gap between the Latin American and Caribbean economies and the industrialized economies of the United States and Western Europe. They argued that the continued poverty, inequalities, and economic underdevelopment in the Latin American and Caribbean societies were largely due to the structural dependency of their economies upon the economies of the advanced capitalist countries, which purchased most of Latin America's exports at cheap prices and sold the region most of its imports at expensive prices.

They criticized the process of unequal exchange associated with this economic dependency and claimed it transferred most of the region's valuable resources and capital to the advanced industrial countries.[7] They also said that because the Latin American and Caribbean economies were so thoroughly penetrated by foreign capital, the process of industrial development taking place in the region was being controlled by foreign investors and transnational corporations so that it served the interests of these investors and corporations rather than the national industrial development of the Latin American and Caribbean countries and the needs of their people. As Chilcote and Edelstein (1986) state in their synthesis of this school of critical thought, "Industrial development [in Latin America] has been led, not by indigenous forces in accordance with national development needs, but by transnational corporations pursuing the needs of their global balance sheets," and "although economic growth and industrialization have taken place, the benefits of growth have not been distributed" to the majority of the people (19).

Most of the advocates of dependency theory also asserted that the Latin American and Caribbean countries would have to pursue a Socialist path (although they disagreed on which Socialist path) to achieve national development based on self-directed industrialization, as well as social justice, popular democracy, and economic equity (Chilcote and Edelstein 1986, 86–132). In general, they disagreed with the orthodox Marxist perspective held by most of the official Communist parties in the 1960s, which argued that these countries would have to first undergo a bourgeois (capitalist) democratic revolution. According to this perspective, a bourgeois capitalist revolution was needed to eliminate the vestiges of "feudalism" in these societies and to lay the foundations for the development of mature capitalist societies in which the preliminary conditions for a genuine Socialist revolution would arise as a result of the class conflict between the capitalists and the working class. In contrast, most of the *dependentistas* argued that there was no feudalism in the Latin American and Caribbean societies and that their national bourgeoisie (local capitalists) was too weak to bring about a bourgeois democratic revolution or to "offer any way out of underdevelopment in Latin America" (Frank 1969, xv). Thus, Frank (1969) argued, the "world capitalist system" had long ago "incorporated and underdeveloped even the farthest outpost of 'traditional' society"; as a result, there was no longer any possibility for the peripheral countries to achieve a "classical national or modern state-capitalist development independent of imperialism" (xv).

The *dependentistas'* views on the underdevelopment of the Latin American and Caribbean countries (and other Third World countries) were sharply criticized by conservative, right-wing, and left-wing critics alike, who called attention to the genuine weaknesses in this perspective and/or opposed it for political and ideological reasons. Some of the more important theoretical and analytical flaws in the dependency perspective identified by its critics included its overemphasis on the "external," as opposed to "internal," forces and conditions responsible for the region's uneven and inequitable process of development, as well as its almost exclusive focus on the relations of external trade and distribution as opposed to the relations of production within the Latin American and Caribbean countries and the world capitalist system.

In addition, leftist critics noted the failure of some of the *dependentistas* to distinguish the differences between the "old" imperialism of the sixteenth, seventeenth, and eighteenth centuries and the "new" imperialism of the nineteenth and twentieth centuries. And both right-wing and some left-wing critics objected to the argument made by the more radical *dependentistas*, such as Frank, who argued that no significant degree of national development could take place in the Latin American and Caribbean countries unless they broke out of the world capitalist system and embarked on a Socialist path of development (Chilcote 2003, 42–45).

In this regard, it is important to note that the Brazilian sociologist Theotônio dos Santos made an important distinction between different types and historical periods of dependency (Dos Santos 1968). Dos Santos argued that "colonial dependency" characterized the relations between the

European imperialist countries and their Latin American and Caribbean colonies during the centuries of colonial domination, but he contended that this colonial form of dependency was replaced by "financial-industrial dependency" in the latter half of the 1800s. After World War II, he contended, a new form of "technological-industrial" dependency replaced the financial-industrial dependency that prevailed in Latin America during the late 1800s and first half of the 1900s. According to Theotônio dos Santos, this "new dependency" was based on the control that U.S. and European transnational corporations had gained over the Latin American and Caribbean economies as a result of their increasing investments in these economies and their use of new technologies that made it possible for them to integrate their branch operations in these economies into their expanding transnational production and distribution networks.

In a similar vein, Cardoso and Faletto (1979) argued that "dependent capitalist development" had been taking place in Latin America as a result of the increasing investments of multinational corporations in the economies of the region, and they contended that this process of development was a new form of monopolistic expansion under the control of these corporations. In the early 1970s, Cardoso and Faletto provided an analysis of the structural composition of the new form of dependent capitalist development they saw unfolding in Brazil and other parts of Latin America. According to them, the new form of dependent development that they saw taking place in the Latin American and Caribbean economies in the 1960s and 1970s involved the collaboration of the state, the multinational (transnational) corporations, and the modern capitalist sectors in these countries. Cardoso and Faletto believed the new form of dependent capitalist development taking place in Latin America was largely propelled by the investments of multinational (transnational) corporations, and they accurately concluded that this form of dependent capitalist development was not compatible with the redistribution of income to the poorer segments of the population.

Ironically, Cardoso subsequently became "part of the problem" he and Faletto critically analyzed in the early 1970s. He was elected and served as president of Brazil from 1995 to 2003. During his presidency, Cardoso was harshly criticized for the neoliberal economic policies followed by his administration. These policies have been severely criticized for favoring the transnational corporations and privileged business elites in Brazil and for following the neoliberal dictates of the IMF and the World Bank (Petras and Veltmeyer 2003). Cardoso's administration contained inflation in Brazil, "stabilized" the Brazilian economy, and provided a favorable climate for foreign investment by holding down the wages of the working class, deregulating the economy, privatizing key sectors and enterprises, and resisting popular demands for income redistribution and other badly needed social reforms.

THE EXTERNAL SHOCKS OF THE 1970S
AND THE "LOST DECADE" OF THE 1980S

During the latter part of this period of contending perspectives on Latin America's underdevelopment, dependency, and development, several external shocks from the international economic system dramatically altered not only the international economic environment of the Latin American and Caribbean economies but also domestic economic conditions in the region. These shocks displaced the debate over the contending perspectives on the region's economic development mentioned above and introduced a new perspective based on neoliberal ideology.

The first of these shocks occurred at the outset of the 1970s, when in 1971 the U.S. government's unilateral decision to suspend the convertibility of the U.S. dollar to gold shook the international economic system. This move ended the relatively stable international monetary system established by the Bretton Woods agreements and created a new international regime of financial and commercial transactions based on variable, instead of fixed, exchange rates. The new exchange rates "proved especially problematical for the Latin American and Caribbean countries, due to the vulnerability of their economies to world market fluctuations and their lack of skilled people for the increased burden of economic management" associated with financial and commercial transactions based on variable exchange rates (Weeks 1995, 110).

This shock was followed by the unprecedented petroleum price increases that occurred in 1973 and 1974 and again in 1979 and 1980. These price increases generated large trade deficits in most export-oriented countries that were heavily dependent upon oil imports (i.e., most of the Latin American and Caribbean countries). To pay for their expensive oil imports, many of the Latin American and Caribbean countries turned to commercial banks in North America and Western Europe to borrow the large sums of money they needed to pay for their imports. These commercial loans enabled countries such as Argentina and Brazil to continue financing the industrialization of their economies beyond the limits of their own financial resources.

The privately owned commercial banks in North America and Western Europe were only too willing to extend the Latin American and Caribbean countries large loans since they were flooded with the "petrodollar" profits the petroleum-exporting countries were giving these banks to invest for them (Theberge 1999, 5). However, these loans brought about a change in the source and composition of the debts held by the Latin American and Caribbean countries. The composition of their debts changed from long-term, low-interest-rate official loans from IFIs to short-term commercial loans with variable, high interest rates. Previously, most of the loans these countries took were from the IMF, the World Bank, the U.S. government, and the governments of other advanced industrial countries, but the new high-interest loans were provided by commercial banks (Theberge 1999).

This change in the sources, interest rates, and composition of loans borrowed by the Latin American and Caribbean countries in the 1970s was a major factor contributing to the "debt crisis" that occurred throughout the region in the 1980s. It is important to note that throughout the 1970s, the U.S. government, the IMF, and the World Bank encouraged the Latin American and Caribbean countries to borrow money from the commercial banks in the United States and Western Europe. They did not consider the growing indebtedness of these countries a long-term risk because the prices of their primary products on the world market were rising (due to inflation but also because of strong demand for them). This faulty assessment of the situation generated ungrounded optimism on all sides about the ability of most of the Latin American and Caribbean countries to service their newly acquired external debts (Weeks 1995, 111).

Thus, between 1975 and 1982, commercial bank loans to Latin America quadrupled the region's external debt from $75 billion in 1975 to more than $314 billion in 1983, which was equivalent to about 50 percent of the region's total GDP. Debt service (interest payments and the repayment of principal) grew from $12 billion in 1975 to $66 billion in 1982 (Theberge 1999, 6). A large share of Latin America's external debt was used to finance the region's growing trade imbalances toward the end of the 1970s. The region's financing needs increased as the interest payments on the debts increased. Moreover, although exports increased at an average rate of 12 percent per year during this period, the service payments on the external debts increased 24 percent per year, creating a growing gap between the income earned from exports and the costs of servicing the region's debts (Theberge 1999).

This borrowing frenzy came to an abrupt end in the early 1980s, when the Latin American and Caribbean economies and other developing economies were again subjected to new and unexpected economic shocks coming from the international system (Theberge 1999). The most serious of these external shocks was the severe economic recession in the advanced industrial countries during 1981 and 1982. This recession brought about a rapid decline in the previously inflated prices of primary commodities (including oil). The recession also generated high international interest rates, as well as falling prices for most of the primary exports of the Latin American and Caribbean countries. As a result, many of the Latin American and Caribbean countries, especially those with the largest debts, found that they could not continue servicing their debts without borrowing more funds. However, the interest rates were much higher than in the 1970s, and the lenders were reluctant to extend these countries new loans (Weeks 1995, 111).

In August 1982, Mexico announced it could not continue to service its huge external debt (even though it was an oil-exporting country). This so-called debt crisis was provoked by the Mexican capitalist class, which had begun shifting its assets abroad in response to the changes taking place in the international economy and the country's growing debt problem. More than $20 billion from the private sector left the country between 1981 and 1982 (Weeks 1995). Continuously falling oil prices on the international market and the reevaluation of the Mexican peso compounded this massive outflow of capital. Together with the increasing financial burden the country faced in servicing its external debt, the massive outflow of capital pushed Mexico into a financial meltdown.

This financial crisis sent shock waves through the international financial establishment and precipitated a larger, international "debt crisis" as other Latin American and Caribbean countries revealed that they too were having increasing difficulty servicing their large external debts. The falling prices of their exports and the increasing interest rates on loans had reduced their financial capacity to service their loans and increased the reluctance of the international commercial banks to make further loans to them to refinance their existing loans (Weeks 1995). Since many of the loans were short-term commercial loans, the refusal of the commercial banks to refinance them created a crisis for the Latin American and Caribbean borrowers when they came due for full payment.

Faced with this worsening financial crisis, the international financial establishment (the IFIs, the large commercial banks, and the top financial officials in the United States and other creditor countries) grew increasingly concerned that other debtor countries might follow Mexico and set off a chain reaction of loan defaults, which in turn might cause the collapse of the commercial banks holding most of the loans of the defaulting countries. Alarm over the potentially catastrophic nature of this financial crisis brought about a significant change in the orientation and priorities of all the international lending agencies. It also brought about a change in the relations between the U.S. government and the governments of the Latin American and Caribbean countries.

Previous commitments (often superficial) to assist the Latin American and Caribbean governments in promoting poverty alleviation and achieving greater equity in income distribution were now replaced with a new emphasis on making sure the Latin American and Caribbean countries continued to service their external debts. As a result, the U.S. government, the IFIs, the commercial banks, and the governments of the countries holding large loans with Latin America joined together to make sure the Latin American and Caribbean countries continued to service their loans. Generally speaking, these external creditors agreed that the Latin American and Caribbean governments should be pressured to continue servicing their countries' debts by creating current account surpluses through the reduction of their government expenditures, the devaluation of their currencies, the encouragement of foreign investments, raising their domestic interest rates, and expanding their exports. As a result, they began pressuring the Latin American and Caribbean governments to implement these measures.

To appease these creditors and stave off the complete financial collapse of their highly indebted economies, most of the Latin American and Caribbean governments were forced to refinance their external debts, devalue their currencies, drastically reduce government expenditures, and restructure their economies according to the dictates of the U.S. government, the IMF, the World Bank, the IDB, and the commercial banks. In response to the conditions set by these IFIs, the commercial banks, and the U.S. government, most of the Latin American and Caribbean governments introduced the required "structural reforms" involving the "liberalization" of both their trade regulations and controls on foreign investments, the devaluation (and "dollarization") of their currencies, the reduction of their expenditures on public services and public subsidies (for basic foods, transportation, etc.), and the privatization of government-owned enterprises and public utilities.

As a result of these so-called structural reforms, the Latin American and Caribbean governments in effect diverted revenues from the public sector and from the incomes of the popular classes to their countries' international creditors, the transnational corporations with investments in their economies, and to the upper-class business elites (who in most cases had been the recipients of the debts owed to the international creditors and/or were linked to the transnational banks and corporations that benefited from the so-called structural reforms). Under these crisis conditions, dependency theory, development (modernization) theory, and the ISI approach to national industrial development were displaced by the new ideology that accompanied the "structural adjustments." To many intellectuals, experts, and policy makers in Latin America, these perspectives no longer seemed to be either relevant or politically viable.

STRUCTURAL ADJUSTMENTS AND NEOLIBERALISM

The IMF and the World Bank assumed the lead role in promoting the "free market" structural adjustment packages in Latin America (Weeks 1995, 115–16). These IFIs required the Latin American and Caribbean governments to make major economic policy changes in return for receiving "bridging loans" and other forms of financial assistance from these institutions. The policy changes imposed by the IFIs in return for their financial assistance were called "policy conditionality" and "policy based lending."

The IMF's conditional loans were primarily aimed at "stabilization" (i.e., at a short-run reduction in inflation and at quick balance-of-payment corrections to create current account surpluses). The World Bank's conditional loans were aimed at "structural adjustments," which involved medium- and long-term "reforms" that transferred resources from domestic production and public services to the production of internationally competitive goods and services—or from what the World Bank economists called "nontradeables" to "tradeables." Since the loans from the IMF and the World Bank tended to go together, this formal division between "stabilization" and "structural adjustments" was difficult to distinguish in practice. By the early 1990s, nearly every Latin American and Caribbean country (and over eighty countries worldwide) had adopted IMF and World Bank stabilization and structural adjustment "reforms." In fact, some even adopted these types of economic policies in anticipation of receiving loans from these two IFIs (Weeks 1995).

It is important to note that the "stabilization" and "structural adjustment" policies that the IFIs and the U.S. government insisted the Latin American and Caribbean governments introduce in the 1980s and 1990s were piloted during the 1970s by the military dictatorship headed by General Augusto Pinochet in Chile (Collins and Lear 1995). Ironically, these policies later became known as "free market reforms," even though they were developed and imposed by General Pinochet's dictatorial regime, which violently replaced the democratically elected Socialist government of President Salvador Allende (1970–1973) in a bloody military coup in September 1973. Once the military had forcibly demobilized and repressed the multiclass popular movement that had brought Allende and his democratic Socialist government into office, they rolled back the policy gains achieved by the popular classes in Chile during the preceding years. They started by introducing policies aimed at dismantling the welfare and income-redistribution policies introduced in the preceding decade. At the same time, they set about the task of restructuring the Chilean economy and the state in favor of transnational capital and the Chilean upper class.

With the help of a team of U.S.-educated Chilean economists called "the Chicago Boys" (so named because they were inspired by the "free market" ideas of Milton Friedman at the University of Chicago) and the assistance of the IFIs and the U.S. government, the Pinochet regime introduced a combination of economic and social "reforms" that drastically reduced Chile's public sector, privatized a large number of the country's government-owned enterprises, deregulated the economy to "open" it up to foreign investments, eliminated price controls on basic necessities, dismantled Chile's progressive labor laws, and reduced or eliminated most of the government programs previously aimed at improving the living conditions of the popular classes (Collins and Lear 1995).

The "free market" ideological justification for this type of "restructuring" in Latin America and the Caribbean is generally called "neoliberalism" by its critics, as well as by most scholars and journalists who write about this subject (Harris 2000; Harris and Seid 2000). This ideology deals with how economies should be structured (i.e., unfettered by government regulations and restraints) to promote private enterprise, "free markets," rapid economic growth, and "free trade." The key concepts in this ideology are "free markets" and "free trade," and the advocates of this ideology use these concepts like a mantra.

This ideology of free market and free trade fundamentalism became the dominant form of contemporary capitalist ideology in the 1980s during the administration of President Ronald Reagan in the United States and the government of Prime Minister Margaret Thatcher in the United Kingdom (Harris 2000). It provided the ideological foundation for what has been called the "Washington Consensus" (Williamson 1993), which is the package of "free market" and "free trade" "structural reforms" that the U.S. government and the three IFIs headquartered in Washington, D.C., began imposing on the Latin American and Caribbean governments during the early 1980s.

This ideology was used to justify the so-called stabilization measures and Structural Adjustment Programs (SAPs) that the U.S. government and IFIs insisted the governments in Latin America and other parts of the world adopt in order to create budget surpluses that would allow them to pay off their debts, "open" their economies to more foreign investments and "free trade," privatize their supposedly inefficient state enterprises and public services, control inflation in their economies, deregulate their supposedly overregulated markets, and increase the "competitiveness" and "integration" of their economies into the global economy (Williamson 1993). This ideology of neoliberalism served as an ideological smokescreen for the largely unpopular and drastic measures that IFI experts and U.S. officials imposed as "conditions" upon the Latin American and Caribbean governments in the 1980s and 1990s in return for loans, credits, and development assistance.

The consequences of these SAPs in terms of loss of jobs, income, and personal savings, cut backs in public services, the transfer of public utilities and state enterprises to private ownership at rock-bottom prices, and the decline in living standards for the majority of the population are truly incalculable. As a result, even prominent U.S. economists have criticized the disastrous effects of these neoliberal policies and programs imposed by the IFIs and the U.S. government during the 1980s and 1990s. For example, Joseph Stiglitz, who was President Bill Clinton's top economic adviser and subsequently senior vice president of the World Bank and the winner of the 2001 Nobel Prize in Economics, has severely criticized these polices and the neoliberal "free market fundamentalism" that justified them. According to Stiglitz (2002), these policies were "an almost certain recipe for job destruction and unemployment creation at the expense of the poor," and they contributed to the instability of the economies where they were implemented (84).

Generally speaking, the pursuit of neoliberal policies that have encouraged foreign investments, the privatization of state assets, and the "opening" up of their economies through deregulation has constrained most of the Latin American and Caribbean governments from implementing policies aimed at combating the inequalities, disparities, injustices, and environmental threats suffered by the majority of the population in their countries (Harris and Seid 2000, 13). The neoliberal policies and programs associated with the Washington Consensus (and the "Post-Washington Consensus") redistributed wealth from the poor to the rich and contributed to a dramatic increase in the number of people living in poverty within the region. As a result, the relative per capita income of the population in most of the Latin American and Caribbean countries was lower in 2000 than it was in 1950 (see table 3.6), and even in those countries where there was some improvement, it was quite modest.

During the first decade of neoliberal economic restructuring (the 1980s), the number of people below the poverty line in Latin America and the Caribbean increased from 136 million in 1980 to 196 million in 1990 (Vilas 1995, 140). This 44 percent increase in the number of people living in poverty over the course of the 1980s was double the 22 percent increase in the region's population during this decade. Between 1990 and 2003, the number of people living in poverty increased to 220 million. While this 12 percent increase represented a much slower rate of increase than during the 1980s, it left 44 percent of the region's population living in poverty in 2003

Table 3.6.   Relative per Capita Income in 2000 as a Percentage of 1950 per Capita Income

Haiti	29%	El Salvador	69%
Nicaragua	36%	Paraguay	72%
Venezuela	42%	Colombia	89%
Bolivia	50%	Chile	97%
Honduras	56%	Panama	114%
Guatemala	61%	Mexico	115%
Peru	61%	Costa Rica	118%
Ecuador	63%	Brazil	125%
Uruguay	63%	Dominican Republic	134%
Argentina	64%		

Source: Frankema (2006, 6).

(González 2003). As a result, instead of wealth trickling down to the poor as promised by the advocates of neoliberalism and globalization, it appears that millions of people trickled down from the middle and working classes into poverty.

Moreover, the "global competitiveness" of the economies of most of the Latin American and Caribbean countries did not improve as a result of their governments' efforts to deregulate and "open" their economies to foreign investments, increase their exports, and make their products more "competitive" in the global economy. In 2001, after at least ten years (and in some cases more than twenty years) of neoliberal "reforms" aimed at "globalizing" the Latin American and Caribbean countries' economies, the IDB reported that Latin America occupied fifth place among the seven major regions of the world in terms of its "global competitiveness" (IDB 2001).

FINAL CONSIDERATIONS

Even a cursory critical examination of the recent economic performance of countries such as Chile, Argentina, and Mexico, which faithfully implemented most of the neoliberal reforms insisted upon by the IFIs and the U.S. government, reveals that their publicized achievements in macroeconomic growth and financial stability were accomplished at great costs to the majority of the population. These costs have included holding down the real wages of their workforces, massive job losses and unemployment, the reduction of public services and social benefits, the rapid growth of the "informal" sector of their economies, and the retarded and imbalanced development of the countries in which these structural "reforms" and policies were implemented. And in the case of Argentina, the "payoff" for being the poster child for the neoliberal agenda of the so-called Washington Consensus was the unprecedented total collapse of its economy, which pushed more than 50 percent of the population below the national poverty line in 2002 (Burbach 2002, 38–40). Indeed, one of the most reprehensible aspects of the SAPs implemented in Latin America and the Caribbean has been the dispassionate disregard their adherents and apologists have shown for the large numbers of people who have suffered and continue to suffer the harmful effects of these neoliberal measures aimed at "restructuring" and "globalizing" the Latin American and Caribbean economies.

Throughout the region, the interests of the popular classes are still largely excluded or underrepresented in the policy-making process, and these classes continue to be inequitably compensated for the wealth they produce, much of which is transferred out of their countries. The existing pseudodemocratic and elite-dominated regimes that prevail throughout the region pay lip service to "the alleviation of poverty," and an increasing number of the political leaders in these countries even pay lip service to replacing the existing neoliberal "reforms" with more progressive policies. However, most governments in the region continue to protect and promote the interests and privileges of the upper-class business elites and the transnational banks and corporations that continue to dominate economic life in the region today. Nevertheless, in an increasing number of these countries, neoliberalism has become a politically bankrupt ideology, and neoliberal policies no longer have any legitimacy except among the elites.

During the 1990s and early 2000s, popular resistance to the existing polyarchical (elite-dominated) and pseudodemocratic regimes in the region and their neoliberal policy agenda increased dramatically. This resistance increased both in intensity and scope throughout the entire region (Harris 2005). In the majority of countries, by the early 2000s, the neoliberal structural reforms and policies had been publicly discredited and repudiated by both popular protests and national elections. In fact, in many of these countries, increasing popular resistance forced the resignation or led to the electoral defeat of the political leaders and parties associated with the unpopular neoliberal policies.

By the end of 2006, in Argentina, Bolivia, Brazil, Ecuador, Nicaragua, Uruguay, and Venezuela, political leaders professing anti-neoliberal views and alternative policy agendas had been elected to office. In most cases and in varying degrees, these political leaders appeared to be committed to promoting inward- and regionally oriented, pro-poor policies, even if these policies involved going against the vested interests of the transnational corporations and local elites that have controlled the economies of these countries since at least the 1970s. Thus, a new page has been turned in the economic and political history of Latin America and the Caribbean. It remains to be seen what the outcome of these new developments will be for the region's future economic development. The final chapter of this book will discuss in greater deal these developments and their implications.

NOTES

1. The Latin American and Caribbean countries and their economies have been variously categorized as "developing," "underdeveloped," "less developed," "peripheral," "dependent," and "Third World." The choice of which of these labels is used in each case reflects the theoretical and/or ideological perspective of the person(s) or organization involved in using them. This chapter uses these labels to categorize the Latin American countries/economies and compare them with other countries/economies. Since all of these labels are biased and imprecise, they will be used generally with quotation marks or preceded by the word "so-called" to indicate their questionable or biased nature.

2. Cuba is again the exception since it has a socialist economy with little or no official unemployment and poverty. Moreover, there is a wide range of difference between the Latin American and Caribbean economies in terms of the extent of unemployment in them, the percentage of the population living in poverty, and the percentage of the workforce engaged in informal employment.

3. In most discussions about economic development, "absolute poverty" generally refers to a universal estimate of what are considered minimum consumption needs for survival (e.g. $2 at purchasing power parity per day), and this estimate is made without reference to the income or consumption levels of the general population. In contrast, "relative poverty" generally refers to a fraction of the average or median income or consumption of the population as a whole (often with adjustments for family size) that is considered too low in comparison to the average of the general population. Absolute poverty is generally updated for price changes only, while relative poverty is updated for changes in the median or mean income or consumption level of the general population. For a discussion of absolute and relative poverty, see Gordon Fisher, "Is There Such a Thing As an Absolute Poverty Line over Time? Evidence from the United States, Britain, Canada, and Australia on the Income Elasticity of the Poverty Line," Poverty Measurement Working Papers, United States Census Bureau, August 22, 2002, available at www.census.gov/hhes/poverty/povmeas/papers/elastap4.html#C1 (accessed December 23, 2006).

4. One of the main features of the Bretton Woods system was an obligation for each country to adopt a monetary policy that maintained the exchange rate of its currency at a fixed value, plus or minus 1 percent, in terms of the value of gold. It was also based on the ability of the International Monetary Fund to bridge temporary imbalances of payments with loans in convertible currency to countries experiencing balance-of-payment difficulties. This system largely collapsed in 1971, when the United States suspended the convertibility of the U.S. dollar to gold. For more information, see the entry on the Bretton Woods system at Wikipedia, the online encyclopedia, at http://en.wikipedia.org/wiki/Bretton_Woods_system (accessed December 11, 2006).

5. For an excellent discussion of the origins and views of the various contributors to dependency theory, see Chilcote and Edelstein (1986, 19–33 and 81–86). For a representative selection of the views of many of the early advocates of dependency theory, see the collection of essays edited by James Cockcroft, André Gunder Frank, and Dale Johnson (1972).

6. This discussion of the financial crisis in Latin America that was precipitated by the Mexican "debt crisis" relies heavily upon the chapter written by Weeks (1995) in the first edition of this book.

7. Weeks (1995) points out a glaring contradiction in the position taken by the IFIs during this period when he notes, "While the governments of developing countries came under heavy external pressure to liberalize trade, the OECD [developed] countries exhibited increasingly protectionist tendencies with respect to both agricultural products and labor intensive manufactures from the Third World" (116). He also notes that "the policy changes demanded of Latin American and Caribbean governments by the multilateral agencies [IFIs] went far beyond what the developed country governments practiced themselves" (116). As an example, he reports that "it

took the United States seven years to reduce its fiscal deficit from six to four percent of gross national product (116)," but the IFIs required the Latin American and Caribbean governments to make much larger reductions in their fiscal deficits within the space of only twelve months.

NOTE

The author of this chapter has placed some suggested resources that you may wish to consult on the book's website at http://www.rowmanlittlefield.com/isbn/ 0742555240.

REFERENCES

Berberoglu, Berch. 1992. *The Political Economy of Development: Development Theory and the Prospects for Change in the Third World*. Albany: State University of New York Press.

Blázquez-Lidoy, Jorge, et al. 2006. "¿Ángel o demonio? Los efectos del comercio chino en los países de América Latina." *Revista de la CEPAL* (Diciembre). Available at www.eclac.cl/publicaciones/xml/6/27636/LCG2323eSantiso.pdf (accessed January 10, 2007).

Burbach, Roger. 2002. "Throw Them All Out: Argentina's Grassroots Rebellion." *NACLA Report on the Americas* 36, no. 1 (July–August 2002): 38–40.

Cárdenas, Enrique, José Antonio Ocampo, and Rosemary Thorp, eds. 2000. *The Export Age*, vol. 1 of *An Economic History of Twentieth-Century Latin America*. New York: Palgrave.

Cardoso, Fernando Henrique, and Enzo Faletto. 1979. *Dependency and Development in Latin America*. Berkeley: University of California Press.

CBSNews.com. 2005. "Trade with Cuba Steadily Rising," November 4. Available at www.cbsnews.com/stories/2005/11/04/politics/main1009953.shtml (accessed January 10, 2007).

Central Intelligence Agency. 2006. *World Fact Book 2006*. Dulles, VA: Potomac Books Inc.

Chilcote, Ronald, ed. 2003. *Development in Theory and Practice: Latin American Perspectives*. Lanham, MD: Rowman & Littlefield.

Chilcote, Ronald, and Joel Edelstein. 1986. *Latin America: Capitalist and Socialist Perspectives of Development and Underdevelopment*. Boulder, CO: Westview Press.

Cockcroft, James, André Gunder Frank, and Dale Johnson, eds. 1972. *Dependence and Underdevelopment: Latin America's Political Economy*. Garden City, NY: Doubleday.

Collins, Joseph, and John Lear. 1995. *Chile's Free-Market Miracle: A Second Look*. Oakland, CA: Food First.

De Gregorio, José. 2004. "Sustained Growth in Latin America." Paper presented to the Latin American Colloquium, Yale University Center for the Study of Globalization, November 19–20. Available at www.ycsg.yale.edu/documents/latin Colloquia.html (accessed December 27, 2006).

Dos Santos, Teotônio. 1968. "El nuevo carácter de la dependencia." *Cuadernos de Estudios Socio-Económicos* 10. Santiago: Centro de Estudios Socio-Económicos, Universidad de Chile.

Economic Commission for Latin America and the Caribbean (ECLAC). 2006a. "Poverty in Latin America Continues to Decrease for the Third Consecutive Year." Press Release. Available at www.eclac.cl/default.asp?idioma=IN (accessed December 31, 2006).

———. 2006b. *Preliminary Overview of the Economies of Latin America and the Caribbean 2006.* Available on the ECLAC website at www.eclac.cl/default.asp? idioma=IN (accessed December 31, 2006).

Evans, Peter. 1979. *Dependent Development: The Alliance of Multinational, State, and Local Capital in Brazil.* Princeton, NJ: Princeton University Press.

Frank, André Gunder. 1969. *Latin America: Underdevelopment or Revolution.* New York: Monthly Review Press.

Frankema, E. H. P. 2006. "A Theil Decomposition of Latin American Income Distribution in the 20th Century: Inverting the Kuznets Curve?" Working Paper of Groningen Growth and Development Centre, University of Groningen, the Netherlands. Available at www.helsinki.fi/iehc2006/papers2/Frankema.pdf (accessed March 30, 2007).

Galbraith, James K., Laura Spagnolo, and Daniel Munevar. 2006. "Pay Inequality in Cuba: The Special Period and After." Working Paper 52, Society for the Study of Economic Inequality (ECINEQ). Available at http://ideas.repec.org/p/inq/inqwps/ecineq2006-52.html (accessed March 6, 2007).

Gallagher, John, and Ronald Robinson. 1953. "The Imperialism of Free Trade." *The Economic History Review,* Second Series 6, no. 1. Available at www.mtholyoke .edu/acad/intrel/ipe/gallagher.htm (accessed December 16, 2006).

Ghosh, Pradip. 1984. *Third World Development: A Basic Needs Approach.* Westport, CT: Greenwood Press.

González, Gustavo. 2003. "Latin America: More Poverty, Fewer Social Services." *Terra Viva Online.* January 13. Available at www.ipsnews.net/fsm2003/eng/note1 .shtnl (accessed March 23, 2003).

Harris, Richard. 2000. "The Effects of Globalization and Neoliberalism in Latin America at the Beginning of the Millennium." In *Critical Perspectives on Globalization and Neoliberalism in the Developing Countries,* ed. Richard Harris and Melinda Seid, 139–62. Leiden: Brill.

———. 2005. "Popular Resistance to Globalization and Neoliberalism in Latin America." In *Globalization and Development in Latin America,* ed. Richard Harris, 273–333. Whitby, Canada: de Sitter Publications.

Harris, Richard, and Melinda Seid. 2000. "Critical Perspectives on Globalization and Neoliberalism in the Developing Countries." In *Critical Perspectives on Globalization and Neoliberalism in the Developing Countries,* ed. Richard Harris and Melinda Seid, 1–26. Leiden: Brill.

Human Rights Watch (HRW). 2002. "Americas Overview." *World Report 2002.* Available at www.hrw.org/wr2k2/americas.html (accessed January 30, 2004).

Inter-American Development Bank (IDB). 2001. "Competitiveness: The Business of Growth: Economic and Social Progress in Latin America." An IDB online report available at www.iadb.org/res/publications/pubfiles/pubB-2001E_235.pdf (accessed April 4, 2005).

International Herald Tribune. 2005. "Latin American Poverty." May 26. Available at www.iht.com/articles/2005/05/25/opinion/edlatin.php (accessed December 13, 2006).

Kaufmann, W. 1951. *British Policy and the Independence of Latin America, 1804–1828.* New Haven, CT: Yale University Press.

Magdoff, Harry. 2003. *Imperialism without Colonies.* New York: Monthly Review Press.

Malik, Mohan. 2006. "China's Growing Involvement in Latin America." *Power and Interest News Report,* June 12. Available at www.pinr.com (accessed December 27, 2006).

Organization for Economic Co-operation and Development (OECD). 2003. "Science, Technology and Industry Scoreboard 2003—Towards a Knowledge-Based Economy." An OECD online report. Available at www1.oecd.org/publications/e-book/92-2003-04-1-7294/C.2.1.htm (accessed November 17, 2006).

Perry, Guillermo, et al. 2006. *Poverty Reduction and Growth: Virtuous and Vicious Circles.* Washington, DC: World Bank.

Petras, James, and Henry Veltmeyer. 2003. *Cardoso's Brazil: A Land for Sale.* Lanham, MD: Rowman & Littlefield.

Prebisch, Raúl. 1950. *The Economic Development of Latin America and Its Principal Problems.* Lake Success, NY: Economic Commission for Latin America.

Rojas, Róbinson. 1993. "Notes on Import-Substitution Strategies for Development." Unpublished paper posted online. Available at www.rrojasdatabank.org/impsub1.htm (accessed January 4, 2007).

Rostow, Walt. 1960. *The Stages of Economic Growth: A Non Communist Manifesto.* Cambridge: Cambridge University Press.

Solimano, Andrés. 2005. "Economic Growth and Macro Management in Latin America: Past, Present and Future Perspectives." Unpublished presentation at the REDIMA II Conference, Lima, Peru, June 21. Available at www.comunidadandina.org/economia/redima2_cepal1.pdf (accessed December 31, 2006).

Stein, Stanley, and Barbara Stein. 1970. *The Colonial Heritage of Latin America: Essays on Economic Dependence in Perspective.* New York: Oxford University Press.

Stiglitz, Joseph. 2002. *Globalization and Its Discontents.* New York: W. W. Norton.

Theberge, Alexander. 1999. "The Latin American Debt Crisis of the 1980s and Its Historical Precursors." Unpublished seminar paper presented at Columbia University, April 8. Available at www.columbia.edu/~ad245/theberge.pdf (accessed December 31, 2006).

United Nations Council for Trade and Development (UNCTAD). 2002. "The Least Developed Countries Report, 2002: Escaping the Poverty Trap." New York: United Nations.

United Nations Development Program (UNDP). 2006. *Human Development Report 2006.* New York: United Nations.

United Nations Population Fund. 2005. *The State of World Population.* New York: United Nations.

U.S. Census Bureau. 2006. International Data Base. Available at www.census.gov/cgi-bin/ipc/agggen (accessed January 12, 2007).

Vilas, Carlos. 1995. "Economic Restructuring, Neoliberal Reforms, and the Working Class in Latin America." In *Capital, Power and Inequality in Latin America,* ed. Sandor Halebsky and Richard L. Harris, 137–64. Boulder, CO: Westview Press.

Weaver, Frederick. 2000. *Latin America in the World Economy: Mercantile Colonialism to Global Capitalism*. Boulder, CO: Westview Press.

Weeks, John. 1995. "The Contemporary Latin American Economies: Neoliberal Reconstruction." In *Capital, Power and Inequality in Latin America*, ed. Sandor Halebsky and Richard L. Harris, 109–36. Boulder, CO: Westview Press.

———. 1999. "Have Workers in Latin America Gained from Liberalization and Regional Integration?" University of London, School of Oriental and African Studies, Center for Development Policy and Research Discussion Paper 1199. Available at www.eldis.org/static/DOC8886.htm (accessed January 24, 2004).

Weisbrot, Mark, and David Rosnick. 2003. "Another Lost Decade? Latin America's Growth Failure Continues into the 21st Century." Unpublished report of the Center for Economic and Policy Research, Washington, DC, November 13. Available at www.cepr.net/publications/latin_america_2003_11.htm (accessed December 27, 2006).

Williamson, John. 1993. "Development and the 'Washington Consensus.'" *World Development* 21:1239–1336.

World Trade Organization. 2006. "Country Profile for Cuba." September. Available at http://stat.wto.org/CountryProfile/WSDBCountryPFView.aspx?Language=E& Country=CU (accessed December 10, 2006).

4

Economic Restructuring, Neoliberalism, and the Working Class

Viviana Patroni

The scope of recent economic change in Latin America has been so profound that no one—whether from among the very few who have benefited from the restructuring or the large segment of the population that has suffered its consequences—can look at the last quarter-century in the region with indifference. Yet, during these years, very little has been delivered in the form of more efficient economies, higher levels of employment, or enhanced regional stability. For most Latin Americans, change in the way they experience work has been sweeping but not positive. On the contrary, they have experienced a number of negative trends: growing unemployment, increasing incidences of precarious and informal forms of work, declining job stability, and stagnant or falling wages. In short, for most people, economic restructuring, mainly in the shape of what we could call market-friendly reforms or neoliberal reforms, has meant labor-market conditions that, for the most part, have involved drastic deteriorations in living standards, both in terms of job quality and prospects for the future. As Silver and Arrighi (2000) point out, the puzzling aspect of the last decades of the past century is that a crisis of capital was transformed into a crisis of labor.

The transformation of Latin American labor markets has been related very closely to the program of reforms implemented in most countries in the region, including privatization, trade liberalization, and labor deregulation. These policies came at a heavy social cost from the very beginning and generated a considerable degree of resistance. However, by the 1990s, governments had managed either to neutralize the opposition or, in some cases, even garner an impressive consensus (although this consensus has started to crumble in many countries) around the need for increased market deregulation. Labor was an important player in this process, sometimes resisting flexibilization policies but at other times accommodating to the dictates of reform. Overall, though, the scope of the transformation of labor processes and markets was such that the capabilities of labor, forged as they were during decades of very limited autonomy, were no match for the conditions that neoliberal approaches unleashed.

This chapter addresses these issues, starting with a brief historical overview of the main events and forces that have shaped the politics of Latin American organized labor. The main focus is on the transformation that workers and their organizations and labor markets generally have experienced since the 1980s. The argument here is that Latin American unions have been in a very weak position to respond effectively to the challenges presented by neoliberalism and that their weakness has been the result of the limitations imposed on unions by their historically very reduced space for autonomy. The chapter concludes with an exploration of the different alternatives emerging from within labor to respond to the devastating consequences of free market thinking.

LABOR AND POLITICS IN LATIN AMERICA: AN OVERVIEW

The composition of the Latin American working class, its relative strength as a social actor, and the strategies it has pursued given these parameters have exhibited a large degree of variation among the different countries of the region. Nonetheless, it is possible to point out some general patterns, trajectories, and features.

Certain historical conditions facilitated the emergence and growth of Latin American labor unions. These conditions usually fostered an increasing sense of common identity among workers. Efforts at unionization encountered the most propitious arena for growth where both a high concentration of workers and dire working conditions facilitated concerted action against employers. In addition, in countries where labor was not in abundant supply, workers were consistently more effective in creating stronger unions. Under such circumstances, labor demands were strengthened even when highly repressive responses increased the cost of labor struggles (Collier and Collier 1991).

While heterogeneity remained a key characteristic of the working class in Latin America, by the early 1930s, at least in major urban centers, significant portions of workers had acquired a culture of their own that transformed them collectively into a distinctive social actor. This emerging working class underwent rapid expansion in the postwar period as industrialization and urbanization proceeded swiftly. The growing social significance of the working class paralleled the transformation of its organizations into primary actors in the promotion of citizenship rights. This political task was undertaken on behalf of not only unions' rank and file but also other subordinate groups. In this way unions acquired a pivotal role as representatives of a much broader segment of the population, which became constituted, through this process and at this critical time in the political history of the region, as "the people" (Roxborough 1998, 227). Through this process, too, the notion of citizenship became much more directly connected to demands for social justice and recognition of the intrinsic dignity of workers. The populist movements that sprang up in Latin America in the 1930s and 1940s gave new language to these demands and legitimized them politically. In turn, particularly when the working class had already been a relatively powerful force, its incorporation into the populist alliance infused into the latter elements of a discourse that conditioned in fundamental ways its nature and appeal as a political force.

Populism came to consolidate the role that in many countries, even if only in incipient form, the state had already acquired as the preferred arena of action for labor and, in fact, labor's more obvious interlocutor (Roxborough 1998, 226). This power of the state can be explained partly by the fact that, in the context of labor's weakness to affect general working conditions through direct action in the workplace, political action at the level of the state or participation within parties with strong capacity either to gain power or to affect policy making became the most effective mechanism to secure protective legislation and higher wages (Drake 1996, 18–19).[1]

Since the end of the 1940s and until the 1970s, import-substitution industrialization (ISI) advanced rapidly in most countries of the region. There were important national differences in the way industrialization and the social transformation that went with it affected political systems. There were also variations in the way in which the labor movement related to political parties and the state. However, the regulation of labor relations acquired under corporatism some common features in several countries of the region. Although corporatism as a system of state-labor relations was consolidated in most countries during the period of populism, it was in reality compatible with a number of political regimes.

Corporatism implied the enactment and entrenchment of labor legislation through which the state both further institutionalized its role in the mediation of labor conflicts and affected in direct ways the nature of union organizational strategies. In general terms, one could say that corporatism resulted in the creation of structures within the labor movement that acted as mechanisms to control workers' demands. However, it is imperative to keep in mind that the trajectory of the relationship between state and labor, as well as between labor leaderships and their rank and file, presented a number of complexities. Thus, if one of the most important outcomes of corporatism was the subordination of labor's demands to broader political strategies pursued by political parties and the state, it was equally true that labor did not relinquish all of its autonomy. In fact, the effectiveness of corporatism as a containment strategy was based on the legitimacy that the leadership was able to maintain vis-à-vis its rank and file, and this implied some capacity to represent effectively the interests of their members. Very often, doing so entailed confronting the state and, of course, labor actions against employers. Ultimately, labor organizations' success in securing improvements in working conditions or a higher share of the national income remained a function of their capacity to exercise direct pressure on the state and employers.

The very delicate balance organized labor maintained in this respect can be appreciated by the fact that not only did corporatist unions at times face stiff opposition from employers and repression from the state, but on several occasions they were also forced to overcome major opposition movements from within their own rank and file. While restrictions on democratic competition within unions were key characteristics of corporatism, they did not prevent the emergence of powerful opposition movements. If the corporatist ties that developed between labor unions and the state set the contours of labor's contemporary history in Latin America, so did the opposition they generated among more progressive labor alternatives.

THE END OF AN ERA

Political variables are certainly key in explaining the significance and endurance of corporatism, but just as important is the shared economic trajectory of most Latin American countries. A reliance on industrialization, the centrality of domestic markets, high levels of protectionism, and the key role assigned to the state in the regulation of the economy formed the core of the economic model that made viable the pattern of labor incorporation just described.

Starting in the 1970s, though, a major shift in economic orientation began to take place. This adjustment happened first in Chile, Argentina, and, to some extent, Brazil, where brutal military regimes imposed economic programs of trade liberalization, privatization, and deregulation that in the 1980s would become the essence of economic restructuring. For the region as a whole, the clearest point of rupture with the previous pattern of accumulation came with the financial crisis several countries confronted after 1982. The appeal of the package of reforms implemented after this time, particularly in the 1990s, was closely connected to the growing influence of a body of ideas that, since the 1970s, had come to question the principal tenets of development thinking as it had evolved in the post–World War II period. This questioning of broadly accepted approaches to development, more specifically industrialization under regimes of high protectionism, coincided with, and was quite certainly related to, rapid and profound changes in the larger international economy that together have come to be known as globalization. The Globalization has entailed a profound transformation in the relation between capital and labor, a major transformation of the productive process away from regulation and toward flexible accumulation, and a radical process of social polarization worldwide (Robinson 2003, 19). The reconfiguration of labor markets in Latin America and elsewhere, particularly the intensification of informal and precarious forms of work, has rendered these changes transparent.

Starting in the 1980s, the implementation of market reforms in Latin America was undertaken by new and ostensibly democratic governments. In most cases, the return to democracy was accompanied by a strong consensus and expectations that the postauthoritarian regimes would address deep-rooted social inequalities and the exclusionary traits that had been typical of the economic growth patterns followed until then. However, rather than these emerging democracies' affecting the nature of economic restructuring, conversely, economic reforms conditioned Latin American democracies and the qualities of citizenship in the postauthoritarian era.

In the opening years of the twenty-first century, and after over two decades of neoliberal structural adjustment, questions regarding the relationship between growth and equity and the relative inclusiveness and/or purported democratic qualities of political regimes in Latin America have acquired a new urgency. In particular, a growing opposition to market reforms has been crucial in raising awareness about neoliberalism's critical shortcomings. Not only is it recognized that neoliberal policies have been only partly successful in fostering economic growth, but it is also clear that they have been undertaken at the expense of creating deteriorating living conditions for large segments of the Latin American population. Neoliberal reforms have not only failed to provide a way to counter the abysmal regional record of inequality (in fact, Latin America is the most unequal region in the world when it comes to income distribution), but they have also contributed to worsening the situation such that poverty has been further deepened (Hoffman and Centeno 2003, 367). Persistent and increasing inequality, combined with low and unstable rates of economic growth, explains the growth of poverty for the region as a whole. Urban poverty affected 29.8 percent of the urban population and 59.9 percent of the rural population in Latin America in 1980. By 2002, the figures were 44 and 61.8 percent, respectively (CEPAL 2005, 119). While these numbers represent a slight improvement when compared to the 1980s—that is, after a decade of unmitigated economic decline—there is still evidence of a dramatic deterioration in welfare suffered by most Latin Americans, regardless of the fact that there were some improvements in the overall growth rate during the 1990s.

Three regional characteristics central to drawing the context within which labor responses developed emerged under neoliberal policies. One was the region's poor economic performance. While there were important country-by-country variations, overall growth was only sporadic and subject to critical structural limitations that served to temper its intensity. Another major feature of the extension of "market-friendly" policies was the notion that previous rigidities in labor markets limited the impact of growth on the absorption of labor. Therefore, reducing labor costs, both directly through the control of wages and indirectly through the reduction of payroll taxes, was considered a fundamental goal of various initiatives aimed at labor-market deregulation. Contrary to what had been promised, however, such liberalization processes did not improve but exacerbated poor labor conditions and led to the rapid growth of precarious forms of employment. In many countries, worsening working conditions coexisted with rising unemployment. Poor economic performance certainly explains some of these trends in the sense that there was a low generation of employment overall. However, it must be stressed that the quality of employment, not just the quantity of jobs available, declined. These changes in the labor market figure prominently as a variable to explain growing poverty, as does the persistence of extremely unequal patterns of income distribution. Finally, as a third regional characteristic evolving with the neoliberal model, it is important to point to the shifting political realities that emerged and created a new environment for (re)constructing the relationship the labor movement had previously developed with political parties and the state. These new political patterns conditioned in fundamental ways labor's capacity to respond to the pressures it had faced since the 1980s. These three characteristics are elaborated below. The first two (i.e., poor economic performance and rigidities in labor markets) are treated together in the following section. The reorganized political context within which the Latin American labor movement came to articulate its response to the neoliberal onslaught is the focus of a separate discussion.

ECONOMIC TRANSFORMATION AND
THE NEW REALITIES OF LABOR MARKETS

The perceived need to bring about an end to the overregulation of markets gave direction to economic policy in Latin America in the post-ISI period. The assumption was that overregulation had created major obstacles to the pace of economic growth and to overcoming the internal and external bottlenecks so characteristic of development patterns in the region. The pace and scope of economic reform varied significantly from country to country, but the general thrust was very similar across the board. There has also been the general realization that structural reforms have failed to produce the outcomes that originally served as their justification.

The growing opposition to the so-called Washington Consensus, which until recently dominated the debate about Latin American development options, is a good indication of the widely perceived failure of the neoliberal model to solve the region's predicaments (Lora and Panizza 2003). In fact, after over two decades of neoliberal reforms, several traits can be observed: (1) Latin American economies have become even more susceptible to external shocks, (2) while exports have grown in some countries, they continue to be based on primary resources, (3) increased international competition has resulted mostly in the destruction of domestic industries, and finally, (4) the privatization of the public sector has simply consolidated private monopolies and further exacerbated inadequacies in access to public services and utilities for a large proportion of the population.

After a decade of crisis and economic decline during the 1980s, the 1990s generated high expectations regarding the potential for improved economic performance. However, growth in this latter decade was not sufficient to undo the setbacks of the previous period. With the exception of Chile and Colombia, all countries experienced negative growth during the 1980s. Economic performance tended to improve overall during the 1990s, but serious financial crises punctuated the decade (the Tequila crisis in 1995, the Asian crisis in 1997 and 1998, and finally the repercussions of Argentina's devastating collapse in 2001 and 2002), creating grave economic difficulties for most countries. While some economies performed better than others, it is overwhelmingly clear that market reforms from the late 1970s right up to the present have delivered very little in terms of economic growth. There has been a lot of pain—in the form of major structural transformations whose negative consequences will be difficult to rectify in future—for very little gain. Moreover, growth rates for the region have remained well below those experienced during the previous protectionist regime: gross domestic product (GDP) per capita grew at an average annual rate of 3 percent between 1960 and 1980, but between 1980 and 2002 growth in GDP per capita remained drastically low at 0.5 percent (Solimano 2006, 3).

The Growth of Unemployment

More to the point of our discussion regarding changes in labor markets, and as mentioned above, volatile and weak economic growth since the 1980s seems to go a long way toward explaining the increasing lag in employment creation. In fact, it is very likely that the general rate of labor absorption[2] in the 1990s was not substantially different from the average rate for the period from 1950 to 1999. Although proponents of neoliberal reforms had argued that more flexible labor markets would encourage a greater use of labor, at the aggregate level this seems not to have been the case. By the same token, and again at a very general level of aggregation, concerns with the likelihood of lower rates of labor absorption might have been misplaced.[3] All this means that growing unemployment until early in the new century was related fundamentally to the poor record in economic growth most of the region experienced during the neoliberal era (Weller 2003, 36).

When compared to the 1980s, the labor supply grew at a slower rate in the 1990s. This slowdown reflected demographic changes since the 1970s—lower birth rates especially—that resulted in a reduction in the rate of expansion of the working-age population. Nonetheless, the global rate of labor force participation[4] increased consistently during the period reflecting, in particular, the increasing participation of women in the labor force. Between 1960 and 1990, women increased their participation in labor markets from 18 to 57 million (Munck 2004, 9). The growing number of workers seeking employment created additional pressure on labor markets. Thus, the tendency during the 1990s was for unemployment to increase; that is, although rates of economic growth were better during the 1990s than in the 1980s, they were not sufficient to absorb the growing rate of labor force participation. Moreover, the various financial crises during the 1990s produced serious economic setbacks that reduced employment markedly. The recovery phase was not sufficient to overturn the problem. Thus, by the end of the 1990s and the beginning of the new century, unemployment levels were higher than those that had been registered during the financial crisis at the beginning of the 1980s (Weller 2003, 37–38).

The recent process of incorporation of women into the labor force has happened, then, at a particularly difficult juncture. According to a recent International Labour Organization (ILO) study (Abramo and Valenzuela 2005), women represent 40 percent of the economically active population (EAP) in the urban sector. While their participation rate was 39 percent in 1990, it had reached 44.6 percent in 2002. However, unemployment also increased substantially for women, from 6.5 percent in 1990 to 13 percent in 2004; that is, female unemployment grew at a higher rate than male unemployment, which increased from 5.3 to 9.1 percent for the same period. Because of the general trends in labor markets, women have found their point of entry through employment primarily in the informal sector. In fact, half of all female employment can be accounted for in this way. Other important sources of employment for women are the public sector (education, health, and state bureaucracy), domestic services, export processing zones (EPZs), and retailing.

Since 2003, the region has experienced a new phase of economic growth with positive results in terms of employment generation. Economic growth for the region as a whole was equivalent to 5.9 percent in 2004 and 4.3

percent in 2005. In 2006, it may reach 4.1 percent (ECLAC 2005, 13). Economic recovery translated into a growing demand for labor that was all the more effective in reducing unemployment since it was accompanied by a slower-growing labor supply in 2004. Thus, unemployment fell from 11.1 percent in 2003 to 10.2 percent in 2004 and to 9.6 percent in 2005 (ILO 2005, iii–iv).

One of the most noticeable aspects of this recent process of economic growth is its unprecedented coexistence with a rising current account surplus.[5] The reasons for the surplus are varied, as noted by the Economic Commission for Latin America and the Caribbean (ECLAC) (2005), but the expansion of the global economy, as well as its impact on the volume of exports and improving terms of trade, figures prominently. Another key variable affecting the state of the current account surplus has been the growing magnitude of foreign remittances from emigrants. In fact, according to the Inter-American Development Bank, remittances reached US $45.8 billion in 2004. This represents a sharp increase given that only as recently as 2001, remittances stood at US $26 billion. Various benefits can be associated with this inflow of resources, particularly when remittances are seen to represent a very substantial share of a country's GDP. For instance, in 2002 in small countries such as Nicaragua, remittances were equivalent to 29 percent of GDP and 127 percent of exports. In large economies such as Mexico, remittances still accounted for 3 percent of the GDP. Foreign income amounted to 7 percent of that perceived for exports (Orozco 2004, 9–10).

A growing body of literature has explored the expanding significance of out-migration in countries of the region and the concomitant rise of remittances. Quite often, these studies focus on the various benefits implied by the existence of remittances as a source of foreign income with the potential to play a countercyclical role and also to become a vital source of investment for individuals, as well as community initiatives. One point must be underscored: the rise in remittances reflects the growing portion of the population that has been forced to leave its home communities and countries as a survival strategy. The remittance phenomenon certainly also points to emerging patterns in migration, particularly the maintenance of transnational bonds with the country of origin, ranging from continuing support for family left behind to consumption of traditional products made available in the migrant-receiving countries. Nonetheless, we must remember that the large movement of workers across Latin American borders (mostly from the South to the North, but not exclusively so) is one of the most tangible and vivid expressions of the exclusionary nature of economic growth in the region. Migrants and their remittances are not simply a manifestation of the growing integration of Latin American countries into the global economy (Orozco 2004, 12). They are additionally, and much more importantly, an expression of the problems the region has faced in terms of generating employment and securing fair wages.[6]

Nowhere Else to Go: Informal and Precarious Work in Latin America

Lower rates of economic growth and unemployment, however, have not been the only variables affecting labor markets. Indeed, a critical change during the 1990s was the low generation of salaried employment, a fact that points to the diminishing weight of formal jobs in terms of overall total employment (Weller 2003, 36–37). The ILO estimates that seven out of ten jobs created in Latin America since 1990 augmented the ranks of the informal sector (ILO 2003). The informal sector encompasses a large diversity of activities undertaken usually within very small enterprises relying on low capital inputs and is, quite often, characterized by low levels of productivity. Representative occupations include the self-employed (excluding professionals and technicians), unpaid family workers, street vendors, those providing various kinds of personal services, domestic workers, and waged workers as characterized above (that is, those working without social security or any other legal protection). Diversity in the universe of occupations within the informal sector is expressed by the multiplicity that exists also around income and educational levels. Taken together, such heterogeneity implies that establishing direct connections between the informal sector and extreme poverty or marginality can be misleading (Feldman and Murmis 2000, 242). Nonetheless, for a very large portion of those employed in the informal economy—whom Portes and Hoffman (2003) identified as the "informal proletariat"—poverty, lack of any social protection, poor and unsafe working conditions, and low wages constitute the most prevalent work scenario.

Another important feature of the informal sector is that it is not necessarily marginal to the formal economy (Vilas 1995, 147). On the contrary, an important segment of microenterprises plays the fundamental role of transforming the labor of those in the informal sector into low-cost goods and services in order to satisfy the demand of individual consumers or, through subcontracting, of enterprises for cheap inputs (Portes and Hoffman 2003, 45). Although the problem of informality in Latin American economies is not new, the 1990s represented a major shift in previous patterns of employment generation because of the rate at which informal employment expanded. During the ISI period, formal employment increased consistently in the region, accounting for 60 percent of total employment generation for the years 1950 to 1980. Certainly this generation level was not sufficient to absorb the growing labor supply most countries faced in the urban sector, a fact that constituted one of the main criticisms raised against the pattern of industrialization followed by the region. However, from the 1990s onward, this problem of informality acquired a completely new meaning as formal employment became increasingly scarce. Part of the difficulty was the drastic fall in employment within the public sector, along with the drop in formal employment within large- and medium-sized industry. Enterprises in these two industrial sectors had accounted for 45 percent of total employment creation up until the 1980s, but during the 1990s their share fell to only 20 percent (Portes and Hoffman 2003, 49).

The growth of informal employment was thus closely related to the performance of the formal economy. Inadequate levels of employment generation in the more advanced sectors of the economy and the lack of any form of unemployment insurance in most countries forced a growing number of Latin American workers to seek refuge from open unemployment through self-employment or through employment in microenterprises or other low-productivity occupations within the informal sector. Among those self-employed in the informal economy were former public servants and other professionals and skilled workers who, as a result of restructuring, had been displaced from their traditional formal occupations. These former employees had no option in terms of securing a living other than attempting to use their skills by creating employment opportunities for themselves. Their participation in the informal economy as microentrepreneurs also generated employment for the growing number of workers in the informal labor market. In fact, microenterprises in the urban sector became a major source of employment during the 1990s, accounting for 30 percent of all new jobs created in the period 1990 to 1998 (Portes and Hoffman 2003, 48).

For the region as a whole, the proportion of informal employment in relation to total urban employment was close to 47 percent. In several countries, the informal sector accounted for over half of the employment for the EAP. That was the case, for example, in countries such as Colombia, Ecuador, Paraguay, and Peru, where workers in the informal economy accounted for almost 60 percent of the total employment figures (ILO 2005, 11).

Increasingly during the 1990s, many jobs also came to be characterized by their precariousness. Changes in labor legislation made it possible for employers to hire workers within the formal economy under conditions that mirrored those faced by workers in the informal economy. Thus, provisions that allowed for temporary contracts, reduced workdays, wages below minimal levels, and subcontracting introduced the flexibility that modern firms sought for their workforces (Zapata n.d., 12). Moreover, even in those cases where labor legislation remained unchanged, deteriorating conditions in labor markets became the context for a de facto flexibilization in contractual relations. According to the ILO, only four out of ten employees in the formal sector in this decade enjoyed the benefits of social security, while only two out of ten in the informal economy did so (ILO 2003).

Women were particularly affected by these trends in the transformation of working conditions. This result was all the more troubling given, as mentioned before, the massive incorporation of women into labor markets, a phenomenon that became especially conspicuous in the service sector. Employment in services actually expanded during the 1990s at a higher rate than total employment, a reflection of the growing tertiarization (expansion of the services sector) of the region's economies. However, growing employment in the service sector was accompanied by diminishing productivity within it. Women's participation in paid employment was concomitant with the increase in self-employment and nonremunerated activities, a factor that clearly points to the growing importance of informal activities and the central participation of women in them.

The drop in formal employment has created a radically different situation for unions. Designing a strategy to counteract the trends identified above will require the ability to organize beyond unions' traditional constituencies. In turn, such an alternative assumes the capacity to forge new identities regardless of the growing disparities in workplace experiences. Worsening working conditions and the stagnation or decline of real average wages for the working class during the 1990s indicate the mounting difficulty of protecting acquired rights and benefits in the context of increasingly narrower opportunities in the labor market. In this sense, it is important to consider the disciplinary role of neoliberalism on the working class (Patroni 2004). High levels of unemployment and the realities of those who labor at the margins of the formal economy do not create a medium conducive to strengthening labor responses to protect, let alone advance, workers' demands. In this context, unions have faced a declining relevance as institutions capable of delivering on issues central to the quality of the lives of their affiliates.

POLITICAL TRANSITIONS AND THE LABOR MOVEMENT

The hardships for the labor movement in Latin America have not been limited to the impact of economic structural changes on labor markets. For example, the transition away from ISI was coupled with an important political transformation. In many countries, this political change implied a return to democratic rule after long and violent dictatorships. In others, civil wars gave way to new regimes that oversaw a very incomplete transition to what many hoped were going to be more inclusionary political alternatives. In all cases, though, democracy, at least in the way that it has unfolded regionally, has proven an inadequate institutional setting in which to struggle against the exclusionary nature of the emerging pattern of development. Moreover, if at one point in history unions were essential actors in the extension of democratic and social rights, their capacity to affect the recent course of political transformation has been limited considerably.

A fundamental element in explaining the rather limited political capabilities of unions during this latest period in Latin America is the redefinition of the relationship between unions and the state and unions and the political parties that previously had facilitated their access to power. The process of the rise and decline in union strength took particular and quite specific forms in each country, but there were noticeable patterns within the region in terms of the political context that made viable the implementation of neoliberal reforms. In several countries, for example, the political viability of market reforms was only achieved through the intervention of political parties or coalitions with deep historical roots as allies of labor and other key social actors within the popular sector. More generally, it was labor's consent to (or, in some cases, its unwillingness to contest) the reforms introduced by the political parties it had historically supported that reduced the amount of opposition these reforms would have otherwise encountered. This response on the part of labor to policies that clearly jeopardized the economic and social foundations upon which its power had been based is the result of a complex process. In the case of Mexico, for instance, neoliberal reforms created a number of serious tensions between the state and organized labor. The reforms also deteriorated the corporatist relationship that from the late 1930s onward was at the core of the interaction between the two. However, corporatism survived throughout the consolidation of neoliberal reforms, and it played a key role in reducing the scope for opposition from within the labor movement.

As early as the mid-1980s, Mexico moved decisively in introducing neoliberal reforms. As it did so, the ruling Institutional Revolutionary Party (PRI) needed to confront two major problems. One was the social costs of reforms that threatened to jeopardize their implementation by generating effective resistance to them. The other was the political costs implied by alienating key actors in the alliance that had sustained the PRI's power. Because labor had been such a central pillar in this alliance, its political standing within the party was a particularly sensitive issue for the PRI's leadership. The tension between the party and the official labor unions was uneven, but the general trend since the 1980s was for the political hierarchy of the PRI to set a number of limits to the power that corporatist unions had previously exercised. The political isolation of the labor leadership within the party might explain in part labor's incapacity to present a viable alternative against the introduction of economic policies that affected its rank and file negatively. However, labor's lack of political independence also set very concrete limits to its capacity to conceive alternatives outside of those proposed by the party and, therefore, by extension, the state (Zapata 1998, 151).

Nonetheless, securing the basis of the corporatist system that had regulated the relationship between the labor movement and the state remained vital for both. In fact, the success of the economic policies followed by the PRI rested in no small part on the implementation of several social pacts through which prices and salaries could be controlled. The support of the official labor movement for these pacts was essential, but to make its participation effective, the power of labor's leadership needed to be protected. It is in this context that the PRI's reluctance to implement changes in the labor legislation that had cemented the power of the official labor movement can be explained. However, while the legislation was not changed, key modifications facilitating the flexibilization of labor relations were introduced through collective agreements (Patroni 2001, 266). Preserving the existing labor legislation meant, then, that corporatism remained an important alternative to isolate the official labor movement from challenges from below by securing, as has been practiced before, their privileged position to organize and represent the demands of the working class.

Against most predictions, the end of the PRI's seventy-year electoral monopoly with the coming to power of an alternative party (the National Action Party) in the presidential elections of 2000 has not posed a major challenge to corporatism (Roman and Velasco Arregui 2006, 97). Lack of change does not mean that the position of corporatist labor organizations will be secure in the long run, but at least during the critical period of transition away from one-party rule in Mexico, the official labor leadership has not been completely marginalized as a key political actor.

A profound transformation in the relationship between party and labor unions was also a characteristic of Argentina's transition away from authoritarianism. The segment of the labor movement associated with the Peronist party, beyond any doubt the dominant labor faction, faced a number of challenges with the return to democratic rule in 1983. For the first time in a free election, the Peronist party was defeated that year, placing the union leadership in a particularly delicate position within the party. Difficult as the situation for labor was at that time, it would become even more complex with the election of the Peronist candidate Carlos Menem to power in 1989. Menem's victory in May of that year initiated a process of rapid change in Argentina propelled by the implementation of a thorough neoliberal program of reforms. While the whole package of reforms introduced by Menem's new Peronist administration rested on potentially very risky measures, the deregulation of labor markets was without question the most daring initiative. The labor reforms Menem proposed were aimed at achieving the deregulation considered essential to "modernizing" labor relations in the country. By 1996, Menem had successfully introduced a number of laws and executive decrees that radically changed social and labor rights in the country.[7]

It was evident to the Menem administration that controlling labor's capacity to oppose the proposed program of labor flexibilization was an unavoidable first step in securing success in other areas of economic reform. Menem's strategy toward the labor movement was successful in the sense that it neutralized the once powerful General Confederation of Labor

(CGT). Moreover, the internal conflict generated by Menem's reform program was substantial enough to split the CGT—this was the first time that the confederation had actually split under a Peronist administration. However, the support that some sectors within the CGT continued to extend to Menem was central to the government's capacity to push forward with implementing reforms while at the same time avoiding the total collapse of its relationship with organized labor.

Later in the 1990s, as his electoral support weakened, Menem agreed to the reversal of some of the labor reforms he had introduced earlier and also to the protection of those prerogatives at the core of the unions' corporatist power, particularly the reaffirmation of industrywide collective agreements and the protection of union health-care programs from private competition. Nevertheless, the existence of these spaces for negotiation did not safeguard the CGT against its increasing marginalization. The mounting incidence of unemployment and underemployment, as well as of precarious and informal forms of employment, affected the power of Argentina's unions in critical ways. However, it was the transformation of the Peronist party itself, and labor's weaker position within it, that created a political crisis for which there appeared to be no resolution.

The case of Argentina shows the very direct and costly consequences of neoliberal reforms on the political power that labor had exercised in the past. Not only did reforms undermine the structural basis of union power, but organized labor's inability or unwillingness to oppose them undermined its previous political clout in critical ways. The emergence of some quite articulate and innovative alternatives within the labor movement further complicated this scenario in Argentina. Nonetheless, unions, and the CGT in particular, managed to retain a not inconsequential amount of power. The election of a new Peronist administration in 2003 under Néstor Kirchner might have created new opportunities for some sectors within the CGT, particularly those that opposed Menem, to reestablish themselves as labor's effective leadership.

The most radical labor-reform program in Latin America was implemented in Chile during the dictatorship of General Augusto Pinochet. The interesting point about the Chilean case is that, regardless of the return to democratic rule in 1990 and the role that more progressive forces have played in the administration of the country's government since then, labor rights have remained seriously curtailed. The explanation for this continued antilabor stance can be found in the particular characteristics of Chile's transition to democratic rule, in particular authoritarianism's endurance within the institutional structures of the country. As importantly, labor's extremely weak political position contrasts sharply with the power gained by employers' associations during the years of dictatorial rule. Labor's capabilities have been further weakened by its increasing political isolation from the parties that traditionally were its main allies, namely, the Christian Democrat, Socialist, and Communist parties (Cook 2002, 26). Under these circumstances, unions' struggles to regain previous labor rights have not been particularly effective. Moreover, the continuation of neoliberal policies under Chilean civilian rule has made the maintenance of flexible labor markets a pivotal aspect of government policy. In short, while labor has attempted to challenge existing labor legislation and while democratic governments have introduced some improvements, the legislative strategy, for the most part, has been to retain the kind of flexibility in labor relations considered essential for the positive functioning of markets (Taylor 2002).

While unionism in Brazil has suffered some important setbacks since the 1990s, its example remains fundamental in tracing the emergence of alternative forms of labor organizing. In fact, the growth and consolidation of a "new unionism" in Brazil since the 1970s allowed the labor movement to challenge prevailing corporatist practices and to become the central actor in the country's struggles surrounding the return to democratic rule. Notwithstanding labor's major historical achievements and its impressive political autonomy and power, the advancement of neoliberal reforms in the 1990s created a challenge difficult for Brazilian labor to confront. As in other countries in the region, the power of neoliberal reforms in Brazil has been felt in the depth of industrial restructuring and in concomitant changes brought about in labor markets. These factors have meant that employers in the modern sectors have been able to hire an increasing number of workers under precarious conditions. The growth of precarious employment within the formal economy has expanded the heterogeneity of the labor market in Brazil, a country already characterized by a large informal sector. Unlike the cases of Mexico and Argentina discussed above, unions in Brazil developed a strategy to deal with the impact of heterogeneity in labor markets as a key component of their struggle against labor flexibilization (Munck 2004, 12). The Unified Workers' Central Organization stands as a pivotal example of the way in which unions can transform themselves into more autonomous and inclusive actors in their efforts to resist neoliberalism. In the case of Brazil, greater political autonomy from the state created the conditions within which the labor movement could construct itself as a challenge to the devastating exclusionary practices that have accompanied the extension of neoliberal reforms.

Workers' Rights and Labor Rights in Export Processing Zones

If historical links with political parties provided only very limited protection against the damaging consequences of neoliberalism for the working class, the reality was certainly not better for workers in countries with weak labor movements or where violent political strife had critically undermined working-class organizations. This was the case for most Central American countries. In the late 1980s, steps were taken toward the resolution of long-lasting armed conflict in the region, along with the adoption of neoliberal policies. One key feature in this ongoing economic transformation has been the rapid expansion of EPZs, or *maquilas*, particularly in the apparel sector. The growth of exports from *maquilas* has been staggering, particularly since the early 1990s. Textile and apparel exports from Central America to the United States increased from $500 million in 1986 (when the U.S. Special Access Program was set in place) to $6.5 billion in 2000. Toward the end of the 1990s, Central American EPZs provided employment to more than three hundred thousand workers, the equivalent of 35 percent of all manufacturing employment for these countries (Frundt 2002, 14). Unions, weakened by years of repression and a strong antiunion stance on the part of employers, paramilitaries, and governments, have faced daunting difficulties in organizing workers in this sector.

As in the rest of the world, most of the workers in the *maquila* industry in Central American countries are young women receiving very low pay and subject to a number of labor and human rights violations. Employers, subcontractors producing for large global retailers, have resisted unionization in a number of ways, including the not-so-idle threat of moving elsewhere if workers' collective action imperils the exercise of management's prerogatives in establishing working conditions. Beyond this problem, organizing workers in *maquilas* presents a number of formidable challenges for which there are no simple solutions. First, in order to address mounting anti-sweatshop campaigns in northern countries, large corporate retailers have promoted the implementation of corporate codes of conduct by their subcontractors to make their operations compatible with international norms. Not surprisingly, companies have circumvented these restrictions by employing yet another tier of subcontractors not subject to monitoring (Frundt 2002, 15). As importantly, insofar as these codes establish the norms that regulate production within a workplace, businesses have in practice displaced domestic labor legislation and undermined legally constituted unions (Zapata, n.d., 10–11; Robinson 2003, 172–3).

Second, organizing very young women as workers, usually with no previous experience and facing a number of vulnerabilities connected to the conditions just cited, has proven to be another very difficult task. The quandary is not so much that these women might be less prone to organize but rather that, as is not uncommon in the rest of Latin America, unions have not been particularly successful in representing and organizing gender-specific demands. Thus, issues related to women's taxing family responsibilities, demands related to daycare and other benefits connected to women's role as the main caregivers for their children, and other problems connected to widespread practices of gender discrimination have not been addressed in an effective way by unions (Frundt 2002, 17). Yet, female workers in the *maquila* sector, as well as those facing similar situations in the modern, export-oriented agricultural sector, have continued to press to secure collective representation.

Finally, in an attempt to overcome the obstacles to organizing that are emerging from both employers' resistance to accepting the role of unions in the workplace and the inadequacy in addressing gender-specific demands, unions have been amenable to joining forces with nonunion actors. The high level of female participation in the *maquila* workforce has become an important subject for a number of women's local and international nongovernmental organizations (NGOs). These organizations have taken on an important role in supporting workers' struggles, contributing to establishing links with broader demands for gender equity and creating a system of support for their organizational drives (Frundt 2005, 32). International solidarity has also been a key component in attempts to organize workplaces and improve working conditions in the *maquila* sector. Both unions and NGOs in the North and the South have been key players in the planning and implementation of international campaigns (Anner 2006). All of these developments are positive in the sense that they attempt to address the obvious and pressing need to develop global responses to capital's global strategies. Yet, it is important to note that solidarity across sectors or nations is not a trouble-free proposition. Conflicts, misgivings, and distrust among various actors need to be addressed directly if their alliances are to engender viable and enduring alternatives to corporate strategies within EPZs.

CONCLUSION: A NEW CENTURY FOR LABOR?

As this chapter suggests, traditional Latin American labor unions have not been able to generate responses forceful enough to alter the pattern of transformation of working conditions imposed by neoliberal restructuring in the region. One reason for unions' inability to protect labor rights and wages has been their own increasing marginality, a position they have come to assume as formal employment, the sector traditionally organized through unions, has diminished in significance. There are forces at play that escape the unions' capacity for intervention, given their overall conservative orientation. One important variable was the growing consensus neoliberalism gained among influential sectors of the population after the traumatic experiences of the 1980s. The political costs of opposition, thus the danger of even greater marginalization, increased for unions as neoliberalism gathered momentum. At the core of the problem was not only the political reliance of unions on the very parties that carried out the reforms but the unions' conservative role as organizations of the working class. Another

factor was the continuation of long-established patterns of union representation and political intervention that rendered the organizations particularly ineffective under a new pattern of accumulation.

Finding alternatives to counteract the power of neoliberalism to transform labor markets into traps of informality and precarious work will require the concerted action of a broad range of actors. In particular, devising
ways to enhance the organizational capacity of the informal sector and
other workers in precarious jobs emerges as a critical first task. The experience of organizations like the Central of Argentine Workers (CTA) provides
a number of insights into both the potential of, and difficulties involved in,
developing more encompassing forms of labor organization. Since its be-
ginnings in the early 1990s, the CTA has been quite successful in attracting
a very wide range of workers, including the unemployed, underemployed,
self-employed, and retirees, as well as a sizeable portion of those employed
in the formal sector. The CTA represents, in this respect, a key force in the
effort to bring together a range of demands from sectors affected in particular ways by the process of restructuring and to articulate them through various, but coordinated, forms of struggle and protest.

Promising as the experience is, it has not been free of problems. One issue is that bringing together the struggles of those sectors marginalized by
the process of restructuring in Argentina is not always a feasible political
task. Because of their vulnerability and marginality, these groups are particularly susceptible to clientelistic manipulation. Moreover, the obstacles to
forging alliances among organizations representing marginalized groups
have proven difficult to overcome. The trajectory of the *piquetero* movement
(mostly organizations representing the unemployed) provides a telling example of the dangers of fragmentation and political isolation.

International solidarity might also contribute to boosting the potential of
alternative forms of labor organizations to confront the power of capital.
The experience of transnational solidarity in the EPZs points to workable
and potentially productive alternatives, notwithstanding the deep-rooted
differences that exist among various actors in different countries. The emergence of continental partnerships like the Hemispheric Social Alliance constitutes another example of the growth of international solidarity with a
strong likelihood of giving origin to further spaces of resistance to neoliberal globalization (Anner 2006). It is possible that international solidarity
and other types of international alliances will help generate the process of
renewal required for Latin American labor to build up its capacity to challenge the current nature of work and work experiences in the region. Without such change, there can be no guarantees that improved economic performance by itself will reduce the burden of informality and poverty.
Ultimately, finding a way out of the shattering experiences of marginality
and poverty faced by so many Latin Americans constitutes the precondition

to convey deeper meaning and structure to the rather weak forms of democratic representation the region has produced to date.

NOTES

The author of this chapter has placed some suggested resources that you may wish to consult on the book's website at http://www.rowmanlittlefield.com/isbn/ 0742555240.

1. However, as Collier and Collier (1991) note, this thesis of "political bargaining" obscures the complementarity that might exist between labor's capabilities in the political arena and its economic significance.

2. This measure is related to the labor elasticity of production, that is, the average change in employment associated with a 1 percent increment in production.

3. Nonetheless, a lower capacity for employment generation was visible in economies where growth was based on the proportionally rapid growth of extractive industries and natural resource–based exports.

4. Labor force participation measures the fraction of the working-age population working or looking for work.

5. It must be noted that there are very significant differences across subregions. Thus, while South American countries registered a current account surplus equivalent to 3 percent of GDP in 2005, the situation was the inverse for Central America and Mexico. In fact, these countries experienced a deficit of 1.8 percent of GDP for the same year.

6. For an alternative view regarding the role remittances play within families and communities of the migrants' country of origin, see the Cuernavaca Declaration of 2005.

7. The right to strike was curtailed (Decree 2184), salaries in the public sector were reduced (Decrees 435 and 612), a number of precarious forms of employment were legalized (Laws 24,013 and 24,467), salary increases were negotiated according to increments in productivity (Decree 470), and the liabilities for work-related accidents were restricted (Law 24,028).

REFERENCES

Abramo, Laís, and María Elena Valenzuela. 2005. "Women's Labour Force Participation Rates in Latin America." *International Labour Review* 144, no. 4: 369–99.

Anner, Mark. 2006. "Labor and the Challenge of Cross-Border, Cross-Sector Alliance." In *Latin America after Neoliberalism: Turning the Tide in the 21st Century?* ed. Eric Hershberg and Fred Rosen, 298–315. New York: The New Press.

Collier, Ruth Berins, and David Collier. 1991. *Shaping the Political Arena: Critical Junctures, the Labor Movement, and Regime Dynamics in Latin America*. Princeton, NJ: Princeton University Press.

Comisión Económica para América Latina y el Caribe (CEPAL). 2005. *Anuario estadístico de América Latina y el Caribe 2004*. Santiago: Publicación de las Naciones Unidas.

Cook, María Lorena. 2002. "Labor Reforms and Dual Transitions in Brazil and the Southern Cone." *Latin American Politics and Society* 44, no. 1 (Spring): 1–34.

Drake, Paul W. 1996. *Labor Movements and Dictatorships: The Southern Cone in Comparative Perspective.* Baltimore: Johns Hopkins University Press.

Economic Commission for Latin America and the Caribbean (ECLAC). 2005. *Preliminary Overview of the Economies of Latin America and the Caribbean 2005.* Santiago: United Nations Publications. Available at www.eclac.org/publicaciones/xml/9/23219/LCG2292_i_Preliminary_Overview.pdf (accessed August 25, 2006).

Feldman, Silvio, and Miguel Murmis. 2000. "Diversidad y organización de trabajadores en actividades informales: Análisis de algunas experiencias pertinentes." In *Informalidad y exclusión social,* ed. Jorge Carpio, Emilio Klein, and Irene Novacovsky, 241–68. Buenos Aires: Organización Internacional del Trabajo y Fondo de Cultura Económica.

Frundt, Henry J. 2002. "Central American Unions in the Era of Globalization." *Latin American Research Review* 37, no. 3: 7–53.

———. 2005. "Movement Theory and International Labor Solidarity." *Labor Studies Journal* 30, no. 2 (Summer): 19–40.

Hoffman, Kelly, and Miguel Angel Centeno. 2003. "The Lopsided Continent: Inequality in Latin America." *Annual Review of Sociology* 29:363–90.

International Labour Organization (ILO). 2003. "Labour Overview: Latin America and the Caribbean." Available at www.oit.org.pe/portal/noticias.php?ddocCodigo=69 (accessed August 4, 2004).

———. 2005. *2005 Labour Overview: Latin America and the Caribbean (First Semester Advanced Report).* Available at www.oit.org.pe/portal/documentos/labover05.pdf (accessed August 3, 2006).

Lora, Eduardo, and Ugo Panizza. 2003. "Latin America's Lost Illusions: The Future of Structural Reform." *Journal of Democracy* 14, no. 2 (April): 123–37.

Munck, Ronaldo. 2004. "Introduction." *Latin American Perspectives* 31, no. 4 (July): 3–20.

Orozco, Manuel. 2004. *Remittances to Latin America and the Caribbean: Issues and Perspectives on Development.* Washington, DC: Report Commissioned by the Organization of American States. Available at www.frbatlanta.org/news/CONFEREN/payments04/orozco.pdf (accessed July 4, 2006).

Patroni, Viviana. 2001. "Labour Legislation Reform in Mexico and Argentina: The Decline and Fall of Corporatism?" *Canadian Journal of Political Science* 34, no. 2 (June): 294–74.

———. 2004. "Disciplining Labor, Creating Poverty: Neoliberal Structural Reform and the Political Conflict in Argentina." *Research in Political Economy* 21:91–119.

Portes, Alejandro, and Kelly Hoffman. 2003. "Latin American Class Structures: Their Composition and Change during the Neoliberal Era." *Latin American Research Review* 38, no. 1: 41–82.

Red Internacional de Migración y Desarrollo. 2005. Cuernavaca Declaration. Available at www.yorku.ca/cerlac/documents/Declaration.pdf (accessed March 25, 2006).

Robinson, William. 2003. *Transnational Conflicts: Central America, Social Change, and Globalization.* London: Verso.

Roman, Richard, and Edur Velasco Arregui. 2006. "The State, the Bourgeoisie, and the Unions. The Recycling of Mexico's System of Labor Control." *Latin American Perspectives* 33, no. 2 (March): 95–103.

Roxborough, Ian. 1998. "Urban Labour Movements in Latin America since 1930." In *Latin America: Politics and Society since 1930,* ed. Leslie Bethell, 219–90. Cambridge: Cambridge University Press.

Silver, Beverly J., and Giovanni Arrighi. 2000. "Workers North and South." In *Socialist Register 2001: Global Classes, Global Realities,* ed. Leo Panitch and Colin Leys, 53–76. London: Merlin Press.

Solimano, Andrés. 2006. "Introduction and Synthesis." In *Vanishing Growth in Latin America: The Late Twentieth Century Experience,* ed. Andrés Solimano, 1–45. Cheltenham, UK: Edward Elgar.

Taylor, Marcus. 2002. "Interrogating the Paradigm of 'Labor Flexibilization': Neoclassical Prescriptions and the Chilean Experience." *Labour, Capital and Society* 35, no. 2. (November): 222–51.

Vilas, Carlos. 1995. "Restructuring, Reforms, and the Working Class in Latin America." In *Capital, Power, and Inequality in Latin America,* ed. Sandor Halebsky and Richard L. Harris, 137–63. Boulder, CO: Westview Press.

Weller, Jürgen. 2003. "Reformas económicas y situación del empleo en América Latina." In *Entre el trabajo y la política: Las reformas de las políticas sociales argentinas en perspectiva comparada,* ed. J. Lindenboim and C. Dañan, 33–56. Buenos Aires: Biblios.

Zapata, Francisco. 1998. "Trade Unions and the Corporatist System in Mexico." In *What Kind of Democracy? What Kind of Market? Latin America in the Age of Neoliberalism,* ed. Philip D. Oxhorn and Graciela Ducatenzeiler, 151–67. University Park: Pennsylvania State University Press.

———. n.d. "Crisis del sindicalismo en América Latina?" Available at www.iisg .nl/labouragain/documents/zapata.pdf (accessed May 26, 2004).

5

Insecurity, Development, and Democracy

A Pan-American Perspective

Jorge Nef

THE PROBLEM OF INSECURITY IN THE AMERICAS

This chapter reexamines the political economy of marginalization and underdevelopment, looking at the last two decades through a prism of complex dependency and human security, or, more properly, insecurity (Nef and Rojas 1984; Nef 1999, 13–26). It also examines marginalization and underdevelopment in the broader context of the entirety of the Americas, rather than confining itself to the exotic "orientalism" (Said 1978)[1] characteristic of studies that focus on "the other" America. From this standpoint, globalization can be seen as a multifaceted process in which transnationalized alliances of elite sectors at the global center and the periphery engage in a regional and global strategy of accumulation and exploitation. Dedemocratization and renewed authoritarian tendencies throughout the hemisphere are the political corollary of these profoundly reactionary socioeconomic processes. The net result is a significant deterioration of the security of most people and the generation of democratic deficits (Nye 2003), not only south of the Rio Grande but also in North America.

The Americas constitute the richest continents in the world. Yet, richest in this sense does not necessarily mean most developed; nor is this wealth synonymous with equitable, let alone secure, development. The region contains three geopolitical "giants": the United States, Canada, and Brazil. Two of these (the United States and Canada) are the most prosperous countries in the world. One is a global superpower, and the other has persistently held one of the highest scores in the United Nation's Human Development Index. These two countries, together with Brazil, possess the largest economies in the hemisphere. From a cultural point of view, and in contrast

118

to xenophobic and ethnocentric perceptions, the societies of "North" and "Latin" America, as well as the Caribbean basin, are an outgrowth of Western civilization. What was once called the New World is today an uneasy combination of three foundational metacultures (indigenous or Native American, Euro American, and Afro American) to which have been added new migratory strains from Asia and the Middle East. This unique multicultural mosaic is found in different degrees from Alaska to Tierra del Fuego.

There are, of course, great differences between the northern and the southern parts of the Western Hemisphere, just as there are dramatic contrasts within the individual countries located within it. Transcending these societal differences, however, is an abysmal and growing gap within *all* the countries of the Americas between the rich and powerful, on the one hand, and the rest of the population, on the other, especially their poorer members.

By most statistical accounts and with very few exceptions (Haiti, Honduras, Bolivia, Nicaragua), the nations south of the Rio Grande comprise the "upper layer" of countries in what was formerly called the Third World. Moreover, unlike most of the Middle East, Africa, and Asia, the ratio of natural resources to population and its biophysical diversity are highly favorable in most of these nations. In this sense, taken together, Latin America and the Caribbean, irrespective of their proximity to the overdeveloped "North," appear at least statistically to have overcome the worst conditions of poverty and to possess some of the best prospects for development (CPRC 2005, 79–82).

However, not only has distributional inequity in this region, deeply rooted in powerlessness and exclusion, continued to exist, but it has become increasingly more pronounced throughout the Americas. Therefore, in discussing this hemispheric conglomerate as a whole, it is a bit misleading to talk about rich countries and poor countries. Underneath this distinction lies the reality of rich people living very well in the poorer countries and poor people living in misery in the richer countries. Thus, according to a 2004 report by the United Nations Economic Commission on Latin America and the Caribbean (ECLAC) (2004), "Latin America is still the region of the planet with the worst [distribution] indicators, which is made worse because in some countries there has been growing income concentration" (1). The same report estimated that by 2002, 44 percent of the population was below the poverty line, and over 19 percent lived in extreme poverty (5). This means that two out of every five Latin Americans are poor and survive under very precarious and insecure circumstances. It is important to understand the processes whereby this inequity is generated and reproduced.

But poverty and exclusion are not just Latin American, or Third World, traits. For all the United States' wealth and power, nearly 14 percent of its population lives in permanent poverty, and income distribution in the United States has persistently worsened over the last decades. In 1979, the top 1 percent of the U.S. population earned on average 33.1 times as much as the lowest 20 percent. In 2000, this indicator of income inequality had grown to 88.5 times as much as the lowest 20 percent (Hogan 2005, 1). On a somewhat smaller scale, poverty and income inequality have also risen in Canada. In 2003, almost 16 percent of the population lived under the poverty line (CIA 2006).

Even when recent economic recovery is factored in, the overall real income levels for most Latin American and Caribbean countries are still below those of 1980 (UN 1994, 2). As in North America, a slow economic recovery has failed to translate into secure employment or social well-being for a large proportion of the population. Nor are there any signs that the extreme inequalities in these countries are being arrested, let alone reversed. Borrowing a Brazilian general's purported comment over a quarter-century ago about Brazil's "economic miracle" at the outset of the 1970s, it can be said today as well that "the economy's doing fine; it's just the people that aren't" (Street 2000).

In the United States, the profound cultural distemper of the Vietnam War, the institutional crisis crystallized by Watergate, and the post–Vietnam War economic recession of the 1980s brought forty years of economic, social, and political "Fordism" to an end. Though not unscathed, the country emerged from this period with a secular democracy, a welfare state, and a significant degree of distributional equity. The real challenge emerged only a few decades later. Paradoxically, the collapse of the Soviet Union and the end of the Cold War created the conditions for an even deeper political crisis. Its precipitators were the 2000 presidential elections, the terrorist attacks of 2001, the ecological disasters of 2005, the military and political fiasco in Iraq, and a profound cultural distemper.

In the post-9/11 period, a much more radicalized, fundamentalist, and messianic power elite now leads the country. The United States has dramatically mutated into a warfare state ruled by a plutocratic regime. Civil society is also more fragmented, with the once discredited militarist fraction again on top, pursuing an unabashedly imperialist agenda (the Project for the New Century) and ostensibly attempting to solve internal contradictions by means of a perpetual war economy. As in the 1960s, the United States is once again engaged in a policy confrontation with its neighbors to the south, including Cuba, Brazil, and the populist governments of Venezuela, Bolivia, and Nicaragua. The rhetoric for intervention has shifted from the Cold War to the "war on terror," now articulated in a new totalitarian regional concept of hemispheric security (Chillier and Freeman 2005, 1–10).

THE PATTERNS OF INTER-AMERICAN RELATIONS

In terms of inter-American affairs, the region is more integrated in a hub-and-spokes relationship with the United States and a growing asymmetry in the limited free trade arrangements known as the North American Free Trade Agreement (NAFTA), the Dominican Republic–Central America Free Trade Agreement (DR-CAFTA), and the Free Trade Area of the Americas (FTAA) (which is presently paralyzed). Military integration in the region, under the Rio Treaty and its structural and ideological mechanisms, has been a fact of life since World War II and much longer in Central America. For contemporary U.S. elites, as was the case for their nineteenth-century forebears, what lies south of the Rio Grande continues to be perceived simultaneously as a resource-rich El Dorado and as a cultural and political threat. In this sense, the "South" is constructed as a source of "evil" in the form of drugs, illegal aliens, undesirable values, and menaces to security (Huntington 2004). Now this threat has also come "indoors" in the form of a growing Hispanic population that has migrated to the United States.

Above and beyond the perceived threats, frequent confrontations, and prejudices, the reality of a growing structural interconnectivity between the "North" and the "South" in the Western Hemisphere is becoming patently clear. This realization points toward the need to study the Americas systemically as an integrated whole, avoiding the facile epistemological divide between two universes: one normal, "up here," the other abnormal, "down there."

I am arguing here—as Karl and Fagen (1986) suggested nearly two decades ago—the usefulness of applying to the study of the Americas the paradigm developed by experts to analyze Eastern Europe (4–8). This conceptual framework posits that Eastern Europe was an integrated region where the Soviet elites enjoyed relational control, or "metapower," over their satellites. Thus, the study of individual countries and the region as a whole started from the premise of penetrated political systems, not sovereign entities. Hardly anybody could have attempted to explain the pre-1989 processes within the subordinate countries behind what was then called the Iron Curtain without reference to the hegemonic and dominating power of the Soviet Union.

In the Western Hemisphere, which has relatively more permeable borders than Eastern Europe did, asymmetrical interpenetration, both formal and informal, is continuously taking place. Northern elites, by themselves or in alliance with their Latin American and Caribbean counterparts, exert relational control, or metapower, over other subordinate groups, classes, and clients in the region. This process is framed within a dominant and messianic economic, ideological, and cultural matrix as dogmatic and compelling as its Soviet counterpart. In this complex exchange system, investment capital, technology, and ideology flow south, while profits and people flow north.

But this sketchy characterization fails to capture the unique dynamic intermeshing taking place in the Americas. For instance, a significant portion of the so-called Hispanic population in the United States (Amerindians, Mexicans, and Puerto Ricans) did not have to cross any border. They were already there. This seemingly amalgamated complexity needs to be analyzed as such in its multiple and nuanced manifestations. The current ideographic and comparative paradigms do not allow for interactive and integrated analysis of this sort. Rather, they obscure the understanding of this complex reality by adopting theoretical assumptions, like the capsular nature of nation-states, as empirical facts.

CRISES WITHOUT REVOLUTIONS

South of the Rio Grande, the occurrence of armed revolutions seems unlikely, at least for the time being—a significant change from the scenario of two decades ago. Guerrilla activity is at its lowest level, and other forms of low-intensity conflict have declined, with the exception of the long-winded war between the Revolutionary Armed Forces of Colombia and the Colombian establishment and the sporadic outbursts in Chiapas. However, the long-term, deep-seated social antagonisms under the seemingly and often constricted democratic veneer of the political regimes have not vanished. Rather, they have manifested themselves in the familiar spiral of crime and institutional, repressive, and insurgent violence. Ineffectiveness, low legitimacy, and corruption have paralyzed the weak civilian governments that replaced the harsh military dictatorships of the past. With the exhaustion of elitist legitimation based upon limited participation and the Washington Consensus, new actors and forms of political mobilization have emerged in opposition to politics as usual.

Since 2000, mass mobilizations and "people's coups" have replaced the once common dynamics of the middle-class military coup d'état (Vilas 2004). This has occurred in Ecuador, Bolivia, and Argentina. Political alienation runs high in the Americas; and this is not confined to Latin America. Symptoms are also present in North America in the form of abstentionism, disaffection from politics, corruption, and a growing crisis of legitimacy. A careful review of the emerging literature and both statistical and qualitative data on the region renders a view that is far from optimistic for both development and democracy. The alleged, but ephemeral, economic boom and official confidence of the late 1990s and early 2000s had little to do with social equity, political democracy, or a real improvement in economic well-being or with the actual material security of the region's inhabitants. Rather, this view rests on the ideological illusion that a felicitous correspondence between market politics and market economics has finally emerged, preventing turbulent social change from below. And if this epiphany fails to maintain credibility, there is always the possibility of falling back on national security and "securitization" (Chillier and Freeman 2005, 1) as the policy software of last resort.

MUTUAL VULNERABILITY IN THE AMERICAS

Three central propositions are advanced here: The first is that the repressive bureaucratic and military regimes of the past in Latin America and today's limited democracies exhibit a greater degree of continuity than the proponents of democratic transition theory and the popular media suggest. Despite the normalization supposedly taking place, persistent violence and political turmoil are not things of the past. The underlying social, economic, and international forces, which have enjoyed extraterritorial power and privilege, still prevail. Contrary to myth, the Americas as a whole, with few exceptions, have not undergone profound social reform. Worse, the very few attempts at reformism have been stunted and reversed. The region's social and economic systems, from Patagonia to Alaska, are mostly conservative and elitist, with occasional symbolic trappings of populist nationalism. Regime stability has been maintained with significant levels of exclusion and official violence.

The second proposition is that this kind of regime stability, in the long run, has hampered sustainable, equitable, and democratic development. In fact, the current style of development hinders real democracy and increases, rather than decreases, poverty and insecurity for most people in the hemisphere. This proposition leads to the third, which is that "deficit" and limited democracy is not only a Latin American phenomenon. North America, especially the United States, has moved in recent years toward dedemocratization and authoritarianism. As the current style of unipolar, imperial globalization (Triska 1986, 4–8) has taken hold, dedemocratization, widespread insecurity, and mutual vulnerability have increased. In fact, it can be argued that "securitization" and militarization lie at the core of human insecurity in the hemisphere.

I have explored the first two propositions in some detail in a previous article (Nef 2005) and only touch upon them tangentially here. Therefore, the bulk of this chapter concentrates on the democratic deficits that have resulted from the alleged democratic "transitions" in Latin America and on the process of dedemocratization that is affecting the Americas as a whole.

DEPENDENT DEVELOPMENT AND INTERVENTION

Structural underdevelopment has been historically and structurally imbedded in the Americas' nation-states and in the pattern of inter-American relations. This tends to generate a self-perpetuating vicious cycle: the more vulnerable and penetrated the states in the region are, the more illegitimate their regimes become. Lack of internal popular support makes them weak and unstable, therefore requiring the substitution of external for internal constituencies. In this context, intervention provides a sort of "insurance policy" to preserve this system. The key function of both the regional and national political systems has been largely the maintenance of a hemispheric and international order based on inequality and dependent development.

Since the onset of the Cold War, the protection of the dependent mode of development has taken the form of counterinsurgency and civic action. The preservation of the existing pattern of privileges and inequities has been the central preoccupation of the region's security forces (Lovell 1971). In the 1950s and 1960s a reorganization of the regional military structure and culture ensued, substantively changing the military's mission and doctrine. This has entailed a shift from defending territorial security (against external aggression) by conventional forces to fighting an "internal enemy" with special forces schooled in the above-mentioned counterinsurgency and civic action. One major result was a further erosion of the already precarious sovereignty of the Latin American states. The U.S. security establishment became the apex of a vertically integrated regional counterinsurgency and counterrevolutionary system. The local military was given a new self-justifying and professional mission to fight "subversion," however loosely defined (Corbett 1972).[2] In a relatively brief period and irrespective of declared intentions, the local military and police forces (the latter through so-called public-safety programs) were transformed into the dominant internal operational units of an integrated hemispheric security regime. This reorientation became manifest as early as 1964, with the Lyndon B. Johnson administration's encouragement and promotion of the Brazilian military's counterrevolution of 1964.

This is not to say that U.S. intervention in Brazil was something radically new. On the contrary, since the Mexican-American War of 1846 to 1848, there has been a continued U.S. military involvement in Central America and the Caribbean. Leaving aside the private ventures and rivalries of Cornelius Vanderbilt and William Walker in Nicaragua in the 1850s, gunboat diplomacy has been a fixture in the region since at least the 1880s. Such involvement has ranged from the Spanish-American War (1898), to the creation and appropriation of Panama (1904), to the Marine occupations of Haiti (1917) and Nicaragua (1927). Most importantly, these imperial undertakings involved long occupations, the establishment of puppet regimes, and the training of local armed forces under U.S. command: the quasiconstabulary national guards. Several strongmen in the region were U.S.-appointed heads of the national guards in their countries.

The Cold War period added two features to the existing neocolonial pattern. One new trait was the shift in the rationales for intervention away from the old discourse: Manifest Destiny, preemption of European intervention under the Monroe Doctrine, and the protection of American investments and properties, or what Theodore Roosevelt referred to as the "chronic immorality" of "Latin" governments (Nef and Núñez 1994). The justification for interventionism shifted during the Cold War to allegedly preventing a Communist/Soviet invasion or revolution—a self-fulfilling prophecy in the case of post-1959 revolutionary Cuba. The second new and related trait was the extension of the theater of intervention from the traditional hunting grounds of Central America and the Caribbean to encompass all of Latin America.

But intervention does not occur in a vacuum. Most regimes in Latin America and the Caribbean are tied to the export of commodities. They suffer from chronic vulnerability and the ups and downs of the fluctuations in international commodity trading. In this context, internal and external factors combine to produce instability. Even in the once more-institutionalized democracies, like Uruguay and Chile, the economic crises of the 1950s and 1960s led first to a weakening, and finally to a breakdown, of consensus and civic confidence. Political conflict and sociopolitical stalemate eroded both the legitimacy and the effectiveness of these regimes. Labor practices inherited from the populist years of the Great Depression and World War II reproduced and accelerated the "push-up" effect of institutionalized social conflict. The latter had the effect of generating and maintaining immobility, political deadlock, and chronic hyperinflation.

The rules of the pluralistic game decomposed in the midst of rapid mass mobilization during the 1960s. In these once more stable and "civic" countries, the existing socioeconomic order, both domestic and international, was maintained by a resort to naked, yet highly bureaucratized, repression under a new political alliance. This alliance involved a coalition between the externally linked business elites, which supported conservative economic policies, and the security establishments, which had become transnationalized by the ideological "professionalism" they adopted during the Cold War.

The military establishments in the Americas today, with very rare exceptions, comprise trained, indoctrinated, and well-financed ultraconservative fractions of the clerical and white-collar middle classes. As armed bureaucrats specializing in coercive and repressive violence, they have provided the force required to keep the population at bay. Their ideological-professional "prime directive" has been—and continues to be—the National Security Doctrine (NSD) developed during the Cold War (Weil, Comblin, and Senese 1979; Rojas 2003).[3] South of the Rio Grande, their professional and ideological indoctrination, as well as financing in strategic areas, tends to be externally generated, which gives the United States an upper hand in controlling their allegiance and attitudes.

THE NATIONAL SECURITY REGIME AND NEOLIBERALISM

The above-mentioned NSD, also called "Pentagonism" by Juan Bosch (Bosch 2000, 5–14), was based on three elements: (1) the existence of an external global enemy manifested in an apocalyptic ideological conflict, (2) an internal enemy ("subversion") supported by the external enemy, and (3) the existence of an external "friend" (the regional security regime dominated by the United States). The adoption of this professional "software" has eroded, and continues to erode, the national character of local military institutions. More than in the former Communist bloc (the Warsaw Treaty), this type of regional security regime has decisively transnationalized the states in the region. The most explicit articulation of this strategic doctrine was the Nixon Doctrine, outlined in the Rockefeller Report of 1969. This report clearly showed a shift in the normative ideal of the U.S. political establishment from democracy and popular participation to the maintenance of law and order through authoritarian measures. An effect of this blueprint was that between 1969 and 1973, the number of military dictatorships in Latin America steadily climbed from ten in 1969 to twelve in 1970, fourteen in 1972, and fifteen in 1973 (Nef 1978).

The authoritarian conceptions of economic liberalism that unfolded under military rule in the 1970s rejected the nationalist and protectionist premises underlying the import-substitution policies of the 1940s, 1950s, and 1960s, as well as other Keynesian economic policies. Instead, economic growth was seen as a function of the reinsertion of the economies of the region into the international division of labor, primarily as exporters of raw materials. This change in economic policies represented a return to the earlier export-based economies of the region's colonial and neocolonial past. Competitiveness meant the maintenance and expansion of three comparative advantages: investment opportunities, cheap natural resources, and, above all, cheap labor. With the exception of Brazil in the late 1960s and the 1970s, economic development under authoritarian rule meant increased reliance on the extraction of resources and exports produced in the primary sector, holding down wages, and heavy borrowing. The aggregate foreign debt, which in 1960 amounted to about one-third of the value of regional annual exports, grew by 1970 to 1.7 times the total value of annual exports. By 1993, the gap had nearly doubled to over 2.7 times the total value.[4] By 2002, in response to drastic debt-reduction measures, it had stabilized at about 1.8 times the total value of exports.[5] The neoliberal strategy of development also involved the creation of favorable conditions for foreign investment through the deregulation, denationalization, and privatization of the national economies and the dismemberment of labor organizations. The combination of repressive policies and the subsequent more hegemonic adjustment recipes in the Washington Consensus enabled both the domestic and transnational elites associated with these policies to increase their share of regional wealth and promote a greater degree of regional economic integration.

The era of manifest national security was not only extreme in its persistent abuses of human rights, but the early neoliberal design of the economic strategies associated with it involved the dismantling of the welfare state and most of the import-substitution industrialization and social safety nets developed since the 1930s. This form of authoritarian, neoliberal capitalism rejected the demand-side policies that were part of the Alliance for Progress initiated by the John F. Kennedy administration. National security, and later economic liberalization, were more concerned with direct containment of perceived security threats and the protection of the status quo than with social and economic development per se.[6] Other than offering "economic miracles" financed by illusive foreign investment, this approach favored monetarism (later identified with the Chicago School of economists) over the structuralist, Keynesian doctrine pursued by ECLAC.

These policies were far more effective as a shock therapy in atomizing labor, freezing wages, letting prices float to world levels, and privatizing the Latin American economies than as a means for raising living standards. They were also effective in the short run as economic weapons in a sociopolitical war that benefited "friends" and punished "foes," rather than bringing about national development. The long-term economic consequences of these measures have been, by and large, catastrophic for the region. So were their social, environmental, and financial implications. In fact, far from generating stability and bringing about prosperity, the combination of dictatorial rule with unrestricted free market policies created a serious governability and corruption problem. This formula of authoritarian regimes with so-called free market economic policies also set the conditions for the subsequent debt crisis and recession of the 1980s suffered by the Latin American and Caribbean countries.

The authoritarian states that emerged in South America, patterned on the example of the post-1964 military regime in Brazil, can be seen as attempts at economic modernization from the top down, combined with strong external inducements. The benefits of this new order accrued to a small

alliance of domestic entrepreneurs and speculators supported by the tech-
nocratic-military middle classes and its business, political, and military associates in the United States, Canada, and Western Europe. This new order's
narrow social base created a persistent crisis of legitimacy managed by three
instruments. The first was the use of military force backed by the alliance
between the military officer corps and the domestic socioeconomic elites.
The second was the inclusion of external, chiefly U.S., surrogate constituencies—military, business, political, and diplomatic—to compensate
for the loss of internal sources of support. The third was the political demobilization and exclusion of the bulk of the population from the political system. Thus, military dictatorship became an intrinsic component of
the strategy to secure economic freedom for the local elites and the U.S.
constituencies associated with these regimes (Letelier 1976, 138, 142).

The social cost for the popular majorities was enormous: living conditions deteriorated, and the social gap between the rich and the poor
widened. With perhaps the sole exception of Chile, these regimes failed to
generate genuine counterrevolutions. At best, the national security regimes
constituted a deterrent against popular mobilization, economic nationalism, and the perceived threat from the political Left. Moreover, their neoliberal policies required large amounts of external financing. This financing was possible in the 1970s and early 1980s due to the truly massive
deposits of petrodollars in Western private banks, which made them willing to extend large loans to most of the Latin American and Caribbean
governments.

DEBT AND REGIME CRISIS

This was not the case after the mid-1980s. As the governments and especially the private sector in the region increased their financial obligations,
the failures of production and exports to keep pace with the level of borrowing and, most importantly, with rising interest rates resulted in a huge
debt crisis. This economic crisis was accompanied by the political crisis of
the dictatorships as they failed to stem the erosion of the political alliances
that had permitted their implementation of repressive social and economic projects. Continued government by force was ultimately untenable,
particularly since the pretended defense of national security was based
upon the insecurity of most of the population. Moreover, these national
security regimes were not really national, but largely occupying, regimes.
The combined impact of economic crises, the growing inability of the military to manage conflict among the internal factions in these regimes, and
a new political coalition in Washington concerned about the long-term effects of authoritarian solutions created the conditions for the military's

withdrawal from the heights of the state. The Linowitz Report, heavily influenced by the views of the Trilateral Commission (Sklar 1980), outlined a transitional strategy in 1975 (Linowitz 1975). This document constituted the blueprint for the James E. Carter administration's initiative to push for democratization.

The new strategy of promoting a "democratic transition" (Siat and Iriarte 1979) became an insurgency-containment modality in Central America, where persistent U.S. support for failed military-civilian dictatorships under the likes of the Somozas in Nicaragua and Efrain Rios Montt in Guatemala had created a serious crisis of domination. This crisis revealed that repression had become unviable and was giving rise to popular revolutionary insurrections. President Kennedy's dictum that revolution would be the inevitable result of the failure to make social reforms in Latin America was now a real possibility in the region. Therefore, a negotiated transition became the only alternative to popular revolution. The Carter administration, with its human rights agenda, provided a "decent interlude" to implement this strategy of containment. But the real substance behind the political and ethical framework it provided was short-lived following Carter's defeat in the 1980 U.S. national elections. As a result, the democratic transition for most of Latin America was largely the outcome of intra-elite negotiation mediated and supervised by external actors. Rather than a true regime transition, this process resulted in the consolidation of a largely nondemocratic socioeconomic order under a formal democratic political facade.

This orderly retreat of the national security regimes left many authoritarian enclaves and extraterritorialities. In this respect, the reemerging democracies shared some of the political characteristics of the older "managed democracies" in Colombia, Venezuela, and Mexico, which did not experience direct military rule during the Cold War. Although authoritarian capitalism had proved largely to be a developmental failure, the radical restructuring of the economies along so-called free market lines by means of political repression was so profound as to prevent a return to the economic nationalism that preceded it.

Likewise, the restructuring and transnationalization of the security establishment made the pursuit of nationalist and nonaligned foreign policies impossible. In this sense, the political regimes that have emerged in Latin America as a result of the formal process of democratization and military withdrawal, while possessing the formal trappings of sovereignty and democracy, are neither truly democratic nor sovereign. They are precariously balanced civilian regimes based on negotiations within the elites. They have exclusionary political agendas and narrow internal support. In these regimes, the popular sectors are effectively kept outside the political arena, while external actors, both economic and military, enjoy de facto veto power over the policies of the state. In addition, these countries have remained saddled with burdensome, and in some cases unmanageable, foreign debts (see table 5.1), not to mention the debt-management conditionalities that have been imposed on them by International Monetary Fund (IMF)–inspired structural adjustment policies (SAPs).

These policies have perpetuated the economic dependence and underdevelopment of the Latin American and Caribbean economies. These structural conditions give rise to the above-mentioned built-in vulnerability to external economic and political influences and require increasing doses of external assistance and financial support. This situation can be dramatically illustrated by the inability of these countries to extricate themselves from their chronic indebtedness—they are caught in a "debt trap" (Martinez 1992; World Bank 1988–1992).[7] Debt management became the number-one political concern in the regional agenda during the early 1980s. The service of the region's debts, both payments of principal and interest, grew from slightly over 40 percent of the total value of annual exports in 1979 to over 65 percent in 1983.

Despite the fact that about one-half of the countries in the region had reduced their debt liabilities by the 1990–1991 period, the overall debt had grown to $421 billion. By 2001, it reached $740 billion, subsequently expanding at an average annual rate of over 5 percent (ECLAC 2001).[8] In fact, out of the seventeen most indebted countries in the world in 1992, twelve were in the Latin American region. On average, annual interest-rate payments fell from 33 percent of all exports in 1987 to 22 percent in 1991 as the "lost decade" of the 1980s came to an end. Between 1992 and 1999, the burden was reduced even further in countries like Brazil and Mexico, which decelerated their rate of indebtedness from staggering triple- to double-digit annual rates. Argentina accelerated its already huge rate of indebtedness from a fifteen-year average annual growth of 178 percent to 256 percent in the thirty years between 1970 and 2000. Venezuela, in turn, went from a yearly increase of 320 percent between 1970 and 1985 to a whopping 465 percent in the 1970 to 2000 period.

The debt problem involved in the inability to pay these debts is staggering, but there are also equally dramatic traits in other aspects of the economies. For instance, the value of debt service in relation to the total value of export earnings for Argentina moved from an already high 34 percent in 1990 to over 71 percent in 2000. For Brazil, the jump was from 23 percent to nearly 91 percent. In 2003, the average annual debt service for Latin America had climbed to an unbelievable 201 percent of the value of exports (World Bank 2001). This means that countries have been going into debt at twice the amount of the increase of their export earnings. So far, despite major economic crises in Mexico (1994), Ecuador (1999), Argentina (2001), Brazil (2002), and Bolivia (2003), most countries in the region

Table 5.1. Latin American Foreign Debt Figures for 1990, 1992, 2000, and 2003

Debt Service	Debt/GDP per Capita				As Percentage of Exports			
	1990	1992	1999	2003	1990	1992	2000	2003
Argentina	79.9	30.3	51.2	—	34.1	34.4	71.3	—
Bolivia	94.3	61.2	65.9	38.0*	39.8	39.0	39.1	166.0
Brazil	28.8	31.2	40.0	54.0	20.8	23.1	90.7	330.0
Chile	74.7	48.9	50.7	67.0	25.9	20.9	26.0	178.0
Colombia	42.4	36.9	44.7	47.0	36.4	38.9	28.6	232.0
Costa Rica	70.9	58.7	33.6	36.0	24.5	20.6	8.2	77.0
Dominican Republic	74.7	57.0	28.7	33.0	10.3	13.5	4.8	71.0
Ecuador	119.9	99.9	107.3	82.0	33.2	27.1	17.3	296.0
El Salvador	36.9	25.5	17.4	55.0	17.1	13.2	6.7	198.0
Guatemala	33.6	24.2	28.6	21.0	13.3	24.0	9.4	115.0
Haiti	37.0	—	30.6	29.0	9.5	—	8.0	214.0
Honduras	116.3	92.0	83.3	54.0	40.4	33.7	19.3	134.0
Mexico	44.5	34.1	33.5	25.0	27.8	44.4	30.2	88.0
Nicaragua	199.4	750.3	231.0	40.0	14.7	21.8	23.0	129.0
Panama	152.0	107.2	55.7	93.0	9.7	12.6	10.0	124.0
Paraguay	44.7	24.6	22.6	51.0	11.0	40.3	10.4	112.0
Peru	83.9	92.7	50.9	60.0	11.0	23.0	42.8	335.0
Uruguay	46.7	46.7	40.1	90.0	41.8	23.2	29.2	353.0
Venezuela	66.1	61.1	71.1	42.0	20.7	19.5	15.7	139.0

Source: World Bank, *World Development Report,* 1990, 1991, and 1992, passim., and 1994, 206–207. Also, 2005 figures were calculated from data contained in the International Bank of Reconstruction and Development/World Bank, *World Development Report 1989* and *World Development Report 1992. Development and the Environment* (New York: Oxford University Press, 1989 and 1992). Tables used include Table 1, "Basic Indicators," Table 21, "Total External Debt," Table 24, "Total External Debt," Table 26, "Total Extern Debt Ratios," and Table 26, "Population Growth and Projections." The 1990 gross national product figure for Nicaragua was estimated on the basis of the 1987 figure and an average decline of 2.5 percent per year. Figures for 2000 came from the United Nations Development Program, *Human Development Report 2002,* 203–205.

* Data from debt-sustainability analysis, Heavily Indebted Poor Countries (HIPC) initiative. Estimates for such countries are for public and publicly guaranteed debt only. Available at www.worldbank.org/date/wdi2005/wditex/Section4.htm.

have not defaulted outright on their debts. The pursuit of this policy of fiscal responsibility has been extremely hard on the general population, which has had to absorb the full impact of the use of a good portion of their countries' export earnings and government revenues for debt payments.

The transition from dictatorship to limited democracy has to be seen in the context of the previous (1970s–1980s) transition to national security regimes, both in the bureaucratic-authoritarian context of the countries of the southern cone of the Americas and in the less institutionalized setting of the countries in Central America. Growing participation and dependent development can coexist only under conditions of economic expansion and for as long as such participation does not threaten the perceived interests of the domestic and regional elites.

The economic factors that undermined the national security regimes were not exclusively experienced by the military dictatorships. The few remaining civilian governments in Latin America during the 1980s, such as Colombia, Venezuela, and Costa Rica, were also severely affected by the debt crisis. Venezuela and Costa Rica were hit particularly hard. The disintegration of the alternation in power between the Christian Democratic party COPEI and the Social Democratic party AD in Venezuela, which paved the way for Hugo Chávez's ascent to power, can be traced precisely to the phenomenal economic dislocation that took place during this period of the so-called lost decade of 1980 to 1990. From being an oil-rich country with many "haves" and abundant resources that could be distributed, Venezuela became primarily a country of "have-nots."

THE RECEIVER STATE

The mounting debt crisis set the conditions for the emergence throughout the Americas in the mid-1980s of a new political configuration I have called a "receiver state," blending limited democracy with neoliberal economics. Highly transnationalized and weak, this type of state acts in political alliance with foreign creditors and international financial institutions as the manager, executor, and liquidator of assets in a country that has experienced bankruptcy. The central function of this state is the administration of national and international debts, combined with the implementation of SAPs. Such policies are geared to assure the payment of debts through the massive privatization of the state's assets and the denationalization of the economy. This state provides very narrow spaces for popular political participation. Generally speaking, national economic and fiscal policies are effectively excluded from domestic political input. Yet, SAP policies define the rules of the game and impose strict limits on all domestic social policies.

The various national incarnations of this type of receivership exhibit some differences, which reflect the nature of the transition process from military to civilian rule, as well as the particular political coloration of the civilian management that has appeared in the postauthoritarian period. On close scrutiny, however, irrespective of the elected nature of the government in charge, the economic agenda of the transition period has a striking resemblance to the agenda imposed under authoritarian rule. Thus, in this sense, the repressive states of the 1970s and the receiver states of the 1990s and 2000s are two different political arrangements made to protect the interests of a similar cluster of elites.

The receiver state expresses the interests of a transnational and conservative coalition, managed by political actors that form moderate rightist to center-left governments. Limited democracy with narrow opportunities for political participation and exclusionary agendas provides a thin cushion over the deep structural problems formerly controlled by repression. The current modality of conflict management, while reducing the most blatant (and uglier) forms of human rights abuses, has left the most pressing and fundamental socioeconomic and political problems largely unresolved. The transnational integration of the domestic elites (economic, military, technocratic, and bureaucratic), combined with the political demobilization and marginalization of the popular sectors, does not provide a formula for stable governance, let alone genuine democracy. In the absence of tangible rewards to buy legitimacy for the ruling regimes, insurgent, repressive, institutionalized, and criminal violence has become common currency in these political systems. While not yet failed states such as those in Africa or Central Asia, political meltdowns—such as those that occurred in Ecuador in 1999, Argentina in 2001, and Bolivia in 2003—have become a distinct possibility throughout Latin America and the Caribbean. Even North America has exhibited symptoms of severe institutional decay, corruption, and the erosion of democratic liberties.

Despite the democratic rhetoric and phasing out of the "old" national security regimes, at present the Americas are not geared up for substantial or sustainable democratization. Formal demilitarization and the return to a limited form of formal democracy are not synonymous with a substantial change in the status quo. Nor is substantive democracy nowadays any more "real" in those countries, including the United States, where civilian governments have remained in formal control for a long time. On the contrary, the prevailing discourse on democracy among the official intelligentsia throughout the Americas involves the equation of a substantially restricted form of participation with neoliberal economics and the protection of national security (Montecinos and Markoff 1993).

This model of democracy amounts at best to a plutocracy with limited popular support, which occasionally resorts to electoral rituals and is ultimately backed up by an elaborate security apparatus. While this "low-intensity democracy" may appeal to the consumption-intensive, high-income core groups throughout the Western Hemisphere, it is not really based on majority rule or popular accountability. It basically corresponds to the same elitist formula articulated by the Trilateral Commission in the mid-1970s, which considered the root cause of the so-called crisis of democracy at the time to be too much democracy (Huntington, Crozier, and Watanuki 1975; Chomsky 1977).[9] Behind a façade of legality, this mode of political conflict management entrenches a corporatist pact among elites that represents basically the same economic, social, and political interests that have sustained antidemocratic regimes. These reactionary coalitions involve the power elite at the core of the international system, along with the military, local bourgeoisie, and upper segments of the middle classes at the domestic level. Democratic development in the Americas, with the qualified exceptions of Canada, Costa Rica, and perhaps contemporary Chile, has been weak and fragile at best throughout the hemisphere.

The regressive socioeconomic policies implemented under authoritarian rule during the 1970s and 1980s have been enshrined both in the pacts of political transition and in ad hoc constitutional mechanisms. Other factors have constrained the redemocratized regimes as well. One is the weakness of the governing political alliances since the transition arrangements effectively prevented most leftist and popular political forces from gaining control of the state. Another is the crucial, highly autonomous role played by the transnationalized security forces as a parallel state institution that, in most cases, has maintained the status quo and prevented the exposure of past and present human rights abuses. Then, there are the above-mentioned odious, massive debt obligations incurred mostly under the previous repressive regimes. They severely limit the rendering of public services to those in need and create formulas of fiscal austerity. The current debt-management programs inevitably cause popular expressions of outrage and protest, followed by increasingly repressive governmental responses.

The negative effects of the debt service on already limited fiscal resources are compounded by the strict conditionalities imposed by the international financial institutions (the IMF, the World Bank, the Inter-American Development Bank [IDB], and private international banks). Structural adjustment policies resulting from such conditionalities have weighed against demands for reform, equity, and social justice, already frozen by the previous dictatorships.

THE IMPACT OF PUBLIC POLICIES

Since the 1980s, the Americas have experienced an expanding and converging set of problems, whose common denominator is a fiscal crisis of the state. In North America, fiscal crises have been a recurring fixture, vaguely masked by neoliberal rhetoric and national security concerns. These crises affect employment, purchasing power, housing, the safety of drinking water, the quality of sanitation, the growing incidence of old and new diseases of epidemic proportions, a deteriorating ecosystem, and a profound inability to meet health challenges. A regional health crisis is unfolding as life-threatening ailments thought to have been eradicated (such as malaria, Chagas, and tuberculosis) are making a dramatic comeback, and new morbidity and mortality factors like HIV/AIDS are on the rise. This has happened at a time when social safety nets and health-delivery mechanisms have been drastically reduced as a consequence of neoliberal structural adjustment policies. The United States has been plagued by an ineffectual and utterly malfunctioning (and expensive) health-care system, driven by insatiable insurance companies and so-called health maintenance organizations (HMOs), which have serious accessibility and coverage problems. Elsewhere in the Americas, the poverty-driven diseases, combined with the dismantling of the institutional mechanisms for disease containment and treatment, have multiplied health insecurity across class and national boundaries (Nef 2004a).

Environmental threats are another example of policy-driven dysfunctionalities. These threats include untreated sewage, expanding waste sites, air pollution, and climate change and also encompass a broader complexity and multiplicity of reciprocating problems. In an earlier study (Nef and Robles 1998), we describe a calamitous situation in which retrofeeding and destructive processes have created a vicious cycle of vulnerabilities. In the United States, all of these contradictions appear to have come to a head in 2005 with Hurricane Katrina's devastating impact on New Orleans, revealing the hitherto hidden dimension of poverty, neglect, and exclusion, combined with inadequate policies and misplaced security priorities.

Current industrial, mining, and agricultural practices, mixed with uncontrolled urbanization,[10] have created an interwoven pattern of biophysical and social stress upon the ecosystems and human populations of the region. For instance, deforestation in Latin America, with its health-related problems, accounts annually for over 40 percent of the global loss of forests. On a per capita basis, this makes Latin America the number-one contributor to forest depletion and loss of biodiversity. Furthermore, in the midst of the widespread expansion of commercial agricultural production for export, food insecurity remains a major threat for large segments of the population, even in the statistically "richer" countries. The pressures to manage debt and its conditionalities put a premium on the production of cash crops instead of food crops for domestic consumption, as well as on the merciless exploitation of natural and human resources.

POVERTY AND INEQUALITY

Between the 1980s and the 1990s, those living below the poverty line in Latin America and the Caribbean increased from above 120 million to over 200 million and from 41 to 46 percent of the population (Robinson 1994; Altimir 1994). The most affected have been those already vulnerable: women, children, the elderly, and ethnic minorities. Though extreme conditions of poverty and indigence have gone down to mid-1990s levels in most countries, overall deprivation is still higher than it was two decades ago, and rural poverty has increased steadily. Central America has been the most seriously affected by the lingering effects of the civil wars of the 1980s and the combined impact of the concentration of wealth and the spread of poverty. In the 1990s, reportedly nearly 80 percent of inhabitants in these countries were unable to secure a basic food basket, and half of these people were destitute (Robinson 1994). Although today the figures for Central America are less dramatic than during the crisis of the 1980s, the legacy of man-made and natural catastrophes is an ever-present reality.

Even the much-hailed economic "miracles" in the region have not produced sustained development. The combination of entrenched elite interests, extreme free market measures, and structural adjustment policies has left a lasting burden of poverty and despair. The areas of public health, education, and community development have suffered continuously, impacting precisely the least protected members of society. Since the boom of the 1970s, the most enduring feature of Brazil's economy has been that its income distribution is the most unequal in the Western Hemisphere, and one of the worst in the world, despite the reformist administrations of President Fernando Henrique Cardoso in the 1990s and, more recently, his more populist, laborite successor, President Luiz Inácio "Lula" da Silva.

Chile's "success story" does not fare much better under close scrutiny. According to our calculations using ECLAC data, between 1970 and 1987, the proportion of Chileans defined as poor increased by an average yearly rate of 7.2 percent. Meanwhile, real income per capita grew at an annual average rate of 0.3 percent. This resulted not from unfathomable economic forces but government policy. Since 1990, with a succession of democratic governments and despite the fact that the speed of impoverishment has been arrested and even reversed, widespread privation persists. Despite impressive gross national product annual growth rates between 4.5 and 10 percent and a generally successful poverty-alleviation package implemented by the administration of President Ricardo Lagos, after Brazil, Chile still stands with Guatemala and Paraguay as having one of the worst income distributions in the region (see appended table 5.3, F; World Bank 2001).

Pauperization and expanding inequity are not limited to these two cases. They are present all over the hemisphere, throughout the Caribbean and in

Argentina, Uruguay, Paraguay, Venezuela, Colombia, Peru, Bolivia, Ecuador, Panama, Costa Rica, the Dominican Republic, Haiti, and particularly Mexico. Poverty and inequality have also significantly expanded in North America, where a similar neoliberal policy model has been followed. As already mentioned, the most affected by this policy model are the rural and urban poor; however, white-collar, middle-class sectors have also seen their economic opportunities and social safety nets dramatically eroded. In fact, in Latin America, as in Canada and the United States today, the middle classes are diminishing in the growing gap between the extremities of wealth and poverty (Robinson 1994).[11]

CONTINUING MILITARY INFLUENCE

Beneath the civilian mantle, praetorianism has a lingering presence. Given the polarized and violent nature of many political conflicts in Latin America, militarization has been a long-standing feature of the Latin American state. With few exceptions, the military establishment has played a disproportionately large role in most of the countries, whether under civilian rule or not. Leaving aside the case of Costa Rica (which does not have a military establishment per se), a careful examination of all the other cases reveals that meddling by the military or military repression has been present. With the withering away of the former national security regimes, their place has been taken not by political systems in which the military is subordinate to civilian control but rather by what can be considered civil-military regimes that contain powerful and relatively autonomous security establishments composed of the military and police.

Since the end of the Cold War, the presence of military officers is less conspicuous in Latin American politics than in the recent past, but closer scrutiny reveals a more complex picture. The end of the civil conflicts in Central America, the declining insurgency threat in Peru, and the effects of structural adjustment packages upon defense budgets suggest a trend toward demilitarization.[12] Yet, overall budget reductions between the 1980s and the early 2000s have not been matched by comparable personnel reductions. Rather, a small increase in military personnel has taken place. The average figures for the region are deceiving since reductions in countries with large military establishments, such as Argentina, Chile, Nicaragua, and Peru, offset the significant increases in most other countries (see table 5.3, G, H; IISS 2001). Twelve out of twenty countries actually increased the size of their armed forces between 1985 and 2002. Colombia topped the list with a 76.7 percent increase, followed by Venezuela (53.1 percent), Guatemala (40.7 percent), and Mexico (35.6 percent). The largest military establishment outside of the United States is that of Brazil, with armed

forces totaling nearly 270,000. Its military establishment grew 7 percent between 1988 and 1993 and averaged an annual increase of 4 percent by 2002
(IISS 2001).

In comparison with the Group of 8 nations and the Middle East, the size
of Latin American forces is relatively modest, but the impact, influence, and
transnationalization of these security establishments, especially of the officer corps, remain extensive in Latin America. In fact, it would not be an exaggeration to suggest that the Latin American military are a branch plant
heavily dependent on the U.S. military and its ideological hegemony. The
current concept of "hemispheric security" in fact encourages the militarization of numerous human-security issues (Chillier and Freeman 2005). Not
including some 760,000 paramilitary and an indeterminate number of reserves, Latin America has over 1.3 million individuals under arms and
spends close to $9 billion on defense (Chillier and Freeman 2005).

Given its economic base and geostrategic situation, Latin America remains overly militarized; the externally controlled security sector is a vora-
cious competitor for the scarce resources needed for development. It also
constitutes a persistent obstacle to the sovereignty of, and the cooperation
among, nations in the region and continues to be the single most serious
threat to political stability, integration, sustainable democracy, and human
rights.

The militarization in most spheres of society has been a constant aspect
of U.S. society since the end of World War II. The United States remains by
far the most militarized country in the hemisphere and among modern
Western societies. The United States possesses the only truly global military
establishment. Its awesome might is combined with a ritualized and extreme patriotism and a political elite always ready to overplay nationalistic
feelings. Consequently, the government of the United States has shown a
proclivity to militarize hemispheric relations. In the long run, this predis-
position presents a clear and present danger to democracy at home and
abroad.

With the end of the Cold War and the reduced threat of regional insurgency, the fundamental security issue in the Americas does not concern how
to protect the Americas from external and internal "enemies" but how to
safeguard the population in most countries within this region from their
own security forces. In this context, we must reconsider civil-military relations and the nature of the prevailing civil-military regimes in the emerging
inter-American order, especially in light of contemporary strategic issues,
like the so-called war on terror. These issues include the lingering of border
tensions, exemplified by flare-ups like the 1995 Ecuadorian-Peruvian border war, the growing militarization of social conflicts (as in the Chiapas region of Mexico), the expansion of Colombia's civil strife, the narcowars in
the Andean region, the reemergence of Haiti's security establishment, the

ongoing confrontation between the United States and Venezuela, and the involvement of Latin American forces in the Middle East conflict. Another more immediate concern is the increasingly conservative, interventionist, and apocalyptic mood that characterizes the current American political elite and the above-mentioned intensive, post-9/11 remilitarization of American society.

LIMITED DEMOCRACY AND ELECTED PLUTOCRACIES

Current political developments in Latin America, while conveying a less repressive picture than in the past, especially in contrast with the somber record of the 1970s, present at best mixed signals. On the positive side, nowadays governments generated through formally free and competitive elections rule most of the region. In an earlier period, Guyana's former president Cheddy Jagan sarcastically called this type of politics "5-minute democracy" (Jagan 1996). In various places, some degree of formal democratic consolidation has taken place as a second or even third cycle of elected officials has assumed office. There have also been sporadic, yet significant, attempts to hold these governments accountable to the electorate. Moreover, the instances of torture, disappearances, and blatant state terrorism have become less frequent, with notable exceptions, such as in Colombia. However, there are also disturbing signs. One of these is the persistence, and even revival, of authoritarian and oligarchic traditions. Political power also continues to remain highly concentrated in small elites. Fundamental democratic values, such as respect for human rights, honest government, and the reduction of discrimination and official abuse, are not widely shared or practiced. Corruption in both parts of the Western Hemisphere is widespread and growing (Nef 2004b).

The electoral processes, while they are a common sight throughout the Americas, are increasingly void of choice and real meaning. Electoral fraud and manipulation still persist. Voters can cast ballots, but the choices and policy options are roughly the same. The socioeconomic and institutional pillars of the current, limited democratic regimes are similar to those of the former national security regimes: large landowners, business elites, foreign investors, and authoritarian elements within the military, judiciary, and technocracy. The large majority of those who committed crimes against humanity remain at large and have not been punished for their murderous misdeeds. Thus, it is hardly surprising that public apathy and cynicism throughout the hemisphere are at an all-time high, while governmental legitimacy is declining (Graham and Sukhatenkar 2003).

Despite the unfolding of formally contested elections during the 1990s and 2000s in all of the countries and the passage of constitutional reforms in a good number of them, these formal processes of democracy have failed to provide real democratic alternatives. The above-mentioned alienation of the population from the political process has resulted in extremely high rates of electoral abstention (Robinson 1994, 8). Colombia tops the list of electoral abstention, with only some 40 percent of the eligible voters casting their ballots in 2000, and this poor example is followed closely by voter participation in the United States.[13] In addition, many of these contests, including the U.S. election of 2000, have been tainted by serious irregularities.

Apart from the ceremonial transfer of office by electoral means and the absence of direct military rule, democracy in the Americas has not been consolidated in this decade. The transition to political democracy remains incomplete, and in some cases, there has been a process of "undoing democracy" (Close 2004, 2–4). The continued existence of oligarchies throughout the continent has shown remarkable continuity with the past. The old practice of executive *continuismo* and dynastic-type succession (the elimination of which was central to the region's past democratic agenda) has resurfaced in unexpected places like Costa Rica and the United States. There is also a remarkable continuity of policy with past regimes. Neoliberal recipes have become entrenched in the conditionalities attached to debt alleviation, regional trade agreements (such as NAFTA or the Mercado Común del Sur, or MERCOSUR), and the so-called macroeconomic equilibrium policies, which effectively remove fiscal, monetary, and credit policy decisions from national political control. In addition, the "new" cold war against terrorism in the context of U.S. unipolarism, with its pseudo-moralistic and messianic discourse, is undermining genuine progress toward greater democracy, sustainable and equitable development, and human security.

FINAL CONSIDERATIONS: ASSESSING REDEMOCRATIZATION AND DEDEMOCRATIZATION

A profound structural contradiction has emerged in the region's systems of governance. If elected governments stress democracy, equity, popular rule, and the interests of the general public (the bulk of the civil society), they encounter relentless opposition and sabotage from the domestic and transnational elites who still dominate the region's economies, leading to their eventual ineffectiveness, if not outright destabilization. Thus, most governments in the region stress economic liberalism and ignore the interests of the majority of society, while ruling in the interests of the elites. In the North American context, Ralph Nader (1992) has labeled this "plutocracy." The political cost of this option is very high in the long run: loss of legitimacy, as well as popular (and national) sovereignty, and the erosion of trust between elected officials and the electorate, a central tenet of both democratic governance and pluralist politics.

Given the level of political alienation throughout the region, it is not surprising that recently angry communities have risen up in popular insurrection to confront the growing threats to their livelihood and dignity in Chiapas (1994), Quito (2000), Buenos Aires (2001), and La Paz (2003 and 2005). These popular insurrections have had broad domestic and international implications. They are specific examples of the Latin American variant of the international antiglobalization movement. They reveal grassroots attempts to re-create the kind of civil society and popular organizations crushed by the double squeeze of military rule in the 1970s and neoliberal economic restructuring in the 1980s and 1990s. They also reveal that in recent years, populism and anti–status quo feelings have been on the rise throughout Latin America.

A more institutional manifestation of this expanding protest movement is the series of electoral victories of populist, nationalist, and left-of-center parties and candidates in Argentina (Néstor Kirchner), Brazil ("Lula" da Silva), Uruguay (Tabaré Vázquez), and Venezuela (Hugo Chávez), all of them at odds with Washington's conservative politics (LatinReporters.com 2004). These developments suggest that popular movements and popular rebellions are still an important element in the new globalized regional order (*Latin America Weekly Report* 1994 a, b) and that inter-American relations dominated by the U.S. monologue and the so-called Washington Consensus are increasingly being challenged. Leftist groups and platforms have reemerged as political options, and it is likely that we may witness more popular mobilizations in the near future. In recent years, elections in Venezuela, Brazil, Uruguay, Bolivia, and Nicaragua have shown a convergence between new social and political movements and a growing antagonism toward Washington and its consensus.

Instability in the regional order, despite the illusion of regional integration characterized by NAFTA, DR-CAFTA, and the efforts to implement the now virtually defunct FTAA umbrella, is increasing. By challenging the legitimacy of the new interelite and transnational regional arrangements, the new modes of resistance reveal the intrinsic weakness and precarious legitimacy of the posttransition regimes. Even the United States is not exempt from this turmoil and protestation. This is quite remarkable in the context of the growing apathy and cynicism in the American body politic. The unexpected mass mobilizations of 2006 brought millions of protesters of mostly Hispanic origin into the streets of Los Angeles, New York, and Chicago to demonstrate against attempts by the right-wing elements in control of the U.S. government to criminalize the large number of undocumented immigrants in the United States under the rubric of the so-called war on terror and the strengthening of "homeland security." This momentous event indicates that social movements against the status quo are becoming ubiquitous throughout the hemisphere.

Thus, from a long-range structural perspective, social upheavals, some of them violent, have not withered away in the region, although their manifestations have changed. My analysis strongly suggests that the politics of limited democratization combined with neoliberal economics, while an improvement over the atrocious human rights abuses of the military dictatorships, imposes built-in constraints that block the realization of a truly stable and sustainable system of democratic politics in the Americas. Nor is this combination of limited democracy with neoliberalism a guarantee against expanding corruption and widespread popular alienation. In fact, the opposite seems to be the case. Moreover, if the neoliberal economic policies continue to fail to produce a better standard of living for the alienated majorities (as is currently the case throughout the Americas), and should the structural crisis deepen, these civilian regimes will likely be replaced once again by repressive civil-military regimes in the name of national security.

A subtler form of national security ideology is the cultural "software" of the security establishments in most countries of the Americas and a regular staple in the training of the military, police, and paramilitary forces throughout the hemisphere. The "Communist" subversion of yesteryear is being replaced by new internal enemies: "terrorism," "anarchy," and "drug traffickers." In fact, anything that threatens the investment climate, or the core elites' interests, qualifies as a threat to national security and as a candidate for enemy status. Growing U.S. military involvement, as in Plan Colombia, is a case in point. Moreover, the post-9/11 atmosphere has had a most deleterious effect on the prospects for democracy in the Americas because it has given those in control of the U.S. government the opportunity to assume a hard-line "counterterrorist" posture that justifies authoritarian measures and the violation of civil rights.

As the entire region becomes more closely integrated, a potentially dysfunctional system of mutual vulnerability is taking shape. Its impact on the life of millions throughout the Americas could be catastrophic. The preservation of the status quo points toward scenarios where unemployment, poverty, violence, criminality, health hazards, environmental threats, drug addiction, refugee flows, massive population displacements, repression, and environmental decay feed upon each other and transcend national boundaries. The regional drug-trading regime is a dramatic illustration of this interconnectedness. The ties that link the drug trade together begin with peasant producers in the economically depressed Andean region and include the crime syndicates that produce, transport, and import these addictive commodities, the corrupt officials who assist them, the local retailers who sell the drugs, and the end users, ranging from the destitute to those in high social standing.

Under these circumstances, the linkages of mutual vulnerability between North and South and their multiple accelerators, including the contingent mode of labor relations, create a spiraling lose-lose situation: a negative-score game. Without profound changes in both the societies of the South and the North, the possibility of arresting or reversing the existing serious threats to human security will remain doubtful. Short of a radical reorganization of the pattern of governance throughout the Americas, including decision making, accountability, and regional cooperation, multiple and critical dysfunctions are likely to increase within these societies.

In recent years, the Americas have been undergoing a rapid and multidimensional process of globalization, a term often used synonymously with modernization and Americanization (Fukuyama 1999).[14] But this process has not necessarily benefited most countries, let alone their people, as Geoffrey Garrett (2004) has observed:

> Middle-income countries have not done nearly as well under globalized markets as either richer or poorer countries, and the ones that have globalized the most have fared the worst. . . . The ultimate irony facing globalization's missing middle may be that the more the free trade project flounders in Latin America, the greater will be the pressure on people in the region to migrate to the United States. Migration will, in turn, squeeze employment and wages for the American manufacturing middle class even more. (Garrett 2004, 96)

Globalization does not involve just a series of purely random, mechanically preordained stages of development operating outside the realm of concrete actors' interests, objectives, and rules. Rather, this process unfolds within a system of intentional regulations (and deregulations) that affect the very way the "game" of globalization and its outcomes play out. Globalization in the Americas is not exempt from these eminently political regulatory policies, which the global actors can create and change. Politics still matters, and what matters in politics is who governs.

Regional security cannot be equated with short-term business confidence, the magic of the marketplace, or a messianic vision of a hemispheric "Manifest Destiny," or "wars" on terrorism, or fending off the "Hispanic threat" (Huntington 2004). On the other hand, a breakdown of democratic development, prosperity, and equity, together with the increase of tensions in the more volatile regions of the hemisphere, would have a direct and most deleterious effect upon the well-being and security of the people all over the Americas. The weakness of democratic institutions and their inability to move from democratic transition and elected plutocracies to the consolidation of popular rule is a critical structural flaw in the security system of the Western Hemisphere. As a 2005 report from the International Institute for Democracy and Electoral Assistance (IDEA) in Sweden indicates (see table 5.2),

Key democratic institutions in the Americas are not performing to the entire satisfaction of citizens. Some segments of the population feel and are effectively excluded from politics and its processes, particularly women, youth and indigenous peoples. In many countries, democratic institutions remain weak, especially political parties and representative bodies. Politicians are mistrusted everywhere, yet the majority of Latin Americans say that political parties are vital to democracy. Once in office, Latin American governments often fail to forge the political alliances needed to govern and to facilitate needed reforms (otherwise known as a "crisis of governability"). (IDEA 2005)

A similar observation could be made of North America (Stoker 2006, 36–37). It is becoming obvious that the Cold War's end did not automatically bring about a Fukuyama-type scenario of the "end of History," with global prosperity, peace, and democracy for all (Fukuyama 1989).

The two-decade-old democratic transition in the region has not been synonymous with either the entrenchment of participatory practices or with responsible government, let alone with the enhancement of human dignity. The "safe," "limited," "low-intensity," and substantially meaningless democracy brokered and supported by Washington and encapsulated in the famous, unilateral "Washington Consensus" is fundamentally flawed. This model of democratic development, peddled by transition theorists and the neoauthoritarians at the core of the hemispheric order, impedes more than facilitates the emergence of a sustainable security community for the whole region. So does the persistence of neoliberal economic dogmatism and the rebirth of national security doctrines designed to fight elusive and perpetual global enemies. That narrowly defined concept of military security as practiced in the Americas is, in fact, a major cause of insecurity. This link

Table 5.2.   Electoral Participation

	High Turnout			Low Turnout	
Country	*1988–1991*	*1998–2001*	*Country*	*1988–1991*	*1998–2000*
Uruguay	96.9	94.6	Peru	56.9	78.6
Argentina	89.4	78.1	Paraguay	56.3	59.4
Chile	88.3	83.1	Haiti	52.7	60.5
Costa Rica	85.1	73.7	Bolivia	51.0	64.5
Brazil	76.6	81.0	Mexico	50.0	48.2
Honduras	75.7	78.0	Dominican Republic	45.8	45.6
Nicaragua	73.3	76.2	El Salvador	44.0	31.1
Venezuela	72.3	46.5	Colombia	40.1	40.5
Panama	70.1	76.1	United States	36.5	46.5
Canada	68.3	54.6			
Ecuador	64.7	48.5			

Source: International Institute for Democracy and Electoral Assistance (IDEA), "Voter Turnout from 1945 to Date," Stockholm, Sweden, 2003, available at www.idea.int/vt/analysis.

Table 5.3a.   Comparative Indicators for Latin America and the Caribbean

Country	A Corrupt (CPI)[a] 2004	B GDP per Capita[b]	C Growth GDP 2003	D Debt/GPD 1999	E Inflation (Annual) 1999	F GINI Index[c] 1999–2002	G Defense Exp./GDP per 1,000 2003	H Forces in 1999	I HDI in millions (thousands)[d] 2002	J Population Index 2004	K Urban 2002	L EDI 2000[e]
Argentina	2.5	12,400	8.8	51.2	−1.2	52.2	1.1	1.9	0.85	39.5	33, 5	0.96
Bolivia	2.2	2,600	2.5	65.9	2.1	44.70	—	4.0	0.68	8.9	5, 58	0.90
Brazil	3.9	8,100	−0.2	40.0	4.9	59.25	1.5	1.8	0.77	186.0	143, 49	—
Chile	7.4	10,700	3.3	−1.1	3.3	57.10	3.5	5.8	0.83	15.9	13, 45	0.96
Colombia	3.8	6,600	3.9	44.7	11.2	57.60	4.0	3.6	0.77	43.0	33, 22	0.86
Costa Rica	4.9	9,600	6.5	33.6	10.0	46.50	—	2.3*	0.83	4.0	2, 23	0.91
Cuba	3.7	3,000	—	80.0	7.0	—	—	5.1	0.80	11.3	8, 52	0.97
Dominican Republic	2.9	6,200	−0.4	28.7	3.0	—	—	2.0	0.73	8.9	5, 73	0.86
Ecuador	2.4	3,700	2.7	107.3	52.3	—	2.4	4.5	0.73	13.3	8, 18	0.92
El Salvador	4.2	4,900	1.8	17.4	0.5	53.20	0.1	2.7	0.72	6.7	4, 00	—
Guatemala	2.2	4,200	2.1	28.6	4.9	59.87	0.5	2.6	0.64	14.7	4, 83	0.74
Haiti	1.5	1,500	0.4	30.6	8.7	—	—	0.7*	0.46	8.1	3, 06	—
Honduras	2.3	2,800	3.0	83.3	11.6	55.00	0.8	1.2	0.67	6.9	3, 70	—
Jamaica	3.3	4,100	2.3	57.6	5.9	37.90	—	1.1	0.76	2.7	1, 49	0.92
Mexico	3.6	9,600	1.3	33.5	16.6	54.60	0.5	1.9	0.80	106.2	75, 41	0.94
Nicaragua	2.7	2,300	2.3	231.0	10.9	43.11	0.9	3.3	0.66	5.4	3, 04	0.73
Panama	3.7	6,900	4.1	55.7	1.3	56.40	—	0.5*	0.79	3.1	1, 67	0.95
Paraguay	1.9	4,800	2.6	22.6	6.8	57.77	0.7	1.4	0.75	6.4	3, 15	0.90
Peru	3.5	5,600	3.8	50.9	3.5	49.80	1.5	4.4	0.75	27.9	19, 65	0.93
Uruguay	6.2	14,500	2.5	40.1	5.6	44.60	1.1	9.8	0.83	3.4	3, 10	0.93
Venezuela	2.3	5,800	−9.4	71.1	23.6	—	1.3	3.3	0.77	25.4	21.92	0.91

[a] Transparency International's *2004 Corruption Perception Index* (CPI).

[b] Gross domestic product per capita (GDP) (in thousands of U.S. dollars). Central Intelligence Agency, in the 2005 *World Fact Book* electronic publication, available at www.cia .gov/cia/publications/factbook.

[c] Gini Index. World Bank, *World Development Indicators*, available also as an electronic publication at http://esdb.cdie.org/cgi-bin2/broker.exe?_service=default&_ program=lacprogs.pov_3.sas&sscode=WDI180800=&cty=AllLC&year=2001+&year=2002+&year=2001+&year=2000+&year=1999+&output=1. *PNUD World Development Report 1999*.

[d] United Nations Human Development Index (HDI) value from *Latin America and the Caribbean: Selected Economic and Social Data 2004*, electronic publication available at http://qesdb.cdie.org/lac/LACbook/chapter01.pdf, EFA GMR 2003, Statistical Annex.

[e] The Educational Development Index (EDI) is a composite combining the four most quantifiable "education for all" (EFA) indicators. The EDI for a country is the arithmetical mean of the observed values of indicators selected for each of the EFA goals. Since these are percentages, the value can vary from 0 to 1. The higher its value, the closer a country is to the EFA goal and the greater is its educational achievement. See www.unesco.org/education/efa_report/zoom_regions_pdf/laamcari.pdf.

* No military forces; only police and other security forces. Income figures are calculated as purchasing power parity (PPP) = parity equivalent in U.S. dollars. For comparative purposes, the figures for North America for all the above variables (A to L) are shown in table 5.3b.

Table 5.3b. North American Comparisons

Country.	A Corrupt (CPI) 2001	B GDP per Capita 1999	C Growth/ GDP 1999	D Debt/GDP 1999	E Inflation (Annual) 1999	F GINI Index 1999	G Defense Exp./GDP 1999	H Forces per 1,000 2002	I Human Development Index 1999	J Population in 1,000s 1999	K Urbanization Index 1999	L Education Index 1999
Canada	8.9	24,800	3.7	93.0*	1.7	31.5	1.6	1.8	0.932	29,512	77.0	0.98
United States	7.6	33,100	4.2	59.3*	2.1	40.8	3.3	5.1	0.927	275,636	77.0	0.98

Note: This table was calculated by the author on the basis of individual country data provided in the International Institute of Strategic Studies (IISS), *The Military Balance 2000–2001* (London: Oxford University Press, 2001), 25, 54, 227–51, and also from the United Nations' PNUD, *Informe Sobre Desarrollo Humano 1999* (Madrid: Mundi Prensa Libros, 1999), 134–241. The IISS figures for the GNP in Latin America and the Caribbean presented in this table, unlike that of the World Bank used to calculate debt/GNP ratio in table 2, are higher than those prepared by UN agencies like the World Bank and the UNDP.

* The bulk of the U.S.—and to a lesser extent Canadian—debt is internal debt, unlike that of the LAC countries, which is foreign debt.

underpins the insurmountable contradiction between globalization and militarization (Benítez-Manaut 2004, 59). In this context, real regime change throughout the Americas is a necessary condition for human security and the well-being of the vast majority of its peoples.

NOTES

The author of this chapter has placed some suggested resources that you may wish to consult on the book's website at http://www.rowmanlittlefield.com/isbn/ 0742555240.

This material was originally presented as "The Political Economy of Social (In)Justice in Latin America: Panels in Honour of Liisa North" to a session of the Seventy-fifth Congress of the Humanities and Social Sciences, sponsored jointly by the IDRC and York University's Centre for Research on Latin America and the Caribbean (CERLAC), June 1–3, Toronto, Ontario, Canada, 2006. It has expanded upon my ongoing research presented on "Globalization and Insecurity in the Americas," a version of which appeared in Jan Black, ed., *Latin America: Its Problems and Its Promise*, 4th ed. (Boulder, CO: Westview Press, 2005), 207–29, as well as a more recent paper presented to the Panel on Globalization, Exclusion, and Violence in Contemporary Latin American Society, Canadian Society of Hispanists, 2005 Congress of the Canadian Learned Societies, University of Western Ontario, London, Ontario, May 30, 2004, and at the Symposium on Global Blues and Sustainable Development: Technology and Bureaucracy, University of South Florida, Tampa, Florida, September 23–24, 2005.

1. This means current Western depictions of non-Western cultures (in Edward Said's specific case, "the Arabs") regard them as irrational, menacing, untrustworthy, threatening, and dishonest. Compare with Lawrence E. Harrison, *Pan-American Dream: Do Latin America's Cultural Values Discourage True Partnership with the United States and Canada?* (Boulder, CO: Westview Press, 1998).

2. Also see "Appendix F: Précis of the Counterinsurgency Course (1963), the Special Warfare School, Fort Bragg, North Carolina," in Willard Barber and Neale Ronning, *Internal Security and Military Power: Counterinsurgency and Civic Action in Latin America* (Columbus: Ohio State University Press, 1966), 275–76, 217–45, as well as U.S. Army Special Warfare School, *Counterinsurgency Planning Guide*, Special Text No. 31-176 (Fort Bragg, NC: May 1964).

3. Also see Robinson Rojas, "Notes on the Doctrine of National Security" (2003) at rrojasdatabank.org/natsec1.

4. Our calculation is based upon ECLAC *Anuario estadístico* data from between 1970 and 1985.

5. According to the United Nations Economic Commission for Latin America and the Caribbean (ECLAC) *Anuario estadístico 2001*, the figures for disbursed foreign debt were US $22.256 million (1980) and US $739.930 million (2000).

6. For a direct view of the "developmental deontology" of counterinsurgency, see U.S. Army Special Warfare School, *Counterinsurgency Planning Guide*, Special Text No. 31-176 (Fort Bragg, NC: May 1964).

7. See also World Bank, *World Development Report*, 1990, 1991 and 1992, and 1994, pp. 206–207; and *World Debt Tables: External Debt of Developing Countries*, 1987–1988, 1989–1990, and 1991–1992 editions, vol. II (Country Tables, WA: The World Bank, 1988, 1989, 1992).

8. Calculations made on the basis of ECLAC *Anuario estadístico 2001* (Santiago: ECLAC, 2001), table 285 and others.

9. It was based upon the "Task Force Report to the Trilateral Commission," prepared for the first plenary meeting of the commission in Tokyo in May 1975; for a critique of this report, see Alan Wolfe, "Capitalism Shows Its Face," *The Nation*, November 29, 1975, 559.

10. Urban population has expanded exponentially in the region at nearly twice the average rate of population growth. While in 1950 only one city (Buenos Aires) was among the ten most populated cities in the World (with five million), by 2000 three Latin American cities were among the world's largest, respectively ranking second, fourth, and tenth: Mexico City (18.5 million), São Paulo (17.8 million), and Buenos Aires (12.6 million). While this expansion of megacities has been dramatic, even more pronounced is the growth of large metropolitan areas (Santiago, Bogota, Caracas, Lima) and secondary cities (Medellín, Curitiba, Córdoba, Concepción, Guadalajara, etc.). This phenomenon is the tip of the iceberg of a looming urban crisis, resulting from migrations rooted in widespread rural poverty (see table 5.1). It has been estimated that by 2050 Latin America will have double the population of North America (US AID, Bureau for Latin America and the Caribbean, *Latin America and the Caribbean: Selected Economic and Social Data 2004*, 2003, available at http://qesdb.cdie.org/lac/LACbook/chapter01.pdf.

11. William Robinson (1994), citing the 1993 UNDP *Human Development Report*, notes that the wealthiest 20 percent of humanity receives 82.7 percent of the world's income. They also control 80 percent of world trade, 95 percent of all loans, 80 percent of all domestic savings, and 80.5 percent of world investments. They consume 70 percent of world energy, 75 percent of all metals, 85 percent of timbers, and 60 percent of food supplies. He notes that, in this context, the middle classes are tending to shrink considerably since the 20 percent of what could be called the world's middle class only receives 11.7 percent of the world's wealth (*NotiSur*, February 18, 1994, 7). A U.S. study by the Levy Institute, based on the 1998 Federal Reserve's Survey of Consumer Finances, indicated that while the top 1 percent of the population controlled 38 percent of the country's net worth, the poorest 40 percent controlled 0.26 percent of it. In the period between 1983 and 1998, the net worth of that top 1 percent increased 42.3 percent, while the bottom 40 percent of the population was 76.5 percent worse off. See Edward Wolff, "Recent Trends in Wealth Ownership, 1983–1998," (Working Paper No. 300, Levy Institute, 2003), tables 2 and 3. All indications are that income concentration has worsened since 1998.

12. Between 1985 and 1991, the region's defense budgets declined by an average of 24.6 percent, or 4.1 percent per year, and twelve out of twenty countries cut defense expenditures by between 59 percent (Chile) and 4.8 percent (Honduras). On the other hand, two rather large countries, Venezuela and Colombia, dramatically increased such expenditures: respectively, by 23 percent and 275 percent. When the number of troops is examined, the overall trend is a seemingly modest increase of 4.2 percent for the region, or 0.7 percent per year (IISS 2001).

13. For purposes of comparison, the rate in the United States for 2002 was 46.6 percent and about 55 percent in Canada (2000). An examination of voting turnout in parliamentary elections held in both Latin and North America in the decade between 1988 and 1991 and 1998 and 2001 shows a low voting turnout in nearly half of the nations by comparison with most European democracies (IDEA 2003).

14. See the interview with Francis Fukuyama, "Economic Globalization and Culture," *Technology and Society Document*, Internet version, February 1, 1999, available at www.ml.com.woml.forum.global.htp.

REFERENCES

Altimir, Oscar. 1994. "Income Distribution and Poverty through Crisis and Adjustment." *CEPAL Review* 52 (April).

Benítez-Manaut, Raúl. 2004. *Mexico and the Challenges of Hemispheric Security*. Washington, DC: The Woodrow Wilson International Center for Scholars, Latin American Program, 59.

Bosch, Juan. 2000. *El Pentagonismo sustituto del imperialismo*. 3rd ed. Santo Domingo: Editora Alfa y Omega, 5–14.

Central Intelligence Agency (CIA). 2006. *The World Factbook*, updated December 19, 2006. Available at https://www.cia.gov/cia/publications/factbook/geos/ca.html.

Chillier, Gaston, and Laurie Freeman. 2005. "Potential Threat: The New OAS Concept of Hemispheric Security." WOLA Special Report. Washington, DC: Washington Office on Latin America, 1–10.

Chomsky, Noam. 1977. "Trilateral's RX for Crisis: Governability Yes, Democracy No." *Seven Days*, February 14.

Chronic Poverty Research Centre (CPRC). 2005. *The Chronic Poverty Report 2004–2005*. Manchester, UK: Institute for Development Policy and Management, University of Manchester, 79–82.

Close, David. 2004. "Undoing Democracy in Nicaragua." In *Undoing Democracy: The Politics of Electoral Caudillismo*, ed. David Close and Kalowatie Deonandan, 2–4. Lanham, MD: Lexington Books.

Comisión Económica para América Latina y el Caribe (CEPAL)/Economic Commission for Latin America and the Caribbean (ECLAC). 2004. *Panorama económico de América Latina 2004*. Santiago: CEPAL, 1, 5.

Corbett, Charles D. (Col., U.S. Army). 1972. *The Latin American Military as a Socio-Political Force: Case Studies of Bolivia and Argentina*. Monographs in International Affairs. Miami: Center for Advanced International Studies, University of Miami, 13–19.

Economic Commission on Latin America and the Caribbean (ECLAC). 2001. *Anuario estadístico 2001*. Santiago: ECLAC.

Fukuyama, Francis. 1989. "The End of History?" *The National Interest* 16 (Summer): 3–18.

Garrett, Geoffrey. 2004. "Globalization's Missing Middle." *Foreign Affairs* 83, no. 6 (November–December): 85, 96.

Graham, Carol, and Sandip Sukhatenkar. 2003. "Is Economic Crisis Reducing the Support for Markets and Democracy in Latin America? Some Evidence from the

Economics of Happiness." Paper presented to the Brookings Institution, Washington, D.C., November.

Hogan, Jenny. 2005. *New Scientist*, March 1, 1.

Huntington, Samuel. 2004. "The Hispanic Threat." *Foreign Policy* (March–April). Available at www.keepmedia.com/pubs/ForeignPolicy/2004/03/01/387925. Original title: "The Hispanic Challenge."

Huntington, Samuel, Michel Crozier, and Joji Watanuki. 1975. *The Crisis of Democracy: Report on the Governability of Democracies to the Trilateral Commission*. Triangle Papers 8. New York: New York University Press, 1–5, 169.

International Institute for Democracy and Electoral Assistance (IDEA). 2005. IDEA Report. Stockholm, Sweden: IDEA. Available at www.idea.int/americas/index.cfm.

International Institute of Strategic Studies (IISS). 2001. *The Military Balance 2000–2001*. London: Oxford University Press, 25, 54, 227–51.

Jagan, Cheddy. 1996. "Sustainable Development in the Americas." Keynote address to the Twenty-seventh Annual Congress of the Canadian Association of Latin American and Caribbean Studies, York University, Toronto, Ontario, Canada, October 31.

Karl, Terry-Lynn, and Richard Fagen. 1986. "The Logic of Hegemony: The United States as a Superpower in Central America." In *Dominant Powers and Subordinate States: The United States in Latin America and the Soviet Union in Eastern Europe*, ed. Jan Triska, 218–38. Durham, NC: Duke University Press, 4–8.

Latin America Weekly Report. 1994a. January 13, 2.

——. 1994b. February 17, 62.

LatinReporters.com. 2004. "Uruguay, Chili et Venezuela votent à gauche; le Brésil se recentre." November 2. Available at www.latinreporters.com/uruguaypol02112004.html.

Letelier, Orlando. 1976. "The 'Chicago Boys' in Chile: Economic 'Freedom's' Awful Toll." *The Nation*, August 28, 138, 142.

Linowitz, Sol. 1975. *The Americas in a Changing World* (Commission on United States–Latin American Relations, Sol Linowitz, chairman). New York: Quadrangle Books.

Lovell, John. 1971. "Military-dominated Regimes and Political Development: A Critique of Some Prominent Views." In *Political Development in Changing Societies: An Analysis of Modernization*, ed. Monte Palmer and Larry Stern, 159–79. Lexington, MA: Heath Books.

Martínez, Osvaldo. 1992. "Debt and Foreign Capital: The Origins of the Crisis." *Latin American Perspectives* 20, no. 1 (Winter): 65.

Montecinos, Verónica, and John Markoff. 1993. "Democrats and Technocrats: Professional Economists and Regime Transition in Latin America." *Canadian Journal of Development Studies* 14, no. 1: 7–22.

Nader, Ralph. 1992. "Plutocracy and the Citizen Agenda for '92 and Beyond." Speech delivered at Harvard Law School, January 15. Available at www.ratical.org/co-globalize/RalphNader/RN01.15.92.html.

Nef, Jorge. 1978. "Myths in the Study of Latin American Politics." In *Canada and the Latin American Challenge*, ed. Jorge Nef, 19–42. Toronto-Ottawa-Guelph: Ontario Cooperative Program in Latin American and Caribbean Studies (OCPLACS), Canadian Association for the Study of Latin America and the Caribbean (CALACS).

———. 1999. *Human Security and Mutual Vulnerability: The Global Political Economy of Development and Underdevelopment.* 2nd ed. Ottawa: IDRC Books, 13–26.

———. 2004a. "Socioeconomic and Political Factors of Health Security and Insecurity in Latin America and the Caribbean." *Journal of Developing Societies* 19, fascicule 2, no. 3: 172–226.

———. 2004b. "Structural Correlates of Government Corruption in Latin America: Explaining and Understanding Empirical Findings." In *Governance in Southern Africa and Beyond,* ed. Dele Olowu and Roy Mukwena, 283–304. Windhoek, Namibia: McMillan-Granberg.

———. 2005. "Globalization and Insecurity in the Americas." In *Latin America: Its Problems and Its Promise,* ed. Jan Black, 207–29. 4th ed. Boulder, CO: Westview Press.

Nef, Jorge, and Ximena Núñez. 1994. "El monólogo interamericano: Una visión histórica." *Política* (Chile) II Época 32 (Spring): 81–112.

Nef, Jorge, and Wilder Robles. 1998. "Environmental Issues, Politics, and Administration in Latin America: An Overview." In *Governmental Response to Environmental Challenges in Global Perspective,* ed. Joseph Jabbra and Onkar Dwivedi, 42–62. Amsterdam: IOS Press.

Nef, Jorge, and Francisco Rojas. 1984. "Dependencia compleja y transnacionalización del estado." *Relaciones Internacionales* 8–9 (December): 101–22.

Nye, Joseph. 2003. *The "Democracy Deficit" in the Global Economy: Enhancing the Legitimacy and Accountability of Global Institutions.* Task Force Report 57. The Trilateral Commission. Available at www.trilateral.org/projwork/tfrsums/tfr57.htm#intro.

Robinson, William. 1994. "Central America: Which Way after the Cold War?" *NotiSur* 4, no. 8 (February 25): 1–9, especially 5.

Rojas, Robinson. 2003. "Notes on the Doctrine of National Security." Available at rrojasdatabank.org/natsec.

Said, Edward. 1978. *Orientalism.* New York: Pantheon Books; London: Routledge and Kegan Paul; Toronto: Random House.

Siat, Arturo, and Gregorio Iriarte. 1979. "De la seguridad nacional al trilateralismo." *Cuadernos de Cristianismo y Sociedad* (Buenos Aires) (May): 23–24.

Sklar, Holly. 1980. "Managing Dependence and Democracy—An Overview." In *Trilateralism: The Trilateral Commission and Elite Planning for World Management,* ed. Holly Sklar, 1–55. Montreal: Black Rose.

Stoker, Gerry. 2006. *Why Politics Matters: Making Democracy Work.* London: Palgrave, 36–37.

Street, Paul. 2000. "The Economy Is Doing Fine, It's Just the People That Aren't." *Z Magazine* (November). Available at www.zmag.org/ZMag/articles/nov00street.htm.

Triska, Jan, ed. 1986. *Dominant Powers and Subordinate States: The United States in Latin America and the Soviet Union in Eastern Europe.* Durham, NC: Duke University Press.

United Nations. 1994. *World Economic and Social Survey 1994.* New York: United Nations, 42.

United Nations Development Program (UNDP). 1999. *Informe sobre desarrollo humano 1999.* Madrid: Mundi Prensa Libros.

Vilas, Carlos. 2004. "Shaky Democracies and Popular Fury: From Military Coups to Peoples' Coups?" *Cuadernos LACS,* 2.

Weil, Jean-Louis, Joseph Comblin, and Judge Senese. 1979. "The Repressive State: The Brazilian National Security Doctrine and Latin America," LARU Studies Doc. 3. Toronto: LARU, 36–73.

World Bank. 1988. *World Debt Tables: External Debt of Developing Countries*, 1987–1988 ed., Vol. 2. Country Tables, WA: The World Bank.

———. 1989. *World Debt Tables: External Debt of Developing Countries*, 1989–1990 ed., Vol. 2. Country Tables, WA: The World Bank.

———. 1990–1992 and 1994. *World Development Report*.

———. 1992. *World Debt Tables: External Debt of Developing Countries*, 1991–1992 ed., Vol. 2. Country Tables, WA: The World Bank.

———. 2001. World Development Indicators (1999–2001). Available at http://esdb.cdie.org/cgi-bin2/broker.exe?_service=default&_program=lacprogs .pov_3.sas&sscode=WDI180800+&cty=ALLC&year=2002+&year=2001+&year= 2000+&year=1999+&output=1.

6

The Riddle of New Social Movements

Who They Are and What They Do

Judith Adler Hellman

What are commonly called popular, grassroots, or social movements have long been a feature of the Latin American and Caribbean landscape. As early as the 1960s, indigenous people from the highlands of Peru were descending on Lima to invade public lands and establish their highly organized squatters' communities, priests and lay people immersed in liberation theology were developing ecclesiastical base communities (CEBs) in cities and villages from El Salvador to Chile, Paulo Freire and his followers were using literacy programs to stimulate the collective struggle of the Brazilian poor for land and social justice, and impoverished Jamaicans were joining their neighbors in "share-pot" groups in the countryside and the "yards" of Kingston slums. However, it is only since the 1980s that the importance and political potential of social movements have been appreciated—if sometimes overstated—by analysts and activists who are looking for grounds for optimism.

Forty years ago, the focus of our attention and hope for progressive change in the Americas was the Cuban Revolution, and students of the region tended to view the future of Latin America and the Caribbean as resting on the possibility of reproducing the Cuban model elsewhere in the hemisphere. Debates centered on the viability of the guerrilla "foco" as a "road to revolution," the feasibility of guerrilla struggle in countries like Argentina and Uruguay that lack Sierra Maestra–type mountains, the relative advantage of rural or urban fronts, and the wisdom of Che Guevara's decision to open a South America–wide foco in Bolivia.

The descants in this discussion were the loud notes sounded by those who asserted that the electoral road to socialism was still viable or that the organized urban workers remained the vanguard class. Arguments raged over the relative revolutionary potential of agricultural wageworkers, small-holding peasants, tenants, sharecroppers, the urban industrial working class, and sometimes even the "new middle classes" and the "progressive national bourgeoisie." It was taken as given, however, by almost all progressive people concerned with Latin America and the Caribbean that Socialist revolution was the model, the acquisition of state power was the goal, and the only open question was what would prove the most appropriate means to that end.

The social movements so central today to our discussions and our hopes for a more humane future in the Americas were not entirely ignored. They tended, however, to be viewed simply as building blocks in the more elaborate project, which was the total revolutionary transformation of society. Squatters' movements, self-help or literacy groups, cooperatives, and community organizations of every sort were seen as comprised of "prepolitical" people[1] taking their first halting steps toward the kind of consciousness and the practical participatory skills that would eventually allow them to become protagonists in a revolutionary scenario.

The triumph of the revolutionary forces in Nicaragua and Grenada inevitably reinforced this view of social movements as building blocks. Grassroots groups, middle-class business associations, labor unions, and peasant movements were all key components in the coalition of forces that brought the Sandinistas to power in Nicaragua. And in Grenada, the victory of Maurice Bishop and his New Jewel Movement was made possible only through the multiclass participation of students, nurses, trade unionists, and the Chamber of Commerce in JEWEL (New Joint Endeavor for Welfare, Education, and Liberation), a social movement made up of community-level organizations, as well as rural and urban workers. Typically, when discussing the social movements that gave support to the Nicaraguan or Grenadian revolutions, most commentators were principally concerned not with the movements themselves but with the contribution they made to the larger revolutionary project.

However, as hopes for Socialist revolution began to recede in the wake of the savage coups in Chile and Grenada, the Contra war and electoral rejection of the Sandinistas, and the defeat of guerrilla forces in Mexico and throughout South America, social movements began to be viewed in a different light. And once disillusionment with the Cuban Revolution began to set in as well, expectations of full-scale revolutionary transformation diminished, and interest and hope increasingly came to focus on small-scale, localized movements.[2]

Thus, with the collapse of the old revolutionary projects, passions were transferred to a huge range and variety of activities that came to be grouped under the ever-broader heading of "social movements" or "new social movements." Indeed, it is astonishing to contemplate the number and variety of collective activities pursued by activists in Latin America and the Caribbean that are referred to in this way. For example, in the first comprehensive collection of writings on the topic, Tilman Evers (1985) provides a list of new social movements that includes squatters' groups, neighborhood councils, church-sponsored base communities, indigenista associations, women's organizations, human rights committees, youth groups, popular cultural and artistic activities, literacy groups, coalitions for the defense of regional traditions, environmental movements, and "a patchwork of self-help groupings among unemployed and poor people" (43). Significantly, Evers also includes under his new movement heading "workers associations organizing independently and even in opposition to traditional trade union structures" (43).

In a later survey of new social movements, Fernando Calderón, Alejandro Piscitelli, and José Luis Reyna (1992) provide examples of the multiplicity of "new sociocultural actors who today produce our societies," including Brazilian ecology activists, the Argentinean Mothers of the Plaza de Mayo, and the Chilean women who "gained the recognition of civil society through their opposition to the authoritarian regime" (19). The authors also cite the Kataristas in the Bolivian altiplano, "a peasant movement of an indigenous nature," which demanded "ethnic autonomy, class transformation and affirmation of citizenship"; the São Paulo metalworkers who opposed "technocratic state policies" and critiqued the "effects of industrial automation . . . on workers' jobs and culture"; and Rastafarians in the Caribbean, whose "political critique and cultural affirmation [are] expressed primarily through dance and music." Nor does this wide range of activities exhaust the authors' examples, which also include Mexicans and Peruvians struggling for the "democratization of microlocal urban territories" and even Sendero Luminoso, which they describe as a Peruvian mixture of millenarianism with authoritarian communism. Calderón, Piscitelli, and Reyna characterize this last movement as "absolute, cruel and disconcerting." However, they group Sendero among their examples of new social movements on the grounds that it reflects "the complex processes of exclusion and disintegration occurring in Peruvian society" (20–23).

In addition to these initiatives, human rights, indigenous peoples', environmental, women's, gay and lesbian, youth, student, debtors', and popular cultural associations are generally included in any comprehensive list of social movements. The definition begins to stretch too wide for some when we move from the "social" to include class-based and partisan struggles. But increasingly, even urban- and rural-based trade unions and progressive political parties are also discussed in the context of social movements or grassroots organizations. So, too, are the activities of cross-border solidarity organizations, Internet exchange groups, an immense array of often highly institutionalized domestic and international nongovernmental organizations

(NGOs), microenterprises of every stripe, particularly "productivist" agricultural cooperatives, and sometimes the entire informal economy, which, in many parts of Latin America, outstrips the formal economy in size!

This list should give the reader an idea of the daunting task involved in establishing a broadly acceptable definition of new social movements. Confronted with the vast number and complexity of new movements, how are we to determine precisely which kinds of struggles are properly listed under this heading?

As noted above, the widest area of agreement regarding the definition of social movements is expressed in the notion that they must be distinguished from what are generally referred to as "traditional" parties and unions. Moreover, it is usually assumed that the "new subjects" who participate in the new movements differ in some fundamental way from "traditional" political actors; either they are different people, or they are the same people acting in different, more spontaneous, democratic, decentralized, and participatory ways. Furthermore, the activities of participants in new social movements are thought to unfold somewhere out in "civil society" or in the "realm of everyday life" rather than in what is normally conceived of as the "political arena" (not to speak of the factory floor!). Movement activists are presumed to be responding in new ways to "new forms of subordination," and their struggles focus on the realm of consumption rather than production. "The common denominator of all the 'new social movements,'" writes Slater, citing Ernesto Laclau and Chantal Mouffe, "would be their differentiation from workers' struggles, considered as 'class' struggles" (Laclau and Mouffe 1985, 159, in Slater 1985, 3).[3]

This much said, we can begin to appreciate the difficulty of squeezing all the movements listed by Evers and Calderón, Piscitelli, and Reyna into even the broadest definition of new social movements. Moreover, although the novelty of their approach and their distinction from traditional class-based struggles are widely accepted as two key characteristics of the new movements, we find students of the phenomenon constantly stretching the limits of even this loose definition. In fact, in the next section, a more detailed look at specific cases reveals that the new social movements are neither so new nor so isolated from class and partisan struggles as some have asserted.

THE LINK TO WORKERS' AND PARTY STRUGGLES

While there is almost perfect agreement among social-movement theorists that such movements transcend traditional conflicts in the sphere of production and differ in some fundamental way from traditional interest groups and class-based organizations, some of the most interesting and significant struggles in recent times have taken place precisely at the point of intersection between trade unions and social movements. The Brazilian metalworkers are a case in point. Those who analyze this movement find a direct and logical link between the struggles of workers in the realm of production and those of neighborhood groups concerned with consumption issues. Lucio Kowarick (1985, 86–89) argues that the "Brazilian miracle" was based on a strategy of exploiting labor in the factories and limiting the goods and services available to the urban poor. Thus, when Brazilian unions mobilized to fight the superexploitation of workers, and the *bairro* associations protested the lack of social services, their activities could be said to have "fused" (Kowarick 1985, 84). Collective action that brings together both forms of protest becomes, by definition, a common struggle on two fronts of the same battle against capitalist exploitation and the "pauperization" it requires (Kowarick 1985, 88).

Likewise, Maria Helena Moreira Alves's work (1984) focuses on the links forged between São Paulo's secular grassroots organizations, progressive Catholic ecclesiastical base communities, and independent trade unions. In her study of the mobilizations of the late 1970s and early 1980s, she shows that the neighborhood or favela associations often originate as part of the personalistic following of politicians intent on establishing a clientelistic relationship with the poor. Yet, these organizations may be transformed into genuine instruments for popular struggle when "the increased political consciousness of working class members allowed [slum dwellers] to set up new associations and maintain a high degree of autonomous political action so as to escape the clientelistic ties of the past" (Moreira Alves 1984, 77).

Yet another good example of a fruitful relationship between a trade union and a new social movement is the case of the Nineteenth of September Garment Workers Union, which developed out of the rubble of the 1985 Mexico City earthquakes, which damaged or destroyed four hundred centers of garment production and left eight hundred workers dead and forty thousand unemployed. Teresa Carrillo (1990) shows how Mexican feminists managed to collaborate with female garment workers to build the first Mexican trade union to be led by women. While the union had only limited success in terms of contract negotiations, it did manage to build a range of services, including day care, health care, a job bank, a training center for women over forty, a popular education program, and some food distribution. Significantly, Carrillo (1990) notes that the union enjoyed high visibility on a national and international level and took on "a central role in initiating communication and collaboration among unionized women in Mexico," extending those linkages "to neighborhood associations and other independent organizations" (232).

When we consider these experiences, the insistence of social movement purists that such movements lie outside the realm of class struggle begins to seem strained at best. In reality, most social movements, like the traditional trade unions and parties from which they can be distinguished, respond to changing conditions in flexible ways. The movement that passionately eschews formal links with unions or political parties today may become engaged in enthusiastic campaign work if the right candidate were to appear tomorrow.

A case in point is the Asamblea de Barrios, a popular urban movement that grew out of the mobilization following the 1985 earthquakes in Mexico City. Initially formed by those left homeless in the disaster, the asamblea outlived the emergency, expanded its membership, and began to organize poor urban people around the demand for affordable housing for slum dwellers in the center of the city and for the extension of urban services (potable water, sewer lines, electricity, schools, clinics, and bus lines) to people living on the periphery of the Federal District. While the asamblea initially rejected any suggestion of involvement in partisan politics, once Cuauhtemoc Cárdenas emerged in 1988 as a progressive alternative to the continued rule of the official party, the Partido Revolucionario Institucional (PRI), the asamblea was quick to cast its lot with the opposition candidate. Asamblea members campaigned for Cárdenas in the neighborhoods where the movement had painstakingly built support. An observer of this process, Jaime Tamayo (1990), wrote, "The sudden politicization of these emergent social movements and their inclusion in cardenismo's national project, has not so far affected their independence. Quite the contrary, it has allowed them to expand their intersectoral alliances without diminishing their autonomy" (134).

The support lent to the Worker's Party by Brazilian social movements provides another clear example of an organic link between such movements and a party that attracted a broad popular class base. Ilse Scherer-Warren (1987) describes the grassroots movements of São Paulo as a "transition" to expanded forms of popular expression or the "conquest of political space" (48). For Scherer-Warren, the autonomy of new social movements from parties is a temporary situation. In the long run, she argues, grassroots movements in Brazil prepared their activists for political participation in the direct elections that were key to the process of transition from military rule to democracy in Brazil. But the new parties of the Left retained the support of the new social movements they had won as electoral allies only by incorporating the movements' demands into their program for transformation.

These cases indicate that the situation of new social movements is more fluid than some theorists have appreciated. The deep distrust of unions, parties, and partisan politics often expressed by social-movement activists in the late 1970s had diminished, in many cases, by the end of the 1980s. To be sure, many movements still fear absorption and demobilization when any kind of coalition with a political party is proposed (Hellman 1992, 53–54). But the 1980s were marked by the steady immiseration of poor people under structural adjustment policies, and the decade also witnessed the weakening and marginalization of many parties of the Left throughout Latin America. Under these adverse circumstances, alliances between new movements and parties of the Left came to look less sinister and problematic to the movements than was previously the case. Indeed, in Mexico, the fraud perpetrated by the official party in the 1988 elections brought even very independent, apolitical groups into a broad movement to protest the assumption of power by the PRI candidate, Carlos Salinas. From that point on, most Mexican movements, with little hesitation, added electoral reform to their list of specific demands.

Moreover, even when new social movements remain aloof from partisan and union politics, they may nonetheless contain many characteristics that we might associate with class-based organizations. As noted above, new social movements are generally defined as struggles that lie outside the realm of production. But the analyses, goals, and activities of some of these movements are, in fact, centered on the problem of access to, or control of, the means of production. This is particularly obvious in the case of rural mobilizations. For example, Calderón, Piscitelli, and Reyna (1992) note that the Bolivian Katarista movement and the Unión de Comuneros "Emiliano Zapata" based in Michoacán, Mexico, both call for communal autonomy and increased political participation, as well as for "changes in the agricultural power structure" (21). What sorts of changes in the agricultural power structure are on the agenda of such movements? Normally, they would include securing access to land and the means to work it productively (that is, water resources, agricultural credit, and technology). Surely these goals, central to virtually all peasant movements, correspond to the identity of the peasantry as a social class, even when they are combined with noneconomic, "cultural" demands the same people might make as an ethnically distinct, indigenous community.

Perhaps this point is most clearly illustrated by the problem of defining the 1994 rebellion in Chiapas, where the Zapatista Army of National Liberation burst onto the international scene on New Year's Day. The links of the Zapatistas to the progressive Catholic clergy and to a broad range of national and international human and indigenous rights organizations have led many to view this formation as a new social movement. Moreover, the examination, if not to say deconstruction, of their published statements, particularly the words of their principal spokesman, Subcomandante Marcos, have led many observers to underscore the distinction between the "discourse" of this group and the "tired old rhetoric of the revolutionary Left."

Indeed, the Zapatistas have been careful to underscore their total autonomy from all existing political parties and organizations in Mexico. They call for cultural liberation as indigenous people, and they demand items like schools and health-care facilities. In all of these respects, the group seems to fit the definition of a new social movement. Yet, the concentration of peasant land in the hands of large commercial owners lies at the heart of the struggle in Chiapas, and the movement grew directly from the alienation of the peasants of Chiapas from the means of production. Under the circumstances, if the Chiapanecos constitute a new social movement in their concern with collective consumption, ethnic identity, and cultural survival, they must, at the same time, be understood as a class-based organization in which peasants are drawn together not only in ethnic solidarity but as a social class made up of agriculturists who have been despoiled of their lands.

It may be that June Nash (2001) is the analyst who has most clearly appreciated that culture and politics are often best understood as inextricably intertwined. In her study of the role of cultural resistance and class consciousness in Bolivian tin miners' communities, Nash (2001) writes, "The cultural roots of resistance to alien control can generate social movements that restructure the society, influencing the choice of timing for political acts of protest as well as the place and form in which rebellion arises" (182). In the case of these industrial miners, Nash (2001) finds that beliefs and rituals surviving from precolonial periods "generate a sense of self that rejects subordination and repression" and that these historical ties are part and parcel of the class consciousness the miners develop as workers and trade unionists (182).

Inasmuch as the definition of social movements is so loose, it corresponds neatly to the needs of progressive people in a post-Communist world who seek to invest their hopes and energies in an appropriate cause. Unfortunately, this vagueness also serves the needs of apologists for neoliberalism who borrow World Bank language to pose self-financing or NGO-financed popular voluntary organizations as the principal promoters of "development with a human face." Indeed, in the neoliberal model, popular self-help organizations fill the vacuum created by the withdrawal of state funding for social services (Macdonald 1995).

Thus, discerning the definitional boundaries of what we should consider a progressive social movement poses some real difficulties, especially for those who assume that anything "popular" is necessarily progressive. In reality, the Christian Right has enjoyed considerable success organizing at the grassroots level in Latin America. And other organizations that fit the definition of popular movements may be as reactionary as the fundamentalist Evangelicals, or they may be turned to conservative purpose when captured by the state or by personalistic populist leaders. Thus, the vast array of activities that come under the heading of social or grassroots movements presents a full range of mixed and often contradictory possibilities. For example, the ecclesiastical base communities that emerged in Brazil generally radicalized slum dwellers there, while in Colombia the CEBs evolved into a tool of the conservative Catholic hierarchy and exerted a conservative influence over the poor people they organized (Levine and Mainwaring 2001). Or, to take another example, microenterprises, a favorite project of international-aid givers, may develop into democratically managed popular cooperative projects, or they may become a further source of inequality and stratification, not to mention tension and even violence, in poor communities (North and Cameron 2003).

Finally, to the definitional confusion we must add the concept of civil society itself. There is general agreement that social movements arise and develop somewhere "out there" in civil society. At times, however, the definition running through such discussions is no more precise than to label as "civil society" all movements that we admire and as "not civil society" those we do not like or trust.

For example, for most analysts and activists, autonomous trade unions are a part of civil society, but *oficialista* unions (and independent unions that have grown corrupt) are not. If we take Mexico as an example, unions that were affiliated with the official party, the PRI, and formed the pillars of support for the consolidation of one-party rule would not be considered part of civil society, but the "democratic currents" that developed within them would. Indeed, the problem of posing all popular organizations as civil society is nowhere demonstrated more clearly than in Mexico. If a union or association of some kind were organized from the top down in order to co-opt and manipulate people, it seems reasonable that we would not think of it as an element of civil society. However, if it were organized from the bottom up, and subseqently co-opted and captured by the state as so many popular organizations in Mexico have been, it is difficult to know at what point we should no longer consider it part of civil society and see it instead as part of the state apparatus.

This conceptual problem is very much with us today when we try to categorize the Bolivarian Circles, neighborhood groups whose popular support is so crucial to the regime of Hugo Chávez in Venezuela. Are these part of civil society? Are they spontaneous grassroots expressions that spring from the soil of popular activity? Or are they more comparable to the kinds of popular organizations that the PRI used to maintain itself in power for seven decades? In Mexico, the further growth of genuine peasant and workers' organizations was stimulated from above when President Lázaro Cárdenas (1934–1940) required popular support to underpin his regime so that he might carry out radical policies like a massive land distribution in 1937 and the nationalization of petroleum resources in 1938. Under Cárdenas, these popular organizations willingly lent their support to his projects; only later did they become tools of top-down rule. Similarly, a glance at the popular organizations crucial to the consolidation of Jean-Bertrand Aristide's Lavalas Party in Haiti raises the same definitional dilemma. These began as authentic grassroots organizations and expressions of civil society, but once consolidated from above, they became instruments of Aristide's own *personalismo* and *continuismo*.

HOW NEW ARE THE NEW MOVEMENTS?

If there is a problem in determining which new social movements are genuinely social rather than political or which movements are genuinely popular rather than imposed from above, even greater is the analytical challenge of determining which movements are really "new" and which are rooted in historical struggles of the past. As Andre Gunder Frank and Marta Fuentes (1989) have asserted, "Social movements in the West, South and East that are commonly called 'new' are with few exceptions new forms of social movements which have existed through the ages" (179–80).

For students of Mexican social movements, a clear cut-off date allows us to distinguish "old" from "new." The student movement of 1968, culminating in the regime's massacre of participants in the Plaza of the Three Cultures on October 2, 1968, is widely understood to mark an undisputable watershed in Mexican history. And thus, as Joe Foweraker (1990) argues, although every contemporary movement has historical forerunners, "the very accumulation of movements after 1968 works a qualitative change in the relationship between popular movements and the political system" (7).

In the case of Mexico, the events of 1968 produced a generation of leaders who fanned out across the country and went on to organize new kinds of popular mobilizations in every corner of the republic. Thus, one way to recognize what is genuinely new in the Mexican context is to look for veterans of the 1968 movement in leadership roles. Another telltale sign is the presence of women: Foweraker (1990) notes that "one specific indication of the novelty of the phenomenon is the important role played by women in the post-1968 popular movements" where the mass base is female, "even if their leadership is still mainly male" (7).

Even in the case of Mexico, however, where the task is simplified by the existence of a broadly accepted watershed moment, we still face the problem of whether we should label as novel movements that strive to construct "new identities" that are, in fact, rooted in the past. In particular, this dilemma arises with respect to indigenous movements that look to precolonial times to find the structures they propose as the framework for a new kind of community. Indeed, this can be said of *indigenista* movements everywhere in Latin America. And in the Caribbean, the Rastafarians whom Calderón, Piscitelli, and Reyna cite enthusiastically as an example of a new movement, are, in fact, engaging in an exercise in identity politics that can be traced to the Back-to-Africa movement of Marcus Garvey in the 1920s, if not beyond to the slave rebellions and the maroon communities of the seventeenth and eighteenth centuries.

In my own consideration of Mexican movements (Hellman 1994b), I have been struck by the continuity, rather than elements of rupture, with the past. In comparing the independent peasant organizations I studied in the late 1960s with contemporary movements, I have noted that neither the fundamental goals nor the strategies and tactics of the rural movements have altered markedly. The strategy of the old organizations—like that of the new—was to establish themselves as a force with which to be reckoned on the local and, eventually, the national scene and thus to wrest concessions from the state. The techniques applied before 1968 were not so different from the mobilizational and pressure tactics used by movements today—although to hear all the excited talk about "new practices," a student of new movements could be forgiven for feeling some confusion on this point. Demonstrations, sit-ins, hunger marches to the capital, petitions, and letter-writing campaigns were the tactics the old movements employed. Then, as now, group members were assembled at or marched or trucked (banners flying) to the Zócalo, the president's official residence, or the appropriate government agency. There they would remain, a public embarrassment to the regime, until they were received by some government functionary who promised to address, if not redress, their grievances.

To be sure, a whole new "repertoire of protest" (Tilly 1978; Tarrow 1994) has been added to the old, including the production of a countercultural pop-culture figure like Superbarrio, a masked *lucha libre* wrestler who embodies the goals of the have-nots of Mexican society, or the ski masks worn by the rebels in Chiapas, which have become an important symbol of resistance appearing on the heads of popular demonstrators throughout Mexico and wherever "antiglobal" protesters assemble. Furthermore, today, urban popular protesters outnumber those who arrive in the capital from the countryside, and contemporary protesters are more likely to address themselves to public opinion through the media, particularly the international media, than exclusively to the agents of the Mexican state (Hellman 1999). On balance, however, at least for students of Mexico, it is far easier to discern signs of historical continuity with respect to the symbols and goals of protest than to find evidence of a clear break with the past (Knight 1990). After all, the Chiapan Zapatistas, with their electronic linkups to world opinion, their skillful management of CNN and *New York Times* correspondents, and their production of glossy, four-color pamphlets for distribution as press releases may be testing new approaches and new limits of protest in Mexico. But they are still "Zapatistas" articulating demands not so different from those voiced in 1915 by the original Zapatistas as they rode through the mountains of Morelos behind their leader, Emiliano Zapata.

Still, if much of what goes on today in Mexico or elsewhere in Latin America and the Caribbean is rooted in past struggles, clearly there are also developments that can properly be seen as new. For example, women have long participated in popular mobilizations in the Americas, and the celebration of motherhood has always been part of Hispano-American culture. But the redefinition of motherhood as a political responsibility and the transfer of the mother's role from the private to the public sphere, where this identity may become a weapon of struggle, are unquestionably new phenomena. This novel conception of women's role developed in the 1970s during the period of totalitarian military rule in the southern cone, and it subsequently spread throughout the region (Jaquette, Feijoó, and Perelli 1991; Schirmer 1993).

Moreover, some movements that have emerged in recent years have few or no historical precedents. To be sure, Jean Meyer (1973–1974) has argued that the activities of the CEBs in Mexico can be traced to the rabble-rousing priests of the Mexican independence movement or the "social Catholicism" of the immediate prerevolutionary and revolutionary period (cited in Knight 1990, 88–89), and undoubtedly historians may uncover other links with the past in other Latin American countries. However, the CEBs, in their most democratic, participatory form represent a genuinely novel experience that would not have been possible before Pope John XXIII, Vatican II, and liberation theology came on the scene. Likewise, the spread of feminism, gay rights, and ecology movements through Latin America marks a new chapter in the development of protest (Escobar and Alvarez 1992).[4] Human rights as a transnational concern in which domestic and foreign activists work together to influence international public opinion is not only new in its conception but, like the feminist, gay, and green movements, relies to a large extent on a network of international communication that has only become feasible in the electronic age. Furthermore, the internationalization of social-movement struggles in the form of the collaborative presence of foreign NGOs in the *barriadas* of Lima, the backlands of Brazil, or the town squares of Chiapas has, for better or worse, transformed the way in which popular movements theorize, strategize, and carry out their activities.

Therefore, the question of novelty turns out to be at least as complicated as the search for a clear, delimiting definition of new social movements. Perhaps the trickiest question of all, however, is not who or what new social movements are, but what they do. The next section of this chapter, thus, focuses on the knotty problem of assessing the goals and impact of the movements, or at least the claims their analysts make for them.

WHAT NEW SOCIAL MOVEMENTS DO

If the image of social movements as the building blocks of Socialist revolution has largely been abandoned, it has been replaced by other expectations. Movements are credited with the capacity to transform consciousness and prepare their members to take a more active, militant, participatory role in society. They are posed as winning concrete concessions for their members. And finally, they are thought to play a key role in the process of democratization in Latin America.

The first assertion regarding the transformation of consciousness is perhaps the most difficult to argue persuasively because, abundant as the anecdotal evidence may be, there is no agreed-upon way to demonstrate, let alone measure, the dimensions of the changes brought about in the participants' subjective feelings about themselves as political or social actors. I collected many such narratives in the course of my research among Mexican neighborhood activists (Hellman 1994a). More or less typical of the evidence provided in such interviews would be the statement made to me by an activist in the Asamblea de Barrios who described the changes she underwent in the course of her participation. She explained,

> I learned about politics. I even learned how to talk about sex without embarrassment. I learned so many things I never knew before. Most important, I learned how to deal with people, to talk to people. And now I know how to get more information out of the people who really know what's going on. I learned that only when we unite do we achieve anything. (Hellman 1994a, 20)

The experience related to me by this woman is the kind of transformation that is generally described by other social-movement analysts as "empowerment." Typically the term is used to refer to women who emerge from the private, isolated sphere of the home to participate in collective mobilizations around consumption issues. Nikki Craske (1993), for example, has drawn a comparison between Mexican women organized within the co-optive structures of the PRI and others who were active in an independent neighborhood group. Craske (1993) found that women in the independent organizations "show greater knowledge of political institutions and the political system, and they are more confident regarding their ability to take on power positions, both personal and institutional; that is, they feel empowered by their experience" (112).

From this statement, one may infer that empowerment has to do with increased knowledge about politics, combined in some way with growing personal confidence and, perhaps, even a greater sense of control over one's life. However, although the literature on new movements is replete with references to empowerment, virtually no one has paused to define the concept; nor is there agreement on exactly how an empowered person differs from someone who has not undergone this transformative process. In short, while Karl Marx provided some guiding principles to predict when a worker could be said to have acquired "worker's consciousness" (Miliband 1977, 31–33), nothing comparable exists in the world of social-movement studies. Thus, although there is a broad consensus that important forms of learning and attitude change occur when new subjects join new movements, beyond these vague assertions, we have no intersubjective indicators of what those changes are, and Craske is one of the few analysts who has even attempted to establish a base line from which the changes might be traced.

This lack of precision just about forces us back into the arms of Gabriel Almond and Sidney Verba (1965) and other behavioralist political scientists of the 1960s who at least provided definitions—like them or not—for what they called "political cognition" and the growth of a sense of "political efficacy" or "political competence." Ironically, it may be that these terms, rather than the "constitution of new subjects and subjectivities," come closest to providing a conceptual vocabulary with which social-movement analysts might meaningfully express their observations regarding the transformation of consciousness undergone by new actors.

Moreover, apart from the lack of precision in the use of the term "empowerment," it is worth noting that while movement participation may have enormous transformative potential, in practice, the outcomes of activism for participants are not always positive. For example, the process of "empowerment" that so many analysts celebrate is almost always confined to the realm of subjective feelings. To be sure, increased self-confidence and the development of organizational skills and practical knowledge (the elements that, for most commentators, constitute the "power" in "empowerment") undoubtedly represent substantial gains for a powerless person. Yet, rarely does empowerment involve the actual acquisition of economic or political power. What is more, with all the talk of empowerment, there is little recognition that people may not only become empowered with the sense of their own expanded capabilities but also "disempowered" and ultimately demobilized.

This kind of disempowerment may occur when a movement is repressed. But, significantly, it may also occur when participants grow discouraged and disillusioned by the dynamics of group participation, the behavior of their coactivists who rise to leadership positions, or the bossiness of foreign or middle- and upper-class cooperants—to cite but a few negative possibilities.

Oddly, many analysts of social movements who have themselves experienced periods of disillusionment in the course of their own lives of political struggle fail to acknowledge, or perhaps even to consider, that a neighborhood activist can get pretty fed up with her neighbors and that such movements decline not only in response to repression or co-optation but due to loss of enthusiasm for collective activity itself on the part of burned-out social activists. In reality, women may not only emerge from the isolation of the patriarchal family to work together with others in a soup kitchen. They may also retreat back into the private sphere of the family,

however oppressive, when relationships with coactivists become too difficult and complex to manage or even to bear.

A second claim made for social movements is that they win key concessions for their adherents. Ironically, this is the area of organizational
achievement that receives the least attention because it appears to be the
one that most embarrasses social-movement analysts (Hellman 1992,
55–56). In reality, new movements often do realize many of their concrete
goals, winning for their members the material goods and services they des-
perately need. But inasmuch as movements often obtain these concessions
only by compromising their independence vis-à-vis the state, the literature
on social movements devotes far less attention to the specifics of organizations' material victories than to their consciousness-raising or democratizing potential. Yet, although for theorists the extraction of output from the
state may be the least important achievement of a new movement, for the
participants themselves, this is often, if not usually, the central issue (Hellman 1994b). As Paul Haber (1990) points out in his study of the Committee for Popular Defense (CDP) in Durango, Mexico,

> The ability to deliver goods and extract concessions from the state, combined
> with inspirational ideological positions articulated by a competent and ideally
> charismatic leadership, is the winning combination for most, if not all, Mexi-
> can [urban popular movements]. Many CDP members are first or second gen-
> eration immigrants from rural Durango and most have very low incomes and
> little or no formal education. Within the political culture of the CDP, as is true
> elsewhere in low-income urban barrios throughout Mexico . . . participation in
> decision-making is simply not valued as much as the demonstrated ability to
> extract governmental concessions and services. (234)

The third area of potential achievement for new social movements has
generated perhaps the greatest interest among analysts. Social movements
are often credited with having an important contribution to make to the
overall process of democratization in Latin America. In general, students of
the transition in South America have emphasized the movements' "democratizing impact on political culture and daily life," and much attention has
been focused on the way in which "grassroots democratic practices [are]
transferred into the realm of political institutions and the state" (Alvarez
and Escobar 1991, 1).

Women's movements, in particular, have been studied in relationship to
democratization. Writing in 1991, Jane Jaquette identified as the central
question of her collection "the role of women and of feminism in the transition from authoritarian to democratic politics" (1), and the place of
women in the defeat of authoritarian regimes in Argentina, Brazil, and
Chile has attracted a great deal of attention to this aspect of women's struggles. Another collection of writings on Latin American women that in fact

covers a much broader range of questions regarding women's political participation carries a publisher's advertisement on the back jacket that shouts in bold letters: "What are the 'new politics' of Latin America? How have women shaped the democratizing process?" (Radcliffe and Westwood 1993). This marketing approach on the part of Routledge is reiterated in the introductory chapter of many dissertations produced in the same period; the presumed connection between democratization and new social movements often serves as the justification for concern with the latter.

While it is relatively easy to demonstrate the relationship between new movements and the consolidation of democracy in some countries, elsewhere in Latin America the connection is not nearly so strong. Moreover, some analysts tend to conflate the internal dynamics of movements with their impact on the political system as a whole. There is, in fact, an important distinction to be drawn between a movement's internal practices (which may or may not be more open, less hierarchical, and more participatory than those of traditional political formations) and its capacity to push the whole political system in that direction. As Renato Boschi (1984) notes, while the movements may "allow for some degree of internal democracy at some point of their trajectory . . . democratization of social relations does not necessarily entail democratization at the institutional level of politics" (8).

A good illustration of this point can be found in the case of Uruguay. Writing on new movements there, Eduardo Canel (1992) found that the grassroots groups that arose during the eleven years of military dictatorship went into decline shortly after the return to democracy in 1984. Although many observers thought of the movements as "embryos of new more democratic social practices, with the potential to transform power relations in daily life" and assumed that they would "play a central role in the process of constructing a . . . qualitatively more democratic society," in fact, the restoration of civilian rule in Uruguay was marked by the return of the most traditional forms of party-based political activity. "In this context," writes Canel (1992), "grass-roots activities declined and many of the new organizations disappeared or were assimilated into more traditional ones. The hope of establishing a new way of doing politics did not materialize and the country missed a good opportunity to develop a more open and democratic political system" (276–77).

In Mexico, social movements have contributed to the push for democracy. Nonetheless, many Mexican movements retain their tendency to fall squarely into the logic of clientelism that has always guided the political strategies and tactics not only of the official party organizations but of Mexican opposition movements as well. These movements are, in fact, deeply enmeshed in clientelistic patterns from which they escape only very rarely. At times, the emergence of a new movement has challenged the old PRI-linked networks based on local strongmen. But often such a movement undermines the control of the caciques only by replacing the old networks with alternative channels that, generally speaking, are also clientelistic in their mode of operation.

Because social movements do not arise in a vacuum and are always, to some degree, products of the political context in which they grow, it may be disappointing, but it is not surprising, that social movements do not manage to democratize the system in every case. Notwithstanding our wishes to the contrary, popular movements do not necessarily bring about an opening of the political system. As Boschi (1984) has noted in the case of Brazilian neighborhood movements, the striking thing is not how radical is the influence of new social movements but rather "how little change they bring about in existing institutional formats" (9).

Thus, not only do we find that movements may not succeed in democratizing the system, but, as I have noted, often their internal structures are not particularly democratic. Instead, their internal organization and practices may reflect the broader political and social culture in which they are embedded. For example, women and illiterate peasants often form the base of social movements in which leadership is exercised by men or middle-class intellectuals, and decision making may even reside in the hands of foreign cooperants. In sum, traditional power differentials often characterize the internal workings of popular movements.

In short, the study of specific movements suggests that there is nothing deterministic about the relationship of new movements to the process of democratization. A movement's own practices may be more open and inclusionary, although often they are not (Hellman 1994b, 133–35). But even when a movement is more participatory and democratic in its internal structures, it does not necessarily change the system simply by making demands upon it.

THE FUTURE OF NEW MOVEMENTS

If the new movements do not, in all cases, function to democratize the system as a whole, this is not to say that they have no positive role to perform. The greatest potential of the movements may well lie in the alliances that many analysts and movement activists have previously identified as a threat to movement survival (Hellman 1992, 53–54).

The preoccupation with the difference between movements and parties, a preoccupation that has sometimes troubled theorists more than activists, has come in the new millennium to seem an exaggerated concern. Social movements may not be able to transform the political system as a whole as some analysts had hoped. However, in key historical moments, they can

link up with other formations—with other movements and even progressive partisan forces, such as the Workers Party in Brazil or the Party of the
Democratic Revolution in Mexico. Moreover, this kind of alliance may be
forged in ways that strengthen both the party and the movement.

That social movements can, with relative ease, establish alliances among
themselves has been demonstrated by the growth of *coordinadoras*, that is,
coordinating committees and other umbrella organizations that allow a
wide assortment of movements to join forces around common goals. That
they can do this in ways that permit individual movements to retain their
distinctive identity has also been demonstrated in practice. Even groups
that begin with very antiorganizational values frequently end up establishing linkages among themselves for their mutual benefit and protection.

In a period like the present, it seems reasonable to predict that alliance
strategies may well gain momentum. Distinctions between class-based organizations and social movements have been a focus of this chapter. It is
precisely these differences that are increasingly likely to be set aside as social movements of all descriptions form links with independent trade
unions and progressive political parties to defend their achievements of the
past and to push forward, however haltingly, with the project of building
social justice.

NOTES

The author of this chapter has placed some suggested resources that you may
wish to consult on the book's website at http://www.rowmanlittlefield.com/isbn/
0742555240.

I would like to thank Steve Hellman and Barry Carr for comments on the second
draft.

1. To borrow the term coined by Eric Hobsbawm (1959), who, in this work on
precapitalist society, describes as "prepolitical" those "who have not yet found, or
only begun to find, a specific language in which to express their aspirations about
the world. Though their movements are thus in many respects blind and groping,
by the standards of modern ones, they are neither unimportant nor marginal" (2).

2. An extended version of this argument can be found in the thirtieth-anniversary
issue of the *NACLA Report on the Americas* (see Hellman 1997).

3. It is not surprising that it should be European observers of Latin American social movements who have placed the strongest emphasis on differentiating the new
social movements from workers' struggles (Slater 1985; Evers 1985; Laclau and
Mouffe 1985). In Europe, the displacement of the organized industrial working
class as the central protagonist in struggle and its replacement by a variety of new
social actors reflect the changing composition of the workforce and the altered social structure of Western European societies (see Berger 1978; Offe 1985). However,
in Latin America, notwithstanding the rhetoric of some Marxist parties and tenden-

cies, the organized working class has never been so dominant a force as to hegemonize popular struggles, although in particular geographical locations (such as the industrial belt around São Paulo) or during given historical moments (such as the rise of Peronism in Argentina), the organized working class could be said to have played a central role, if not actually to have served as the "vanguard" of struggle. Thus, it may be that the issue of differentiating class-based from "popular" struggles is not so urgent in Latin America as it may have become for analysts of Western European movements.

4. This said, historians of women's movements in Latin America can point to intellectual and social precursors for the feminism that has emerged since the 1970s, and with respect to environmentalism, Alan Knight (1990) writes, "A formally ecological movement is a new phenomenon in Mexico, although protests against ecological abuses (which are not easy to distinguish from movements of economic self-defense) are far from new. Recent campaigns . . . bear comparison with earlier twentieth-century protests against the devastation wrought by the oil companies—notably the Dos Bocas blowout (1908) and the 1910 gusher, Potrero del Llano No. 4" (101).

REFERENCES

Almond, Gabriel A., and Sidney Verba. 1965. *The Civic Culture*. Boston: Little, Brown.

Alvarez, Sonia E., and Arturo Escobar 1991. "New Social Movements in Latin America: Identity, Strategy, and Democracy." Panel proposal made to the Latin American Studies Association Meetings, Washington, DC.

Berger, Suzanne. 1979. "Politics and Antipolitics in Western Europe in the Seventies." *Daedalus* 108:27–50.

Boschi, Renato. 1984. "On Social Movements and Democratization: Theoretical Issues." *Stanford-Berkeley Occasional Papers in Latin American Studies* 9 (Spring): 1–17.

Calderón, Fernando, Alejandro Piscitelli, and José Luis Reyna. 1992. "Social Movements: Actors, Theories, Expectations." In *New Social Movements in Latin America: Identity, Strategy, and Democracy*, ed. Arturo Escobar and Sonia E. Alvarez, 19–36. Boulder, CO: Westview Press.

Canel, Eduardo. 1992. "Democratization and the Decline of Urban Social Movements in Uruguay: A Political-Institutional Account." In *New Social Movements in Latin America: Identity, Strategy, and Democracy*, ed. Arturo Escobar and Sonia E. Alvarez, 276–90. Boulder, CO: Westview Press.

Carrillo, Teresa. 1990. "Women and Independent Unionism in the Garment Industry." In *Popular Movements and Political Change in Mexico*, ed. Joe Foweraker and Ann L. Craig, 213–33. Boulder, CO: Lynne Rienner Publishers.

Craske, Nikki. 1993. "Women's Political Participation in Colonias Populares in Guadalajara, Mexico." In *Viva: Women and Popular Protest in Latin America*, ed. Sarah A. Radcliffe and Sallie Westwood, 112–35. London: Routledge.

Escobar, Arturo, and Sonia E. Alvarez, eds. 1992. *New Social Movements in Latin America: Identity, Strategy, and Democracy*. Boulder, CO: Westview Press.

Evers, Tilman. 1985. "Identity: The Hidden Side of New Social Movements in Latin America." In *New Social Movements and the State in Latin America*, ed. David Slater, 43–72. Amsterdam: CEDLA.

Feijoó, María del Carmen. 1991. "The Challenge of Constructing Civilian Peace: Women and Democracy in Argentina." In *The Women's Movement in Latin America: Feminism and the Transition to Democracy*, ed. Jane S. Jaquette, 72–94. Boulder, CO: Westview Press.

Foweraker, Joe. 1990. "Popular Movements and Political Change in Mexico." In *Popular Movements and Political Change in Mexico*, ed. Joe Foweraker and Ann L. Craig, 3–20. Boulder, CO: Lynne Rienner Publishers.

Frank, Andre Gunder, and Marta Fuentes. 1989. "Ten Theses on Social Movements." *World Development* 17, no. 2: 179–89.

Haber, Paul Lawrence. 1990. "Cárdenas, Salinas y Los movimientos populares urbanos en México: El caso del Comité de Defensa Popular, General Francisco Villa de Durango." In *Movimientos sociales en México*, ed. Sergio Zermeño and Aurelio Cuevas, 221–52. México, DF: Universidad Nacional Autonoma de México.

Hellman, Judith Adler. 1992. "The Study of New Social Movements in Latin America and the Question of Autonomy." In *New Social Movements in Latin America: Identity, Strategy, and Democracy*, ed. Arturo Escobar and Sonia E. Alvarez, 52–61. Boulder, CO: Westview Press.

———. 1994a. *Mexican Lives*. New York: The New Press.

———. 1994b. "Mexican Popular Movements, Clientelism, and the Process of Democratization." *Latin American Perspectives* 21, no. 2 (Spring): 124–42.

———. 1997. "Social Movements: Revolution, Reform and Reaction." *NACLA Report on the Americas* 30, no. 6 (May/June): 13–18.

———. 1999. "Real and Virtual Chiapas: Magic Realism and the Left." In *Socialist Register, 2000*, ed. Leo Panitch and Colin Leys, 156–80. London: Merlin Press.

Hobsbawm, Eric. 1959. *Primitive Rebels*. New York: W. W. Norton.

Jaquette, Jane S., ed. 1991. *The Women's Movement in Latin America: Feminism and the Transition to Democracy*. Boulder, CO: Westview Press.

Knight, Alan. 1990. "Historical Continuities in Social Movements." In *Popular Movements and Political Change in Mexico*, ed. Joe Foweraker and Ann L. Craig, 78–102. Boulder, CO: Lynne Rienner Publishers.

Kowarick, Lucio. 1985. "The Pathways to Encounter: Reflections on the Social Struggle in São Paulo." In *New Social Movements and the State in Latin America*, ed. David Slater, 73–93. Amsterdam: CEDLA.

Laclau, Ernesto, and Chantal Mouffe. 1985. *Hegemony and Socialist Strategy: Toward a Radical Democratic Politics*. London: Verso Books.

Levine, Daniel H., and Scott Mainwaring. 2001. "Religion and Popular Protest in Latin America: Contrasting Experiences." In *Power and Popular Protest: Latin American Social Movements*, ed. Susan Eckstein, 203–40. Berkeley: University of California Press.

Macdonald, Laura. 1995. "A Mixed Blessing: The NGO Boom in Latin America." *NACLA Report on the Americas* 28, no. 5 (March/April): 30–35.

Meyer, Jean. 1973–1974. *La Cristiada*. 3 vols. México, DF: Siglo Veintiuno Editores.

Miliband, Ralph. 1977. *Marxism and Politics*. Oxford: Oxford University Press.

Moreira Alves, Maria Helena. 1984. "Grassroots Organizations, Trade Unions and the Church: A Challenge to the Controlled Abertura in Brazil." *Latin American Perspectives* 11, no. 1 (Winter): 73–102.

Nash, June. 2001. "Cultural Resistance and Class Consciousness in Bolivian Tin-Mining Communities." In *Power and Popular Protest: Latin American Social Movements*, ed. Susan Eckstein, 182–202. Berkeley: University of California Press.

North, Liisa L., and John D. Cameron, eds. 2003. *Rural Progress, Rural Decay: Neoliberal Adjustment Policies and Local Initiatives.* Bloomfield, CT: Kumerian Press.

Offe, Claus. 1985. "New Social Movements: Challenging the Boundaries of Institutional Politics." *Social Research* 52, no. 4 (Winter): 817–68.

Perelli, Carina. 1991. "Putting Conservatism to Good Use: Women and Unorthodox Politics in Uruguay, from Breakdown to Transition." In *The Women's Movement in Latin America: Feminism and the Transition to Democracy*, ed. Jane S. Jaquette, 95–113. Boulder, CO: Westview Press.

Radcliffe, Sarah A., and Sallie Westwood, eds. 1993. *Viva: Women and Popular Protest in Latin America.* London: Routledge.

Scherer-Warren, Ilse. 1987. "O carater dos novos movimentos socais." In *Uma revolucão no cotidiano? Os novos movimentos socais na América do Sul*, ed. Ilse Scherer-Warren and Paulo J. Krischke, 35–53. São Paulo: Editora Brasiliense.

Schirmer, Jennifer. 1993. "The Seeking of Truth and the Gendering of Consciousness: The Comadres of El Salvador and the Conavigua Widows of Guatemala." In *Viva: Women and Popular Protest in Latin America*, ed. Sarah A. Radcliffe and Sallie Westwood, 30–64. London: Routledge.

Slater, David. 1985. "Social Movements and a Recasting of the Political." In *New Social Movements and the State in Latin America*, ed. David Slater, 1–25. Amsterdam: CEDLA.

Tamayo, Jaime. 1990. "Neoliberalism Encounters Neocardenism." In *Popular Movements and Political Change in Mexico*, ed. Joe Foweraker and Ann L. Craig, 121–36. Boulder, CO: Lynne Rienner Publishers.

Tarrow, Sidney. 1994. *Power in Movement: Collective Action, Social Movements and Politics.* New York: Cambridge University Press.

Tilly, Charles. 1978. *From Mobilization to Revolution.* Englewood Cliffs, NJ: Prentice Hall.

7

Women in the Social, Political, and Economic Transformation of Latin America and the Caribbean

Francesca Miller

One of the most striking phenomena of the past three decades is the extent to which women are effectively articulating the central concerns of contemporary life: access to housing, employment, and health care; freedom from violence; full citizenship for all people; and preservation of the environment. Historically, women activists in Latin America, while insisting on the validity and specificity of the female experience, have posited their work as part of the search for social, economic, and political justice for all people. This chapter focuses on the history of women's activism as influenced by, and exerting influence on, contemporary social movements. Theoretical insights emerge from the comparison of Latin American women's movements as they developed in specific historical contexts; considerations of class, generational change, and ethnicity, as well as gender, inform the analysis.

In the early twenty-first century, a focus on women in Latin America reveals the profound changes that have occurred in the region since the late 1970s. Far more women now live in urban areas—many in and around megacities such as São Paulo, Buenos Aires, and Mexico City, D.F.—than live in rural regions. Between 1970 and 2006, the number of women employed in the formal economy rose by 83 percent in all regions of Latin America except the Caribbean, where the wages of women are often sustaining, transmitted from transnational female emigrants to family at home. Access to education for girls has risen steadily since 1950. In Mexico and Brazil, the number of children a woman will bear in her lifetime has dropped by half; in Cuba, Venezuela, Uruguay, and Costa Rica, birth rates are comparable to those in southern Europe. Additionally, whereas in 1970 most Latin American women could be described as culturally Catholic, church attendance has dropped precipitously. Pentacostalism and protestant evangelicism have attracted women for reasons discussed below, but contemporary women's lives are imbued with a secular worldview that is reinforced by global communications, internal and international migration, and increased personal autonomy and mobility.

Such a profile masks deep regional variations both within nations and from one country to another. With 189 million people, Brazil is the largest and most populous of the Latin American nations. If statistics are taken from Brazil's industrialized Central South, female education and employment levels are comparable to those of Colombia, Mexico, Venezuela, and Chile. But if the calculations are derived from the country's North and Northeast, they resemble those of Peru and Ecuador, where infant mortality and fertility rates are the highest in South America.

More importantly, the pattern of greater female involvement in the formal labor force, a pattern driven at least in part by deteriorating standards of living brought about by crippling inflation and neoliberal responses to the international debt pressures of the 1980s and 1990s, exists simultaneously with the growth in concrete numbers of women whose economic status is precarious in the extreme. Since the 1990s, an estimated 130 million women and children, living primarily in the urban periphery—*pueblos jóvenes, favelas, barrios pobres*—have been attempting to eke out a daily living in the informal economy as petty vendors, laundresses, and part-time domestics.

The present situation raises the following central questions: What do the ongoing changes, many of which are linked to the internationalization of the economy, portend for women and their families? Does the entry of women into the paid labor force in unprecedented numbers indicate not the promise of greater economic and personal independence for women but the "atomization of the labor force" and "deteriorating conditions" (Fernández-Kelly 1993)? Recent statistics bear out this darker view: since 2005, more women are in wage-earning jobs, but men are being forced out of stable, salaried work. The female workforce is seen as cheaper, pliable, and transient. Such a picture does not bode well for the family and places even harsher burdens on the female worker (Hite and Viterna 2005).

What role are Latin American women playing in trying to shape the future? The issues women are identifying as central to their present and future circumstances are visible in the focus of the hundreds of women's organizations—local, national, transnational—that are a hallmark of contemporary Latin America. The history of these organizing efforts offers us an understanding of their potential for the future.

A SENSE OF PLACE

Every observer of Latin America soon learns that the term "Latin America" serves more to obscure than to illuminate an understanding of the thirty-odd countries and dozen territories that lie between the Rio Grande in the north and Tierra del Fuego in the south. Similarly, it is soon discovered that there is no single type of Latin American woman. Factors of time and place, class, race, ethnicity, age, sexual identity, and marital status, among others, are important considerations, whether these women are Mexican, Brazilian, Haitian, or Guyanese and who would not necessarily be able to speak to one another as their respective national tongues are Spanish, Portuguese, French, and English. Moreover, it is not unlikely that a Guatemalan woman's first language might be Maya or Quiché, not Spanish, that a woman of the Andes might speak only Quechua or a woman of the Amazon, a Tupí dialect.

The classical understanding of the peopling of the Americas is built on the deeply sexual metaphor of the "Contact Period," when seafaring European men encountered the indigenous women of Middle, Central, and South America and produced "a new race." The story of Malinche/Malintzin (1504?–1538), a Tabascan woman given as tribute to the conquistador Hernán Cortés and who, through her knowledge of languages, subsequently played a pivotal role in the Spanish overthrow of the Aztec regime in central Mexico, became a founding myth of modern Mexico. But this paradigm ignores the presence of French, Spanish, and Portuguese women who began to arrive as early as 1498 and leaves out women, both free and slave, who came to the Americas from sub-Saharan Africa.

Additionally, since the late nineteenth century, the large Latin American nations have received successive waves of immigrants from Europe and Asia. Spanish, Portuguese, Italian, and German immigrants settled in significant numbers in Mexico, Argentina, Uruguay, Chile, and southern Brazil. Brazil has the largest number of citizens of Japanese descent of any nation other than the United States or Japan itself. Koreans, Chinese, and Southeast Asians have emigrated to Brazil and other Latin American nations. In the past forty years, immigrants from India, Pakistan, Syria, Lebanon, Iran, and Iraq have made their way to South America. Though in some cases the first immigrant generation settled in rural areas, the daughters and granddaughters of the European, Asian, and Middle Eastern immigrants live in the cities and should be understood as Latin American women.

Recent research challenges many long-held preconceptions about the roles women played in colonial society (Lavrin 1989; Seed 1988). Distinctions of class, racial heritage, and ethnicity were sharply reinforced by an economy that rested on the institution of forced labor. Prior to the Contact

Period, female roles in indigenous societies varied as widely as did the societies themselves: women were priestesses, physicians, agricultural laborers, artisans, market vendors, prostitutes, and slaves. The degree to which colonization disrupted the customs of the indigenous peoples depended on the extent of contact.

Family, church, and state were the central institutions that governed colonial life, especially for Iberian and mestiza women, though the Catholic Church touched all sectors of society through conversion and in the rituals of baptism, confirmation, marriage, and burial. The church determined social mores and reinforced the structures that propertied families placed on their daughters, for whom marriage or a religious vocation were the respectable choices. The image of the cloistered upper-class Iberian woman, however, must be balanced against examples of the upper-class woman who actively participated in the economy by running large estates and overseeing complex familial business affairs. Similarly, the diverse experiences of poor women should not be subsumed under blanket assumptions that differentiate their lives from that of their male counterparts only by their biological functions.

Women of African descent were present in every region of the Americas. In Brazil, where slavery was not finally abolished until 1888, female slaves were found in larger concentrations in urban areas, working in households or earning money for their owners as street vendors, wet nurses, craftswomen, or prostitutes. To the extent that their particular situations enabled them to do so, they kept alive their religious and cultural practices and deeply influenced the formative national cultures in Brazil, the Caribbean, Colombia, and Venezuela.

One of the best-known women of the colonial era is Sor Juana Inés de la Cruz (1648–1695), who is considered one of the great lyric poets ever to write in Spanish. Because of her status as a great woman, an exception, Sor Juana cannot be used as an example of women in colonial Latin America. But perhaps the point is that no woman can be, whether she is a domestic slave of Afro-Brazilian heritage in Salvador, Brazil; an Aymará woman of the Bolivian Andes whose male kin were taken by the Spanish to work the silver mines; the mestiza wife of a cattle rancher in northern Mexico; or the illegitimate daughter of a Creole mother, as was Sor Juana, born Juana Ramirez de Azbaje. It is with a sense of this rich and diverse heritage that the contemporary history of Latin American women must be approached.

Historically, the voices of women activists in Latin America have articulated ideas that have driven forward a politics of inclusion. This is traceable in the nineteenth-century push for the education of women, which, in the twentieth century, was articulated as the drive for universal education. It is visible in the history of universal suffrage, despite the ofttimes limited intentions of the early woman suffragists and their male allies.

The following metaphor invoked by a Chilean woman at the IV Encuentro Feminista Latinoamericano y del Caribe (Fourth Feminist Encounter of Latin America and the Caribbean), which convened in Taxco, Mexico, October 19–25, 1987, is apt:

> I think that, from the most radical feminism, deeply transformative ideas have emerged. The early feminists gave the first kick to the soccer ball, the ball is now circulating through the field and is not always controlled by the players themselves and the score is sometimes scored by people who haven't been participating, but who suddenly succeed in passing a law. On the one hand, the feminist movement appears to be marginal, but on the other, it is obvious that it has permeated everything.

WOMEN AND NATIONAL FORMATION

The issue of full citizenship for women and access to education for girls was raised in the immediate aftermath of the Wars of Independence (1790–1823). A 1924 petition presented to the government of Zacatecas, Mexico, states, "Women also wish to have the title of citizen . . . to see themselves counted in the census as *una ciudadana.*" Women patriots were vital to the success of the independence movements. The histories of these women were used at the time to rouse patriotic fervor. In later years, Latin American women pointed to the patriotism of their precursors in the effort to claim their own right to civil, political, and economic independence.

A central arena for the debate of women's role in the new nations took place around the issue of education. In the struggle between secular and liberal values and religious corporatist politics that marked the nineteenth century, the question of who would educate young women was played out among Catholic female teaching orders, independent dames' schools, and the new public schools, which were established to impart a modicum of learning, along with household skills, to poor young women.

Women who founded girls' schools were among the first voices calling for women's rights in Latin America. The periodical or political journal first appeared as a central forum for the public debate of women's issues in Latin America in the early nineteenth century. Argentine writer Juana Manuela Gorriti founded *La Alborada del Plata* (1850), which engaged in the intense international debate surrounding women's role in the modern state. Juana Manso, while in exile from Argentina in Brazil, founded *O Jornal de Senhoras*, which dealt primarily with the discussion of female education and politics. Similar journals appeared in Mexico (*La Semana de las Señoritas Mejicanas*, 1851–1852), Cuba (*Album Cubano de lo Bueno y lo Bello*, founded in 1860 by Gertrudis Gomez de Avellaneda), Peru and Bolivia (*El Album*,

1860s), and elsewhere (Stoner 1989). The linkage of the ideas of independence, the abolition of slavery, and the drive for political and economic modernity with full citizenship for women permeates the writings of these early feminists.

By the latter half of the nineteenth century, arguments for women's equality were cast in terms of progressivism and the hope for a better life in the New World. The first issue of *O Sexo Feminino*, edited by Francisco Motta Diniz, was "dedicated to the emancipation of women" and appeared in Campanha, Minas Gerais, Brazil, on September 7, 1873. September 7 commemorates Brazil's independence day; the use of national patriotic symbols by Latin American women activists has a long history. *O Sexo Feminino* declared, "It will be seen that America will give the cry of independence for women, showing the Old World what it means to be civilized, that women are as apt for education as young men." *La Mujer*, published in Chile in the 1890s, was committed to the idea that "the woman is the basis for universal progress."

Women and the Process of Modernization

The emergence of women novelists, poets, journalists, and political activists and the development of a shared feminist consciousness in Latin America are directly linked to trends that combined to produce a process of modernization in certain nations. Women speaking out on behalf of women found their voice—and their audience—in Argentina, Uruguay, Chile, and Brazil, states that received thousands of European immigrants, whose urban centers became true cities, and where social and political reform movements were mounted, as well as in Mexico and Cuba, where major social upheavals took place. Women workers were at the heart of the great Rio Blanco textile strike of 1907, and schoolteachers and factory workers played a crucial role in the politics that led to the Mexican Revolution of 1910.

The turn of the twentieth century also marked the entry of women into the paid workforce in significant numbers. Women factory workers and piece workers, drawn from the immigrant and rural-to-urban migrant peasant population, were the primary laborers in the textile, food-processing, and tobacco industries. They faced great difficulties in organizing to improve their working conditions. The hostility of employers and officials, little support from their male cohorts, long working hours, and family demands left scant energy for union work. The call of São Paulo seamstresses Tecla Fabbri, Teres Cari, and Maria Lopes in the Brazilian anarchist newspaper *Terra Livre* (July 29, 1906) reflects these frustrations: "Comrades! Shake off the apathy that dominates you. In this city where we are so exploited, resolve to make a new attempt to defend us all!"

Women in the white-collar urban workforce were predominantly young single women employed as clerks and in service-related jobs in government and commerce. The Liga de Empleadas Católicas (League of Catholic Women Employees), established in the 1920s by the Catholic Church with branches throughout Latin America, was founded to respond to the needs of young working women while keeping them within the Catholic fold. These women were part of the formative urban middle and working classes in Santiago, Mexico City, Havana, Caracas, Rio de Janeiro, São Paulo, Montevideo, and Buenos Aires. The Argentine writer Alfonsina Storni (1892–1938) addressed the concerns of this new population in her articles in the newspaper *La Nación*. Working women and their occupations, the relationship of women to national and cultural tradition, and the role of the Catholic Church in women's lives were frequent themes not only in her work but also throughout the contemporary press (Kirkpatrick 1990).

Though women were entering new fields in urban areas, in the 1920s the great majority of women were rural. In Andean America, Paraguay, parts of Brazil, southern Mexico, Guatemala, and Venezuela, that population was predominantly indigenous. Rural women's work was immensely varied: women carried out ancient mining-related tasks in Potosí; worked communal agricultural plots and ran trade networks in the Peruvian sierra; hulled and sorted spices in the Caribbean; worked the sugar, rubber, and banana plantations of Brazil, Haiti, and Cuba; harvested the wheat and grapes of Chile and Argentina; and did domestic labor at the big house on the ranch, *finca*, and *hacienda*. And everywhere women prepared daily meals, cared for children, cleaned, and washed clothes for their own households in addition to whatever other work they might perform.

Apparent in the examination of women's occupations in the early twentieth century is the emergence of two antithetical patterns that have persisted and intensified over time. One is the new presence of the middle-sector workingwoman: skilled and unskilled factory workers, teachers, government employees, writers, and sales clerks. Although there are great differences in the social and economic status of these women, their pay and relative job security differentiate them as a group from women whose work lies in the unregulated, informal sector of the economy, which includes female domestics, market women, vendors, laundresses, prostitutes, and nearly all women working in rural areas.

Female schoolteachers formed the nucleus of the first women's groups to articulate what may be defined as a feminist critique of society, that is, to protest the pervasive inequality of the sexes in legal status, rights over children, marriage, and access to education and political and economic power. The teachers represented a new group in Latin American society, the educated middle sector, which included skilled workers, clerks, and government employees, as well as educators. They were in touch with one another through their institutions of learning and through professional associations, forums in which they could share their common experiences. The critical change was that their activities were collective, not individual.

In Mexico in 1870, the poet and educator Rita Cetina Gutierrez, Cristina Farfan de Garcia Montero, and several primary school teachers formed La Siempreviva, a female society dedicated to overcoming women's unequal status in society and to combating social problems by improving hygiene and educating mothers in nutrition and child care. In their decision to found a publication to espouse their ideas and to open schools to train a new generation, the members of La Siempreviva employed tactics used by the earlier advocates of women's rights.

In South America, a collective female critique of discriminatory practices based on gender was visible at a series of scientific congresses held between 1898 and 1909. Men and women delegates presented papers on health care, hygiene, mothers' welfare, and scientific research. In conference discussions, the divisive issue proved to be female education: should women have equal access or be educated only in "suitable" professions, such as primary school teaching? The women delegates were indignant that the debate should be cast in these terms and broadened the discussion into a wide-ranging attack on the pervasive inequality of the sexes within their societies (Miller 1992).

In the next decades, women called numerous conferences to discuss these issues. On May 10, 1910, the date of the centennial celebration of Argentine independence, the first Congreso Femenino Internacional (International Congress of Women) convened in Buenos Aires with more than two hundred women from Argentina, Uruguay, Peru, Paraguay, and Chile in attendance. The congress was organized by the Consejo Nacional de Mujeres (National Council of Women) and presided over by Cecilia Grierson. Sponsoring groups included the Asociación Nacional del Profesorado (National Association of Professors), the Asociación Nacional Argentina Contra la Trata de Blancas (National Argentine Association against the White Slave Trade), the Centro Socialista Femenino (Socialist Women's Center), Escuela Normal de Maestras de Tucumán (Teacher's Normal School of Tucumán), Grupo Femenino Unión y Labor (Women's Union and Labor Group), Liga Nacional de Mujeres Librepensadores (National League of Free-Thinking Women), and many more.

The wide differences in the political orientation of the women at the Congreso Femenino Internacional reflected the great political diversity present in Buenos Aires, Montevideo, São Paulo, Santiago, and Lima in that period. Many of the reformist women belonged to the Socialist Party; others rejected the Socialist platform as too concerned with class and labor and aligned themselves with the anarchists, whose platform called for a complete reform of the bourgeois household. The loyalties of others lay with the

Argentine Radical Party, a more conventional form of political opposition. Topics addressed ranged from international law, particularly as it related to the rights of married women to retain their citizenship, to health care, the problems of the married workingwoman, and equal pay for equal work. A resolution commending the government of Uruguay for the enactment of a bill of divorce in 1907, the first in Latin America, was also passed.

Universal suffrage was part of the Socialist Party platform and was debated at women's congresses in Latin America during the first half of the twentieth century. In 1916, two feminist congresses were convened in Mexico to discuss the role of women in postrevolutionary Mexico and to attempt to influence the Mexican Constitutional Convention then meeting in Queretaro. On its promulgation in 1917, the Mexican Constitution was hailed as the most advanced social and political document of its day. Political rights, including the right to vote, were granted "to all Mexican citizens." Women, however, were excluded from the category of citizen (Soto 1979).

The history of feminism in Peru offers an example of the women's movement in a country where a strong middle class did not develop in the early twentieth century and secularization of schools did not occur. Maria Jesús Alvarado Rivera, who studied at the private school for girls formed by the feminist thinker and author Elvira García y García, founded Evolución Femenina in 1914 to discuss "the woman question." The core group of members had all attended the Congreso Femenino Internacional in 1910. The conservatism and class bias of the Peruvian political milieu is apparent in the women's twelve-year campaign not for access to government positions but for the right of women to be appointed as directors of the powerful private charitable organization, Sociedades de Beneficencia Pública (Societies for Public Beneficence).

In the 1920s and 1930s, a number of national and international women's conferences met to discuss civil, legal, and educational reform, suffrage, and the rights of working women. In 1922, with the example of U.S. women's successful drive for suffrage (1920) and in the wake of the war to "make the world safe for democracy," two thousand women from throughout the hemisphere convened in Baltimore and formed the Pan-American Association for the Advancement of Women. Veterans of the scientific congresses, such as Amanda Labarca of Chile and Flora de Oliveira Lima of Brazil, were among the Latin American delegates, as were a rising generation of feminist leaders that included Elena Torres, who was at that time designing the radical rural literacy program in postrevolutionary Mexico; Sara Casal de Quiroz of Costa Rica; and Bertha Lutz, founder of the Liga para Emancipação Intelectual Feminina (League for the Intellectual Emancipation of Women) in Rio de Janeiro (1920). Lutz's vision of feminism was that "in Brazil, the true leaders of feminism are the young women who work in industry, in commerce, in teaching" (Hahner 1991).

In the 1920s, Cuban women were heavily involved in the effort to establish democracy and social equality in their newly independent nation. In 1923, the Club Femenino de Cuba (Women's Club of Cuba), which was founded in 1917, formed the Federación Nacional de Asociaciones Femeninas (National Federation of Women's Associations), an umbrella group of thirty-one women's organizations, which planned the First National Women's Congress in Havana on April 1–7, 1923. Government officials were invited to the event in an effort to influence national reform policy. A second women's congress met in Havana in 1925 to call for (1) social equality between men and women, (2) child protection, (3) equal pay for equal work, (4) equality for illegitimate children, (5) the elimination of prostitution, and (6) the prohibition of the unequal treatment of women.

In Mexico, in July 1925, Sofia Villa de Buentello organized the Congreso de Mujeres de la Raza (Congress of Women of the Race), where the class and ideological splits that characterized the women's movement in the hemisphere in the following decades first appeared. Irreconcilable differences emerged between the Socialists, who insisted on the economic basis of women's problems, and the conservatives and moderates, who believed female inequality to be rooted in social and moral conditions.

In Argentina, feminists Alicia Moreau de Justo and Elvira Rawson joined with other reformist groups, including the conservative Catholic women's trades' union, to support passage of protective legislation for women industrial workers in 1924. Encouraged by this success, the National Feminist Union and the Women's Rights Association formed a coalition to push a comprehensive reform of the civil code through the Argentine congress in 1926; the reform granted married women equal civil rights with adult men, mothers parental rights over their children, and married women the right to enter professions, make contracts, and dispose of their earnings without spousal permission. In order to maintain the coalition, the Argentine National Women's Council agreed not to connect the reform to the divisive issue of women's suffrage.

In 1928, Cuban women's associations hosted women from all over the hemisphere who came to Havana as unofficial delegates to the Sixth International Conference of American States. By the end of the conference, the women had presented an equal rights treaty for the consideration of the governments of the hemisphere and successfully lobbied for the creation of an officially designated body, the Comisión Interamericana de Mujeres (Inter-American Women's Commission, or CIM), which was charged with the investigation of the legal status of women in the twenty-one member states. The use of the international forum for the discussion of women's issues proved particularly efficacious for those Latin American women who found it difficult to create sympathetic political spaces in their home countries.

Bringing international attention to an issue was a political strategy that Latin American feminists helped to pioneer, and it was one that would serve them well over time (Miller 1992).

The Change in the Legal and Civil Status of Women

Prior to the early twentieth century, the legal and civil status of Latin American women was governed by a complex body of legislation rooted in Iberian and ecclesiastical law; in practice, the legal status of most women was determined by their relationship to the male head of household. Indigenous women living within their traditional communities (Maya, Guajira, Aymará, Guaraní) were governed according to the customs of that community. Although elaborate sets of laws governing slave women had evolved by the nineteenth century, individual slave women had little recourse to these laws. In all cases, full citizenship was limited to men of property.

The history of female suffrage illustrates the politics involved in seeking redress through legal change. Effective universal suffrage, male or female, did not exist in any Latin American nation until after World War II. Property, type of employment, and residence requirements restricted the vote to certain sectors of the population. Moreover, irregular transitions in power and the suspension of civil liberties, including the right to hold elections, characterized the political scene in many Latin American nations during the period between 1929, when Ecuador became the first Latin American country to make female suffrage the law, and 1961, when women finally received the right to vote in Paraguay, the last country in Latin America to do so. Three periods of enactment may be distinguished:

1. Pre–World War II: Ecuador, 1929; Brazil and Uruguay, 1932; and Cuba, 1934
2. World War II: El Salvador, 1939; the Dominican Republic, 1942; Panama and Guatemala, 1945
3. Post–World War II: Venezuela and Argentina, 1947; Chile and Costa Rica, 1949; Haiti, 1950; Bolivia, 1952; Mexico, 1953; Honduras, Nicaragua, and Peru, 1955; Colombia, 1957; and Paraguay, 1961

The enactment of female suffrage should not be viewed, however, as a signpost that the women's program had triumphed in any one country. An examination of the first group of states to enact suffrage for women reveals that a variety of motives prompted the governments of Brazil, Uruguay, and Cuba to bring women into the national polity. The enactment of suffrage in these countries was the result of years of hard work and carefully planned campaigns by groups of women and their male allies, who were prepared to act when a political opening occurred. When the Brazilian Revolution of

1930 brought a reformist government to power, the Federação Brasileira pe-olo Progresso Feminino (Brazilian Federation for Women's Progress), led by Bertha Lutz and Carolota Pereira de Queiroz, presented the leaders with a platform of thirteen principles, which included female suffrage and equality before the law. In Cuba, numerous women's organizations, including the Alianza Naciónal Feminista, the Partido Naciónal Sufragista, and the Partido Democrático, were in the forefront of groups fighting for political reform and poised to demand the extension of the franchise to women when the new provisional constitution was drafted in 1934.

By way of contrast, in Ecuador, the political coalition that lobbied for the female vote was deeply conservative; it viewed women as loyal to the Catholic Church and politically malleable and believed the female vote would buttress the Conservatives' political base vis-à-vis a challenge from the Socialist Party. Ironically, many members of the political Left concurred with the Conservative Party's assessment of women's political acumen.

In Argentina, Eva Maria Duarte de Perón is often credited with the passage of female suffrage, but by 1947, Argentine women had waged a half-century-long campaign for the vote, suffrage laws had been passed in many other Western Hemisphere nations, and commitment to equal political rights was part of the United Nations Charter, to which Argentina was a signatory. What Eva Perón did was deliver the new female vote for the Peronist party.

Despite the passage of female suffrage laws in every Latin American country by 1961, language and literacy requirements continued to limit the right of women to vote. Rural women were especially affected by these requirements. In some countries, such as Guatemala, male suffrage was universal, but female suffrage was restricted to women who could read and speak Spanish. In Peru, Quechua-speaking Peruvians did not receive the franchise until 1980, a restriction that affected women who stayed in the sierra and maintained the home community, while the men migrated out of the area to work or fulfill military service.

Although female literacy remained comparatively low in most Latin American countries until the 1960s, by the late 1920s the number of women attending postelementary schools was nearly equal to that of male students in Cuba, Argentina, Uruguay, and Chile. New associations of women seeking broad-based reform, including women's suffrage, appeared in the 1930s. One was the Movimiento Pro-Emancipación de la Mujer Chilena (Movement for the Emancipation of Chilean Women) (1935–1955), established by Chilean university women (Antezana-Pernet 1994). Journals such as Nelly Merino Carvallo's *Mujeres de America* (1930–1935, Buenos Aires) appealed to an international audience and carried articles written by Bolivian, Paraguayan, Peruvian, and Uruguayan women, as well as Argentines; themes of peace and transnational sisterhood were among those discussed.

Women leaders also emerged within the political Left, although their politics as spokeswomen on behalf of their own sex often put them in dire conflict with their male comrades, as is illustrated by the career of Patricia Galvão, known as Pagú, who joined the Partido Comunista Brasileiro (Communist Party of Brazil, or PCB) in 1930. Pagú, like most radical women, felt scorn for bourgeois feminists, but she had a feminist vision of her own. In her book *Parque Industrial* (1933), she describes the sexual discrimination and duress experienced by female industrial workers. Pagú had the temerity to link sexism with racism in the Brazilian workforce and, thereby, so outraged the male leadership of the PCB that they ordered her book destroyed.

In Mexico, women loyal to the Revolutionary Party were deeply disappointed when the reformist president Lázaro Cárdenas (1934–1940) failed to fulfill his promise to reform the constitution to grant equal rights. At the Eighth International Conference of American States (Lima, 1938), the Mexican delegation to the CIM, led by Amalia Caballero Castillo de Ledón, successfully lobbied for the passage of the Declaration in Favor of Women's Rights. The resolution established the precedent for the incorporation of the phrase "the equal rights of men and women" into the draft of the United Nations Charter in Chapultepec, Mexico, in March 1945.

The democratic opening that followed World War II in many Latin American nations was brief. The Rio Treaty, signed in 1947 at the Inter-American Conference for the Maintenance of Continental Peace and Security in Petrópolis, Brazil, marked the beginning of the Cold War in the Western Hemisphere and served as the blueprint for the North American Treaty Organization (NATO). Less well known is the history of the Primer Congreso Interamericano de Mujeres (First International Congress of Women), convened that same year by women from every nation in the Western Hemisphere to protest the arming of the Americas and to plead that the Rio Conference turn its attention and resources not to a military buildup but to social and economic problems. The women's agenda did not prevail. The congress's resolutions on the peaceful use of atomic power, the dedication of financial resources to economic and social development rather than military buildup, and the denunciation of dictatorships in Honduras, the Dominican Republic, and Haiti were not included in the Rio Treaty.

The concerns voiced at this women's conference did persist, however. Some years later, they were at the heart of the Alliance for Progress and burned bright in the declarations for social justice made by liberation theologians, reformers, and revolutionaries in the 1960s and in the rising concern for human rights in the 1970s.

From 1959 to 1990, the triumphalism of the Cuban Revolution echoed throughout the hemisphere. Whether women supported revolution, favored reform, or were ardent counterrevolutionaries, hemispheric politics were deeply affected. Throughout the region, among those committed to change through revolution, women were most active in the urban movements. Young women made up almost half of the "soldiers" of the urban revolutionary Tupumaro movement in Montevideo, Uruguay. Among rural guerrilla groups, women were more apt to be seen as *compañeras*, companions of the male revolutionaries. "Tania" (Haydée Tamara Bunke Bider, 1937–1967) was an exception; she played a key role in Che Guevara's effort to establish a revolutionary front in Bolivia and became a martyr to a generation of young women after her death under fire.

Liberation theology, which emerged from the Latin American Catholic Church in the wake of Vatican II (1962) and the Medellín Conference (1968), did not address the specific needs of women. However, women of the church—laywomen, nuns, congregants, and participants in base communities—were deeply involved in the church's commitment to the poorest of the poor. Women were also active in defending the traditional ways of life they believed were threatened. In Brazil in 1964 and Chile in 1972, upper- and middle-class women organized street demonstrations to protest the erosion of homemakers' buying power, the specter of communism, the supposed threat to the family, and to call on the military "to restore order."

Taking their cue from the Cuban Revolution, women who joined the revolutionary Left in the 1960s adopted a class analysis that repudiated feminism as bourgeois and divisive to the cause. But it was from this generation of women activists, the most highly educated generation of women in Latin American history, that the feminists of the 1970s emerged, giving up not a whit of their commitment to social change but adding to it a new, gendered brand of social criticism. By 1985, this generation of Latin American feminists had developed a stinging critique of the traditional Left within their own communities, challenged the "First World" view of feminists from Europe and the United States, and contributed organizational models, political strategies, and a new understanding of grassroots social movements and global feminism.

In 1975, the Conferencia Mundial del Año Internacional de la Mujer (World Conference of the International Women's Year) convened in Mexico City to draw up the "world plan of action" for the United Nations Decade for Women (1976–1985). It was at sessions of the Tribune for Nongovernmental Organizations, held in parallel with the conference, that nongovernmental organizations and individuals could speak and where the Latin American women were especially influential. The majority of the six thousand women who attended the tribune came from North, Central, and South America; two thousand were from Mexico alone. The lines of debate that dominated the first half of the UN Decade emerged in the confrontation between Betty Friedan and Domitila Barrios de Chungara, who came to Mexico to represent the Housewives' Committee of Siglo XX, an organization of Bolivian tin miners' wives.

By 1977, women's movements emerging throughout Latin America included a feminist political critique. During the next decade, more than two hundred newsletters, feminist journals, and women's movement periodicals appeared, indicating the presence of women's groups in every region of the continent. One of the earliest and most notable was *fem*, published since 1976 by a collective editorship, Nueva Cultura Feminista, in Mexico City. The subjects addressed in the periodical provide a microcosm of the concerns of Mexican feminists over the years: abortion, work, sexuality, feminism, language, family, education, mothers and children, women writers, the history of women in Mexico, women in the struggle for social justice, and so on. *MUJER/fempress*, published monthly in Santiago, Chile, beginning in 1981, carried articles by correspondents from every country in the hemisphere.

In 1984, the Grupo de Estudios sobre la Condición de la Mujer en Uruguay (Study Group on the Condition of Women in Uruguay) began the publication of *La Cacerola* (the Casserole), explaining, "The name has many meanings, but one above all: in these months of perilous transition to democracy, the casserole has been converted into a symbol of liberation." In Peru, the Centro de Flora Tristán published *VIVA*; the Movimiento Manuela Ramos ("Manuela Ramos" signifies "everywoman") issued pamphlets on health and community resources; and *Mujer y Sociedad* addressed the politics of violence in the nation and in the home. Brazilian women were leaders in the innovative use of film and succeeded in incorporating the concerns of the women's movement into popular *telenovelas*, long-running stories of Brazilian life, such as *Malu mujer*. *Enfoques de Mujer*, published in Paraguay in the late 1980s and early 1990s by the Grupo de Estudios de la Mujer Paraguaya, was, like its counterparts in Brazil, Argentina, Uruguay, and Chile, founded by Paraguayan women participants in the struggle to end the military dictatorship and bring democracy to their country.

Many of the women's groups also established documentation centers, realizing how little information was available on women. And without adequate data, a critical analysis of women's situation was not possible. In Chile ISIS International went online in the early 1990s with information and publications about women across the hemisphere, and today it coordinates, via computer, the Women's Health Network of Latin America and the Caribbean and the Program for Information and Politics on Violence against Women.

In 1992, the Facultad Latinoamericana de Ciencias Sociales (the Latin American Faculty of Sciences, or FLACSO, www.flacso.org) in Santiago, Chile, began publication of a new country-by-country series entitled *Mujeres Latinoamericanas en Cifras*. The editors state in the preface,

> Mujeres Latinoamericanas is the first systematic, universal effort to document in numbers the situation of women in a continent of multiple hues and geog-

raphies, that also takes into account the great political, social, ethnic, cultural and economic disparities that exist in the hemisphere. The subordination of women, broadly debated throughout the whole world, is today an inarguable reality. . . . Mujeres Latinoamericanas en Cifras is intended to be an instrument for the transformation of this situation.

Statistics, gathered from sources each country-team deemed most reliable, were presented in sophisticated graphics offering socioeconomic and demographic profiles for each of the nineteen countries covered in the series, including statistics on women in the workforce, education, and the political process; medical and actuarial statistics; legislation affecting women; and at the end of each volume, a listing of *organismos y acción de promoción de la mujer* (organizations and actions concerned with the promotion of women).

The Chilean editors write that the latter section proved the most difficult to find information on "due to the lack of official sources and the nonexistence of central data repositories" (*Mujeres Latinoamericanas en Cifras* 1992, 127). Pointing to informational lacunae is part of the political intent of these documentation centers. In contexts where people's very lives have been "disappeared" from the official story, the creation of a new historical record in which women's lives are visible has potent meaning.

In 2006, we can see the powerful legacy of these pioneering efforts to gather and disperse information by and for women on the Internet. FLACSO itself has online publications of information in every Latin American nation, including the site Latinoamericanas en Cifras. A quick look at the listings of the Latin American Network Information Center reveals the minutes of the 10th Encuentro Feminista de Latinoamericana y del Caribe held in São Paulo, Brazil, in 2005, the website of the Caribbean Crisis Centers and Agencies Working to Eradicate Violence against Women, and the Comité de América Latina y el Caribe para la Defensa de los Derechos de la Mujer (Committee of Latin America and the Caribbean for the Defense of Women's Rights). Country-by-country resources are listed, including, for example, *Geledes*, the online publication of the Institute for Black Women in Brazil; Saúde de Mujer (Women's Health); and Gay.Brasil.com. The diversity and wealth of information available in 2006 is a tribute to the underfunded and often unsupported work carried out by women activists in past years.

The strategies developed by Latin American women activists over the past century have been widely adopted in other areas of the world. The Organizaciones de Trabajadores del Hogar de America Latina y del Caribe (Organizations of Latin American and Caribbean Home Workers), founded in 1988 by women household workers, has been a model for similar organizations in Africa and Southeast Asia. Violence against women, in all its forms, is a central concern of the contemporary women's movement in

Latin America. The celebration of November 25 as the International Day against Violence against Women was initiated in 1987 by Latin American feminists at the IV Encuentro Feminista in Mexico to commemorate the tortured deaths of six Dominican peasant women for resisting sexual violation at the hands of military troops. In 1992, the United Nations declared November 25 a global day of commemoration with regard to violence against women.

The Encuentro's resolution was intended to protest violence against women perpetrated by the state as well as in the home. Since the proclamation of this day, thousands of women have gathered in public squares across Latin America to show their solidarity on this issue. This event is a quintessential expression of Latin American feminism since it has involved the use—in this case, the creation—of an official, international event to make a statement in the local arena and, thereby, gather a bit of political *sombra*, or protective shade. November 25 is a protest against the violence women experience on a daily basis at the hands of the men with whom they share their lives, and it is a protest against official tolerance of rape and domestic battery.

In instituting the International Day against Violence against Women, Latin American feminists did not attempt to separate public from private or national politics from domestic concerns. Their activism obviates neat distinctions between what is "feminist" (for example, a gendered understanding of women's position within the family) and the gendered expression of a larger political issue (e.g., violent, state-sponsored political repression). The blending of the political activism of women on the Left with the feminists' gendered analysis has produced a profoundly ethical expression of principle that abhors both state-sponsored violence against the general populace and the day-to-day violence women withstand because they are women.

THE CONTEMPORARY HISTORICAL CONTEXT

A striking phenomenon in the 1995–2005 decade is the number of Latin American women who have entered the wage economy. However, statistical profiles also show that under the neoliberal reforms of the last fifteen years, as Latin American women entered the wage economy in greater numbers, the employment of male workers dropped, a result of employers' seeking a cheaper and more pliant workforce (PAHO 2005). Thus, the overall picture is one of more precarious employment for women and men and more poorly recompensed employment for men in the lower economic tiers, not a general improvement in employment conditions with women rising to equity with male counterparts.

Access to education continues to improve for women, and there is near equity with male counterparts in most urban areas, but recent reports show the persistence of less access for indigenous women and women of Afro-American descent. There are also serious questions about the quality of education, documented in the 2006 *Report Card on Education in Latin America: Quantity without Quality.*

Politically, male voters continue to outnumber female, and women have less access to political positions. Fierce ongoing debate within the women's movement continues over the strength of autonomy versus integration, but over the last two decades, influenced by pressure from women within the national community, the transnational women's movement, and the United Nations, most parliaments in the region have created parliamentary commissions focused on legislative issues related to women, for example, the Bicameral Commission for Women's Rights in Argentina (1995), the Committee for Gender and Generational Issues in Bolivia (1997), the Commission for the Family in Chile (1991), and the Commission for Equity and Gender in Venezuela (1997).

The results of the institutionalization of women's issues, or "state feminism," as it is sometimes called, may be seen in Chile's Servicio Nacional de la Mujer (SERNAM), which articulates a discourse of women's equality and a set of objectives around which to mobilize. SERNAM links up previously dispersed groups and addresses sources of women's marginalization, such as gender, class, and ethnicity. It has been successful in sponsoring legislation that criminalizes sexual violence, expands women's rights within the family, and protects women within their jobs; it is effective in disseminating information to women about their rights and examining gender-specific forms of poverty.

The need for autonomous women's groups remains strong, and the Internet facilitates communication across physical and social divisions to the extent that the new technologies, machinery, and skills are put into the hands of all people and do not create new "digital divides." Feminist organizers in Mexico assert that the new technology is excellent for getting information across vast territories and for getting the word out, "but does not replace the value of face-to-face meetings" in which direct argument, conversation, and the development of personal relationships can take place (quoted in Franceschet 2003, 9).

THE TWENTY-FIRST CENTURY: EMBODYING THE LOCAL AND THE GLOBAL

The locus within the women's movement, the tensions between local and global economic contexts, and particularly the effects of neoliberalism illuminate a significant degree of change within the last decade. Women's attempts to raise public consciousness have merged with the efforts of Socialists, populists, liberal reformers, theologians, and revolutionaries to publicize the plight of the poor. The fusion of a radical critique of economic, political, and social injustice with a gendered analysis has resulted in a syncretic understanding that has transformed both feminism and the politics of social change in Latin America and deeply influenced the global women's movement.

Eugenia Rodriguez Sáenz's 2005 book, *Un Siglo de Luchas Femeninas en América Latina: Ayer y Hoy: Mujeres Haciendo Historia* (in English, *A Century of Feminist Struggles in Latin America, Yesterday and Today: Women Making History*), published in honor of the fiftieth anniversary of the winning of women's suffrage in Costa Rica, documents that various aspects of society, the economy, and daily life have changed, but the specific tracing of the introduction of gender studies into the university, documented in the second half of the book, illustrates the incremental pace and the hard-fought battles to win significant space and funding; it also serves as a metaphor for the need for tenacity and perseverance in the search for social justice.

The emphasis on individual fulfillment that characterized the mainstream women's movement in the United States remains muted in the Latin American context. In Latin America, a process of *conscientización* developed in which women sought to awaken one another's awareness and understanding of their specific historical situation, while providing the analytic tools and organizational modes to participate in the transformation of social conditions. This is notable in the striking appeal of evangelical religions to women. "Pentecostal evangelicism is part of the broad activism of women in Latin America" and involves an estimated 130 million women (Hallum 2003). Analyzing evangelicism as a women's movement, Maxine Molyneux writes that evangelical communities address "practical gender interests in which women join together around such issues as food availability, utility services, economic demands and strategic gender issues such as inadequate health care, food availability, abusive men, [and] low self-esteem." Women come seeking help for their families, for a sick child, for support. Many become leaders as healers.

The increasing immediacy of the global in the personal is notable. In this contemporary construct, feminist understandings of the world and challenges to patriarchal structures are taking on new voices, forms, and strengths no longer mediated by the nation-state. For example, the concluding statement of the conference Los Diálogos Feministas, held in Porto Alegre, Brazil, in 2005, begins,

> Conscious, as feminists, that our bodies are replete with cultural and social signifiers, we also propose that the bodies of women are key sites in political and

moral struggles. It is across the body of women that the community, the state, the family, fundamentalist forces (state and non-state), religion, and the marketplace try to define themselves. These forces and institutions, across a plethora of patriarchal controls, transform the bodies of women into expressions of power relations. The bodies of women, then, are at the center of authoritarian or democratic authority. (*Nota Conceptual del los Diálogos Feministas, Porto Alegre, Brasil, 2005*)

NOTE

The author of this chapter has placed some suggested resources that you may wish to consult on the book's website at http://www.rowmanlittlefield.com/isbn/0742555240.

REFERENCES

Alvarez, Sonia E. 1990. *Engendering Democracy in Brazil: Women's Movements in Transitional Politics.* Princeton, NJ: Princeton University Press.

Antezana-Pernet, Corinne. 1994. "Peace in the World and Democracy at Home: The Chilean Women's Movement in the 1940s." In *Latin America in the 1940s: War and Power Transitions,* ed. David Rock, 166–86. Berkeley: University of California Press.

Bergmann, Emily. 1990. "Sor Juana Inés de la Cruz: Dreaming in a Double Voice." In *Women, Culture and Politics in Latin America,* ed. Seminar on Feminism and Culture in Latin America, 151–72. Berkeley: University of California Press.

Chaney, Elsa, and Mary Garcia Castro. 1989. *Muchachas No More: Household Workers in Latin America and the Caribbean.* Philadelphia: Temple University Press.

Conference of Nicaraguan Women. 1993. "Diverse but United: Minutes." *La Boletina* (January): 3.

Dore, Elizabeth, and Maxine Molyneux, eds. 2000. *Hidden Histories of Gender and the State in Latin America.* Durham, NC: Duke University Press.

Enloe, Cynthia. 1993. *The Morning After: Sexual Politics at the End of the Cold War.* Berkeley: University of California Press.

Feijoó, Maria del Carmen. 1982. "Las feministas." In *La Vida de Nuestro Pueblo: Una Historia de Hombres, Cosas Trabajos, y Lugares,* no. 9. Buenos Aires: Centro Editor de América Latina.

Fernández-Kelly, Maria Patricia. 1993. "Political Economy and Gender in Latin America: The Emerging Dilemmas." Paper presented at the Seminar on Women in Latin America, Woodrow Wilson Center, Smithsonian Institute, Washington, D.C., October 29.

Franceschet, Susan. 2003. "State Feminism and Women's Movements." *Latin American Research Review* 38, no. 1: 3–40.

Friedman, Elisabeth Jay. 2005. "The Reality of Virtual Reality: The Internet and Gender Equality Advocacy in Latin America." *Latin American Politics and Society* 47, no. 4: 209–11.

Greenberg, Janet. 1990. "Toward a History of Women's Periodicals in Latin America: A Working Bibliography." In *Women, Culture and Politics in Latin America*, ed. Seminar on Feminism and Culture in Latin America, 130–50. Berkeley: University of California Press.

Hahner, June. 1991. *Emancipating the Female Sex: The Struggle for Women's Rights in Brazil, 1850–1940*. Durham, NC: Duke University Press.

Hallum, Anne Motely. 2003. "Taking Stock and Building Bridges: Feminism, Women's Movements and Pentacostalism in Latin America." *Latin American Research Review* 38, no. 1: 169–86.

Hite, Amy Bellone, and Jocelyn S. Viterna. 2005. "Gendering Class in Latin America: How Women Reflect and Experience Change in the Class Structure." *Latin American Research Review* 40, no. 3: 50–82.

Jaquette, Jane, ed. 1989. *The Women's Movement in Latin America*. Boston: Unwin Hyman.

Kirkpatrick, Gwen. 1990. "The Journalism of Alfonsina Storni: A New Approach to Women's History in Argentina." In *Women, Culture and Politics in Latin America*, ed. Seminar on Feminism and Culture in Latin America, 105–29. Berkeley: University of California Press.

Lavrin, Asunción, ed. 1978. *Latin American Women: Historical Perspectives*. Westport, CT: Greenwood Press.

———. 1989. *Sexuality and Marriage in Colonial Latin America*. Lincoln: University of Nebraska Press.

Leitinger, Ilse, ed. 1994. *The Costa Rica Women's Reader*. Pittsburgh: University of Pittsburgh Press.

Macías, Anna. 1982. *Against All Odds: The Feminist Movement in Mexico to 1940*. Westport, CT: Greenwood Press.

Masiello, Francine. 1990. "Women State and Family in Latin American Literature of the 1920s." In *Women, Culture and Politics in Latin America*, ed. Seminar on Feminism and Culture in Latin America, 27–47. Berkeley: University of California Press.

Miller, Francesca. 1990. "Latin American Feminism and the Transnational Arena." In *Women, Culture and Politics in Latin America*, ed. Seminar on Feminism and Culture in Latin America, 10–26. Berkeley: University of California Press.

———. 1992. *Latin American Women and the Search for Social Justice*. Hanover, NH: University Press of New England.

Monterrey, Luz. 1993. "Interview." *La Boletina* (January).

Morello-Frosch, Marta. 1990. "Alfonsina Storni: The Tradition of the Feminine Subject." In *Women, Culture and Politics in Latin America*, ed. Seminar on Feminism and Culture in Latin America, 90–104. Berkeley: University of California Press.

Mujeres Latinoamericanas en Cifras. 1992. Facultad Latinoamericana de Ciencias Sociales con la colaboracion del Servicio Nacional de la Mujer (SERNAM). Sixteen books, each edited within the country under study. Editado por el Instituto de la Mujer, Madrid, y FLACSO, Chile.

Pan American Health Organization (PAHO). 2005. *Gender, Health and Development in the Americas: Basic Indicators 2005.*, Washington, D.C., PAHO, Gender, Ethnicity and Health. Available at www.paho.org.

Partnership for Educational Revitalization in the Americas. 2006. *2006: Quantity without Quality: A Report Card on Education in Latin America.* Inter-American Dialogue, Washington, DC.

Pratt, Mary Louise. 1990. "Women, Literature, and National Brotherhood." In *Women, Culture and Politics in Latin America,* ed. Seminar on Feminism and Culture in Latin America, 48–73. Berkeley: University of California Press.

Programa Interdisciplinario de Estudios de Mujer (PIEM). 1987. *Presencia y transparencia: La mujer en la historia de Mexico.* Mexico City: Colegio de Mexico.

Randall, Margaret. 1994. *Gathering Rage: The Failure of Twentieth-Century Revolutions to Develop a Feminist Agenda.* New York: Monthly Review Press.

Sáenz, Eugenia Rodríguez, ed. 2005. *Un siglo de luchas femeninas en América Latina.* San José: Universidad de Costa Rica.

Seed, Patricia. 1988. *To Love, Honor and Obey in Colonial Mexico.* Stanford, CA: Stanford University Press.

Seminar on Feminism and Culture in Latin America. 1990. *Women, Culture and Politics in Latin America.* Berkeley: University of California Press.

Soto, Shirlene. 1979. *The Mexican Woman: A Study of Her Participation in the Revolution, 1910–1940.* Palo Alto, CA: R&R Research Associates.

Stoner, K. Lynn. 1989. *From the House to the Streets: The Cuban Women's Movement for Legal Reform, 1898–1940.* Durham, NC: Duke University Press.

Valdés, Teresa, and Enrique Gomariz, eds. 1993. *Latinoamericanas en cifras: Chile.* Santiago: Facultad Latinoamericana de Ciencias Sociales (FLACSO-Chile).

Vargas, Virginia. 1983. In *Congresso de investigación acerca de la mujer en la region Andina,* ed. Jeanine Anderson de Velasco. Lima: Asociación Perú-Mujer.

———. 2006. "Las nuevas dinámicas feministas en el nuevo milenio." *Latin American Studies Forum* (Centro de Flora Tristán, Lima) 37 (Winter): 1.

8

Indigenous Peoples

Changing Identities and Forms of Resistance

Michael Kearney and Stefano Varese

Any attempt to make meaningful and valid generalizations about the contemporary indigenous peoples of the Americas is a daunting task, given their vast geographical extension and wide variation in social forms and living conditions. There are tens of millions of indigenous peoples, First Nations, or *indígenas* in the Americas. They range from a majority of the population in Bolivia, Peru, and Guatemala to significantly large minorities in Mexico, Colombia, Venezuela, Ecuador, Paraguay, and Chile. In the vastness of Brazil, they are a small minority, but as is demonstrated below, in spite of their small numbers, they have recently acquired unanticipated importance in Brazilian politics. The same could be said in the case of Canada.

We can gain an understanding of contemporary indigenous identities by examining them historically and identifying several major epochs that have shaped the economic and political conditions affecting them, as well as their responses to these conditions. Furthermore, just as the conditions affecting *indígenas* have changed and continue to change, anthropological understandings about indigenous identity have also evolved. Therefore, in reviewing the status of the contemporary *indígenas* in the region, it will also be necessary to comment on the development of the concepts that have been used to interpret these identities.

There are various ways of thinking about the history and identity of indigenous peoples. The approach that dominated anthropological thinking until recently can be referred to as the assimilation model. In this view, the *indígenas* possess "traditional" social forms and cultures that will eventually give way to "modern" society. This process is supposed to occur through the acceptance of the technology and cultural forms of modernity, and in this process *indígenas* are supposed to be "acculturated" into modern society.

This perspective sees contemporary indigenous identities as largely remnants from earlier periods, especially pre-Columbian times. This acculturation perspective implies that indigenous communities are destined to disappear as successive generations lose their traditional traits and assimilate into modern society. To be sure, there has been much acculturation and assimilation of *indígenas* who have merged into the respective national societies surrounding them and retained few traits of their former cultures. Hundreds of local indigenous communities and their languages have completely disappeared over the last five hundred years. At the same time, however, many *indígenas* have displayed a remarkable staying power, and in recent years, their presence has become evermore notable.

These largely unanticipated events require a different theoretical perspective. As noted above, much in the assimilation view of indigenous history has come to pass, but the persistence of nonmodern forms implies the presence also of a logic of difference in contemporary history. The basic working idea here is that people's social identities are formed largely out of opposition with others in a dialectic of constructing the "other" and self-attribution. The rest of this chapter explores this double tendency for leveling and differentiation and assumes that it is inherent not only in local, but also in global, economic, and cultural relations. We begin with a brief historical overview of the incorporation of the indigenous peoples of the Americas into such global relationships.

FROM PRE-COLUMBIAN TO COLONIAL SOCIETIES

At the end of the fifteenth century, when the first appreciable numbers of Europeans came into their midst, the native peoples of what is now North, Central, and South America and the Caribbean were arrayed in numerous and diverse types of societies ranging from nomadic foraging bands to complex state civilizations comparable to those of Asia and Europe. In the two centuries after the arrival of Columbus, the devastating impact of this encounter shaped the destinies of *indígenas* of the region; numerous communities disappeared completely, while others typically suffered population declines of from 80 to 100 percent of their pre-Columbian numbers (for an overview of the human tragedy associated with the conquest, see Galeano 1973). During the ensuing three hundred years, the basic condition shaping the identity of the original inhabitants was their subordinate position as colonized subjects and then, later, as subordinated ethnic groups within the postcolonial nation-states dominated by Europeans.

The conquest irrevocably incorporated the indigenous peoples into global relationships with European states in what was becoming a world capitalist system (see Wolf 1982). As the logic of that new world order was understood by the political leaders of the time, European nations, to prosper and to be strong vis-à-vis other nations, needed colonies as sources of wealth. According to the theory of mercantilism, which gained favor in Europe in the sixteenth century and influenced economic thought through the eighteenth, colonies ideally contained natural resources and native populations that could be mobilized to extract them. The resources produced by cheap labor in the colonies could supply industries in the home countries, which in turn would produce merchandise for sale back to the colonies and on the world market in general.

The identity of the Amerindian peoples during the conquest and colonial periods was shaped mainly by Spanish, Portuguese, French, and English policies designed to maintain distinctions between the European nations and their colonies in the "New World," as well as to maintain, within the colonies, the distinctions between Europeans and the various types of non-Europeans found there. Spanish occupation of the Americas and Spanish colonial policies regarding the natives contrasted sharply with those of the English in their colonial project in North America, which was affected largely by the migration of prosperous dissident religious communities consisting of entire families. Imbued with notions of religious and economic freedom, they sought worldly and spiritual salvation through industry and commerce in which the indigenous peoples were seen as having no significant role. Indeed, the English colonists of North America saw the First Nations more as obstacles to their projects than as resources for their realization.

At the time of its conquest of the Americas, Spain had just emerged from several hundred years of military struggle against the Moorish communities in the Iberian Peninsula. Indeed, the final battle in that long war, the fall of Granada in 1492, coincided with Columbus's first voyage to the islands of the Caribbean. To a great extent, the subsequent "conquest" of what became Spanish America was a continuation of the "reconquest" of Spain and was carried out largely in the form of a military and religious crusade. Whereas English settlement in North America was to a large extent an integral cloning of English communities, battle-hardened military men, for the most part unaccompanied by women and children, occupied Spanish America. Furthermore, whereas the English settlers went to North America to stay, the first waves of Spanish into the Western Hemisphere went to acquire wealth with which to improve their status upon their return to Europe. Unlike the English in North America who largely saw "the Indians" as obstacles to their enterprises, the Spanish regarded indigenous labor as essential for the extraction of wealth from gold and silver mines, as well as plantations that produced commodities such as sugar, silk, indigo, and cochineal for the world market.

In Spanish America, the indigenous peoples were regarded as an essential economic resource that needed to be protected so that it might be perpetually exploited. To this end, many existing indigenous communities were legally recognized and given resources so that they might endure as a labor force and generate wealth for the Spanish Crown, the Spanish colonists, the church, and various Catholic religious orders. Moreover, the catastrophic postconquest population declines noted above made labor scarce. This necessitated stronger policies for the husbandry of these communities. The subsequent social identities and destinies of the *indígenas* and their communities in Spanish America thus developed under markedly different conditions than in the English colonies.

Whereas in North America the indigenous peoples were not greatly valued as an economic resource and were mostly either exterminated outright or forced onto reservations, in Spanish Latin America the larger populations of *indígenas* were concentrated into communities that were in effect internal colonies. In Brazil, on the other hand, the Portuguese colonists regarded the natives much as the English (and subsequently the Americans) in North America. Although many *indígenas* were incorporated into rubber tapping and mining, African slaves assumed a much more important role in the overall economy than they did in most of Spanish America. Similarly, in the Caribbean islands, which faced the initial brunt of Spanish invasion and witnessed the "great death" of indigenous peoples, the surviving communities played a minor role in the colonial economy, while African slaves, mulattoes, and mestizos became the major labor force.

FROM "INDEPENDENCE" TO THE MID-TWENTIETH CENTURY

By the early nineteenth century, *criollos* (creoles) throughout Spanish America had come to think of themselves as more American than Spanish, that is, as residents of the regions in which they were born and with which they identified. When these sentiments culminated in successful independence movements, the independent *criollos* faced the challenge of building nation-states out of the former colonies. Central to the concept of a modern nation-state was the idea of a common national cultural identity.

The postcolonial nation-states, striving as they were to create more or less culturally homogeneous citizenries, swept away colonial laws that defined peoples as members of racial castes (e.g., "Indian," "white," "black," and combinations thereof). Although racism did not disappear, it now became imbricated more in a social structure based on class. The main distinctions in this class structure had to do with the way in which one earned a living, and the major divide was between those who did manual labor and those who did not. Needless to say, the *indígenas* fell almost exclusively into the former category. Thus, although the formal structure of the colonial caste system was dismantled, the position of the *indígenas* on the bottom rung of the social hierarchy was perpetuated. Indigenous communities in the Andes and Mesoamerica became the main provider of "captive" labor for the Spanish colonial economy, especially in plantations, *haciendas*, mines, *obrajes* or small industries, and even cattle and sheep ranches.

By the mid-eighteenth century, the mestizo population had begun to replace indigenous labor in the Spanish enterprises. The colonial system could not create, however, a wholly developed commodity- and labor-market system that would be the precursor of fully developed capitalism.

The architects of the Latin American nation-states assumed that the *indígenas* would disappear from history along with the old caste system. And toward this end, some of them enacted reform programs in the mid-nineteenth century aimed at eliminating the colonial laws that protected the indigenous communities. In Mexico, for example, the liberal pro-capitalist elements that enacted the 1857 constitution dissolved the corporate legal basis of the indigenous communities that had prevailed during the colonial period. The assumption was that exposure of the *indígenas'* communal resources (primarily communal lands) to market forces would break down the "backwardness" of these communities. Thus, they ceased to be regarded as primarily economic resources and were now seen as barriers to the development of the types of modern agriculture and manufacturing taking place to the north in the United States. Indeed, the liberals saw development in the United States as due in large part to the absence of large indigenous peasant communities such as those in Latin America. In contrast to the colonial period, therefore, in which the *indígenas* were seen as sources of wealth, the native communities were now regarded as pockets of backwardness that were inhibiting progress.

This situation prevailed for the most part until after World War II, when the United States took a renewed interest in Latin America in the context of the Cold War. Concerned to maintain its hegemony in the Western Hemisphere in the face of a presumed Communist threat, the United States and various international agencies such as the World Bank sought to promote economic development in Latin America. Indeed, the policies and projects of this period were variations on nineteenth-century developmental goals, except that now they were promoted within the context of the Cold War, with the U.S. government and international agencies assuming considerable responsibility for the economic and political development of "backward" communities.

In this period, the "Indians" were largely identified as "peasants." That is to say, they were seen in terms of economic and developmental criteria rather than in terms of their identities as indigenous peoples. The assumption was that "underdeveloped" communities would be transformed into modern, developed ones.

This period in Latin America was one of rapid population growth in many countries of the hemisphere that exceeded the rates of socioeconomic development measured in terms of job creation and improved standards of living. This explosive population growth also occurred in the indigenous communities, thus contradicting the prognostications about their demise. Indeed, the simultaneous growth in poverty and the numbers of the indigenous peoples suggested that modern history was taking a turn other than that predicted by the architects of the modern Latin American states and development theorists.

THE PERSISTENCE OF THE *INDÍGENAS*

After the disastrous initial biological holocaust caused by the epidemics of the "Columbian exchange" (Crosby 1972), which produced probably the greatest population decline in human history (Borah and Cook 1963; Dobyns 1966; Denevan 1976), the indigenous peoples of colonial Spanish and Portuguese America began a slow demographic recovery, which, by the early 1990s, had brought their population to the vicinity of forty million inhabitants (Mayer and Masferrer 1979; World Bank 1991). This number, however, is far below the estimates of the original indigenous population of the hemisphere.

There is an intriguing paradox in regard to this obstinate biological and cultural perseverance of the Native American people: how could they outlast the initial European military invasion, the resulting massive biological disaster, the systematic "ecological imperialism" they have suffered (Crosby 1986), and the meticulous destruction of their institutions, yet still undergo a process of cultural, social, and political recuperation that has allowed for their continuous and increasing presence in the social and biological history of the continent? The answer to this question must be sought in the complex forms of resistance and adaptation of the various indigenous peoples over the past five centuries. Four fundamental forms of ethnic resilience and opposition recur in this long history. The first is what we may call the moral management of the cosmos, a type of environmental ethic and practice found in the majority of the "indigenous societies" (Varese 2001).

The second is an economic rationality and a social philosophy within the indigenous communities that contrasts with the individualism and market-based economies of modern societies. This "moral economy," as Scott (1976, 1985) refers to it, occurs among some peasant societies and operates according to a logic informed by the ecological cosmology noted above. It seeks to preserve the common resources of the community and minimize internal economic differentiation. Within such a community, basic economic resources are held in common, and access to them is determined by good citizenship, defined in terms of willingness to serve the community in ways that often involve considerable self-sacrifice. Such an economy is centered more on use value than exchange value, and economic transactions are mediated primarily by reciprocity rather than market or profit considerations.

Related to the specifically indigenous nature of these two factors, there is a third: the tendency of *indígenas* to "clandestinize" their ethnobiological knowledge, while maintaining an active exploration, investigation, and conservation of, as well as experimentation with, biodiversity. Finally, indigenous peoples have demonstrated extreme adaptability in restructuring their political action to respond to a constantly changing world.

This chapter explores these characteristics of indigenous communities with respect to the challenge of establishing new, decolonized institutional political and cultural relationships among themselves and between them and the nonindigenous peoples of the Americas. A reconfiguration of this nature implies a demise of nineteenth-century nationalistic ideology and practices, as well as the negotiation of autonomy and sovereignty with national and international entities (the nation-states, intergovernmental organs, transnational corporations, etc.).

Since the European invasion of the Americas, indigenous societies have attempted to keep their biotic and biotechnological knowledge hidden, knowing too well that this was among the most contested cultural domains of the colonial mercantile and evangelical enterprise. For most of the indigenous peoples, agricultural and food production, as well as environmental management, were infused with religious and spiritual significance; consequently, as social practices, they were extremely vulnerable to repression by the colonial authorities.

It is well documented that the Spaniards' early ambiguous attitudes toward the Native American biotic heritage induced a series of repressive measures against the cultivation and use of certain plants and resources. The most notorious example is the Mesoamerican alegria (amaranth, called *tzoalli* and *huautli* by the Mexicans), whose cultivation, trade, and consumption were banned throughout New Spain during the early colonial period based on the argument that it was a "pagan sacrificial plant." However, the use of medicinal and psychotropic plants and substances, of stimulants like coca, and of animal and insect foods, as well as techniques for the preparation of food and fermented beverages and food production (e.g., various types of swidden cultivation), have been contentious areas of cultural and political control since the colonial period up to the present.

In Mexico, Bishop Juan de Zumárraga "wished to outlaw pulque in 1529 because it smacked of idolatry," and for the missionary, "drinking, with its ritual vestiges, was a major obstacle to evangelical expansion" (Super 1988, 75). But similar aspirations are still at the core of various types of evangelical fundamentalism practiced, for example, by the Summer Institute of Linguistics or by many Protestant missionaries involved with indigenous peoples in Latin America (Stoll 1985). In sum, European colonialism brought to the Americas definite ideas about food and food production that are still very much part of the hegemonic culture of Latin America and the ideology that informs most "development" planning and policy that affects the indigenous regions.

The indigenous peoples did not simply react to colonial impositions. Their responses reflected a variety of strategic accommodations and initiatives. For example, immediately following the Spanish invasion of Mexico, the Mayan people of the Yucatan initiated repeated actions of resistance that frequently turned into armed insurrections. These rebellions were motivated by a call to reconstitute the social and cultural precolonial order and return to the world's sacredness: to purify a nature contaminated by foreign oppressors. In 1546, the *chilam* (prophet-diviner) Anbal brought together a coalition of the Mayan people. On the calendar date of Death and End (November 9), they initiated a war of liberation that sought to kill the invaders, finish colonial domination, and purify the earth. The rebels killed Spaniards and their Mayan slaves in sacrificial rites and meted out the same fate to all the plants and domesticated animals brought by the Europeans (Barabás 1987; Bartolomé 1984).

In 1786, the Totonacs of Papantla, in southeastern Mexico, rose in rebellion against the threat Spanish authorities posed to their trees. A Spanish source mentioned the Indians' reasons: "The trees give shade to people and help them to persevere, are useful to tie animals, protect houses from fires, and the branches and leaves are used as fodder for animals" (Taylor 1979, 137).

Earlier, in 1742, in the Amazon jungle of Peru, a Quechua messiah, Juan Santos Atahualpa Apu Capac Huayna, fomented a rebellion. His insurrection mobilized thousands of Ashaninka, Quechua, and a dozen other ethnic groups and kept the Spaniards and Peruvians out of the region for a century. Some of the insurgents' revolutionary demands and proposals were informed by a moral ecology: the right to live in dispersed villages and households to allow a rational use of the tropical rain forest, the eradication of European pigs considered harmful to farming and people's health, the right to freely cultivate and use coca, known as the "the herb of God," and the right to produce and ceremonially drink masato, a fermented manioc beverage of substantial nutritional value (Brown, forthcoming; Varese 1973, 2001; Zarzar 1989).

Two centuries later, in 1973, among the Chinantecs of Oaxaca, Mexico, an intense messianic movement flared up in opposition to the construction of a dam that would flood their territory and force them into exile to distant lands (Barabás and Bartolomé 1973; Barabás 1987). To defend the ecological integrity of their territory, which they considered sacred, the Chinantecs resorted to a diversified strategy that ranged from legal and bureaucratic negotiations with the government and alliance building with poor mestizo peasants to the mobilization of shamans, the "caretakers of the lines" (the ethnic borders) whose "lightings," or *nahuals*, would kill the president of Mexico, Luis Echeverría. The Chinantec messianic movement legitimized itself culturally and socially with the sacred appearance of the Virgin of Guadalupe and the "Engineer Great God," who ordered the performance of a series of collective rituals to strengthen the physical and spiritual integrity of certain ecocultural features, such as rivers, mountains, trees, springs, caves, and trails.

On January 1, 1994, Tzeltal, Tzotzil, Chol, Tojolabal, and Zoque Mayan *indígenas* organized into the Zapatista National Liberation Army (Ejército Zapatista de Liberación Nacional, or EZLN), announced a surprising "declaration of war," and launched the military occupation of four major municipalities in the state of Chiapas, Mexico. An *indígena* army of eight hundred combatants occupied the city of San Cristóbal de las Casas, seized the municipal palace, and distributed a proclamation describing their opposition to the "undeclared genocidal war against our people by the dictators" and their "struggle for work, land, shelter, food, health, education, independence, freedom, democracy, justice and peace" (Comunicados 1994; Stephens 2002).

Of the six points stated in the EZLN's declaration of war, five referred to the rules of war that would guide their army, and the last stated that they would "suspend the looting of our natural resources in areas controlled by the EZLN." This armed movement of an estimated two thousand people essentially comprised the Mayan ethnic groups noted above. A fundamental objective of the insurrection was the defense of their lands and natural resources. In other public declarations and communiqués to the press, the EZLN also stressed its opposition to the North American Free Trade Agreement (NAFTA), which it considered a "death certificate" for the indigenous peasants, and to the modification of Article 27 of the Mexican Constitution permitting the privatization of indigenous and peasant collective and communal lands. "This article 27 of the Constitution, they changed it without asking us, without requesting our input. Now it is time for them to listen to us, because to take our land is to take our life" (*Chiapas Digest* 1994). These few examples taken from innumerable historic and contemporary cases illustrate the moral economy that has guided indigenous resistance to economic exploitation and political oppression.

Nevertheless, since at least the mid-seventeenth century, local indigenous communities have participated in an economic system in which part of the production satisfies subsistence needs, while the rest, the surplus, enters circuits of commercial exchange (Varese 1991a). Contemporary indigenous communities are thus not uncontaminated citadels of precapitalist economy. They are ruled first by the basic principles of a moral economy founded on the logic of reciprocity and the "right to subsistence" and, secondarily, by the necessity of exchange with the surrounding capitalist market. Both of these principles permeate the social life of prepeasant, peasant, and even some postpeasant *indígenas* who, self-exiled from their communities because of poverty, partially reconstitute this moral economy as urban subproletarian or transnational migrant workers in the agricultural fields of California (Kearney and Nagengast 1989; Zabin et al. 1993).

An analysis of Indian social movements that gives attention to forms of internal resistance based on reciprocity and ecological treatment of the cosmos reveals a history of parallel forms of existence. The indigenous and dominant national communities reproduce themselves with contradictory cultural principles that are negotiated over and over again, at times violently. When cornered by the oppressor and unable to avoid direct confrontation, an indigenous community is often forced to choose the desperate option of open opposition. In this sense, the violent rebellions of indigenous people embody and condense in heroic moments the ongoing struggle that they wage on a daily basis in nonviolent forms of resistance. Among such forms of resistance is their indifference to the logic of economic accumulation and, contrarily, their commitment to the dictates of reciprocity, ceremonial squander, and other forms of social generosity, which help to impoverish them economically while equalizing and empowering them politically (Varese and Escárcega 2006a).

NEW CONDITIONS AND NEW IDENTITIES

For the sake of discussion, the contemporary period can be seen as beginning in the late 1970s and early 1980s and extending into the twenty-first century. Several notable events have punctuated this contemporary period. For one, the five-hundredth anniversary of the first encounter of Native Americans with Europeans occurred in 1992. More than just symbolic, this anniversary served to announce that even after five centuries of colonization and oppression, as well as the best efforts of modern nation-states and their international agencies to develop them out of existence, the *indígenas* were still very much present and, in many cases, growing in numbers and political significance. Rather than being passive subjects of history made by Europeans and other nonnative peoples, they have assumed new social forms and new relationships with the nation-states that seek to contain them, and, indeed, in many cases they are assuming new identities that no one had previously imagined. The contemporary situation thus requires a shift in the way in which *indígenas* are conceptualized and equally, if not more importantly, the ways in which they conceptualize themselves.

With respect to the unanticipated turns in the demography and identity of indigenous communities noted above, several major contemporary themes can be identified. The failure of modern history to bring about the cultural demise of the First Nations and to contain their demographic expansion and political power is associated with the stagnation of overall economic development that has been unable to stay ahead of growing poverty and population in many areas of the Americas. Indeed, some observers have noted that the global economy has entered a "postdevelopment" phase of history (e.g., see Escobar 1992).

In contrast to the "classical" economic and social development of the First World countries, which was based on relatively immobile extractive and heavy industries, "postdevelopment economies" are based on flexible, light manufacturing and service industries organized on a global scale to take advantage of the most competitive sources of supplies, labor, and markets. These kinds of industries do not provide their employees with the kind of working conditions that have traditionally been the basis for a stable working class. Most of their employees are paid low wages, receive no benefits, and have no job security. These conditions apply today also to North America. Related to this expansion of "flexible capital" is the growth throughout Latin America of small-scale informal economic activities such as independent home manufacturing and street vending.

In the 1980s, throughout the Americas, neoliberal development reforms dismantled previous import-substitution and protectionist policies. With the removal of tariffs and other forms of protection affected by the General Agreement on Trade and Tariffs and the formation of free trade agreements such as NAFTA between Mexico, the United States, and Canada, the balance-of-payment problems for many of the Latin American countries have been alleviated, but, typically, at a tremendous cost to the middle and lower classes, which have suffered a general decline in income and standard of living. The inhabitants of urban shantytowns and peasant communities have been especially hard hit by these trends (see chapters 2 and 3).

The proliferation of flexible capital, the spread of the informal economy, and the rapid population growth mock the orthodox modernist visions of development and their supposed power to level social and cultural differences. Increasing numbers of indigenous peoples are being drawn into these kinds of postdevelopment conditions of production and reproduction. It is in such contexts that indigenous identities are not only being destroyed but re-created. That is to say, these contexts both dissolve and preserve "traditional" social and cultural forms, but even more notable is the fact that they also stimulate and support the emergence of forms of indigenous identity and resistance that are, strictly speaking, neither modern nor traditional. Indeed, one of the most notable characteristics of the contemporary era is the collapse of the distinction between modern and traditional. An understanding of this rather novel cultural, economic, and political context is essential to comprehending the formation of contemporary indigenous identities. A major feature of this new context is that it is increasingly a transnational space.

TRANSNATIONALIZATION

Modernist theories of indigenous societies assumed that the main context within which the identities of indigenous peoples were being modified was that of the nation-states that encapsulated them. But the dynamics of identity formation in the contemporary era are increasingly being affected by influences emanating from beyond the bounds of the nation-state. Furthermore, specific groups of indigenous peoples have begun to operate outside of the nations in which they have historically been confined. In other words, identity formation is no longer restricted mainly to national contexts.

In many Latin American countries, indigenous groups span the borders of nation-states. This transnational, transborder, transstate character of Native Americans is a historical fact that goes back to colonial territorial partitions and to their postcolonial confirmation. To mention just a few cases, there are Aymara in Peru, Bolivia, Chile, and Argentina; Quechuas in Bolivia, Ecuador, and Peru; Shuar-Aguajun in Ecuador and Peru; Embera in Panama and Colombia; Yanomamo in Brazil and Venezuela; Miskito and Garifunas in Belize, Honduras, and Nicaragua; Mayas in Mexico, Guatemala, and Belize; Mapuches in Chile and Argentina; Yaqui, Kikapoo, and O'hotam (known also as Papago) in Mexico and the United States; Mohawk and Ojibwa in Canada and the United States; and so on. The transnational nature of numerous indigenous peoples is also accentuated by their migration across national boundaries.

Thus, the conventional anthropological image of indigenous people living in relatively isolated and stable rural agricultural communities is challenged by a new and more complex reality in which *indígenas* from Mexico and Central and South America migrate to the United States as rural and urban workers and as political and economic refugees. Mixtecs, Zapotecs, Chinantecs, Triques, Purepechas, Kanjobales, Quiche, Keqchi, Mam, Ixil, Garifuna, Miskito, and even Peruvian Quechua and Ecuadorian Quichua have become a substantial component of the so-called Latino community of the United States (Altamirano 1991; Zabin et al. 1993; Varese 1991b; Varese and Escárcega 2004; Fox and Rivera-Salgado 2004).

Since the early 1970s, massive demographic movements of indigenous peoples in Latin America have taken the shape of migrations to other rural areas and to urban centers with better economic opportunities, both within the same country and in other countries. In fact, the rural-urban migration of *indígenas* has created what Albo (1991) calls "cities of Indians," such as Cochabamba in Bolivia. Throughout Latin America, indigenous peoples unable to make ends meet in the countryside have been forced to move into urban areas. They typically retain close ties with their families and communities in the countryside. Indeed, in many cases, households and entire communities are able to endure from year to year because of complex strategies that effectively blur the distinctions between "rural" and "urban" identities and spaces. The large number of *indígenas* in many Latin American cities is comparable to the situation in the United States where more Native Americans now live in urban areas than reside on reservations.

Just as pollution and ozone depletion in the atmosphere do not obey national boundaries, concern with the ecological well-being of the planet and the rights of indigenous peoples in general are imminent global issues. In recent years, concern for the health of the planet has become linked to the well-being of indigenous peoples in Latin America and elsewhere. Indeed, as concern with the degradation of ecosystems rises, people in and outside of Latin America have increasingly come to appreciate how the *indígenas* have most often lived for centuries in ecological balance with their environments and how this might offer alternative models to the environmentally destructive nature of contemporary forms of development. Consequently, indigenous communities, whose organizations may be numerically quite small or otherwise relatively powerless within their own national contexts, have come to find that they have potentially powerful allies elsewhere in the world.

International concerns about protecting the global ecosystem have drawn indigenous peoples out of their encapsulation within national spaces into the international area. In a similar manner, the growing international concern with the protection of human rights has also brought indigenous peoples to the attention of potential allies outside of Latin America. Sometimes both types of concerns are intermixed, as, for example, when mining, oil, and timber companies, cattle ranchers, or nonindigenous colonists invade indigenous life spaces and begin to destroy them. Until recently, awareness of, and concern with, such conflicts did not extend significantly beyond local regions or national boundaries.

Now, however, the presence of international nongovernmental organizations (NGOs) concerned with environmental issues and human rights in Latin America and elsewhere make extensive use of sophisticated networking and communication facilities to bring rapid and extensive international publicity to the plight of indigenous communities faced with the violation of their environments and rights. One of numerous examples in which the human rights of *indígenas* and ecological issues were interwoven was the international mobilization to protest the assassination of Chico Mendez, leader of the Amazonian rubber tappers' union.

In responding to the invasion of their life spaces and the depredation of their natural resources, indigenous peoples have resorted to legal strategies that often involve seeking territorial rights, semiautonomy within the nation-state, cultural autonomy, and/or recognition of their indigenous languages, as well as judicial reforms that recognize indigenous legal forms (e.g., see Stavenhagen 1988). By advancing such causes and occasionally winning them, existing indigenous identities are not only reinforced but acquire new dimensions and content.

The old units of anthropological analysis and policy making—the rural agrarian community, the indigenous region, multiethnic areas, and even the nation-state—alone are inadequate for comprehending the emergent transnational and transstate networks of indigenous and nonindigenous peoples concerned with the environment and human rights. Latin American indigenous peoples who were formerly marginalized are now actively engaged in the establishment of a transnational civil society, attempting to bypass state mediation and situate themselves in a global civil society while maintaining strong ethnic, cultural, and local loyalties (Brecher et al. 1993; Brysk 1992, 2000; Kearney 1991).

The existence of transnational indigenous peoples' movements that articulate local struggles for communal sovereignty with an agenda of universal political, cultural, and environmental indigenous rights demands a corresponding analytical paradigm and political praxis. Today, transnational, multiethnic indigenous organizations understand clearly that the economic and political power that threatens local indigenous sovereignty is unevenly distributed between transnational corporations, intergovernmental institutions, and national governments. They understand that the proposed "new world order" is a form of neoimperial globalization that is changing the rules of the game and debilitating nation-state sovereignties in order to open more space for the transnational corporations that are the primary organizers of the global political economy.

Most important for the indigenous leadership is the understanding that in the last five centuries, the entrenchment and consolidation of the colonial and republican states have been based on the maximization of labor exploitation carefully organized along the lines of ethnic divisions and ethnoterritorial delineation. The incorporation of indigenous ethnicity into the global division of labor has shaped intra-ethnic class differentiation, as well as interethnic economic inequality and differential access to political power. The result of the differential treatment of ethnic groups and regions by states and by capital has produced a complex class structure that cuts across and permeates the multiethnic configuration of the societies. In this regard, it is interesting to note that indigenous intellectuals in Mexico have coined the term "ethnocracy" to define the contemporary Latin American states, ruled and controlled by cliques of nonindigenous people (CONEI 1994). An intricate panorama of indigenous political organizations and platforms with different levels of class and ethnic consciousness has emerged within this complex ethnoclass structure.

One common characteristic, however, appears throughout the hemispheric indigenous movement and its national and transnational organizations: the organized indigenous peoples display a lukewarm national loyalty, a nonconformity and opposition to the nation-state's political project that has been, after all, the class and cultural expression of mestizo and creole elites and that for centuries has assaulted indigenous sovereignties with racist and ethnocentric arguments. This indigenous tendency toward denationalization is a fertile ideological and cultural terrain for developing collective identities based on alternative forms of ethnopolitical identification.

Indigenous organizations are thus increasingly taking their fight for the ethnic sovereignty of their constituencies beyond the national spaces that contain them into transnational spaces where the balance of power between nation and ethnicity is realigned, often to the benefit of the latter. One form of such realignment stems from the confrontation between indigenous peoples and transnational corporations that seek to intrude into indigenous areas to appropriate resources, usually counting on the complicity or indifference of the reigning nation-state to facilitate their operations. The long struggle of Ecuador's Amazonian Indian communities against twenty-two transnational oil companies is a good example of this trend (SAIIC 1991). The foreign companies operate in indigenous territories under army protection provided by the Ecuadorian government in a style reminiscent of colonial military occupations. In this conflict, indigenous communities defending their ethnic heritage (territory, environment, and natural resources) directly confront multinational development agencies and transnational corporations.

As soon as the revolutionary Sandinista government of Nicaragua was replaced in 1990, the Sumo, a small ethnic group on the Atlantic Coast, were besieged by the transnational Taiwanese company Equipe Enterprise, which had obtained a concession of 350,000 hectares of tropical rain forest on indigenous territory from the newly elected conservative government. The Sumo responded by looking for support from international NGOs, thus avoiding engagement with the government (SAIIC 1991). The Huaorani of Ecuador were able to mobilize national and international environmental groups against the planned oil exploitation of their territory by DuPont-Conoco Oil Company. The Huaorani campaign, which counted on the support of an indigenous international organization, the South and Mesoamerican Indian Information Center (SAIIC) of Oakland, California, and the Sierra Club Legal Defense Club was successful, and the oil company halted its operation in the Huaorani's territory (SAIIC 1991). Peruvian Amazonian indigenous organizations obtained a similar victory when, in September 1991, the Houston-based Texas Crude Oil Company canceled its contract with the Peruvian government for the exploration of the Pacaya Samiria Indian region (SAIIC 1991).

The strategy of internationalizing the defense of collective indigenous rights appears to be more successful than the exclusive exercise of conventional mobilizations at the national level. By globalizing the conflict, the indigenous organizations open fronts at various levels in the international arena and, thus, gain the support of international environmental and human rights movements, as well as the legal defense and financial and technical assistance of international NGOs and intergovernmental organizations, such as the International Labor Organization. Finally, since the early 1980s, the indigenous peoples of the Americas have carried their struggles to the United Nations, demanding that it become more democratic and adopt less nationalist positions and a more stateless orientation. Similar international pressure has also moved the World Bank and the Inter-American Development Bank to reformulate their policies for indigenous regions. Also, new spaces for the defense of indigenous peoples have opened within international law (Anaya 1994) and within the United Nations with the formation of the United Nations Draft Declaration on the Rights of Indigenous People and the International Labor Organization's Convention on Indigenous and Tribal Peoples (Barsh 1994; Coulter 1994; see also Stavenhagen 1988).

CHANGING FORMS OF POLITICAL AND SYMBOLIC REPRESENTATION

As new indigenous political issues connected with environmentalism and human rights have emerged, new organizational forms have also appeared as vehicles to express these issues. Generally speaking, they have taken the form of "new social movements" (NSMs), which have become prominent expressions of grassroots politics (as discussed in chapter 6). Forsaking conventional organizational forms, such as parties and unions, these NSMs tend to be looser networks of individuals and groups, often formed around a single issue. A particular organization may have a name and officers, but its structure and membership tend to be fluid and prone to fragmentation and lack of cohesion.

Nevertheless, the more recent general history of the formation of new indigenous movements in Latin America has been one of a growing coalescence

of smaller ones into larger alliances and confederations. Thus, local groups may form a regional alliance that then joins with other regional groups to form an overarching national or supranational organization, which coordinates its member organizations. This tendency for expansion has now reached the continental level via, for example, the efforts of the International Treaty Council and SAIIC to "link natives of North and South America" (Brysk 2000). Such a historic organizational "transboundarization" between North American and Latin American groups is a logical progression of the political and cultural self-assertion of the aboriginal peoples of the Western Hemisphere. Whereas at the time of their first contact with Europeans, the peoples of the Americas were largely isolated from each other by distance and local differences, now, well into the twenty-first century, they are creating transnational organizations that span from within the Arctic Circle to Tierra del Fuego.

Brysk (1996 and 2000) has observed that the Indian rights movement internationalized so quickly because *indígenas* were forced to turn to the international arena as a result of their domestic powerlessness, and contrary to the implicit assumptions of a levels of analysis model, international activity required fewer resources than domestic mobilization and was more amenable to information politics. In other words, Brysk argues that they were able to turn their "weakness into strength." The development of indigenous organizations has been greatly facilitated by the international prominence given them by the global media of communications that have allowed them to go from oral history to sound bites in one generation (Brysk 2000), as well as by the direct utilization of electronic means of communication such as facsimile machines, videocassettes, and electronic networks.

In the late twentieth century, individual indigenous personalities started to emerge in public spaces on a par with other notable mainstream personalities. Formerly, only mythic personalities appeared in public space, that is, individuals glorified after their death, such as Tupac Amaru or Montezuma. Now, living persons are becoming world figures in real time, rather than in some mythic past. Parallel to the remarkable appearance of major indigenous political figures in the international media is the recent emergence on the international scene of a new type of literature that portrays the lives of *indígenas*. Perhaps the most notable example is that of Rigoberta Menchú (1984), a Mayan woman of Guatemala who received the 1992 Nobel Peace Prize for her autobiography. Menchú's book is a prime example of testimonial literature, a form that has been advanced in large measure by *indígenas* who are increasingly speaking up for themselves, rather than being the passive subjects described by nonindigenous writers. Such testimonial literature is especially notable in that it has been produced, to a great extent, by women (Gugelberger and Kearney 1991).

Debate over the indigenous movement has centered on two main issues: are these "new" organizations legitimate, and is their autonomous presence on the political scene a divisive force within the Left and popular movements? For the last twenty years, social scientists, as well as mestizo and *criollo* political activists, politicians, and policy makers, have debated these questions. Only occasionally have invitations to participate in these discussions been extended to indigenous leaders and intellectuals. Charges of illegitimacy and suggestions that they should submit to the strategic subordination of nonindigenous political parties have been the main focus of debate and struggle. It is obviously risky to generalize such a complex and diverse reality in one broad statement. Nevertheless, it can be argued that the indigenous organizations throughout the Americas, with the exception of those of Mexico, have generally perceived political parties as an extension of the neocolonial state (see Smith 1985).

With the support of marginal sectors of the Catholic Church and a handful of progressive social scientists, a new generation of indigenous grassroots organizations has emerged within the spaces of the neoliberal state and multiplied, expanded, and consolidated support (for an extended discussion of these developments, see Albo 1990; Juncosa 1992). In view of the critical situation of the organized Left, the demise of the Socialist bloc, the profound cultural crisis of both liberal and Marxist utopias, and the messianic escapism of Left-Communist groups like the now defunct Shining Path guerrillas of Peru, it is reasonable to argue that the indigenous movements of the 1990s in Latin America provide a strong and coherent, although multifaceted and plural, voice of opposition, as well as cultural and political innovation.

This perspective on the indigenous movements contrasts in nearly all respects with the reductionist approach of mainstream social scientists to indigenous social and cultural history, which sees indigenous movements only in terms of how they are subordinated to the dominant society's social agenda and confines the analytical discussion to narrow political dimensions and shallow historical perspectives. Their episodic historiography and fragmented ethnography, informed by a Eurocentric epistemology of eventfulness, has obscured the cultural history of the First Nations. In this approach, the political resistance of indigenous people appears to have no historical depth; it begins to take on significance only when they behave like Europeans and use an idiom that nonindigenous peoples recognize and consider politically valid. This conception of the *indígenas* is permeated with the ideology of expanding capitalism and colonialism and is based on the assumption that intellectual and ethical innovations have been diffused from the European center to a passive, uncivilized native periphery.

But the actual chronicle of postconquest history reveals that the indigenous peoples of the Americas have confronted profound and radical issues throughout five centuries of resistance. Proposals for a radical change of the global economic and political system, criticism of the social order imposed on the Americas by the Europeans, and denunciations of the disruption of nature caused by colonialism have motivated numerous indigenous uprisings, provided the basis for persistent daily forms of resistance, and served as an integral part of the critique of the dominant culture developed by the indigenous intelligentsia. For five centuries, the indigenous peoples of the Americas have striven to maintain a critical distance from the worldview and values of the colonizers in an effort to preserve the minimum conditions for their moral autonomy, cultural independence, and political sovereignty.

The rapid growth of transnational indigenous political movements indicates that the indigenous peoples have been able to turn their domestic weakness and marginality into a basis for international recognition and support. Under the contemporary conditions of globalization from the top, the *indígenas* have been able to respond with a "globalization-from-below" (Falk 1993) by shifting the target of their activism from national governments to international political and economic actors.

An extended conception of ethnicity, which incorporates a political project that encompasses the whole multicommunal territory and biocultural resources of a state or region, requires dramatic changes in the political culture, social practices, and organizational forms of those affected by this conception. Larger, more complex ethnopolitical organizations, which require extensive innovations in management and new indigenous democratic mechanisms, must be imagined and implemented. The following examples, drawn from Amazonia and Mesoamerica, illustrate these new indigenous political and cultural forms.

BUILDING INDIAN SOVEREIGNTY IN THE AMAZON

The creation of the Federation of Shuar Centers in 1964 represents an important benchmark in the development of new forms of persistent resistance by indigenous peoples in Latin America. This surprising form of political organization had incorporated by 1987 some 240 centers and more than forty thousand Shuar people into a unique social program of economic and cultural self-determination. Four years after the Shuar federation was formed, the Amuesha people (Yanesha) of the Peruvian upper Amazon convened the first Amuesha Congress, which was later transformed into a permanent political body called the Amuesha Federation.

Between 1970 and 1974, in an intense series of mobilizations, Colombian *indígenas* organized the Indian Regional Council of Cauca and several other organizations. During the 1970s in Peru, the indigenous people of the Amazon region formed a myriad of local organizations and regional federations (e.g., the Ashaninka Congress of the Central Jungle, the Shipibo Congress and Defense Front, and the Aguaruna Huambisa Council). In the highlands of Bolivia, the Katarist movement shaped the initial organized expressions of a strong Aymara and Quechua nationalism. To the south in Chile, under the safeguard of Salvador Allende's Socialist government, the Mapuches participated in the elaboration and implementation of a *Ley de Indígenas* (Law of the *Indígenas*). This short-lived taste of multiethnicity was followed in 1973 by General Augusto Pinochet's military dictatorship and the death, imprisonment, and exile of the Mapuche leadership.

In March 1984, representatives of five indigenous organizations from the Amazonian countries of Brazil, Bolivia, Colombia, Ecuador, and Peru met in Lima and founded an international organization called the Coordinating Body of Indigenous Peoples' Organizations of the Amazon Basin (Coordinadora de las Organizaciones *Indígenas* de la Cuenca Amazónica, or COICA). COICA's main political objective was to become a coordinating body that would present a common policy position for all of the organized *indígenas* of the greater Amazon basin before the region's governments and the international community. COICA's origins can be traced to the three regional community-based organizations of the early 1960s noted above: the Shuar federation in Ecuador, the Congress of Amuesha Communities in Peru, and the Regional Indigenous Council of the Cauca in Colombia (Smith 1993). These local organizations, initially unknown to each other, established a model of social mobilization that gave voice to each local community's problems of territorial loss, human rights abuses, and cultural oppression. Throughout the 1970s, numerous other organizations emerged among the Amazonian peoples and began to establish contacts facilitated by the solidarity of various nonindigenous groups, such as sympathetic Catholic missionaries, pro-indigenous NGOs, and environmentalists.

COICA has been concerned mainly with issues of territorial and environmental rights; human, cultural, and linguistic rights; and rights to economic and political self-determination (Smith 1993; Varese 1991a). Today, COICA consists of more than one hundred interethnic confederations of Amazonian groups from Bolivia, Brazil, Colombia, Ecuador, Guyana, French Guiana, Peru, Suriname, and Venezuela, which represent approximately 1.5 million indigenous peoples (Chirif, Garcia Hierro, and Smith 1991; Chirif in Varese 2006a; Smith 1993; Varese and Escárcega 2006b).

COICA's active involvement in the United Nations' Working Group on Indigenous Peoples' Rights, in the discussions concerning the International Labor Organization's Covenant 169 on Indigenous and Tribal People approved in 1989, and in various committees of the Amazon Treaty Cooperation sponsored by the Inter-American Indigenous Institute brought the members of the organization into contact with an increasing number of international bureaucrats, advocates, indigenous support groups, the leaders of other ethnic minorities, parties, labor organizations, the European Green movement, and funding agencies. In 1986, COICA won an ecological prize, the Right Livelihood award, which brought the organization to the front pages of the international press and gave it major exposure to official circles. In 1989, COICA was recognized by the World Bank and had established official contact with the European Community. In 1991, COICA gained official advisory status with the Indigenous Commission of the Amazon Cooperation Treaty. Moreover, between 1990 and 1991, COICA was one of the founding members of the Alliance for Protecting the Forest and Climate formed with representatives from more than one hundred cities in five European countries (Smith 1993).

This relatively rapid success brought to light some shortcomings of this transnational indigenous organization, particularly structural limitations in representing its constituencies and the lack of means and methods for efficient communications between the community-based units, the regional and national federations, and the central administrative body of COICA. Most significantly, the central administration had become somewhat autocratic (Smith 1993). By 1992, a general congress of COICA had decided unanimously to reorganize the body's internal structure into a less hierarchical body and to facilitate communications and accountability by decentralizing decision making. COICA headquarters were also moved from Lima to Quito.

MESOAMERICAN INDIGENOUS
PEOPLES IN THE UNITED STATES

The activities of migrants from Guatemala and Southern Mexico to the United States have been among the most notable instances in the history of the formation of new organizations of Latin American indigenous peoples. Since the outbreak of civil war in Guatemala during the late 1970s between several indigenous-based guerrilla groups and the government, it has been estimated that some tens of thousands of *indígenas* have been killed, and many thousands more have fled the country to seek sanctuary either in Mexico or the United States. Those who have fled to the United States in the last twenty-five years or so have settled mainly in Los Angeles. Within the Guatemalan indigenous community in Los Angeles, many different ethnic groups are represented, each from a distinct community that speaks its own Mayan language. Whereas these refugees, when in Guatemala, were isolated by distance and culture, they have been thrown together in the sprawling Latino neighborhoods of Los Angeles where they have found common cultural and political bonds. On the basis of this shared heritage, the need to defend themselves as "aliens" in a strange and often hostile land has motivated them to form several interethnic associations. The largest of these, known as Ixim, takes its name from the Mayan word for "maize," which in cognate forms is found in the languages of all the Guatemalan indigenous peoples in Los Angeles.

Comparable to the presence of indigenous Guatemalan refugees in Los Angeles is the presence in California of tens of thousands of *indígenas* from the state of Oaxaca in southern Mexico. In 1993, it was estimated that at any given time there were some twenty-five to forty thousand Mixtec migrant farmworkers in California (Runsten and Kearney 1994). Whereas the Guatemalan *indígenas* were refugees of a horrendous war waged against them, the Mixtecs were mainly economic refugees from a region in which the environment had been steadily deteriorating and undermining subsistence farming, which was their primary livelihood. In the 1980s, Mixtec migrants from various towns formed self-help associations based on their communities of origin, and by the early 1990s, these local groups had come together to form a common Mixtec front.

Since the 1960s, uncounted thousands of Zapotecs from Oaxaca have migrated to California to work temporarily or to settle primarily in the Los Angeles area. As in the Mixtec case, the Zapotecs have formed migrant associations based on their communities of origin, some twenty of which came together in the late 1980s to create a coordinating body, the Oaxacan Regional Organization. The objectives of the Zapotec and Mixtec federations are binational in scope in that they seek to protect and promote the well-being of their members in the United States and also to defend and otherwise support their communities of origin in Oaxaca through financial and symbolic support and by intervening in government policies directed at the indigenous communities. A major milestone in Oaxacan political developments in California was the coming together in 1991 of most of the Mixtec and Zapotec groups to form the Mixtec-Zapotec Binational Front, which has since acquired considerable legitimacy with the Mexican government and international agencies. In 1994, other indigenous groups from Oaxaca requested entry into the front. These groups represented Mixe, Triques, and Chatinos, thus occasioning another name change, this time to the all-inclusive Frente Indígena Oaxaqueña Binacional (Binational Indigenous Oaxacan Front), which can without terminological inconsistency now accept groups representing any of the sixteen indigenous peoples of Oaxaca.

In 2006, a massive social movement, mostly of indigenous peoples, took place in the state of Oaxaca, Mexico. In May of that year, more than seventy thousand schoolteachers serving 1.3 million students declared themselves on strike, demanding an increment to their meager incomes, better classrooms, uniforms for students, free breakfast and lunch for impoverished students, and free textbooks. Most of the teachers were indigenous themselves, reflecting the ethnic demography of the state of Oaxaca, where more than 60 percent of the population belongs to one of the sixteen indigenous groups. The response of the state governor to the demands was to send the police to remove violently the strikers from the main plaza of the city of Oaxaca. The entire Oaxacan community, from the city to the rural areas, revolted against the governor, set up a large umbrella organization of more than three hundred grassroots groups calling itself the Popular Assembly of the People of Oaxaca (APPO), called for a statewide civil disobedience movement, and demanded the resignation of the governor. After months of mobilization, many marches (which, in one instance, assembled half a million people from all over the state), the permanent popular occupation of the central square of the city of Oaxaca, and the occupation of two radio stations and one TV broadcaster, the governor responded with more violence. After six months of occupation of the city by the teachers, APPO, and representatives of indigenous communities, the federal government sent in federal police forces to dislodge the strikers and the supporting peoples from downtown Oaxaca. The movement simply transferred its encampment from the plaza to another important tourist attraction center: the atrium of Santo Domingo. During these months of civil resistance, the governor's paramilitary forces killed at least fifteen people (including a U.S. journalist), practiced the extrajudicial detention and disappearance of hundreds of people, and presumably infiltrated the APPO and the teachers' organization to provoke violence, blaming the civil disobedience for the lack of security and instability in the region. As of the autumn of 2007, the situation remained unsolved, and a false sense of tranquillity had been established by occupying the city with heavily armed police forces.

Some statistics can highlight the deep historical roots of this indigenous and popular uprising:

- The state of Oaxaca has a population of 3.2 million, of which more than half lives below the poverty line (calculated at an income of $5 per day).
- Of the adult population (older than fifteen years of age), 21.5 percent is illiterate.
- The average schooling is 5.6 years.
- Of the 1.3 million students served by the seventy thousand schoolteachers, 780,000 are indigenous and may be monolingual in Indian languages or barely bilingual in Native-Spanish languages.
- At least forty-two thousand Oaxacan teachers are indigenous.

The state of Oaxaca is the second poorest state of Mexico; most of its gross product is from remittances sent by circulatory migrants from the United States. International tourism is the second major provider of hard currency. There are at any given moment between two hundred fifty thousand and four hundred thousand Oaxacan migrants in the United States; most are indigenous and undocumented.

What are some of the lessons that we can derive from the Oaxacan popular and indigenous social movement? Indigenous peoples in Latin America are extensively interconnected, at least at the level of their leadership and activism. The United Nations' Indigenous Forum that meets every year in New York, the United Nations Work Group on Indigenous Population that meets every other year in Geneva, and other various initiatives and forums, including the World Social Forum, as well as the massive presence of the Internet in practically all indigenous territories, including the Amazon, together allow for an extensive, profound, and permanent communication between indigenous peoples. In the third millennium, very few indigenous groups in Latin America live in isolation. The great majority of indigenous peoples has access to regional, national, and, for some of their leadership, international communication and information.

There have also been successful political struggles, achievements that are milestones in the eyes and collective consciousness of the indigenous peoples. In Ecuador, Indians were able to play a major role in the removal of two presidents and now have Indian professionals regularly appointed to important government offices. Bolivia was also a case of tremendous success: a Quechua-Aymara historical, ethnopolitical movement was able to elect the first-ever Indian president of a South American country. In Guatemala, a Maya-Jakaltec served as minister of peace in 2004 and 2005 and was in charge of overseeing the peace accords signed by the army and the revolutionary guerrillas. The Nobel Peace Prize was awarded to Mayan peace activist Rigoberta Menchú. Last, but not least, is the long, ongoing struggle for autonomy of the Mayan Zapatista movement in Chiapas, Mexico.

The Oaxacan indigenous and popular social movement of 2006 is a manifestation of the growing sociopolitical awareness and deep discontent of the Latin American Indians with their subordinate position, their economic exploitation, the ethnic and racial discrimination against them, and the political oppression that they face in their daily lives. As the late Brazilian anthropologist Darcy Ribeiro pessimistically forecast, the world of the third millennium will witness two major challenges: ethnic wars and environmental wars. It is now up to a younger and more sensitive generation of world people to avoid the occurrence of these catastrophic predictions.

The history of the formation of the Guatemalan and Oaxacan indigenous groups in California is perhaps the most notable example of the transnationalization of Latin American indigenous politics. The primary locus of these international groups has been not only outside of the home territory of the groups in question but also outside of Latin America. In their organizational forms, as in their personal lives, the members of these groups transcend the boundaries between the United States, Guatemala, and Mexico, as well as between the so-called First and Third Worlds, a distinction that has become largely obsolete as Mesoamerican indigenous peoples increasingly live transnational lives.

LESSONS FROM EXPERIENCE AND FUTURE PERSPECTIVES

An assessment of the First Nations' movement in the 1990s reveals two crucial concerns of the indigenous people. The first is the political rights of indigenous people to self-government and autonomy. These rights are becoming an increasingly prominent part of the democratization process in various Latin American countries and beyond. The demands of the Mayan rebels of Chiapas presented to the Mexican government in 1994 are a good example. As mentioned above, the indigenous insurgents demanded communal and regional autonomy, free elections, self-rule, and guarantees of nonintervention on the part of the government in their internal affairs. The second issue of crucial concern to indigenous people is their rights to territorial and resource sovereignty. Their demands for ethnic self-determination and autonomy include full control over the lands, water, and resources included within their newly defined ethnic boundaries.

The recovery of ethnic territories and political autonomy is based on three principles. The first is the historical depth of the claim. The current territorial fragmentation and reduction result from centuries of colonial and postcolonial expropriation; therefore restitution of land and reparations are part of the grievance that indigenous people hold against the existing states. The second principle is based on the ethnobiological integrity of territories traditionally occupied by specific indigenous groups. In other words, bioregions and ethnoregions were largely coincident before the externally imposed disturbances of the Europeans. There is no such thing in the contemporary period as natural, untouched landscape: rational intervention by *indígenas* over the millennia has shaped and molded the environment and the biotic resources (see Chirif, Garcia Hierro, and Smith 1991). The third principle is the repudiation of any solution to territorial and environmental claims that would rely on mechanisms that involve the commoditization of nature. As one indigenous leader is reported to have stated in objection to the celebrated debt-for-nature swaps promoted by some northern environmentalists, "It is our nature—and it's not our debt" (Brysk 1992, 2000).

Recognition of, and respect for, these three principles must constitute the ethical framework of any political and economic negotiations between the indigenous peoples and national and international entities on issues of political, territorial, and resource sovereignty. Some of the specific practical aspects of ethnosovereignty rights that will have to be jointly addressed by indigenous and nonindigenous peoples are briefly mentioned below.

A central issue is the recognition of the social and spatial definition of indigenous peoples and groups. According to the "indigenistic" legislation of various national governments, the indigenous ethnic groups are legally defined by their respective constituent communities (e.g., the *resguardo* in Colombia, the *comunidad nativa* and *comunidad campesina* in Peru, the *comunidad indígena* and *ejido* in Mexico). The whole ethnic group, even if legally recognized in some capacity by the state, does not constitute a juridical subject. Nevertheless, the indigenous organizations of Ecuador have succeeded in obtaining the state's recognition of the term "nationalities" for the various indigenous ethnic communities, but this is definitively an exception in Latin America.

In view of the lack of agreement and confusion throughout the continent about ethnosocial definitions and boundaries, indigenous intellectuals and leaders are addressing two levels of sovereignty that are rather complementary. One is "communal sovereignty," which is usually legally recognized by the state. At this level, there are local indigenous institutions, authorities, and clear social-ethnic boundaries but rather murky and more complicated biotic boundaries, therefore a more complex problem of genetic and resource sovereignty.

In contrast, the concept of "ethnic sovereignty" is legally rare or nonexistent from the state's point of view. However, some groups are beginning to define this type of sovereignty (Varese 1988). Total ethnic sovereignty is represented in the numerous indigenous ethnic organizations that have a legal and fully institutional existence. In this case, negotiated restitutions and formal interinstitutional agreements are required at various organizational levels, including the local community, ethnic organizations, local and central government agencies, and external investors and/or scientific parties. In instances of this type, the issue of biotic, cultural, and resource boundaries is easiest to resolve since there may be an approximate coincidence between ethnopolitical and ethnobiotic boundaries. By ethnopolitical boundaries, the indigenous people mean the historically traceable ethnic frontiers, even if they are not actually under ethnic control and are being reclaimed by the organization as a political objective.

Finally, there is the challenge of further developing organizational and legal forms that recognize and meet the needs of the ever-growing numbers of deterritorialized indigenous peoples who reside in cities and in nations far removed from their traditional homelands and modes of existence. These issues of boundaries and identities, of sovereignty and self-determination, promise to be increasingly salient issues of concern to the indigenous peoples of Latin America in the twenty-first century.

NOTE

The authors of this chapter have placed some suggested resources that you may wish to consult on the book's website at http://www.rowmanlittlefield.com/isbn/ 0742555240.

REFERENCES

Albo, Xavier. 1990. "De MNRistas a kataristas a Katari." In *Resistencia rebelión y conciencia campesina en los Andes*, ed. Steve Stern. Lima: Instituto de Estudios Peruanos.
———. 1991. "El retorno del Indio." *Revista Andina* 9, no. 2, December.
Altamirano, Teófilo. 1991. "Pastores Quechuas en el Oeste Norteamericano." *America Indígena* 2-3.
Anaya, S. James. 1994. "International Law and Indigenous Peoples." *Cultural Survival Quarterly* 1:42-44.
Barabás, Alicia M. 1987. *Utopias Indias: Movimientos socio-religiosos en México*. Mexico City: Grijalbo.
Barabás, Alicia M., and Miguel A. Bartolomé. 1973. *Hydraulic Development and Ethnocide: The Mazatec and Chinantec People of Oaxaca, Mexico*. Document No. 15. Copenhagen: IWGIA.
Barsh, Russell L. 1994. "Making the Most of ILO Convention 169." *Cultural Survival Quarterly* 1: 45, 41-47.
Bartolomé, Miguel A. 1984. "La dinámica social de los mayas de Yucatán." PhD dissertation, Facultad de Ciencias Politicas y Sociales de la UNAM, Mexico City.
Borah, Woodrow, and S. F. Cook. 1963. *The Aboriginal Population of Central Mexico on the Eve of the Spanish Conquest*. Berkeley: University of California Press.
Brecher, Jeremy, J. Brown, Robert Childs, and James Cuttler. 1993. *Global Visions: Beyond the New World Order*. Boston: South End Press.
Brown, Michael F. Forthcoming. "Facing the State, Facing the World: Amazonia's Native Leaders and the New Politics of Identity." In *L'homme: Anthopologie et Histoire des Societes Amazoniennes*.
Brysk, Alison. 1992. "Acting Globally: International Relations and the Indian Rights in Latin America." Paper presented at the Seventeenth International Congress of the Latin American Studies Association, Los Angeles, September 24-27.
———. 1996. "Turning Weakness into Strength: The Internationalization of Indian Rights." *Latin American Perspectives* 18, no. 4: 38-57.
———. 2000. *From Tribal Village to Global Village: Indian Rights and International Relations in Latin America*. Stanford, CA: Stanford University Press.
Chiapas Digest. 1994. Issued by the Institute for Agriculture and Trade Policy via e-mail.
Chirif, A., P. Garcia Hierro, and Robert C. Smith. 1991. "El indígena y su territorio son uno solo: Estrategia para la defensa de los pueblos y territorios indígenas en la cuenca amazónica." Lima, Peru: OXFAM.

Comunicados del Ejército Zapatista de Liberacíon Nacional. 1994. January 1, 6, 11, 12, and 13. Available at http://en.wikipedia.org/wiki/Zapatista_Army_of_National_Liberation.

Convencíon Nacional Electoral Indígena (CONEI). 1994. "Declaracíon de los pueblos indios de México en torno a la respuesta del gobierno al EZLN." In Maya Lorena Pérez Ruiz, "El movimiento Indígena Nacional," *Revista Mexicana de Ciencias Políticas* (Mexico City) 188–89: 103–18.

Coulter, Robert T. 1994. "Commentary on the UN Draft Declaration on the Rights of Indigenous Peoples." *Cultural Survival Quarterly* 1:37–41.

Crosby, Alfred W. 1972. *The Columbian Exchange: Biological and Cultural Consequences of 1492*. Westport, CT: Greenwood Press.

———. 1986. *Ecological Imperialism: The Biological Expansion of Europe, 900–1900*. Cambridge: Cambridge University Press.

Denevan, William M., ed. 1976. *The Native Population of the Americas in 1492*. Madison: University of Wisconsin Press.

Dobyns, Henry F. 1966. "Estimating Aboriginal American Populations: An Appraisal of Techniques with a New Hemispheric Estimate." *Current Anthropology* 7: 395–416.

Escobar, Arturo. 1992. "Imagining a Post-Development Era? Critical Thought, Development and Social Movements." *Social Text* 31/32: 20–56.

Falk, Richard. 1993. "The Making of Global Citizenship." In *Global Visions*, ed. Jeremy Brecher et al. Boston: South End Press.

Fox, Jonathan, and Gaspar Rivera-Salgado, eds. 2004. *Indigenous Mexican Migrants in the United States*. La Jolla, CA: Center for U.S.-Mexican Studies and Center for Comparative Immigration Studies, University of California, San Diego.

Galeano, Eduardo. 1973. *The Open Veins of Latin America*. New York: Monthly Review Press.

Gugelberger, Georg, and Michael Kearney. 1991. "Voices for the Voiceless: Testimonial Literature in Latin America." *Latin American Perspectives* 18, no. 3: 3–14.

Juncosa, José, ed. 1991, 1992. *Documentos indios: Declaraciones y pronunciamientos*, nos. 32 and 57. Quito: Ediciones Abya Yala, Colección 500 Años.

Kearney, Michael. 1991. "Borders and Boundaries of the State and Self at the End of Empire." *Journal of Historical Sociology* 4, no. 1: 52–74.

Kearney, Michael, and Carole Nagengast. 1989. "Anthropological Perspective on Transnational Communities in Rural California." Working Paper No. 3 of the Working Group on Farm Labor and Rural Poverty. Davis: California Institute for Rural Studies.

Mayer, Enrique, and E. Masferrer. 1979. "La población indígena de América en 1978." *América Indígena* 39, no. 2.

Menchú, Rigoberta. 1984. *I, Rigoberta Menchú: An Indian Woman in Guatemala*. London: Verso.

Runsten, David, and Michael Kearney. 1994. *A Survey of Oaxacan Village Networks in California Agriculture*. Davis: California Institute for Rural Studies.

Scott, James. 1976. *The Moral Economy of the Peasant: Rebellion and Subsistence in Southeast Asia*. New Haven, CT: Yale University Press.

————. 1985. *Weapons of the Weak: Everyday Forms of Peasant Resistance.* New Haven, CT: Yale University Press.

Smith, Richard C. 1985. "A Search for Unity within Diversity: Peasant Unions, Ethnic Federations, and Indianist Movements in the Andean Republics." In *Native Peoples and Economic Development: Six Case Studies from Latin America,* ed. Theodore Macdonald Jr. Occasional Paper 16. Cambridge: Cultural Survival.

————. 1993. "COICA and the Amazon Basin: The Internationalization of Indigenous Peoples' Demands." Paper presented at the Session on Native Rights and Ethnicity, Thirteenth International Congress of Anthropological and Ethnological Sciences, Mexico City, July 29–August 5.

South and Mesoamerican Indian Information Center (SAIIC). 1991. *SAIIC Newsletter* 6, no. 1–2 (Spring–Summer).

Stavenhagen, Rodolfo. 1988. *Derecho indígena y derechos humanos en América Latina.* Mexico City: El Colegio de México and Instituto Interamericano de Derechos Humanos.

Stephens, Lynn. 2002. *Zapata Lives! Histories and Cultural Politics in Southern Mexico.* Berkeley: University of California Press.

Stoll, David. 1985. *Pescadores de hombres o fundadores de imperio?* Lima: DESCO.

Super, John C. 1988. *Food, Conquest, and Colonization in Sixteenth-Century Spanish America.* Albuquerque: University of New Mexico Press.

Taylor, William B. 1979. *Drinking, Homicide, and Rebellion in Colonial Mexican Villages.* Stanford, CA: Stanford University Press.

Varese, Stefano. 1973. *La sal de los cerros: Una aproximacíon al mundo campa.* Lima: Ediciones Retablo de Papel. English edition: *Salt of the Mountain: History and Resistance in the Peruvian Jungle.* Norman: University of Oklahoma Press, 2002.

————. 1988. "Multi-ethnicity and Hegemonic Construction: Indian Plans and the Future." In *Ethnicities and Nations,* ed. Remo Guidieri, F. Pellizzi, and S. Tomiah. Austin: University of Texas Press.

————. 1991a. "The Ethnopolitics of Indian Resistance in Latin America." Working Paper, Center for International Studies, Massachusetts Institute of Technology.

————. 1991b. "Think Locally, Act Globally." *NACLA Report on the Americas* 25, no. 3.

————. 2001. "The Territorial Roots of Latin American Indigenous Peoples' Movement for Sovereignty." *HAGAR-International Social Science Review* 2, no. 2: 201–17.

Varese, Stefano, and Sylvia Escárcega, eds. 2004. *La ruta Mixteca: El impacto etnopolítico de la migración transnacional de los pueblos indigenas de México.* México: Universidad Nacional Autónoma de México (UNAM).

————. 2006a. *La sal de los cerros: Resistencia y utopía en la Amazonía Peruana.* Lima: Fondo Editorial del Congreso del Perú.

————. 2006b. *Witness to Sovereignty: Essays on the Indian Movement in Latin America.* Copenhagen: International Work Group for Indigenous Affairs.

Wolf, Eric R. 1982. *Europe and the People without History.* Berkeley: University of California Press.

World Bank. 1991. *Informe sobre el desarrollo mundial.* Washington, DC: World Bank.

Zabin, Carol, et al. 1993. *A New Cycle of Poverty: Mixtec Migrants in California Agriculture.* Davis: California Institute for Rural Studies.

Zarzar, Alonso. 1989. *Apo Capac Huayna, Jesús Sacramentado: Mito, utopia y milenarismo en el pensamiento de Juan Santos Atahualpa.* Lima: Ediciones CAAP.

9

Liberation Theology, Christian Base Communities, and Solidarity Movements

A Historical Reflection

Wilder Robles

This chapter examines the interrelationships among liberation theology, Christian base communities (in Spanish, they are abbreviated CEBs), and solidarity movements in Latin America. Its main premise is that liberation theology and CEB created a legacy that endures today in contemporary solidarity movements such as Brazil's Landless Rural Workers Movement (popularly known as the MST). Liberation theology and CEBs were generated by new theological and religious experiences. These movements put forward a broad vision of social change and strongly encouraged grassroots mobilization. The CEB movement, which spread rapidly throughout Latin America during the 1970s and 1980s, reflected the teachings of liberation theology. These communities were small groups of ordinary believers who met for Bible study and worked together to meet their needs. Eventually, the CEBs became a powerful force to be reckoned with. Their involvement in political protest, particularly in the Nicaraguan Revolution (1979) and the Salvadoran Civil War (1980–1992), led to dissension within the Catholic Church and conflict with Latin America's authoritarian regimes. Two main factors contributed to the decline of liberation theology and CEBs: rejection by the Vatican in the 1980s and the arrival of democracy in Latin America in the 1990s. This chapter concludes that the teachings and practices of liberation theology and CEBs are more important than ever in light of growing global poverty, inequality, violence, and environmental degradation. Solidarity movements have a crucial role to play in addressing human suffering and environmental destruction.

It has been almost four decades since liberation theology erupted in Latin America. The term was coined by Peruvian Catholic theologian Gustavo Gutiérrez in 1971. The English version of his book, *A Theology of Liberation*, created a storm when it was published in 1973. Gutiérrez's book immediately produced strong criticism from influential conservative bishops, theologians, and priests, who viewed it as a dangerous "politicization" of Christian doctrine. The new theology challenged the church to work for social justice. To this day, liberation theology is considered one of the most important theological movements of the twentieth century. Its message is straightforward: Jesus Christ is not only the savior, but also the liberator, of the poor and oppressed. Gutiérrez elaborated a clear sociotheological message that linked faith to action; that is, he focused on the role of Christian faith in the context of poverty, inequality, and violence: Gutiérrez called Christians to express their love for God and their neighbors by transforming structural violence in society. Eventually, liberation theology and the CEBs contributed to the transformation of the Catholic Church and the empowerment of the poor.

THE CATHOLIC CHURCH IN HISTORICAL PERSPECTIVE

Since colonial times, the Roman Catholic Church in Latin America has been an influential force: it has contributed to the shaping of the social and religious fabric of Latin American societies. The church has been both an important mechanism of social and political control and a source of solidarity and hope for Latin America's poor. Despite substantial changes in the religious composition of Latin America in the last four decades, the church remains an influential institution with complex and extensive networks. For instance, the church influences Latin America's education system by controlling the best and largest network of private higher education. Many Catholic universities, such as the Pontifical Catholic University of Rio de Janeiro, the Pontifical Catholic University of São Paulo, and the Pontifical Catholic University of Lima, are well-known centers of academic excellence with exceptional international reputations. The same is true with secondary private education. Other Catholic universities, such as the Central American University in El Salvador, are well known for their transformative pedagogical philosophies. The church also maintains its influence in Latin America's informal social-welfare system by running an extensive network of programs to assist migrants, the poor, the sick, and the homeless.

THE CATHOLIC CHURCH IN THE COLONIAL PERIOD (1492–1809)

An examination of the role of the Catholic Church and the influence of liberation theology in Latin America must begin with a historical perspective.

In the colonial period, the church played a vital role in the conquest and colonization of indigenous peoples (Schwaller 2000). The Spanish monarchy exercised control over the church's missionary work under the terms of the Patronato Real (a set of formal agreements between the church and the Spanish Crown) in 1501 and 1508. These agreements formalized the church's subordination to the crown, but simultaneously implied the church's involvement in the state's affairs.

The conversion of indigenous peoples was the church's initial colonial missionary task. For the Franciscan, Jesuit, Dominican, and Augustinian orders, this mission presented enormous challenges. These included the social organization of the indigenous populations (a complex tangle of religious, cultural, and linguistic elements totally alien to the Spanish culture), the use of armed force by the conquistadores in the subjugation of the indigenous peoples, and the abuses prevalent in the *encomienda* (a system by which Indians were assigned to landholding Spaniards to work the land and receive instruction in the Christian faith).

The missionary task was carried out in two different ways. Within the *encomienda* system, priests were assigned to look after the conversion, indoctrination, and pastoral care of the indigenous peoples. In addition, itinerant priests traveled from village to village, often with great hardships, as they went about preaching, instructing, and baptizing the natives and defending them against abuse by the *encomenderos* (landlords). The missionaries paid special attention to the members of the indigenous peoples' ruling classes in the knowledge that commoners tended to follow the examples of their leaders.

During the conversion period, the church's religious interests often clashed with the economic interests of the crown (Burkholder and Johnson 2004). The *evangelizadores*, led by Antonio de Montesinos and Bartolomé de las Casas, were critical of the harsh treatment the indigenous peoples received from the conquistadores. In the seventeenth and eighteenth centuries, the Franciscans, Dominicans, and Jesuits tried to protect the indigenous peoples from this situation by establishing Indian villages, called *reducciones*, in Mexico, Colombia, Ecuador, Peru, Venezuela, Paraguay, and Brazil. The *reducciones* reflected the theocratic and paternalistic character of the religious orders. They were economically self-sustaining religious communities, strictly organized along Christian principles, with enforced manual labor, partial common property, strict spiritual and moral discipline, and unquestioned obedience to the priests. As the colonial economy depended on indigenous labor, the development of *reducciones* inevitably led to conflict between the priests and the colonizers. In almost all cases, the Spanish monarchy sided with the claims of the wealthy colonial elite and moved to restrict, and in some cases to disband, these indigenous communities.

The "spiritual conquest" of Latin America had two major consequences. First, it produced a syncretic Catholic-indigenous religion embedded with a strong message of fatalism. This religion was Catholic in its organizational structure and rituals but indigenous in some of its fundamental beliefs and practices. Second, the conversion of the indigenous peoples led to social practices that undermined the indigenous peoples' potential for rebellion against authority: Catholicism taught them to accept their fate.

By the end of the colonial period, the church was one of the wealthiest and most powerful institutions in Spanish and Portuguese Latin America. It was central to the establishment of the social, economic, and political structures of the colonial system. Ultimately, wealth and power blurred the church's mission in society. As Burns and Charlip (2002) clearly state,

> Wealth reinforced the conservative inclinations of the Iberian Church. After the initial phase of evangelizing, it too exploited the Indians as well as the African slaves, to till Church lands or to erect larger and more opulent edifices. To the masses it preached resignation. . . . Poverty was to have its reward in the next life. . . . In wealth, power, prestige, and monopoly of education, the Roman Catholic Church by the end of the eighteenth century ranked as an omnipotent institution in the Western Hemisphere. Its influence weighed heavily, not only in the social and religious life of the community, but in politics and economics as well. (51)

THE CATHOLIC CHURCH IN THE INDEPENDENCE PERIOD (1810–1825)

By the early nineteenth century, the church was facing an identity crisis as country after country in Spanish America declared its independence from Spain. The creole elites were the driving force behind the emancipation movement (Chasteen 2005). They strongly resented the Spanish Crown's economic and political monopoly over the colonies. Under the influence of the European Enlightenment (which promoted the use of reason, not religion, as a means of establishing an authoritative system of secular governance), the creole elites articulated the ideological basis for the independence movement. Aware of the church's influence in the colonial system, the leaders of the independence movement fueled anticlerical sentiments among the people.

The wars of independence divided the Spanish American clergy (Gibson 1966). The majority of the episcopacy, most of whom were conservative, Spanish-born churchmen, opposed the independence movement, while many native-born, low-ranking clergy supported it. In Central America, for example, the conservative bishops opposed the independence movement, employing excommunication against republican-minded priests.

By the early 1830s, with the triumph and consolidation of the independence movement and the refusal of the papacy to recognize the new states, the church in Latin America faced a growing organizational crisis. This situation disrupted both the church's ability to defend its interests and its power to influence political developments in the newly independent nations. The legacy of the Patronato Real—the control of education, authority over the ceremony of marriage, and the disposition of church property—were the main issues that strained church-state relations during this period. Liberal and conservative political leaders were deeply divided over the religious question. As Burns and Charlip (2002) rightly say,

> While the views of liberals and conservatives varied on many issues from nation to nation, and even region to region, they were steadfast in their views of the Church. The conservatives invariably favored the status quo of the Church, supporting its spiritual and temporal powers, privileges, and prestige. Just as invariably, the liberals challenged the temporal powers of the Church. They uncompromisingly demanded that the state exercise patronage and thus temporal control of the Church. (97)

To protect itself from anticlerical liberals and keep its traditional role in society, the church allied itself with the pro-clerical, conservative forces. This situation added to the tensions between liberals and conservatives during the nineteenth century. In Mexico, under the leadership of Benito Juárez, the liberal government introduced reforms in 1855 that eventually allowed the state to seize most of the church's property and to progressively disenfranchise the church in many other ways.

The wars of independence did not substantially change the basis of the church's relationship to the state: the Patronato Real was simply transferred from the Spanish Crown to the new republics. In most Latin American countries, Catholicism was declared the state's official religion. As a result, the church continued to receive state subsidies and retained its vast landholdings. For the political elite, the church was an indispensable ally.

THE CATHOLIC CHURCH IN THE
EARLY TWENTIETH CENTURY (1920–1950)

In the 1920s and 1930s, the church established new mechanisms of coexistence with the state. New constitutions and concordats brought increasing liberty for most religious groups. In some countries, such as Peru, Argentina, and Paraguay, Catholicism continued to be the state's official religion. In other countries, church and state were formally separated, and civil marriage and divorce were legalized. Yet, even there, the church also continued to provide first-class education to the children of the elite.

The church's political coexistence with the secular state, its close social links with the dominant classes, and its spiritual role within the military, contributed to the stability of church-state relations during the first three decades of the twentieth century. Mexico was a notable exception: the Mexican state limited the role of the church in the educational, social, and political life of the country (Galarza 2003). Church-state relations remained cool and distant until late in the twentieth century. After 1930, the church faced new challenges in Latin America (Schmitt 1972). The social upheaval that swept the region after the Great Depression in 1929 threatened the interests of the church and the local oligarchies. Socioeconomic discontent gave rise to new political movements in Latin America, such as anarchism, communism, and socialism. These secular European-born ideologies appealed strongly to the emergent Latin American working and middle classes. The church, fearing the anticlerical tendencies of these secular ideologies, responded by deepening its intellectual hegemony over the republics. Many Catholic elementary and secondary schools were founded, as well as universities in Bogotá (1937), Lima (1942), Medellín (1945), and Rio de Janeiro and São Paulo (1947). The church also established Acción Católica (Catholic Action) to influence political developments in Latin American (Cleary 1985).

The origin of Catholic Action goes back to Leo XIII's (1878–1903) and Pius XI's (1922–1939) calls for social justice. Leo's encyclical *Rerum novarum* (Of New Things) strongly condemned unrestricted capitalism, individualistic liberalism, and revolutionary socialism, while advocating the right of workers to form associations and calling upon Christians to get involved in the struggle for social justice. Pius XI's encyclical *Quadragesimo anno* (After Forty Years) expanded and developed the social teachings of Leo XIII by advocating fundamental changes in the socioeconomic order. He denounced social injustices, the exploitation of labor, and the unfair gap between rich and poor countries. These two encyclicals laid the foundation for Catholic social thought and influenced the formation of lay movements such as Catholic Action and political parties such as Christian Democracy, first in Europe and later in Latin America.

Catholic Action was basically a lay movement under clerical control. It was directed at raising the Christian conscience, particularly that of the well-to-do, with respect to the needs of the poor. Catholic Action was active in Cuba as early as 1920, reaching Brazil in 1928, Argentina in 1930, Peru in 1935, and Bolivia in 1938. In addition to Catholic Action, there were parallel organizations of Christian inspiration such as Catholic University Students and Catholic Youth Workers. These groups were controlled by the church and served as its political arm in promoting the church's social doctrine. The Christian identity of these groups gave them legitimacy in crucial social groups whose social backgrounds made them hostile to anarchism, communism, and socialism.

Despite the militancy of Catholic Action, by the late 1940s, the church's political leverage in most Latin American countries was limited and its influence in the societies of the region seemed to be incompatible with the aspirations of the majority of the people. Mainwaring (1989) succinctly summarizes the church's standing in society:

> In the period just after the Second World War, the Catholic Church in Latin America seemed an antiquated ornament of a social order that was passing away. The trends of the twentieth century appeared unalterably against it. The Traditional institutional interests that composed the Church agenda had ceased to be important political issues. The Church was a marginal factor in the play of politics, particularly in the populist regimes emerging in many countries in that time. As such, the Church was relatively content to exist in a *modus vivendi* with the state in most countries. This political relationship implied, in turn, an alliance with dominant elites, a broader identification with the existing distribution of power that increasingly faced fundamental challenges. The Church had almost wholly lost contact with the masses in rapidly urbanizing and increasingly secularized societies. The majority lived beyond the limited reach of its institutions and, as the Church itself recognized in the 1950s, beyond its social influence as well. (1)

In the mid-1950s, Catholic Action shifted tactics from a concentration on doctrinal issues to existential priorities. The changes emphasized liturgical renewal and religious reflection directed toward social action. As a result, Catholic Action became more relevant, contributing to the emergence of strong Christian Democratic (PDC) movements in many Latin American countries. Despite these developments, by the late 1960s, many Catholic thinkers were forced to recognize that the gradual reformism and harmonization of class interests advocated by the PDCs was incompatible with the socioeconomic realities of Latin America. This realization led many young Latin American theologians to question the theological rationale behind lay movements and the church's mission in society. The church needed to elaborate a theology that could challenge Christians to a more radical commitment to social justice. Gustavo Gutiérrez, a Peruvian theologian and adviser to Catholic university students in Lima, began outlining the principles of this new theology, later to be called liberation theology. Gutiérrez's new theological insights dramatically influenced the transformation of the church vis-à-vis society in the following decades.

THE TRANSFORMATION OF THE CATHOLIC CHURCH (1951–1990)

The church's transformation from an ally of the oligarchy to an advocate of the poor and oppressed was a gradual process that grew out of several previous developments (Cleary 1985) First, the creation of the Latin American Episcopal Conference (CELAM) in 1955 gave the church a formal unity and coherence in formulating ecclesiastical policy in the region. Second, the massive missionary influx from the United States, Canada, and Europe during the 1960s brought new social values and political attitudes prevalent in Western societies. The situation of appalling poverty in the region moved the new *evangelizadores* to work toward social justice. Finally, the Second Vatican Council (Vatican II, 1963–1965) had a strong impact upon the church, particularly among progressive bishops in the region. The charismatic leadership of these bishops, such as Hélder Cámara from Brazil and Raúl Silva Henríquez from Chile, contributed greatly to the implementation of the council's recommendations in Latin America.

In 1961, Pope John XXIII (1958–1962) called the Second Vatican Council. Elected to the papacy in his later years, Pope John XXIII was a charismatic figure deeply committed to the church's mission in a changing world. He stressed the church's need for *aggiornamento* (to be brought up to date) in order to deal with the problems facing the modern world. Vatican II had an immensely liberalizing effect on the Roman Catholic Church worldwide. The final document of the meetings called for ecumenism, tolerance of secular ideas, greater lay participation in the church, and an active role for Christians in the promotion of social justice. The council's final draft called the church to dialogue with the world, to live within it, and to influence it.

Vatican II redefined the concept of church as understood in traditional Catholic theology. The new theological typology envisioned the church as a community of believers (the pilgrim people of God) in which all members are entrusted with the task of living and proclaiming the Gospel. This model did not emphasize hierarchical structures. In Latin America, the concept of the church as the pilgrim people of God would have profound consequences for liturgical practices, sacramental theology, pastoral activity, and even ecclesial structures in the following decades (Cleary 1990).

In 1968, CELAM held its second gathering at Medellín, Colombia, to reflect on the social aspirations of the masses in light of Vatican II. Influenced by the ideals of the latter and the emergent theological insights of liberation theology, the bishops reformulated traditional church social doctrine in the context of the socioeconomic reality of Latin America. In their discussions, the bishops dealt with issues of poverty, liturgy, lay movements, and violence. The bishops' final document denounced "institutionalized violence" in Latin America, calling it a "situation of sin." This condition, they said, was particularly "scandalous" on a continent considered Christian. The bishops also stated that the dominant

classes and "foreign monopolies," representing an "international imperialism of money," were responsible for the poverty and oppression of
the masses, who yearned for "liberation of all servitude" (Eagleson and
Scharper 1979). In this situation of poverty and exploitation, the bishops argued, there was a strong temptation to resort to violence to overcome this situation. However, the bishops warned that revolution tends
to give rise to new injustices.

Instead, the bishops called for structural changes in Latin American society and declared a "preferential option for the poor" as the basis of the
church's social mission. They proposed to help transform the conditions of
the masses through changes in Catholic liturgy, "consciousness raising," the
education and evangelization of the masses, and the strengthening of the
CEB movement. The bishops thought that with these new pastoral initiatives the laity would become active in the promotion of social justice, thus
collaborators with God in the fulfillment of His Kingdom. The 1968 Synod
of Medellín set the church into motion.

The Medellín document raised many fears among the conservative Latin
American clergy. They argued that advocating structural reforms would inevitably lead to the use of subversive violence as the only means to end "institutionalized violence" in the region (Cleary 1985). They were also dis-
turbed by the theological language of the document, which was drafted
mainly by young theologians advocating the "preferential option for the
poor" (Eagleson and Scharper 1979, 128). At the next CELAM conference
in 1979 in Puebla, Mexico, the bishops reaffirmed the church's "preferential option for the poor." The Puebla document stated,

> We brand the situation of inhuman poverty in which millions of Latin Ameri-
> cans live as the most devastating and humiliating kind of scourge. . . . This
> poverty is the product of economic, social, and political situations and struc-
> tures. . . . Hence this reality calls for personal conversion and profound struc-
> tural changes that will meet the legitimate aspirations of the people for au-
> thentic social justice. (Eagleson and Scharper 1979, 128)

In the context of military rule in most Latin American countries at that
time, the bishops at Puebla made harsh judgments about capitalism, Marxism, and the national security ideology (NSI), the political "theology" of
the military regimes. They condemned capitalism for increasing the gap between rich and poor, Marxism for creating false utopias sustained by force,
and the NSI for legitimizing dictatorships that abused police powers to vi-
olate basic human rights. The Puebla reaffirmation of the "preferential option for the poor" manifested the church's fundamental break with the past.
The church moved away from teaching the poor to accept their social situation passively to instructing them to change it actively.

THEORIES OF CHURCH CHANGE

Three main theories have attempted to explain the transformation of the church vis-à-vis society in Latin America. The first theory is the *institutional approach*. The main advocates of this theory are Western scholars. This theory argues that the transformation of the church was primarily a product of the church hierarchy's initiatives as a response to a variety of religious and secular pressures it faced. Some of these pressures were (1) the advance of communism, socialism, and evangelicalism; (2) the challenge of modernization to traditional religious control; and (3) the pressure from international Catholic hierarchies for the Latin American Catholic Church to speak out more decisively on issues of social justice.

In the Brazilian case, for instance, Bruneau (1982) argues that the hierarchy initiated the transformation of the church as a response to religious and political pressures. From 1950 to 1964, the church hierarchy reoriented its pastoral strategy in order to cope with the worsening living conditions of the working classes, the erosion of its religious influence among the masses, and new challenges to the church's influence from secular popular movements (especially on the political Left). In this context, the church's new strategy attempted to make religious influence more meaningful among the Brazilian population, particularly for the lower classes. This new strategy was reinforced by Vatican II and gained dynamism from the social and political developments following the 1964 military coup. Although initially some sectors of the church hierarchy welcomed the military coup on the grounds that it prevented the country from an "imminent" communist takeover, the church eventually came into conflict with the regime as repression intensified against workers, students, peasants, and religious personnel. The repressive nature of the military regime and the highly inequitable social cost of the Brazilian "economic miracle" forced the church to denounce the military regime.

The second theory is the *people-centered approach*. The main advocates of this theory are Latin American scholars. This theory contends that changes in the church were "bottom up," arising from the prophetic role played by the dominated classes. For example, Dussel (1981) says that the impetus for the transformation of the Latin American church did not come from the hierarchy but from the "people-rooted" church (i.e., CEBs), which emerged in the 1960s and brought a new spiritual dynamism into the institutional church. Following this argument, Gutiérrez argues that this "people-rooted" church originated with the social eruption of Latin America's oppressed masses, who made their presence felt in society through a concrete struggle for liberation. Similarly, Maduro (1982) argues that changes within the Latin American church occurred as a result of class conflict, coinciding with the rise of the national security state of the military regimes during the

1960s and early 1970s. In response to the suppression of their economic and social aspirations, the masses turned to the church as the only available space where they could organize their opposition to the authoritarian regimes. This was particularly the case, he says, in Brazil. The active presence of the CEBs challenged the authoritarian regime and moved the church to a more active role in the promotion of social justice.

Finally, the *middle-way approach* asserts that the changes within the church were due to an interplay between the hierarchy and grassroots forces. Mainwaring (1989) argues that the transformation of the Latin American church resulted not simply from directives from the "top" or pressures from "below" but from an intricate dialectic between the two. He also points to the Brazilian church as an example, explaining that the changes came about from a complex interaction among various levels of the church. As Mainwaring (1989) says,

> Grass-roots movements alone were not, however, responsible for the Church's transformation. On the contrary, without support from the hierarchy these movements could not have transformed the Church. The transformation process was dialectical. Only because of institutional receptivity could radical lay movements emerge, and it was only when the hierarchy actively supported change that the Church strongly defended human rights. Given the hierarchical structure of the Catholic Church, movements not supported by the bishops remain relatively isolated and are more incapable of changing the thrust of the institution's weight. (15)

Thus, the transformation of the church occurred neither suddenly nor in direct response to sociopolitical developments; rather, it was a gradual and dialectical process rooted in the experience of previous lay movements. The changes in the church gained momentum when charismatic bishops realized the need for the church to reevaluate its mission in society in light of new conceptions of faith, new theologies, and new pastoral practices. Mainwaring, however, recognizes that in the case of Brazil, these changes were influenced by sociopolitical events from the 1960s to the mid-1980s.

Mainwaring's *middle-way approach* integrates elements of the institutional and grassroots approaches. The result is an inclusive theory that takes into consideration the complex and dynamic character of the church's transformation and its subsequent impact upon society. The Brazilian church, like the Salvadoran church, was transformed by a dynamic interaction of hierarchical and grassroots forces. The changes brought about by Vatican II, Medellín, and Puebla, liberation theology, and the CEBs made Catholicism more attractive and meaningful to ordinary people and profoundly changed the church's stance toward society in general and the state in particular.

Contrary to generalized views, the transformation of the Latin American church varied widely from country to country. In Brazil, Chile, Peru, and El

Salvador, for example, the church took on a more independent and prophetic role, distancing itself from authoritarian regimes and taking a strong stand on social justice. By contrast, in Argentina, Colombia, and Venezuela, the church hierarchy strongly resisted any changes that could affect its relations with the state and the dominant classes and insisted on theological orthodoxy.

THE FUNDAMENTALS OF LIBERATION THEOLOGY

If Vatican II and the Medellín and Puebla conferences provided the "hardware" for changing the church's attitude toward social issues, liberation theology provided the "software" for the church's new theological and pastoral practices. Liberation theology embodied a critical, transformist, and radical meaning of the Christian message as revealed in scripture. This message challenged both ecclesiastical and political powers. Liberation theology had an immense impact on Latin American society: it not only reshaped the church's role in society but also inspired broad-based popular struggles. Its influence within the CEBs would eventually become a source of enormous tension within the church's hierarchy.

Liberation theology delineated the profound changes in the Latin American church. The combination of theological thinking and Christian living, in the context of social deprivation, gave birth to a new theology that solidly integrated the spiritual and social dimensions of the Gospel. The liberating message of the Gospel was perceived in liberation theology as liberation from the spiritual and social chains of oppression (Boff and Boff 1987). This radical way of interpreting the Christian traditional message of salvation found its full theological significance among a small group of professional theologians, such as Gustavo Gutiérrez (Peru), Leonardo Boff (Brazil), José Miguez Bonino (Argentina), Juan Luíz Segundo (Uruguay), Jon Sobrino (El Salvador), Ruben Alves (Brazil) and Ronaldo Muñoz (Chile). They called themselves "organic intellectuals," that is, intellectuals who do not serve the promotion of mainstream culture but instead identify themselves with the people at the base and try to think through and articulate the insights of theological literature relevant to the social and spiritual needs of the people of God, the community of believers struggling for liberation. These Latin American theologians were the pioneers of a new theological movement that challenged the hegemony of the United States in Latin America, questioned the interests of the church vis-à-vis the state, and condemned unjust social structures.

Many of these theologians came from the ecumenical organization Church and Society in Latin America and the short-lived, but influential,

Christians for Socialism movement, which began in 1971 in Chile. In their final 1972 meeting, the Christians for Socialism stated,

> The economic and social structures of our Latin American countries are grounded on oppression and injustice, which in turn is a result of our capitalist dependence on the great power centers. . . . We commit ourselves to the task of fashioning socialism because it is our objective conclusion . . . that this is the only effective way to combat imperialism and to break away from our situation of dependence. . . . There is a great growing awareness that revolutionary Christians must form a strategic allegiance with Marxists within the liberation process on this continent. . . . Socialism presents itself as the only acceptable option for getting beyond a class-based society. (Ferm 1986, 14)

Despite conventional wisdom, liberation theology has its roots in the thinking of both European and Latin American intellectuals. The teachings of European theologians, such as Jürgen Moltmann, Johannes Baptist Metz, and Dietrich Bonhoeffer, and the ideas of Latin American sociologists and educators, such as Fernando Henrique Cardoso, Teotônio Dos Santos, José Nun, and Paulo Freire, all contributed to the liberationist message. Moltmann argued that the notion of the Kingdom of God gave the church a transformative vision of society as opposed to a merely private vision of personal salvation. Metz contended that faith had a political dimension and that the church must be socially critical. Bonhoeffer stressed Christian solidarity and encouraged Christians to see the world from the perspective of the poor and oppressed. Cardoso, Dos Santos, and Nun explained Latin America's poverty and inequality as manifestations of an unjust capitalist economic order that favored affluent and powerful countries. Freire taught that critical, dialogical education designed to raise individual and social consciousness could transform oppressive social structures. Liberation theology incorporated all of these teachings and contextualized them within the particular socioeconomic situation of poverty and oppression.

Liberation theology developed in three distinctive stages. The first stage, the preparatory phase (1962–1968), started with Vatican II. The second stage, the formative phase (1968–1979), started with the Medellín and Puebla conferences. It was during the formative phase that liberation theology influenced the thinking of other theologies, such as black theology, feminist theology, and eventually ecotheology. In the third stage, the expansionist phase (1979 to the present), liberation theology gained influence in many parts of the world, particularly in African and Asian countries and even North America. During all these stages, liberation theology gained new concepts that redefined and expanded the early liberationist message. Despite its evolution, liberation theology has maintained four fundamental themes, which include the preferential option for the poor, structural violence, social sin, and orthopraxis.

PREFERENTIAL OPTION FOR THE POOR

Liberation theology argues that the church must be in solidarity with the poor and oppressed as they deserve justice. The preferential option for the poor calls on the church to create conditions for marginalized voices to be heard, to defend the defenseless, and to assess social institutions that harm the poor. Gutiérrez (1988) argues that the concept of the preferential option for the poor has a basis in scripture and the early church. Such insistence has led to charges that liberation theology advocates class struggle. However, liberation theology did not invent the division of society into a wealthy elite and an impoverished majority: the church helped to create and sanction this unjust social order. Liberation theology's understanding of the preferential option for the poor was aimed at shifting the church's political loyalties.

Liberation theology uses the concept of structural violence to describe the inhumane situation in which millions of Latin Americans live. Structural violence involves the concentration of resources in the hands of a privileged group, leading either to dominance over other nations or to the exploitation of the underprivileged in their own societies; that is, structural violence is closely related to unjust social and political arrangements that create hunger, poverty, and oppression. The identification of violence with injustice has led to charges that liberation theology implicitly justifies revolutionary counterviolence. Certainly, this is not quite the case. For liberation theologians, structural violence means enormous imbalances in power that lead to human suffering.

Liberation theologians argue that there exists a larger, social dimension of sin beyond individual wrongdoing. There are sins of commission but also sins of omission; that is, there is a social dimension to sin that is more than the sum of individual acts. Structural sin is the generator of poverty and oppression and an affront to God's love for humanity. Structural sin is caused by sinful social structures that distort human solidarity, reciprocity, and equality (Gutiérrez 1988). Accordingly, structural poverty is a manifestation of structural sin. Liberation theology views the relentless competitive basis of capitalism as socially sinful because it legitimizes oppressive and exploitative socioeconomic arrangements. The church must respond to this situation by stressing Christ's redemptive work for humanity; that is, Christ's victory over sin symbolizes more than the redemption of individual sins. It must also lead to the redemption and transformation of the social realities of human life.

Liberation theology coined the term Christian "orthopraxis" as a corrective to Christian orthodoxy. The latter insists on correct belief, yet is complacent about structural violence. Liberation theology states that correct action that leads to human liberation is most important. Thus, orthopraxis stresses Christian action on behalf of the poor and oppressed (Boff and Boff 1987). It also denotes a way of relating faith to action: it seeks to avoid unreflective faith that does not lead to transformative action in the world. Such an emphasis has led to charges that liberation theology disregards Christian orthodoxy, that its emphasis on orthopraxis at the expense of orthodoxy is theologically dangerous.

CHRISTIAN BASE COMMUNITIES

The emergence and growth of CEBs was one of the most important expressions of religious renewal within the Latin American church during the 1970s and 1980s. In Brazil, Peru, Nicaragua, and El Salvador, the CEBs became centers of religious and political reflection, as well as catalysts for community action. According to one estimate, there were during the 1980s more than one hundred thousand communities in Brazil alone and more than eighty thousand in the rest of Latin America (Cook 1985, 7). The emergence of CEBs was a response to the crises within Catholicism. At the first CELAM conference in Rio de Janeiro (1955), the bishops acknowledged severe problems facing the church, including the scarcity of ordained priests, the alienating formality of the traditional Latin mass, and the growing inroads of evangelicalism, socialism, and communism. While the church's reorientation of its religious and social teachings after the Medellín (1968) and Puebla (1979) meetings contributed to the growth of the CEBs, Boff argues that their creation was not a calculated undertaking initiated by clerical leaders but rather a manifestation of the outpouring of the Holy Spirit in the lives of the common people and their response to the liberating message of Jesus Christ.

The CEBs contributed not only to the spiritual renewal of the church but also to the political ferment that rocked Latin America during the 1970s and 1980s. The CEBs were instrumental in awakening the social consciousness of the poor and encouraging the formation of progressive popular organizations. The CEBs helped to transform traditional fatalistic folk Catholicism into an innovative and progressive politicoreligious force. The CEBs embraced the liberationist Gospel with commitment and determination. In relating biblical reflection to the realities of their daily lives (i.e., the exodus from slavery, the prophets' calls to social justice, and Christ's proclamation of God's coming kingdom), CEBs participants discovered a new understanding of their faith that challenged them to become active participants in the promotion of social justice. The ecclesiastical praxis of the CEBs—the centrality of the Gospel, the "priesthood of all believers," and the integration of evangelism and social justice—challenged the institutional church to return to its historical roots, the simplicities of its New

Testament origins, and its early commitment to the cause of the poor and oppressed. Following the Medellín and Puebla conferences, the religious and political dynamism within the CEBs created anxieties and growing concerns among traditionally conservative sectors of the church in Latin America.

CEBs were created in a variety of ways. Some arose from Bible study groups in the local parishes or neighborhoods or from the motivation of a priest, sister, or even a layperson who came to live and work with the poor in the city slums or rural areas. In other cases, CEBs were created by the sole initiative of the parish priest, who decided to divide his parish into small groups in order to encourage his parishioners to share their faith and read the scriptures. Once established, the CEBs gained a dynamic of their own, with their theological reflection, liturgy, and spiritual communion intended to raise the religious and social consciousness of the believers.

The CEBs gained legitimization within church circles after the Medellín and Puebla conferences. Progressive bishops in Brazil, Peru, and El Salvador, for example, wholeheartedly embraced the CEBs on the grounds that the movement represented the embodiment of spiritual renewal within the church. Adding to the momentum, the influx of large numbers of priests from the United States, Canada, and Europe contributed to the organizational vitality of the CEBs, the establishment of close links with the church's hierarchy, and the legitimization of the movement among the Catholic faithful. Peruvian Evangelical theologian Samuel Escobar (1986), writing about the CEBs in 1986, came to the following conclusion:

> Over the past ten years [CEBs] have multiplied and matured, particularly in some countries, so that now they are one of the causes of joy and hope in the church. In communion with their bishops, and in line with Medellín's request, they have become centers of evangelization and moving forces for liberation and development. The vitality of the CEBs is now beginning to bear fruit. They have been one of the sources for the increase in lay ministers, who are now acting as leaders and organizers of their communities, as catechists, and as missionaries. (3)

The CEBs challenged not only unjust social systems but the internal structures of the church. They attempted to change the hierarchical structure of the church, which had over the centuries systematically excluded the laity (men and women) from active participation within the church. The CEBs proposed a more inclusive, democratic church. They wanted to keep their Catholic identity, their Catholic roots, and their Catholic spirituality, aspects that were very important in attempting to reach out to the broader Catholic community.

The conservative wing of the church bitterly denounced the CEBs' tendency to question the church's internal structure on the grounds that this tendency constituted an abdication of church authority, tradition, and dogma. If the progressive church welcomed the CEBs, the conservative church became suspicious of them. As the CEBs became more dynamic and militant in seeking spiritual renewal and social change, particularly in societies experiencing revolutionary fervor, the church hierarchy became embroiled in internal debates and divisions regarding the CEBs' social and religious role. In sum, the CEBs provided opportunities to the poor for religious and political reflection and action. Within these communities, they learned the fundamental principles of grassroots democratic organization, which was based on active participation centered on collective leadership.

REACTIONS TO LIBERATION THEOLOGY
AND CHRISTIAN BASE COMMUNITIES

By the early 1980s, liberation theology had become very controversial. The CEBs' involvement in the Nicaraguan Revolution in 1979 intensified unease among conservative clergy about the direction liberation theology was taking. In Nicaragua, Christians and Marxists had joined hands to topple the brutal regime of Anastasio ("Tachito") Somoza Debayle. In El Salvador and Guatemala, Christians had started to join revolutionary movements, such as the Farabundo Marti National Liberation Front and the Guatemalan National Revolutionary Unity, respectively. These developments deeply alarmed the newly elected Pope John Paul II (1978–2005), who openly held anti-Communist views. Likewise, Washington was alarmed by the revolutionary fervor sweeping Central America and viewed a Christian-Marxist alliance as a serious political threat to the whole Western Hemisphere. In 1980, a blueprint drawn up by conservative Evangelical supporters of the presidential candidate Ronald Reagan urged, "U.S. policy must begin to counter Liberation Theology as it is utilized in Latin America by the Liberation Theology clergy" (Committee of Santa Fe 1980, 2).

The election of Reagan in 1981 opened the door to a concerted attack on liberation theology. Conservative American academics and theologians led by Ronald Nash and Michael Novak soon began campaigning to discredit liberation theology. Their criticism centered on three theological and sociological categories used by liberation theology: theology as critical reflection, the centrality of the poor in Christian theology, and Marxist analysis.

THEOLOGY AS CRITICAL REFLECTION

Liberation theology was controversial because of its unconventional approach to theological reflection. While traditional Western theologies have tended to be intellectual exercises geared purely toward spiritual life and re-moved from worldly concerns, liberation theology has tended to be a criti-cal articulation of the Christian faith that essentially responds to the human struggle for genuine liberation from oppression. For Gutiérrez, theology cannot escape addressing social problems. Theological reflection ought to be an instrument for liberation.

According to Gutiérrez (1988), theology was not simply talk about God or reflection on faith totally dissociated from worldly concerns. Neither was it the articulation of dogmas and doctrines that made up the Christian faith: rather, theology was reflection on social reality in the light of God's Word. Liberation theology was then a critical reflection on liberation praxis (action-reflection). It was a protest against both the social and political con-ditions that perpetuated poverty and oppression in Latin America. As such, it was a theology intrinsically linked to concrete social structures, a theol-ogy critical of the power relationships existing between social groups and that called for social justice. Nash (1988) argued that liberation theology's radical approach to theological thinking was at odds with objective, critical, and epistemological criteria for interpreting the Christian faith.

THE CENTRALITY OF THE POOR IN CHRISTIAN THEOLOGY

The centrality of the poor was the fundamental assumption in liberation theology. For Gutiérrez, poverty was violence; violence was an affront to God and called for solidarity with the poor. Christians had to be united with the poor and the exploited in this world in accordance with the bibli-cal message of salvation. But spiritual salvation alone was not enough. Lib-eration theology addressed a real social problem and presented a solution based on concern for the poor in society. In Gutiérrez's view, the Kingdom of God symbolizes justice in society. Thus, the Gospel's call for justice, love, peace, and repentance cannot be understood only in terms of its spiritual interpretation; it must also be seen in terms of its social dimension. The message of the Gospel is clear: salvation embraces all people and all aspects of life. Conservative theologians could not accept this view. Colombian conservative Bishop Alfonso López Trujillo accused liberation theologians of undermining the spiritual significance of Christ's victory over sin.

LIBERATION THEOLOGY AND MARXISM

The necessity of reevaluating the liberationist meaning of the Gospel within the context of poverty and oppression forced liberation theologians to make use of the social sciences, particularly Marxism. In the context of Latin

America during the 1960s and 1970s, this situation was unavoidable. In academic circles, Marxism was not only the dominant school of thought in the region but also an effective mechanism to explain unjust social structures. Liberation theologians made use of dependency theory, partially rooted in Marxian social thought, to explain the socioeconomic conditions of the poor in Latin America. Using dependency theory purely as an instrument of social analysis, they argued that capitalist forms of productions prevalent in Latin America had created social, economic, and political structures that conditioned the majority of people living in the region to endure poverty and oppression. Liberation theology rejected Western "developmentalism" on the grounds that it had failed to cope with the growing social and economic disparities in the region and concluded that systemic poverty and inequality were products of the region's dependence on advanced Western economies.

The use of dependency theory and Marxian categories of social analysis by liberation theologians caused a great deal of controversy within the church. For instance, Novak (1986) argued that liberation theology was Marxism disguised as Christianity and insisted that Marxism's commitment to atheism and class struggle were incompatible with traditional Christian beliefs. Exiled conservative Cuban priest Enrique Rueda affirmed this view before a U.S. Senate hearing on security and terrorism in 1984:

> There is little doubt that what we are seeing in Liberation Theology is nothing less than an attempt by Marxist ideology to subvert not only the Christian religious foundations of the West, but the very liberal democratic and free-market economic system that offers the only possibility for true development of mankind today. (Tantardini 1991, 1)

Humberto Belli, a Nicaraguan conservative thinker and a close ally of the Reagan administration in the 1980s, had a more sarcastic view of liberation theology. Writing in 1986, he concluded,

> In the liberation theology being preached in Latin America, the revolutionary Christians identified sin with capitalism, Satan with the bourgeoisie and U.S. imperialism; salvation or deliverance from sin with revolution. . . . All of this was the Marxist-Leninist worldview and scatology; only the terms changed. (Tantardini 1991, 49–50)

By the mid-1980s, the Vatican had taken serious measures to rein in the influence of liberation theology within the church. In 1985, the Congregation for the Doctrine of the Faith, directed at that time by Cardinal Joseph Ratzinger (now Pope Benedict XVI), silenced Leonardo Boff for a year for publishing his book *Church: Charisma and Power*. The church could not tolerate Boff's ideas of democratizing ecclesiastical structures. In 1992, the

Vatican prevented Boff from speaking at the Eco-92 Earth Summit in Rio de Janeiro. In response, Boff decided to leave the church. The Vatican also limited the influence of progressive bishops and named additional conservative bishops, particularly those associated with the ultraconservative Opus Dei. Under Vatican orders, some seminaries sympathetic to liberation theology were closed, and others had their curricula drastically changed. Gutiérrez was quietly removed from his parish in Lima and sent abroad to teach theology in prestigious Western universities. Currently, he is a full-time professor at the University of Notre Dame.

Similarly, the CEBs suffered a "top-down," deliberate process of demobilization. Bishops withdrew or limited their support for the CEBs. Ultimately, liberation theology and the CEBs lost their role as important catalysts for critical reflection and grassroots popular mobilization. They continued to exist, but without much support within the church. Boff has persisted in advancing the liberationist message by addressing environmental, indigenous, and minority issues. Similarly, Gutiérrez has continued to expand his theological thinking but from a subtler perspective.

THE CHANGING RELIGIOUS FACE OF LATIN AMERICA

By the early 1990s, the Latin American church's main concern was no longer liberation theology or the CEBs but once again the rapid expansion of Evangelical Christianity (Stoll 1991). The Brazilian Pentecostal leader Caio Fabio d'Araujo once said that "the Catholic Church opted for the poor, but the poor opted for the Evangelicals." This is an overstatement because the poor have been attracted not only to Catholicism and evangelicalism but also to African and indigenous religions. In Bolivia, Peru, and Ecuador, for instance, indigenous peoples are rediscovering and reasserting their ancient beliefs and practices, posing a challenge to Latin American Christianity in general. Caution is then necessary when evaluating the religious transformation underway in Latin America. This is not to deny the fact that Evangelical Christianity has made considerable inroads in Latin America. At the beginning of the 1980s, there were 18.6 million Evangelicals in Latin America. According to CELAM, there are now close to sixty million (12 percent of the entire Latin American population). In Brazil, the percentage is 15 percent; in Guatemala, it is 20 percent; in Peru and Uruguay, it is below 7 percent, respectively. However, recent studies indicate that the growth of Evangelical Christianity has slowed in Latin America (Cleary 2004).

The social implications of the Evangelicals' "Great Awakening" are not yet very clear (Smith and Prokopy 2005). On the one hand, some scholars have criticized the repressive and corporatist nature of the Evangelical churches, which are viewed as reproducing traditional authoritarian and U.S.-centered forms of social control. On the other hand, some scholars have stressed the progressive nature of the Evangelical churches, which are viewed as producing modern forms of democratic participation. Regardless, one thing is certain: Evangelicals have played, and continue to play, an important role in Latin America's democratization process (Freston 2006). One glaring exception was the authoritarian and disastrous rule of born-again José Efrain Rios Montt in Guatemala in the early 1980s, which deeply embarrassed the Evangelical community in Latin America.

CHURCH, DEMOCRACY, AND SOLIDARITY MOVEMENTS: THE CASE OF THE MST

In Brazil, the church took a very critical stance against the military regime (1964–1985) and provided a vital space for organized opposition. The CEBs, especially its women members, played a vital role in the transition to democracy by openly challenging the military regime. The CEBs advocated *cidadania* (citizenship), or the real exercise of fundamental political rights, as the means of expanding and sustaining democracy. The arrival of democracy brought not only hope to the poor but also new spaces for political participation. Unfortunately, the long-term outcome for the poor has been growing despair and marginalization.

Latin American democratic governments have continued to marginalize the poor. They have embraced neoliberalism as the solution to their socio-economic problems. The collapse of the Socialist dream in Eastern Europe and the decline of traditional leftist parties facilitated neoliberalism's implementation. Initially, the introduction of neoliberal macroeconomic stabilization policies abruptly halted hyperinflation, stimulated economic growth, and attracted foreign investment. In addition, the privatization of inefficient state-owned corporations relieved governments of unnecessary financial burdens. All of these contributed to a positive view of neoliberalism among the electorate. However, this triumphalism ended by the late 1990s as country after country confronted enormous economic problems.

Neoliberalism has not produced the expected results. Latin America continues to face an absurd structural contradiction: extreme material abundance for the few amidst extreme poverty for the vast majority; that is, the gap between rich and poor has remained stubbornly high in Latin America. Not only has neoliberalism opened up Latin American countries to the world economy, but it has also exposed them to new internal and external political pressures. Moreover, tighter economic constraints have limited governments' abilities to promote progressive social policies throughout the Americas. All of this has depressed political participation and eroded government accountability, in turn encouraging systemic corruption and social inequities. As a result, democratic governments in the region are suffering from profound deficiencies.

A 2004 study conducted in Latin America by the United Nations Development Program (UNDP) confirms the perils of democratic governance in Latin America. Some of the evidence contained in this report is striking. For instance, opinion surveys conducted for the report in eighteen Latin American countries indicate that just 43 percent of Latin Americans support democracy, 30.5 percent express ambivalence, and 26.5 percent hold nondemocratic views. Another striking example: almost 55 percent of all Latin Americans say they would support an authoritarian regime over democratic government if authoritarian rule could "resolve" their economic problems (UNDP 2004).

There is a growing gap in Latin America today between the theory and practice of democracy. Democratic governments are failing to respond to citizens' interests. The persistence of growing poverty and inequality, the inability of democratic governments to address historical social demands, and the corruption-prone state institutions (particularly the judiciary) have brought into question the sustainability of democratic governance in the region. Thus, democratic transition has not led to democratic transformation; that is, it has not changed the structures of power that benefit the affluent and powerful at the expense of the poor and powerless. Instead, it has often exchanged dictatorship for meaningless electoral democracy.

Social movements are attempting to narrow the democratic deficit by redefining and expanding democratic citizenship. Since the mid-1990s, these social movements, particularly peasant and indigenous movements, have injected a significant measure of popular participation into the limited democratic process (Cleary and Steigenga 2004). They have built decentralized and autonomous national organizations, established international solidarity networks, created political education centers, and forged multiclass political coalitions. All this has strengthened the organizational and operational capacity of such movements to effectively contest entrenched power structures (Robles 2001).

In the early twenty-first century in Latin America, the organized poor are the main force for democratic transformation (Petras and Veltmeyer 2005). This is particularly the case in Brazil with the MST. This movement has been heavily influenced by the teachings and practices of liberation theology and the CEBs (Robles 2000). The MST has incorporated the liberationist message of liberation theology and the collective leadership style of the CEBs. Its key leaders came from the CEBs and the Catholic Church Commission on Land Reform. This Brazilian peasant movement is the largest and most influential peasant movement in Latin America today. The MST offers the rural poor hope for a better future. It was established in 1984 in the city of Cascavel, State of Paraná, to pursue land reform through the occupation of uncultivated private and public lands. Under the charismatic, democratic, and very capable leadership of João Pedro Stédile, the MST has transformed, and continues to transform, Brazil's rural landscape. During the course of its political journey, the MST has developed both a formidable landless peasant organization capable of contesting Brazil's extreme concentration of landownership and an innovative community-based model of land reform that effectively promotes sustainable rural livelihoods. This model addresses structural poverty, enhances peasant identity, strengthens democratic participation, and promotes environmental stewardship.

The MST advocates the transformation of politics by practicing the politics of transformation. Specifically, it advocates the transformation of Brazil's skewed power structures by nonviolent means. The MST has an immense capacity to empower the rural poor: it challenges them to become active agents of social transformation. This movement has a strong political base, effective organization, common purpose, extensive social networks, and favorable public support. All of these have enabled the MST to advance new visions and practices of political and economic democracy in Brazil and beyond.

The MST has achieved remarkable results over the last two decades. First, it has compelled the Brazilian government to redistribute over seven million hectares of land. Second, it has considerably expanded its membership. At present, it has almost 1.5 million members spread across twenty-three Brazilian states. Third, the MST has obtained land titles for more than three hundred thousand landless peasant families. Another 140,000 landless peasant families currently living in camps are awaiting land titles. Fourth, it has established hundreds of agricultural settlements, several alternative media outlets, an extensive welfare system, and dozens of agricultural cooperatives and food-processing plants. Finally, the MST has greatly contributed to the effective globalization of peasant struggles by actively participating in the Via Campesina. The latter is an international movement made up of peasant organizations, agricultural workers, and indigenous communities from Asia, Africa, America, and Europe and the World Social Forum, an antiglobalization forum that coordinates world advocacy campaigns.

In sum, the decline of liberation theology and the CEBs coincided with the emergence of grassroots solidarity movements of leftist inspiration. The MST is just one example. This movement has been influenced by the message, mysticism, symbolism, and activism of liberation theology and CEBs (Stédile and Fernandes 1999). The MST is a movement driven by more than mere material interests: it is an ethically oriented movement working toward a more egalitarian and just society. Its discourse and praxis are truly empowering. The MST expresses the meaning of agrarian justice in a simple, but effective manner: *Reforma agraria é a luta pela vida e dignidade humana e reforma agraria é a luta de todos* (land reform is a struggle for human life and dignity, and land reform is everybody's struggle). This message resonates among the landless peasants. The MST has challenged the poor to become actively engaged in a historical project of societal transformation: to change skewed power relations that legitimize social exclusion, environmental degradation, and gender inequity.

CONCLUSION

In the first place, liberation theology and the CEBs contributed enormously to the transformation of the Catholic Church in Latin America. Despite its conservative look, the church today is a sharply different institution than it was centuries ago. Second, liberation theology changed the church's understanding and justification of poverty in Latin America. Liberation theology proposed a new social vision and, through the CEBs, advanced new forms of grassroots mobilization. Liberation theology and CEBs became powerful tools to empower the poor. Ultimately, these movements fell victim to powerful forces within and outside the church. The deliberate marginalization of liberation theology and demobilization of the CEBs sharply limited these movements' operational capacities and led to their decline. Third, the significant inroads made by Evangelical and Pentecostal Christianity in the last four decades have contributed to progressive religious pluralism in Latin American society. Even so, women remain marginalized within organized Christianity. Fourth, the vast majority of Latin American Christians remains largely poor. Democracy has so far failed to address their needs and aspirations. Finally, liberation theology and the CEBs influenced the formation and operation of solidarity movements contesting structural poverty and violence. The MST is the best example of these movements. Its emergence coincided with the decline of the CEBs. The MST has reenergized, redefined, and reaffirmed the liberationist message in the context of a global human and environmental crisis. It promotes the politics of hope as an alternative to the politics of despair. Solidarity movements have a difficult task of advancing new liberationist visions and strategies that address holistically social, political, economic, cultural, and environmental concerns. In light of these challenges, the teachings and practices of liberation theology and the CEBS are more important than ever.

NOTE

The author of this chapter has placed some suggested resources that you may wish to consult on the book's website at http://www.rowmanlittlefield.com/isbn/ 0742555240.

REFERENCES

Boff, Leonardo, and Clodovis Boff. 1987. *Introducing Liberation Theology*. Maryknoll, NY: Orbis Books.

Bruneau, Thomas. 1982. *The Church in Brazil: The Politics of Religion*. Austin: University of Texas Press.

Burkholder, Mark A., and Lyman L. Johnson. 2004. *Colonial Latin America*. Oxford: Oxford University Press.

Burns, E. Bradford, and Julie A. Charlip. 2002. *Latin America: A Concise Interpretive History*. Upper Saddle River, NJ: Prentice Hall.

Chasteen, John Charles. 2005. *Born in Blood and Fire: A Concise History of Latin America*. 2nd ed. New York: W. W. Norton.

Cleary, Edward L. 1985. *Crisis and Change: The Church in Latin America Today*. New York: Orbis Books.

———. 1990. *Born of the Poor: The Latin American Church since Medellin*. Notre Dame, IN: University of Notre Dame Press.

———. 2004. "Shopping Around: Questions about Latin American Conversions." *International Bulletin of Missionary Research* 28:50–54.

Cleary, Edward L., and Timothy Steigenga, eds. 2004. *Resurgent Voices in Latin America: Indigenous Peoples, Political Mobilization, and Religious Change*. New Brunswick, NJ: Rutgers University Press.

Committee of Santa Fe. 1980. "A New Inter-American Policy for the Eighties." Council on Inter-American Security, Washington, D.C., May, 2.

Cook, Guillermo. 1985. *The Expectation of the Poor: Latin American Base Ecclesial Communities in Protestant Perspective*. Maryknoll, NY: Orbis Books.

Dussel, Enrique. 1981. "Current Events in Latin America, 1972–80." In *The Challenge of Basic Christian Communities*, ed. Sergio Torres and John Eagleson, 77–102. Maryknoll, NY: Orbis Books.

Eagleson, John, and Philip Scharper. 1979. *Puebla and Beyond: Documentation and Commentary*. Maryknoll, NY: Orbis Books.

Escobar, Samuel. 1986. "Christian Base Communities in Historical Perspective." *Transformation* 3 (July–September).

Ferm, Deane William. 1986. *Third World Liberation Theologies: An Introductory Survey*. Maryknoll, NY: Orbis Books.

Freston, Paul. 2006. *Evangelical Christianity and Democracy in Latin America*. New York: Oxford University Press.

Galarza, Ernest. 2003. *Roman Catholic Church in Mexico*. Kila, MT: Kessinger Publishing.

Gibson, Charles. 1966. *Spain in America*. New York: Harper and Row.

Gutiérrez, Gustavo. 1988. *A Theology of Liberation: History, Politics and Salvation*. 2nd ed. Maryknoll, NY: Orbis Books.

Maduro, Otto. 1982. *Religion and Social Conflict*. Maryknoll, NY: Orbis Books.

Mainwaring, Scott. 1989. *The Progressive Church in Latin America*. Notre Dame, IN: University of Notre Dame Press.

Nash, Ronald H. 1988. *Liberation Theology*. Grand Rapids, MI: Baker Publishing Group.

Novak, Michael. 1986. *Will It Liberate? Questions about Liberation Theology*. New York: Paulist Press.

Petras, James, and Henry Veltmeyer. 2005. *Social Movements and State Power: Argentina, Brazil, Bolivia, Ecuador*. Ann Arbor, MI: Pluto Press.

Robles, Wilder. 2000. "Beyond the Politics of Protest: The Landless Rural Workers Movement in Brazil." *Canadian Journal of Development Studies* 21, no. 3: 657–91.

———. 2001. "The Landless Rural Workers Movement in Brazil." *Journal of Peasant Studies* 28, no. 2: 146–61.

Schmitt, Karl M. 1972. *The Roman Catholic Church in Modern Latin America*. New York: Knopf.

Schwaller, John F., ed. 2000. *The Church in Colonial Latin America*. Wilmington, DE: SR Books.

Smith, Christian, and Joshua Prokopy, eds. 2005. *Latin American Religion in Motion*. Boca Raton, FL: Taylor and Francis Group.

Stédile, João Pedro, and Bernardo Mançano Fernandes. 1999. *Brava gente: A trajetória do MST e a luta pela terra no Brasil*. São Paulo: Editora Fundação Perseu Abramo.

Stoll, David. 1991. *Is Latin America Turning Protestant? The Politics of Evangelical Growth*. Berkeley: University of California Press.

Tantardini, Mark. 1991. "Liberation Theology and the Christian-Marxist Convergence." MA thesis, University of Guelph, Canada, 1.

United Nations Development Program (UNDP). 2004. *La democracia en América Latina: Hacia una democracia de ciudadanas y ciudadanos*. Buenos Aires: Aguilar, Altea, Taurus, Alfaguara, S.A.

10

Ecological Crisis, Sustainable Development, and Capitalism

Guido Pascual Galafassi

This chapter addresses the social and ecological crisis in Latin America in relation to the regional processes of social and economic development. Poverty, social exclusion, and environmental conflicts are some of the general consequences of the contradictions that characterize growth without balanced and ecologically sustainable development. To analyze the conditions underpinning these contradictions, it is necessary to take into account three main factors. The first is the contradiction between capital and other factors of production, such as nature, space, and labor power. The second is the underdeveloped nature of the economy, with high levels of inequality and social exploitation. The third is the utilization of natural resources based on an economic strategy of pillage.

Above all, Latin America is largely a derivative market economy: a peripheral copy of the growth economies in the North, exhibiting extreme income concentration and uneven development. The acceleration of economic growth, when it has taken place, has gone hand in hand with the deceleration of national socioeconomic development. While quantitative macroeconomic indices improve, the indicators that measure qualitative changes have generally deteriorated.

In this context, to explain the ecological crisis in Latin America, it is important to consider not only the different environmental impacts but also the socioeconomic factors and contradictions extant in derivative capitalistic development. This chapter concentrates on two interconnected issues. One is the general pattern that social and economic development has taken. The other is the relationship among industrialization, natural resource exploitation, and urbanization.

In order to study the relationship between development and ecological crisis, it is important to pay attention to new perspectives that can give us more analytical insight into the relationship between society and nature. Traditional interpretations of Latin American development have not taken into account the complexity of the existing relations among socioeconomic, political, and environmental factors. These interpretations mainly conceive society as "disconnected" from its natural surroundings. This perspective does not consider the interrelations, influences, and conditions that define the concrete historical processes, which are always (directly or indirectly) forged by the interaction between social and natural processes.

To study the relationship between society, nature, and development, we need to begin by considering one of the basic tendencies of capitalism: to debilitate and destroy its own conditions of production, as noted by O'Connor (1988). These conditions include the physical environment, the regional or urban infrastructure, and human labor power. This basic tendency of capitalism is what O'Connor calls the second contradiction of capitalism (O'Connor 1988). The first contradiction of capitalism (between forces and relations of production, or capital versus labor) is internal to the system and has nothing to do with the conditions of production. The second contradiction "focuses on the way that the combined power of capitalist production relations and productive forces self-destruct by impairing or destroying rather than reproducing their own conditions—'conditions' defined in terms of both their social and material dimensions" (O'Connor 1988, 12). Thus, the second contradiction involves capital against nature, labor power, and space. An intense and continuous exploitation of natural resources, space, and labor power is required for capital to increase its value. As O'Connor puts it, "The basic cause of the second contradiction is capitalism's . . . self-destructive appropriation and use of labor power, urban infrastructure and space, and external nature or [the] environment" (O'Connor 1988, 13). It is self-destructive because the costs of health and education, urban transport, housing and commercial rents, and extracting capital from nature rise, and private costs are turned into social costs.

In the first contradiction of capitalism, the rate of exploitation of labor is a clearly identifiable element. In the second contradiction, a unique term that summarizes the totality of the human-environmental contradiction does not exist. It is possible today to find a multiplicity of social movements with diverse grievances clustered around this second contradiction. These new social movements, together with the historical labor movement, are the agents of current social struggle and transformation. They represent the force of new social struggles that, among others, involve the nature of production, the workplace, health and safety, toxic-waste generation and disposal, air pollution, natural resource depletion, the deteriorating conditions of urban life, and radical democracy as a way to solve social and ecological problems and to make social and political decisions.

GENERAL CHARACTERISTICS
OF DEVELOPMENT IN LATIN AMERICA

We can characterize the historical process of development in Latin America by dividing it into four periods: (1) colonial mercantilism (1500s–1750s), (2) outward growth liberalism dependent on primary exports (1750s–1914), (3) the crisis of the "liberal model" of growth (1914–1950), and (4) the current period of transnational capitalism. Structural underdevelopment and dependency in Latin America[1] started in the colonial period; as the prominent Latin American historian Bagú (1949) stated, "Production was not directed by the needs of national consumers, and not even by the interests of local producers. The lines of production were structured and transformed to conform to an order determined by the imperial metropolis. The colonial economy was consequently shaped by its complementary character" (23).

Throughout the nineteenth century, the politically dominant groups that led the independence movements in the region retained the primary export economies created during the colonial period. They did not attempt to transform the internal productive structures; they only eliminated Iberian interference in the trade of products with England and northern Europe. The logic of the productive system in this period of outwardly directed development was not conducive to the creation of a large industrial sector in Latin America and the Caribbean (Valenzuela and Valenzuela 1998).

This situation changed in the first half of the twentieth century. The world wars and the Great Depression produced a crisis in the export-oriented economies through the collapse of external demand, and this situation limited their capacity to import. Fiscal and monetary policies were adopted to try to promote the internal market and to avoid the negative effects of the external disequilibria. In this context, a favorable climate was created for the growth of an industrial sector under national governmental protection and support. The import-substitution-industrialization (ISI) policies introduced during this period employed the available foreign exchange to acquire the capital goods needed to manufacture substitute products for those that could no longer be imported.

This type of industrialization started to decline after World War II. The transformations in the center of the world system generated a new period of "transnational capitalism." The dependency of the peripheral economies acquired a new character: the growing multinational corporations sought new markets and cheaper production sites for their increasingly technology-based manufacturing processes. These big corporations invested in the periphery and cornered the internal market. As Cardoso and Faletto (1969) note in their classic study, this process involved the "internationalization of the internal market" in the peripheral countries. In addition, two other tendencies can be mentioned. The first was "a new international division of labor in which the periphery acquires capital goods, technology, and raw materials from the central nations, and exports profits, along with its traditional raw materials and a few manufactured items produced by multinational subsidiaries" (Cardoso and Faletto 1969, 34). The second was the denationalization of the import-substituting industries established in the previous period (Valenzuela and Valenzuela 1998).

Various writers have criticized the different approaches to Latin American development[2] from the perspective of sustainable development (Mansilla 1991; Tudela 1990; Gudynas 1999; Leff 1999; Guimaraes 1999). They have noted that Latin American development efforts have been based largely on the ideology of progress and a mechanistic view of society that necessarily equates progress with growth. Capital accumulation, increased productivity, and efficiency are the indicators of advancement in this approach to development. In this context, these writers note that all the tendencies, whether liberal, neoliberal, Marxist, or neo-Marxist, consider economic growth paramount. They argue that the differences among the paradigms relate to the role of the state, the market, the social classes, and so on, but not to the intrinsic sustainability of their models of economic and social development.

Nature generally does not appear in these theories, and when it does, it is only in a residual form. The environmental restrictions on development as growth have been minimized and, in some cases, even ignored. Nature has been replaced by the concept of natural resources, and each one is considered separately. Moreover, these natural resources are assumed to be infinite and to have the capacity to support an unlimited rate of exploitation. Thus, nature does not pose any limitations on material progress.

The concept of "sustainable development" has acquired some importance in the last decades in Latin America, although the concept of sustainability does not mean the same thing for everybody. Many Latin American thinkers (Sanchez 1983; Gallopín 1987; CEPAL 1992; Leff 1994; Sejenovich and Panario 1996; Guimaraes 2001) believe the main objective of sustainable development is to improve the quality of life. This improvement is considered possible through the maximum utilization of the productive potential of the ecosystem, through the use of socially as well as environmentally appropriate technology, and through the active participation of the people in making the fundamental decisions about development.

All of these sustainable-development approaches take into account the conditions of underdevelopment and the ecological crisis. The concept of sustainability raises serious doubts about the possibility of finding an effective solution to the social and environmental problems resulting from the growth economies in the South. Taking into account the process of boundless accumulation and competition in the present globalized context, Latouche (1999) has argued that "the concept of sustainable development is but the latest attempt to ally the bad sides of economic growth" (505). Latouche argues that sustainable development integrates environmental elements into economic calculation in a way that does not address the root causes of the ecological crisis. To reduce the process of environmental and social degradation, it is necessary to modify not only the nature of the market economy but also the logic of modernity. Taking a Marxist approach, O'Connor has strongly criticized the concept of sustainability since he argues that it is not possible to resolve the two contradictions of capitalism. O'Connor maintains that sustainable capitalism is impossible since capitalism has an inherent tendency to self-destruction, and the market economy inevitably increases poverty and ecological devastation (O'Connor 1998).

INDUSTRIALIZATION, DEINDUSTRIALIZATION, AND ECOLOGICAL CRISIS

The modern approaches to development present in Latin America and the Caribbean during the last century have produced a high social and environmental impact. The economic development in the South is a bad copy of the development approaches in the North. Most of the social, economic, and ecological crises in the South have to do with the spread of the "growth economy" approach to development (Fotopoulos 1997). Whereas the market economy has improved the living conditions of most of society in the North, the imported market economy in the South has resulted in a much more uneven pattern of development than in the North and led to a bad copy of the latter's growth-oriented economies.

The industrialization process that began in the 1930s and 1940s in Latin America and the Caribbean is one of the most important causes of the social and spatial transformations that have taken place in the region, as well as the origin of both its rural and urban ecological crises. The demand for labor brought about by this industrialization process accelerated migration from the countryside to the cities and gave rise to the exponential growth the Latin American cities. The urban population, which comprised 40 percent of the total population in 1950, grew to 56 percent in 1970 and reached 67 percent by the mid-1980s.[3] Obviously, there are differences among countries: in Chile, Argentina, and Uruguay, more than 80 percent of the population lives in urban areas, while in Haiti, Honduras, Guatemala, and Bolivia, only approximately 50 percent live in urban areas. But the tendency is for urban growth to continue. The fact is that Latin American and Caribbean countries have been transformed from agrarian to urban countries since the second half of the twentieth century.

It is necessary to distinguish between industrialization and urbanization. The industrialization process was the main cause of the urban growth from

1930 to 1950. However, in the last decades of the twentieth century, the urban population continued to grow (although at a much slower rate), while the number of industrial workers has not only stopped growing but started to decrease.

Urbanization has been accompanied by an increase in commercial, financial, and construction activities, which in turn have generated serious communication and transportation problems. Moreover, most Latin American and Caribbean cities have experienced a profound degradation of their physical environment, and increasing noise, rubbish, and pollution are the most common expressions of the expanding urbanscape. Industrialization and urbanization have generated very high levels of energy consumption. The increase in industrial production and consumption has been based on the exigencies of industrial growth rather than on any kind of integrated social and economic view of development (Vitale 1983).

To promote such industrial growth, Latin American and Caribbean governments have attracted transnational capital to finance, establish, and manage new industries. This transnational capital has brought with it new capital-intensive technologies that have not been effectively incorporated locally. This technological exogeneity has also increased the level of dependency of the Latin American and Caribbean economies on transnational capital.

One of the consequences of haphazard industrial growth has been the generation of new forms of pollution, which in many cases have been outlawed in the more advanced capitalist countries. In their haste to promote industrial development, the Latin American and Caribbean governments have not paid much attention to the environmental impact of this kind of development.

The crisis of this pattern of industrialization started in the 1970s. Structural reforms and the opening of the economy to foreign capital have been central elements in the new economic policies since the 1980s. The respect for "market rules" associated with these new policies has resulted in extensive privatization, deindustrialization, and economic concentration. As a result, there has been an increase in unemployment, poverty, inequality, social exclusion, and the wholesale looting of the region's natural resources.

The renewed specialization of Latin America and the Caribbean as a region that exports raw materials has had a heavy impact on the natural environment. There has been a sharp increase in the rates of natural resource depletion without significant regard for replacement and conservation. The basic characteristics of a "pillage economy" exist with regard to natural resource extraction. The logic followed in this economy is to extract resources as quickly as possible, then move on to new sites when nature cannot provide anything more. This logic of natural resource extraction has led to the exploitation of the region's natural resources without any investment in regeneration in the case of renewable resources or the rational use in the medium or long term of nonrenewable resources. Some historical examples of this logic of extraction to the point of exhaustion are the exploitation of quebracho in the Argentinian Chaco, guano in northern Chile, and silver in Bolivia.

A remarkable contradiction is present in this mode of exploitation. The logic of extracting resources as quickly as possible undermines continuous production. It can be clearly characterized as irrational, especially in those cases of small and medium producers with limited alternatives for changing to the extraction of other types of resources. However, it is clearly profitable for large mobile capital that can afford to go elsewhere once the damage is done and an area's natural resources have been exhausted. This pillage-and-move strategy of mobile megacapital is much more evident today due to the increase in foreign investments over the last decades.

Perhaps the most illustrative example is mining activity. In the context of the new open-market policies since the 1980s, these types of activities are exclusively extractive with no regard to conservation, environmental protection, or the rational social use of resources. These activities are managed by big multinational firms whose productive and investment territory is the whole world. Thus, their method involves two steps: they swiftly exploit the resources involved through extractive processes that minimize costs and maximize profits, and then, once they have exhausted the resources at the site, they move quickly to another region to repeat the process all over again.

Examining the impact of the dominant style of development in the region on the environment, it is possible to identify a series of relevant and significant features that have persisted throughout the region's contemporary history (Galafassi 2004). These features reflect the relationships between contemporary society and the natural environment, particularly the impact of the methods of exploitation that have been used to extract natural resources. They can be summed up as follows:

The natural endowment of resources in the region has played a preponderant role in the pattern of development that has been created in the region. Because of this endowment of resources, the economies in the region are based on agriculture and export-oriented mining. Latin America specializes in the production and export of primary products. A new version of this specialization is represented by the deep integration into the global economy and the region of genetically modified organisms (Dimitriu, Howard, and Reynolds 2002; Kneen 2002)—hence the importance of considering the contradiction between capital and nature as an important aspect of the current development process.

Despite the fact that land is one of the most abundant resources in the region, it represents a limited means of production for most of the population due to the structure of land ownership and use. There is a high degree of monopolization in the ownership of land within Latin America and the Caribbean. A small elite owns most of the productive land, which still represents their main source of wealth and power. Although this concentration of land underwent some modifications in the twentieth century through agrarian reforms, *latifundia* (large estates) are a persistent feature of the region. This has affected urban life since the cities have attracted the large numbers of rural migrants who have been driven off the land or cannot find sufficient employment in the rural areas. The large numbers of rural migrants to the cities have created severe spatial and social imbalances.

The high natural productivity of certain ecosystems in the region has led to the concentration of primary agroexport production in these areas for a long time. The extent of exploitation of the natural environment in these ecosystems has increased over time largely because of the relative resilience of the environment in these ecosystems instead of the higher levels of technological innovation in agriculture. Because of both factors, however, there have been severe signs of soil exhaustion in these areas over the last few decades, which reveals once again the contradiction between capitalism and nature.

There is a notable contrast between the urban lowland systems and the urban systems located in mountainous areas. The different environmental conditions in these two types of urban settings are responsible for marked differences in terms of traffic congestion, access to fresh water, the self-purification capacity of ground-water systems, air circulation, flood problems, and the like. Buenos Aires, for example, is located in a vast plain surrounded by major courses of water. This location creates flood problems but allows for great air circulation. These natural conditions contrast notably with those in Santiago (Chile) and Mexico City, both of which are located in mountainous areas with water-provision problems and a high level of air contamination due to the reduced air circulation in the valleys where they are located.

The dominant pattern and mind-set of development in the region have always considered everything that is natural on the surface as an obstacle that must be removed (forests, fauna, and biodiversity) in order to use the soil for farming, mining, or urban purposes. This approach gives more value to the soil than the rest of the natural resources. Since the mid-nineteenth century, the elite in power have privatized the public lands and all the natural resources that have profitable use, which were previously snatched from the native inhabitants during the colonial period. Thus, the soil is the fundamental resource for the present and future usufruct.

The supposition that there is an unlimited supply of resources has resulted in a slow, and in some cases increasingly deep, process of edaphic, landscape, and biodiversity deterioration. The high natural fertility of certain regions has often hidden this deterioration process until recent times.

The production strategy has been, as mentioned above in the case of mining, to pillage new spaces instead of investing in resource renewal (e.g., reforestation) and conservation. The capitalist logic of minimizing cost and maximizing profits results in increasing resource exhaustion through the geographic mobility of the transnational companies and foreign investments involved in the process. Needless to say, the remaining vast virgin lands in Latin America are an incomparable natural treasure waiting to be pillaged.

The dominant style of development is characterized by a unimodal approach that assumes all regional ecosystems have the same stability and resistance. This assumption has led to the depletion and deterioration of the most fragile ecosystems. In addition, productive practices have acquired a pattern of uniformity and homogeneity that has given rise to the depletion of biodiversity and the destruction of indigenous and peasant cultural variability. The present advance of soy production, with its complex and dependent technological package, represents a new manifestation of this phenomenon.

URBAN AND REGIONAL SOCIOECOLOGICAL CONDITIONS

To analyze the nexus between social and environmental conditions in the urban regions, one needs to take into consideration three main factors: (1) the high population density, (2) the rapid and concomitant territorial growth of the urban regions during the second half of the twentieth century, and, last but not least, (3) the virtual nonexistence of an integrated development strategy aimed at improving the quality of life of the majority of the populations (Galafassi 2002b).

Numerous forms of pollution and environmental degradation, the absence of an appropriate infrastructure, and widespread poverty are the consequences of the contradictions associated with capitalism and the lack of an integrated model of environmentally sustainable development. Poor housing conditions, health problems, food insecurity, and a dearth of basic utilities, among other ills, are mainly determined by the low incomes of a large part of the population (Hardoy and Satterthwaite 1987; Di Pace, Federovisky, and Hardoy 1990; Hardoy, Mitlin, and Satterthwaite 2001). Under these circumstances, it is easy to recognize the reasons for the social and ecological crisis confronting most of the urban regions in Latin America and the Caribbean. This crisis has been made worse by the implementation of neoliberal policies in the last decades.

The domestic habitat of poor families in Latin America is characterized by unsanitary conditions. Approximately 20 to 50 percent of the inhabitants in most urban areas live in inadequate housing (Killen and Rahamn 2001;

Hardoy, Mitlin, and Satterthwaite 2001); up to fifteen people can live in the same dwelling. In addition, the rapid increase in the cities' populations has resulted in the building of illegal communities over swampy areas with contaminated water. These "poor suburbs" have grown more quickly than the rest of the cities, and in most of them there is a lack of running water, drainage, garbage collection, sewage systems, and paved streets (Hardoy and Satterthwaite 1987; Hordijk 1999; Harth Daneke and Silve 1982; Moser 1982; Connolly 1982; Hardoy, Mitlin, and Satterthwaite 2001). Environmental quality is generally sacrificed in favor of more immediate necessities for people's survival, such as housing.

It is possible to establish a difference between the settlements of people who live in precarious houses built under illegal conditions and of those who live in deplorable conditions but in houses or apartments built under legal conditions. The first kind of settlement is referred to as a "shantytown" in English and as a *favela, callampa, cantegrile, pueblo jóvene,* or *villa de emergencia* in Portuguese and Spanish, depending upon the particular country in Latin America. The second kind of housing settlements are generally referred to as "slums" or "tenement houses" in English and are called *asentamientos* or *conventillos* in the Spanish-speaking areas.

Most of the shantytowns have dismal living conditions and appear in precarious geographic locations. There are shantytowns on the sides of mountains where mud slides and avalanches occasionally occur—for example, in Rio de Janeiro (Brazil), Guatemala City (Guatemala), La Paz (Bolivia), and Caracas (Venezuela). There are also shantytowns in some sandy desert areas, such as those surrounding Lima (Peru), and in some flood-prone areas, such as Guayaquil (Ecuador), Recife (Brazil), and Resistencia and Buenos Aires (Argentina). In Mexico City, approximately 1.5 million inhabitants live on the Texcoco lake bed, which is dry most of the year, except when it rains. This place is exposed to dust storms during the dry season and turns into a muddy plain when it rains.

Industrialization has led some cities of Latin America and the Caribbean to have an important concentration of factories. These cities have serious pollution problems compared to the pollution problems in developed countries (Cherni 2001). Actually, these problems are sometimes more dramatic for two reasons. First, the growth of industrial production in some countries has taken place in a context of a thoroughly inefficient system of urban planning and land-use regulation. In general, the faster the increase of industrial production, the higher the probability that environmental problems will be worse since the control of industrial pollution is an important concern neither for the governments involved nor for most of the people. Second, industrial production is commonly concentrated in one or two areas. Despite some government efforts to decentralize industrial development, most new industries have been located on the periphery of larger metropolitan areas. It is well known that the low level of regulatory control in the global South has made it possible for some of the most highly contaminating industries to relocate there. Multinational corporations have exported their high-pollution factories to Latin America and the Caribbean to avoid paying the costs associated with the stricter contamination controls and worker health and safety rules in the advanced capitalist countries.[4]

"Regional impact" is an important factor to consider in Latin America and the Caribbean since the disorderly growth of big cities affects the nearby territories in different ways. Big cities are big production and consumption centers and demand a great quantity of resources like water, fossil fuels, land, and all the other materials that urban activities require. But the cities are also great centers of pollution and contamination, so their regional impacts can be divided into two categories. The first stems from the extraction of natural resources required by urban activities. The second encompasses the urban spillover effects on the environment of the regions surrounding cities. Obviously, both subcategories are closely related, and the type of urban production and consumption defines the natural resources needed, as well as the kind of waste and pollution spread into nearby territories. Furthermore, this permanent exchange of resources in return for waste and pollution makes it difficult to separate the rural areas from the urban areas.

There is a permanent relation between urban and rural areas. The impoverishment of the rural population leads to migration from the countryside into the cities. The cities grow and expand into the surrounding areas, where the agricultural producers and workers are expelled from their lands. New urban areas occupy these lands, generally without consideration of the provision of urban services and their impact on the natural setting, with possibly catastrophic consequences. Likewise, growing population pressure brings about greater demands on water and other resources from the surrounding areas and can have counterproductive effects, such as increased salinization of the water supply in the surrounding rural areas and their desertification.

According to some authors, a parasitic relationship has developed between the cities and their nearby lands. This relationship is based on the evolution of the economic value of the natural resources, particularly the soil, the subsoil, the vegetation, and other geographical features, such as water resources. The growth of cities, therefore, decreases or eliminates the diversity of natural ecosystems affected by their growth, as it reduces the species and changes the geographical features of the areas affected and the potential fertility of the soil in these areas for food production (Rees 1999, 2001).[5]

MODERNIZATION AND SOCIOECOLOGICAL MOBILIZATION

The ideology of modernization has influenced all the development processes in Latin America. As a consequence, the socioecological evolution and the social mobilization processes in the region have been closely related to this ideological paradigm of development. Modernization, as a subsidiary justification for a particular type of material progress, is sustained chiefly by mobilizing vast human capacities to transform material reality through developing productive forces, allegedly to increase the well-being of the population involved. Economic growth, technological innovation, the exploitation of labor, and nature are the main axes of modern progress. This pattern of development, even when presenting certain temporal and spatial variations, maintains an essential continuity throughout most of the history of contemporary Latin America and the Caribbean. Economic growth and technological development have always been at the core of Latin American and Caribbean politics, from the populist period of the 1940s and the developmentalism of the postwar period to the increasing authoritarian neoliberalism of the 1970s and 1980s and the pseudodemocratic neoliberalism of the turn of the century. What differs between countries is the degree to which wealth is distributed and the specific aspects of industrialization, urbanization, agriculture, regional development modes, and the extent of exploitation of both nature and labor in each country.

As a result of these parameters, a diverse range of organizations and social movements has emerged to oppose this dominant model of society, its sociopolitical and economic, as well as its ecological, aspects. These opposing forces include those who criticize capitalism and those who intensely point out the faults of modern progress itself. Criticism of capitalism does not necessarily imply a questioning of the modern development process per se. On the other hand, judging modernity from an ecological perspective involves a critical examination of economic growth as a product of both capitalist and Socialist productivism.

The theoretical frameworks with which social movements are currently researched (often functionalistic or influenced by the postmodern ideology of methodological individualism) tend to differentiate between "old" and "new" social movements, as well as between "old" and "new" political paradigms (Offe 1985; Melucci 1980; Tarrow 1994; McAdam, McCarthy, and Zald 1996). The old movements were enrolled in the classic class struggle in which the dominant social subjects were both the institutionalized groups and the political parties that promoted the values of social mobility. The new movements, on the other hand, are guided by open and flexible networks responding to noninstitutionalized politics in a context in which class struggles are not paramount. Instead of following this theoretical line of argument, we prefer to think of Latin American social reality in terms of complex processes in which the mechanical divisions (between, for example, old and new social movements) do not correspond to the historical present and where the diverse manifestations of social movements interrelate and interact and always express some opposition between classes or fractions of classes (Galafassi 2006).

In the 1960s and 1970s, the differences were more marked, but at present a paradigmatic confluence is taking place. The countercultural and environmentalist movements of the 1960s and 1970s directed their criticism against the above-mentioned ideology of modern progress. They tried to achieve a "return to nature," initiating a new communal life related to a "radical democratic philosophy," thus breaking down the modern concept of private and individualistic life. In so doing, they tried to generate a new social model without industries and cities, decrying modernization and challenging the essential tenets of modern progress. This model also included a general and often inexplicit critique of capitalism.

However, there were also movements identified with left-wing tendencies and class organizations (the labor movement, urban guerrilla movements, peasant movements, etc.) that considered capitalism to be the root of social alienation, and they paid little attention to socioecological and "radical democratic" issues. The predominant prescription was the so-called two-step strategy: first, to gain state power; second, to transform the world (Wallerstein 2002). To attain this objective, a strong and rigid, Leninist-type political organization was seen as a necessity.

Nevertheless, over the last decades, a convergence among tendencies and movements has been emerging in Latin America and the Caribbean, paralleling a similar tendency at the global level. Although significant differences persist among environmentalist groups, they are not as marked as they used to be. The centrality of environmental problems, the criticism regarding state concentration of power, the related emphasis on participatory democracy, and respect for cultural and biological diversity are all standard features of the new social movements. These views are also now increasingly combined with a class-based critique of capitalism and the call for the construction of political organizations that will be able to win elections and form progressive governments, which are features similar to those of the old social movements.

For example, Petras (2002) has identified three waves of overlapping and interrelated new social movements since the end of the 1970s. The first wave comprised human rights, ecology, feminist, and racial/ethnic rights movements, as well as numerous nongovernmental organizations (NGOs). This first wave of new social movements had the military and civilian authoritarian regimes of that time as the main focus of their protest. A new manifestation of this generation of social movements is the popular assemblies that have appeared in recent years and have focused their actions on specific environmental problems.

Two examples of these are the Self-assembled Neighbors of Gualeguaychú (Vecinos Autoconvocados de Gualeguaychú), which protests the construction of new paper mills in Uruguay, and the myriad array of assemblies in Patagonia, the Argentine Andes, and Peru, which have opposed mining projects. The Esquel Assembly in the Patagonian Andes is paradigmatic of this type of popular mobilization. Meridian Gold, Inc., headquartered in Reno, Nevada, proposed to develop an open-pit gold mine seven kilometers upstream from the town of Esquel (population approximately thirty thousand). The mobilization against the proposal started in 2001, and since then the protests have gradually grown in scope and intensity. In March 2003, residents of Esquel responded with a resounding no to a referendum on the mine. More than 80 percent of the citizens of the region voted against the project and against any policy opening the way to natural resource depletion. This experience has been replicated in other places. For instance, the Patagonian Coordinating Assembly against Resource Pillaging was created shortly after Esquel. This assembly works in close relation with other local assemblies opposing mining in the Andean region and also with the aforementioned Gualeguaychú assembly in Uruguay.

A second wave of social movements that emerged in the mid-1980s comprises peasants and rural workers engaged in direct action to promote and defend communal styles of production and political organization. The Zapatistas in Mexico, the Rural Landless Workers of Brazil (the Movimento dos Trabalhadores Rurais sem Terra, or MST), the Cocaleros and other peasant organizations in Bolivia, the National Peasant Federation in Paraguay, and the peasant-Indian confederation in Ecuador are the most prominent movements in this second wave. It could be suggested that even the Revolutionary Armed Forces of Colombia, a more "classical" form of guerrilla organization, has adopted some traits of these new peasant movements. Despite the fact that both their tactics and specific local demands have varied, these movements have in all cases considered "neoliberalism" and "imperialism" broadly defined as the strategic "enemy."[6] These organizations have developed actions and strategies opposing the neoliberal economic regime and the growing concentration of wealth in the hands of local and foreign elites. Specifically, they have struggled for land redistribution, national and communitarian autonomy, and the conservation of the natural resources needed for their subsistence. They have fought against U.S. intervention in the form of coca-eradication programs, the colonization of territory for military bases, the penetration of national police and military institutions through U.S. advisers and training, and the militarization of social conflicts through projects such as Plan Colombia and the Andean Initiative.

The Zapatista Army of National Liberation (EZLN) represents the rights of the indigenous population but also sees itself, and is seen, as part of a wider anticapitalist movement. The Zapatistas oppose corporate globalization and neoliberalism and advocate a communitarian perspective in which a harmonic and sustainable relationship between society and nature is fundamental to their ideology and practice. They see themselves as Emiliano Zapata's ideological heirs and also as heirs to five hundred years of indigenous resistance against imperialism. The EZLN has been fighting primarily for the autonomy of the indigenous population as a solution to poverty.

They seek to create a kind of state within a state where people can retain their own government and communal ways of life, yet receive outside support in basic areas. The Zapatistas have gradually formed several autonomous municipalities (*caracoles*) independent of the Mexican government. These municipalities have evolved into local government juntas, implementing communitarian food-producing programs and health and school systems, which are supported partly by NGOs. The Zapatistas do not tax the inhabitants and decide through assemblies to work on communitarian projects. Members in the juntas rotate continuously so that everybody in the community can have an opportunity to serve and also to prevent people in office from becoming used to power, or corrupted.

Brazil's Landless Workers Movement, the MST, is the largest social movement in Latin America with an estimated 1.5 million landless members organized in twenty-three out of Brazil's twenty-seven states. The MST has been carrying out long-overdue land reform largely without the government's help in a country mired in unjust land distribution. In Brazil, 1.6 percent of the landowners control roughly half (46.8 percent) of the land. The top 3 percent of the population owns two-thirds of all arable lands in Brazil.

Since 1985, the MST has peacefully occupied unused lands, where they have established cooperative farms; built houses, schools for children and adults, and clinics; promoted indigenous cultures; and created a healthy sustainable environment and gender equality. The MST has won land titles for more than 350,000 families in two thousand settlements as a result of their actions, while 180,000 encamped families currently await government recognition. The MST holds that land occupations are recognized in the Brazilian Constitution, which states that land that remains unproductive should be used for a "larger social function." The MST's success lies in its ability to organize and educate a large number of people from different areas and different social categories. The organization's members have not only managed to secure land, which means food security for their families, but they are involved in developing a sustainable socioeconomic model that offers a concrete alternative to today's corporate-dominated globalization that puts profits before people and the well-being of humankind.

More recently, new multisectoral movements similar to the MST in Brazil have launched mass struggles that integrate farm workers and small and medium-sized farmers in Colombia, Mexico, and Paraguay. Their actions and protests are aimed at improving the conditions of peasant production and commercialization; however, environmental aspects are not central to their agendas.

Urban areas are the social space in which the third and newest wave of social movements is centered. This new wave of social movements includes the dynamic neighborhood-based mass movements of unemployed workers in Argentina—the picketers (*piqueteros*)—and organizations that have mobilized the unemployed and poor members of the urban population in the Caribbean basin countries (e.g., Venezuela and the Dominican Republic). Communitarian, democratic, and sustainable-development values are prominent aspects of their political agendas.

One of the main traits all these movements share is the rejection of the traditional patron-client, or patronage, style of politics that has been practiced by political party bosses and trade union bureaucrats in the past and in current populist political regimes. Instead, these movements rely strongly on self-organization and direct action. The Unemployed Workers Movement and the Unemployed Workers Union in Argentina are examples of these kinds of movements. They have a decentralized organizational structure based on *barrio* or neighborhood organizations. Each local-level organization is directed by a general assembly in which all the active members participate. Political and economic autonomy is very important for these organizations. Many of these local organizations have developed a wide variety of autonomous productive enterprises, and a significant number have developed a deep relationship with peasant movements (for instance, in the area of goods for exchange and barter). The management of human and natural resources and communitarian development are central issues in the social and political strategies of these movements of the unemployed.

Complementing these local-based movements, there has been a reemergence of grassroots workers movements, such as the Inter-Sindical Clasista (Classist Union Coalition) in Argentina. Workers participating in this coalition define themselves as classist, combative, and antibureaucratic. In this case, however, the relation between nature and society is not an important concern.

Therefore, the present scene reveals a combination of the features of the old and new social movements. The different profiles of these social movements represent diverse manifestations of antagonisms and conflicts and various common aspirations. The inequitable distribution of power, wealth, and resources among classes and social actors is the structural condition that underlies all social conflicts in the region.

CONCLUSION

The Latin American and Caribbean region is still burdened by the restraints of the so-called Washington Consensus, the U.S.-made project to manage the postdictatorship order based on strictly limited democracy and the rules of a largely unregulated market economy (Galafassi 2002a). These policies have led to the privatization of the state and the shrinkage of its functions, as well as to the destruction of the incipient and fragmented industrial development generated during the period of ISI policies. These policies have led to an increase in the pillaging of the region's natural resources and the degradation of its ecosystems (thereby deepening the contradictions between capital and nature). They have been accompanied by economic concentration, a widening gap between the rich and the poor, and high levels of unemployment. Moreover, the hegemony of neoliberal ideology has prevented the adoption of ecologically sustainable, integrated, and democratic approaches to economic and social development. On the contrary, they have intensified the two basic contradictions of capitalism referred to early in this chapter.

During the ISI period, the main objective was to establish national industries that could produce consumer goods for the domestic market. The ecological effects of this process of industrialization were not taken into consideration, although there were many environmental consequences of ISI. Between the 1930s and the 1960s, the process of national industrial development undertaken throughout the region did in fact improve the living standards of a significant part of the population. But this approach to economic and social development was replaced by the neoliberal, market-driven approach to economic growth adopted by most of the Latin American and Caribbean countries in the 1980s and 1990s.

During the last two decades of the twentieth century, when the environmentalist movement gained prominence in the advanced capitalist countries of the North, neoliberal policies were being imposed on the Latin American and Caribbean countries without regard to their environmental consequences or the growing ecological crises in the region. Thus, efforts to address these ecological crises and the promotion of ecologically and socially sustainable development were put forward by civil society organizations, that is, by new social movements, certain NGOs, and academics.

New social movements have emerged in both the rural and urban areas as an expression not only of the traditional contradiction between capital and labor but also of capital's contradiction with its own natural conditions of production. In the rural areas, the most important issues addressed by these new social movements are those connected with the ownership of land, poverty, and the deteriorating conditions of agricultural production, all of which are intertwined with environmental issues. In the urban areas, some of the new social movements are concerned primarily with ecological issues. These ecologist organizations mainly represent the concerns of the middle class regarding air, water, and food pollution, traffic congestion, and the loss of biodiversity. However, many of these social movements are also interested in "traditional" issues, such as unemployment, urban poverty, and other social and economic problems.

Together with ecological and sociopolitical issues, democracy, particularly representative democracy, has also reached a crisis point throughout the region. Because the limited forms of democracy in the region have lost legitimacy during the last decades as the state has failed to meet the demands of the popular classes, a growing number of people are increasingly questioning democratic representation, as well as the neoliberal capitalist regimes. In this political context, attempts have been made to resurrect different forms of communal and participatory democracy.

In this context, new social movements have emerged with the clear intention of resisting market expansion (Luke 2001; Gezerlis 2002). These new social movements have adopted direct and participatory democratic forms of consensual decision making to resolve political, economic, social, and ecological problems. The notion of community (involving ecumenicity, autonomy, and democracy) has acquired central importance among many of these new social movements. An incipient articulation of the idea of confederated communities has taken hold. In some cases, solidarity alliances among different popular organizations have started to emerge. As a result, a new form of democracy is evolving as networks of movements organize on a regional basis to deal with common problems.

Some examples of this tendency are the networks that have developed among local popular assemblies to oppose new mining projects in the Andes region, the landless peasant organizations, and the new organizations of unemployed rural and urban workers. In these cases, ecological devastation and the pillage of natural resources constitute the crucible around which these popular organizations have structured their resistance against neoliberalism and the forms of natural and human resource exploitation that it promotes.

NOTES

The author of this chapter has placed some suggested resources that you may wish to consult on the book's website at http://www.rowmanlittlefield.com/isbn/0742555240.

1. To quote Sunkel and Paz (1970), "Both underdevelopment and development are aspects of the same phenomenon, both are historically simultaneous, both are linked functionally and, therefore, interact and condition each other mutually. This

results . . . in the division of the world between industrial, advanced or 'central' countries, and underdeveloped, backward or 'peripheral' countries."

2. An interesting critical analysis on the ideology of "developmentalism" and "globalization" can be found in Wallerstein (2005).

3. Latin American and Caribbean (LAC) Population Database compiled by the Centro Internacional de Agricultura Tropical (CIAT), United Nations Environment Program (UNEP), Center for International Earth Science Information Network (CIESIN), Columbia University, and the World Bank (2005) Latin American and Caribbean Population Database. Available at www.na.unep.net/datasets/datalist .php3 or http://gisweb.ciat.cgiar.org/population/dataset.htm (accessed January 23, 2007).

4. See recent examples of the relocation of asbestos manufacturing in Hardoy and Satterthwaite (1987) and mercury contamination in Street (1981).

5. Some studies on this topic in Argentina are Rodríguez et al. (1996) and Morello and Rodriguez (2001).

6. For specific information about popular mobilization versus neoliberal democracy in Mexico, see Stolle-McAllister (2005), McLeod (2005), Wise and Mendoza (2005), and Labrecque (2005).

REFERENCES

Bagú, Sergio. 1949. *Economía de la sociedad colonial.* Buenos Aires: Editorial Ateneo.

Cardoso, F., and E. Faletto. 1969. *Dependencia y desarrollo en América Latina.* Mexico City: Siglo XXI.

Cherni, J. 2001. "Globalisation and Environmental Sustainability in Cities of Developed and Developing Countries." *Theomai Journal: Society, Nature and Development Studies* 4 (second semester of 2001): 106–18. Available at http://revista-theomai.unq.edu.ar/numero4 (accessed September 27, 2007).

Comisión Económica de América Latina y el Caribe (CEPAL). 1992. *Transformación productiva con equidad.* Santiago: ONU.

Connolly, P. 1982. "Uncontrolled Settlements and Self-Build: What Kind of Solution? The Mexico City Case." In *Self-Help Housing: A Critique,* ed. Peter M. Ward, 141–74. London: Mansell.

Di Pace, M., S. Federovisky, and J. Hardoy. 1990. *Los problemas ambientales en las areas urbanas de la Argentina.* Buenos Aires: IIED.

Dimitriu, Andrés, Pat Howard, and Paul Reynolds. 2002. "Genes as Commodities, Science and Crisis." *Theomai Journal: Society, Nature and Development Studies* 5 (first semester of 2002): 59–62. Available at http://revista-theomai.unq .edu.ar/number5 (accessed September 27, 2007).

Fotopoulos, T. 1997. *Towards an Inclusive Democracy.* London: Cassell.

Galafassi, Guido. 2002a. "Argentina on Fire: People's Rebellion Facing the Deep Crisis of the Neoliberal Market Economy." *Democracy and Nature* 8, no. 2 (July): 331–36.

———. 2002b. "Ecological Crisis, Poverty and Urban Development in Latin America." *Democracy and Nature* 8, no. 1 (March): 117–30.

———. 2003. "Inclusive Democracy, Social Movements and Conflicts in Argentina." *Democracy and Nature* 9, no. 3 (November): 393–400.

———. 2004. "Segregación espacial y manejo de recursos naturales en la Argentina del siglo XX. Reflexiones a partir de la contradicción capital-naturaleza." *Anuario IHES* 19:173–90.

———. 2006. "Cuando el árbol no deja ver el bosque. Neofuncionalismo y posmodernismo y posmodernidad en los estudios sobre movimientos sociales." *Theomai Journal: Society, Nature and Development Studies* 14 (second semester of 2006): 37–57. Available at http://revista-theomai.unq.edu.ar/number14 (accessed September 27, 2007).

Gallopín, G. 1987. *Prospectiva ecológica de América Latina*. Buenos Aires: Conferencia Científica Anual "Alejandro von Humboldt."

Gezerlis, Alexandros. 2002. "Latin America: Popular Movements in Neoliberal Modernity." *Democracy and Nature* 8, no. 1 (March): 87–116.

Gudynas, E. 1999. "Concepciones de la naturaleza y desarrollo en América Latina." *Persona y Sociedad* 13, no. 1.

Guimaraes, R. 1999. "Aspectos políticos y éticos de la sustentabilidad y su significado para la formulación de políticas de desarrollo." *Persona y Sociedad* 13, no. 1.

———. 2001. "El nuevo paradigma del desarrollo sustentable." *Encrucijadas UBA* 1, no. 10 (August): 25–36.

Hardoy, J., D. Mitlin, and D. Satterthwaite. 2001. *Environmental Problems in an Urbanizing World*. London: Earthscan Publications.

Hardoy, J. E., and D. Satterthwaite. 1987. *Las ciudades del tercer mundo y el medio ambiente de la pobreza*. Buenos Aires: GEL.

Harth Daneke, A., and M. Silve. 1982. "Mutual Help and Progressive Development Housing: For What Purpose? Notes on the Salvadorean Experience." In *Self-Help Housing: A Critique*, ed. Peter M. Ward, 84–98. London: Mansell.

Hordijk, M. 1999. "A Dream of Green and Water: Community-Based Formulation of a Local Agenda 21 in Peri-urban Lima." *Environment and Urbanization* 11, no. 2 (October): 56–73.

Killen, D., and A. Rahamn. 2001. "Poverty and Environment." In *Opinion IIED*. London: IIED.

Kneen, Brewster. 2002. "The Geo-politics of Genetic Modified Organisms." *Theomai Journal: Society, Nature and Development Studies* 5 (first semester of 2002): 105–17. Available at http://revista-theomai.unq.edu.ar/number5 (accessed September 27, 2007).

Labrecque, Marie France. 2005. "Cultural Appreciation and Economic Depreciation of the Mayas of Northern Yucatán, Mexico." *Latin American Perspectives* 32, no. 4 (July): 87–105.

Latouche, Serge. 1999. "The Paradox of Ecological Economics and Sustainable Development." *Democracy and Nature* 5, no. 3 (November): 501–10.

Leff, E. 1994. *Ecología y capital*. Mexico City: FCE.

———. 1999. *La Complejidad Ambienta*. Mexico City: Siglo XXI/UNAM/PNUMA.

Luke, Timothy W. 2001. "Globalization, Popular Resistance and Postmodernity." *Democracy and Nature* 7, no. 2 (July): 317–29.

Mansilla, H. 1991. *La percepción social de fenómenos ecológicos en América Latina*. La Paz: CEBEM.

McAdam, Doug, John D. McCarthy, and Mayer N. Zald, eds. 1996. *Comparative Perspectives on Social Movements.* Cambridge, U.K.: Cambridge University Press.

McLeod, Dag. 2005. "Privatization and the Limits of State Autonomy in Mexico: Rethinking the Orthodox Paradox." *Latin American Perspectives* 32, no. 4 (July): 36–64.

Melucci, Alberto. 1980. "The New Social Movements: A Theoretical Approach." *Social Science Information* 19:101–19

Morello, J., and A. Rodriguez. 2001. "Adiós, pampa mía: Parasitismo y mutualismo entre Buenos Aires y La Pampa." *Encrucijadas UBA* 1, no. 10 (August): 80–89.

Moser, C. O. 1982. "A Home of One's Own: Squatter Housing Strategies in Guayaquil, Ecuador." In *Urbanization in Contemporary Latin American Critical Approaches to the Analysis of Urban Issues,* ed. Alan Gilbert, Jorge Hardoy, and Ronaldo Ramirez, 159–90. New York: John Wiley and Sons.

O'Connor, J. 1988. "Capitalism, Nature; Socialism. A Theoretical Introduction." *Capitalism, Nature and Socialism* (November): 2–23.

———. 1998. *Natural Causes: Essays in Ecological Marxism.* New York: Guilford Press.

Offe, Claus. 1985. "New Social Movements: Challenging the Boundaries of Institutional Politics." *Social Research* 52, no. 4 (Winter): 119–34.

Petras, James. 2002. "The Unemployed Workers Movement in Argentina." *Monthly Review* 53, no. 8 (January): 94–109.

Rees, W. E. 1999. "The Built Environment and the Ecosphere: A Global Perspective." *Building Research and Information* 27, nos. 4–5: 206–20.

———. 2001. "Concept of Ecological Footprint." In *Encyclopedia of Biodiversity,* Vol. 2, 229–44. New York: Academic Press.

Rodriguez, A., J. Morello, G. D. Buzai, A. Nussbaum, and A. Soto. 1996. "Configuración ecológica del sistema periurbano del Gran Buenos Aires." In *II Simposium sobre especies naturales en áreas metropolitanas y periurbanas.* Barcelona: Diputación de Barcelona.

Sanchez, V. 1983. *En torno al ecodesarrollo.* Mexico City: Editorial Universitaria Estatal a Distancia.

Sejenovich, H. and D. Panario. 1996. *Hacia otro desarrollo: Una perspectiva ambiental.* Montevideo: Nordan-Comunidad.

Stolle-McAllister, John. 2005. "What Does Democracy Look Like? Local Movements Challenge the Mexican Transition." *Latin American Perspectives* 32, no. 4 (July): 15–35.

Street, A. 1981. "Nicaraguans Cite Pennwalth, U.S. Company Has Poisoned Its Workers, and Lake Managua." *Multinational Monitor* 12, no. 5: 25–26.

Sunkel, O., and P. Paz. 1970. *El subdesarrollo latinoamericano y la teoría del desarrollo.* Mexico City: Fondo de Cultura Economica.

Tarrow, Sydney. 1994. *Power in Movement: Social Movements, Collective Action and Mass Politics in the Modern State.* Cambridge: Cambridge University Press.

Tudela, F. 1990. *Diez tesis sobre desarrollo y medio ambiente en América Latina y el Caribe.* Michoacán, Mexico: El Colegio de Michoacán.

Valenzuela, S., and A. Valenzuela. 1998. "Modernization and Dependency: Alternative Perspectives in the Study of Latin American Underdevelopment." In *Development and Underdevelopment: The Political Economy of Global Inequality,* ed. Mitchell Seligson and John Passé-Smith, 263–76. Boulder, CO: Lynne Rienner.

Vitale, L. 1983. *Hacia una historia del ambiente en América Latina*. Buenos Aires: Nueva Imagen.

Wallerstein, Immanuel. 2002. "New Revolts against the System." *New Left Review* 18 (November–December): 29–39.

———. 2005. "After Developmentalism and Globalization, What?" *Theomai Journal: Society, Nature and Development Studies* 11 (first semester of 2005): 73–88. Available at http://revista-theomai.unq.edu.ar/numero11 (accessed September 27, 2007).

Wise, Raúl Delgado, and Rubén del Pozo Mendoza. 2005. "Mexicanization, Privatization and Large Mining Capital in Mexico." *Latin American Perspectives* 32, no. 4 (July): 65–86.

11

Globalization and Regionalization in the Americas

Richard L. Harris and Jorge Nef

This chapter analyzes the Americas and inter-American relations from a global perspective. The much used and contested concept of "globalization" is employed to describe the alignment of the Latin American and Caribbean countries within the new international division of labor that is a central structural element of the contemporary world capitalist system (Harris 2002). This alignment or integration with the system's new "globalized" division of labor has affected more than the "external" relations and the "economic" life of these societies. Since capitalism is "internal" and embedded in nearly all aspects of these countries, their insertion in the world capitalist system's new division of labor has affected them both internally and externally and in a multifaceted manner.

The historical development of these societies within the world capitalist system has shaped their economies, technology, politics, social relations, cultures, religion, life styles, educational institutions, communications and media, and relations with the natural environment. Their early incorporation into this historical structure and process took place when they were colonies of the protocapitalist European nation-states that conquered and colonized the Americas five hundred years ago.[1] Most of the conditions and problems analyzed in the preceding chapters of this volume are directly or indirectly related to the capitalist nature of these societies. They are the legacy of their past development, as well as their contemporary articulation within a highly stratified, inequitable, and evolving international division of labor.

The striking degree of extreme inequality that exists between the privileged elites and the impoverished majorities in the Americas is one of the past and contemporary effects of capitalism on the economic, social, cultural, and political development of this important region of the world (Harris 2000). Not only has such skewed development fostered extreme economic and social imbalances, but it is also largely responsible for deep inequities and injustices. It has fostered polyarchical political regimes, monopolistic or oligopolistic transnational corporations, uneven and truncated development, export dependency, unfair terms of trade (undermining the countries' economic stability and draining them of capital), neoliberal and consumerist ideologies, and the dominant political and economic role exercised by the United States in the entire hemisphere.

These key structural aspects of the Americas largely relate to the historical evolution and global expansion of capitalism. The contradictions created by the contemporary structures and expansion of this system have also provoked significant popular resistance and demands for systemic change. In recent years, there has been a remarkable degree of popular political opposition to the so-called globalization, denationalization, and structural adjustments (privatization and austerity programs) that have taken place in the Latin American and Caribbean countries. In fact, the systemic contradictions within these nations and the contemporary world capitalist system have given rise to antisystemic forces that seek to radically transform the existing economic, political, and social structures this system has created. Taking a global standpoint and using the critical lenses provided by the concepts of capital, power, and inequality, it is possible to see how these changes in the expanding world capitalist system have set the stage for both these antisystemic forces, as well as the transnational capitalist forces that are attempting to integrate these countries into the system's new global division of labor.

THE CURRENT PHASE OF
CAPITALIST EXPANSION IN THE AMERICAS

This system increasingly functions as a single planetary network of production, distribution, and capital accumulation.[2] The contemporary "globalization" or "integration" of the Americas into this global system is taking place under the dominant influence of a relatively cohesive bloc of transnational capitalist forces (Robinson and Harris 2000). This historic bloc consists of the executives and owners of the transnational corporations and major financial institutions, the elites that manage the intergovernmental economic-planning agencies, such as the International Monetary Fund (IMF) and World Bank, the leaders of the dominant political parties and media conglomerates, and the technocratic elites and state managers in the countries of both the North and South. The goals, ideology, politics, and policies of this ruling bloc are conditioned by the new global structure of capitalist production, distribution, and accumulation. Over the last four decades, this transnational bloc has promoted the integration of the hemisphere's national economies into the world economy through measures ostensibly aimed at creating "free markets," greater "competition," and "free trade" (Harris 2000).

This bloc of transnational elites has insisted that the governments in the region harmonize their fiscal, industrial, and trade policies so that the major transnational corporations and financial institutions that operate in the region can move their funds and products freely across national borders. They have also insisted that these governments pursue common or compatible trade, fiscal, monetary, exchange, and environmental policies that have "opened" their economies to relatively unrestricted foreign investments, private capital flows, and tariff-free imports. In general, these policies have involved a combination of (1) "deregulation" measures that reduce the state's control over national economic affairs and encourage transnational capital investments, cross-border transactions, and transnational commercial ventures, and (2) "privatization" measures that reduce or eliminate all state activities that place public interests over private profit making.

The model of economic development pursued by these neoconservative coalitions has sought to create "the conditions for the profitable ('efficient') renewal of capital accumulation through new globalized circuits" and "the subordination and integration of each national economy into the global economy" (Robinson and Harris 2000, 44). In fact, the process of denationalization, subordination, and integration, masked by the term "globalization," being carried out by these forces "parallels the nation building stage of early capitalism that constructed an integrated national market with common laws, taxes, currency, and political consolidation around a common state" (Robinson and Harris 2000, 44). Yet, in this case the so-called process of "globalization is repeating this process . . . on a world scale" rather than a national scale (Robinson and Harris 2000, 44).

The basic underlying objectives of the contemporary "globalizing" forces are largely the same as the driving forces that propelled capitalist expansion throughout the region (and the world) in the past. They seek to eliminate the barriers to capital accumulation and mobility, to secure "safe" areas for capital investments, to control and expand markets, to extract the region's natural resources as cheaply and easily as possible, and to exploit the large reserves of cheap labor in the region to produce "global products" for the world economy. However, these ends are being pursued under conditions that are new and through the use of means that in some respects are very different from those that characterized preceding periods of capitalist expansion. As Amin (2000, 2001a) has noted, the world capitalist system has been reorganizing itself around five new monopolies that benefit the triad of advanced and dominant capitalist countries (the United States, the European Union [EU], and Japan). This triad monopolizes "the control of technology; global financial flows (through the banks, insurance cartels, and pension funds of the center); access to the planet's natural resources; media and communications; and weapons of mass destruction"(Amin 2000). These monopolies have produced "a new hierarchy in the distribution of income on a world scale, more unequal than ever, while making subalterns of the peripheries' industries" (Amin 2000).

The contemporary phase of capitalist expansion involves the introduction of new communications technologies, new means of production, new forms of commoditization, and new ideological justifications for the expansion and integration of the system. These characteristics of contemporary capitalism have been described in some detail in several of the preceding chapters in this volume. As Cristóbal Kay notes in chapter 2, modern capitalist farms and agroindustrial complexes, some owned directly by transnational corporations, have replaced the once dominant *haciendas* or *latifundios* (large landed estates), family farms, and peasant production. Moreover, the former state-supported and national capitalist development of the Latin American and Caribbean economies has been replaced by a new pattern of globalized and privatized export-oriented development that has greatly weakened the peasantry, commercialized the agricultural sector, and strengthened the control of the agricultural capitalists over the agricultural labor force.

The commercialization and industrialization of agriculture have produced a massive out-migration of the population from the rural areas that has partly "ruralized" the urban areas, while rural areas have become increasingly urbanized. In addition, urban and rural labor markets have become more closely interconnected. Moreover, the rural land market has become more "competitive," which has allowed urban investors and transnational capital to gain greater access over the region's natural resources.

Thus, as Guido Pascual Galafassi emphasizes in chapter 10, the largely unregulated urbanization and exploitation of natural resources accompanying the recent capitalist expansion and economic restructuring of the Americas have brought about an ecological crisis. The growing number and size of cities throughout the region have created a profound physical degradation of the natural environment. Noise, waste, and pollution are the most common expressions of this largely unregulated and privatized urbanization. The continued specialization of Latin America and the Caribbean in the export of raw materials and agricultural products has also resulted in increasing pressures on the natural environment and the reduction of the biodiversity necessary for the survival of the ecosystems upon which the biosphere depends.

As Galafassi notes, there has been a sharp increase in the rate of natural resource depletion without any significant efforts being made toward renewal and conservation. Basically, when it comes to the extraction of natural resources, a "pillage economy" exists throughout Latin America and the Caribbean. In this economy, the main agents operate according to the logic of extracting natural resources as quickly as possible without regard to the effects on the natural environment, then move on to new sites where the profitable extraction of resources can be continued until they too are exhausted. This style of resource extraction needs to be replaced with one based on renewable resources and the enforcement of rational limits upon resource extraction in the case of nonrenewable resources. However, this approach runs counter to the logic of contemporary capitalist expansion and the accelerated accumulation associated with the current nonsustainable process of global integration (Ikerd 2005).

Chapter 7 by Francesca Miller and chapter 4 by Viviana Patroni call attention to the large numbers of women that have entered the wage-earning labor force as a result of the economic transformations associated with the evolution and expansion of capitalism in the Americas. Patroni points out that under the neoliberal macroeconomic reforms of the last few decades, employers have hired women in greater numbers, while their employment of male workers has dropped. As Miller points out, many employers prefer to hire women because they can pay them less, and consider them more submissive, than men. The overall picture is one of precarious forms of employment for both women and men. Moreover, the ongoing process of economic restructuring has created poorly paid employment for both men and women in the lower tiers of the workforce, rather than a general improvement in employment conditions and greater equity for women with regard to their male counterparts.

Patroni's analysis reveals that the recent restructuring of the Latin American and Caribbean economies has indeed been profound in terms of its impact—both for the very few who have benefited from this restructuring and for the large segments of the population that have suffered the adverse consequences of the far-reaching economic changes that have taken place. For most workers throughout the Americas, the way they experience work has undergone sweeping changes, most of which have not been positive. On the contrary, there has been a number of negative consequences: loss of well-paying jobs, job instability, and stagnant or falling wages.

Patroni indicates that the neoliberal "market-friendly reforms" have created in most cases a drastic deterioration in the working conditions of the labor force, both in terms of the quality of their work lives and in their prospects for future advancement and improvement. Moreover, Patroni's chapter reveals the very direct and costly consequences of the neoliberal reforms on the political power and influence of organized labor. These reforms undermined the structural basis of unions and weakened labor laws that protected workers' rights to organize and bargain for better working conditions. They have also created a political environment in many of the region's countries in which organized labor has been unable or unwilling to oppose these so-called reforms. Thus, they have undermined in critical ways the previous political influence of the trade unions and the most organized sectors of the workforce.

Other chapters (Nef and Galafassi) reveal how the globalization of the region's economies can be seen as a multifaceted process in which transnational alliances between the economic and political elites in both the center and the periphery are pursuing a regional and global strategy of eliminating the barriers that stand in the way of exploiting the region's abundant supply of cheap labor. This strategy involves rolling back the labor rights gained during earlier periods of popular mobilization at the national level. It also involves privatizing the public sphere and deregulating the extraction of the region's valuable, but in many cases nonrenewable, natural resources.

The exclusive nature of the type of "democracy" that has emerged in the Americas and the continuing authoritarian tendencies in most of the region's political systems have facilitated the implementation of the profoundly reactionary measures that have been introduced in the sphere of employer-labor relations. The net result is a significant deterioration in the employment security of most working people and the generation of democratic deficits—not only in the countries that lie south of the Rio Grande but also in those that lie north of this international, but increasingly porous and artificial, boundary.

Asymmetrical penetration, both formal and informal, is continuously taking place between the northern and southern regions of the hemisphere. Northern elites, by themselves or in alliance with their Latin American and Caribbean counterparts, exert hegemonic control over the subordinate groups, classes, and clients in the region. In the complex international division of labor that has developed between the capitalist centers in the North and the markets and labor forces of the South, investment capital, technology, and ideology flow south, while profits and people in search of employment flow north.

Despite the neoliberal rhetoric that has been used to justify the so-called structural adjustments made in the region's economies since the 1980s, these transformations have not improved the "competitiveness" of these economies in the global economy or their industrial strength; nor have they raised the standards and quality of living of the majority of the population. Putting all rhetoric aside, they have been undertaken to facilitate the more effective mobility of transnational capital and the transfer of increasing amounts of wealth from these economies to the headquarters of the transnational corporations and the private transnational banks in the advanced capitalist countries in the North. Behind the mantra of "free market" and "free trade," which provide an ideological camouflage for the real purposes of the restructuring, the evidence overwhelmingly indicates that the neoliberal structural "reforms" have succeeded in transferring much of the wealth created in the region to the transnational corporations and financial institutions that are based in the centers of the world capitalist system.

As many mainstream economists have acknowledged, the last several decades have been marked by "a tremendous increase in the mobility of international capital" (Kohli 2003, 2), as well as a decline in the flow of "official capital" (from governmental and intergovernmental sources) into the so-called developing countries (i.e., the peripheral societies of the world capitalist system). In the region, loans and financial assistance from the U.S. government and the international financial institutions (IFIs) have drastically declined, while the flow of private capital into and out of the economies of the Latin American and Caribbean countries (and other peripheral countries around the world) has increased dramatically. The flows and backflows of private capital have been facilitated by the Latin American and Caribbean governments, which, under the spell of the Washington Consensus, have removed or weakened their controls on the financial sectors of their economies and on the investments and profit repatriation of the transnational corporations. As a result, private capital flows now dominate, and official flows of capital have been "reduced to a trickle" (Kohli 2003).

The IMF data in table 11.1 reveal that the flow of private capital into Latin America and the Caribbean is much greater than the flow of official capital into the region. Moreover, the data reveal that between 2000 and 2006, the total amount of capital that flowed out of the region was much greater than the total amount that flowed into the region. Depending upon the year in question, there was a net transfer of capital out of the region in the form of private portfolio flows, other private capital flows, and/or official capital flows, plus a continuing outflow of service payments on the large external debts of many of the countries in the region. As table 11.1 indicates, the combination of these outflows every year exceeded the total amount of foreign (private) direct investment and private portfolio flows that went into the region during these years.

In fact, according to the Inter-American Development Bank (IDB) (2005), the estimated net outflow of capital in 2004, which was $12.5 billion, was greater than the outflow of capital during the worst years of the 1980s, when the region suffered both a severe debt crisis and capital flight in dramatic proportions. But at least during the 1980s, the outflow of capital from the region was offset somewhat by the inflow of loans from official sources and other financial mechanisms (IDB 2005). Since these

Table 11.1.   Western Hemisphere[a]: Selected Financial Indicators, 2000–2006 (in billions of U.S. dollars)

Financial Indicators	2000	2001	2002	2003	2004	2005	2006
Foreign direct investment[b]	69.7	66.4	46.4	36.8	46.0	49.2	46.1
Net private portfolio flows[b]	2.6	−7.5	−14.4	−8.8	−13.8	25.3	4.2
Net of other private capital flows[b]	−21.1	−34.7	−28.2	−10.7	−31.0	−60.6	−37.6
Net official capital flows[c]	−6.3	25.2	17.5	4.4	−9.0	−30.0	−12.5
Total debt service	−189.6	−172.3	−154.6	−164.4	−159.0	−200.3	−186.2
Total external debt	764.6	776.7	767.6	789.5	795.6	754.1	742.0

Source: International Monetary Fund (IMF), World Economic Outlook Database, www.imf.org/external/pubs/ft/weo/2006/02/data/index.aspx (accessed January 22, 2007).

[a] The IMF grouping entitled "Western Hemisphere" consists of thirty-three countries: Antigua and Barbuda, Argentina, the Bahamas, Barbados, Belize, Bolivia, Brazil, Chile, Colombia, Costa Rica, Dominica, the Dominican Republic, Ecuador, El Salvador, Grenada, Guatemala, Guyana, Haiti, Honduras, Jamaica, Mexico, Netherlands Antilles, Nicaragua, Panama, Paraguay, Peru, St. Kitts and Nevis, St. Lucia, St. Vincent and the Grenadines, Suriname, Trinidad and Tobago, Uruguay, and Venezuela.

[b] Foreign direct investment (FDI) is the total of all long-term investment by foreign direct investors in an enterprise resident in an economy other than that in which the foreign direct investor is based. The FDI relationship consists of a parent enterprise and a foreign affiliate, which together form a transnational corporation. In order to qualify as FDI, the investment must afford the parent enterprise control over its foreign affiliate. The United Nations defines control in this case as owning 10 percent or more of the ordinary shares or voting power of an incorporated firm or its equivalent for an unincorporated firm. Private capital flows include private debt flows, FDI, and portfolio equity flows. It is the net total of all capital flows from both domestic and external sources. Private foreign capital can be divided into four main types of flows: (1) foreign direct equity investment (divided in turn into new direct equity and earnings from existing equity that are reinvested in the company rather than expatriated); (2) foreign portfolio equity investment, or new equity (or reinvested earnings on existing equity) that is less than 10 percent of the equity value of a company; (3) foreign direct nonequity investment, which includes loans provided by related (parent or affiliated) companies to the company in the recipient country; and (4) other investment, representing loans from unrelated companies and less formalized, short-term credit to companies for trade and services payments (Martin 2004, 5).

[c] Net official capital flows include the net total of all loans and other forms of financial assistance from governmental and intergovernmental sources.

official flows have been reduced to a trickle in more recent years, they no longer offset the outflow of repatriated profits and the sizable loan payments on external debts.

According to data collected by the United Nations Economic Commission for Latin America and the Caribbean (ECLAC) (2005, 173), there has been a net outward transfer of financial resources from Latin America and the Caribbean every year since 1999 (not to mention the years before this). In 2005, the total amount of this outflow of resources was valued at over $67 billion, with Brazil contributing $27.4 billion, Venezuela another $23.6 billion, and Chile $9.6 billion. These negative net transfers of financial resources mean that these countries lose invaluable financial resources that could be used to finance their own development. Instead, they transfer these financial resources to the companies, transnational banks, and IFIs in the United States and other advanced capitalist countries that are the recipients of these transfers.

More specifically, these net transfers represent a reduction in the financial resources available for domestic consumption and investment, as well as improving real per capita incomes (Kregel 2004, 6–8). It must be noted that since 2002 the countries with negative net resource transfers contain the majority of the region's population. Thus, these transfers have affected the consumption and per capita income of the majority of the population living in Latin America and the Caribbean.

The authors of the ECLAC report that contains the data on net transfers mentioned above downplay the significance of the net outflow of capital from the region. They state that these negative transfers represent merely a deficit in accounting terms because most of the capital transferred was used to pay down the external debts and build up the foreign reserve accounts of the countries involved (ECLAC 2005, 42–43). However, Kregel (2004), who has researched negative net transfers as part of his responsibilities at the United Nations Financing for Development Office, contends these negative net resource transfers are the price that many developing countries with large external debts have to pay to remain current on their external payments and to obtain the IMF's "seal of approval." According to Kregel (2004), negative net resource transfers of capital characterized most of the 1980s in the Latin American countries recovering from the 1982 debt crisis under IMF-mandated stabilization and macroeconomic restructuring programs. By the beginning of the 1990s, private capital began to flow into the region, and the net transfer of capital turned positive in most of the Latin American and Caribbean economies. The capital flow turned negative again, however, in the late 1990s. This pattern of negative financial flows reflects the cost of the IMF's "seal of approval." In order to obtain the IMF's approval, these countries have been forced to follow macroeconomic policies that restrict domestic demand so that their economies produce a surplus from their trade in goods and services. However, this surplus has not been sufficient in most cases for them to build up their reserves and/or pay down their existing debts. As a result, these countries continue to depend on new inflows of external private capital to remain current on their external payments and build up their reserves (Kregel 2004, 6–7). Kregel further notes that in order to receive the IMF's continued seal of approval, the Latin American and Caribbean governments have continued the IMF's mandated policies of keeping high real interest rates and large fiscal surpluses, even though these mandated monetary restraints make it almost impossible for them to finance the rapid growth of their economies.

This situation involves the transfer of a sizable amount of the wealth that is generated by the producers in these countries to the transnational elites in the advanced capitalist societies. The neoliberal economic policies and economic restructuring have also transferred wealth from the popular classes to the upper classes in the region. The latter have, for the most part, been eager local collaborators in the restructuring and denationalization of their economies. They have in essence facilitated the transfer of capital accumulated in their countries to the executives and owners of the large transnational corporations (both production and financial companies) based in the United States, the European Union, and Japan (Robinson 2004).

For the popular classes in Latin America and the Caribbean, which produce the exports that earn their countries the foreign exchange used to pay their countries' external debts, the financial resource transfers have cost them dearly. They have suffered declining wages and lower real incomes, double-digit unemployment, the loss of savings and property, the elimination of benefits and pensions, and declining social services (e.g., health and education) as a result of the restructuring of their economies. They have also suffered increases in the cost of the basic commodities they consume, as well as the costs of housing and transportation, which combined with their declining wages and/or lower real incomes have been responsible for their falling or stagnant standards of living and their impoverishment.

In view of the continuing net transfer of capital out of their economies and the unfair terms of trade that limit their export earnings and development, the vast majority of the Latin American and Caribbean countries has little chance of "catching up" with the advanced capitalist countries or becoming genuinely "competitive" participants in the "global economy" in the near future. They are especially unlikely to achieve either of these outcomes if their governments continue to follow the neoliberal prescriptions of the IFIs, the World Trade Organization (WTO), and the Group of 7 governments led by Washington. These powerful guardians of the contemporary world capitalist system insist these countries must completely open their economies to foreign competition and hold down their wages so that they will be forced to become more efficient and productive and supposedly more competitive in the global marketplace. However, the uneven development of these economies, the unfavorable terms of trade that handicap them, their shortage of finance capital, and their extremely inequitable distribution of income cannot be solved by further opening up their economies and holding down their wages so that they obey the "objective laws of the market" as advocated by the IFIs, the U.S. government, the transnational corporations, and the WTO.

Most of these countries cannot improve the "competitiveness" of their economies in the global economy because their present lack of competitiveness is the product of a complex cluster of constraining economic, political, and social conditions that have been imposed on them by the world capitalist system and by the nature of their past historical development within this system (Amin 2001b, 15). That is to say, the power relations and international structures that regulate the global system obstruct their economic, political, and social development. The structures of this system provide a stratified political and economic exoskeleton that constrains all national efforts to pursue any significant degree of self-directed, inward-oriented, and environmentally sustainable development. Indeed, the geopolitical power structures that preserve and support the world capitalist system have made it almost impossible for the populations of the less developed countries in the periphery of the system to pursue a path of inward-oriented and sustainable development (Amin 2001b, 20).

More specifically, in the present expansive phase of capitalist globalization, the development of the so-called less competitive economies within the world system is effectively constrained by the international financial and trade regimes created to regulate this system. These structures regulate the system in the interests of the new transnational bloc that dominates the system. At the national level, the hierarchical power structures within the peripheral countries are dominated by what Petras (2003) has called "the collaborator classes whose function it is to organize the state and economy in accordance with the core definitions of the international division of labor" (170). These classes impede the autonomous and sustainable development of their countries. Indeed, as progressive critics have contended for some time, the development of these societies is obstructed and largely sacrificed for the sake of the expansion and accumulation of capital in the advanced centers of the world economy.

The pressures and demands placed on the governments, economies, and populations of the peripheral countries by the dominant centers of the world capitalist system and by the collaborative domestic elites within these neocolonial countries in the periphery of the system have created a host of contradictions and problems in these societies. On the one hand, these countries are subjected to the conditions for loans, credits, debt payments, investments, developmental assistance, and trade that are set by the IMF, the World Bank, the IDB, the WTO, the transnational corporations (including the major transnational banks), the U.S. government, and the governments of the other advanced capitalist countries. These power structures have pressured and coerced the governments of the Latin American and Caribbean countries into pursuing economic policies that have denationalized their economies and stunted their own national development. Under the hegemony of the bloc of transnational forces that largely control the system, the governments and elites of these peripheral countries have relinquished control over their economies by "opening" them up to transnational capital. The powerful guardians of the world capitalist system have required them to create a "favorable business climate" for the investments, goods, and services of the transnational corporations and investors that are the main agents of the present global expansion and integration of the capitalist system (Harris and Seid 2000, 7–11).

As indicated above, the hierarchical power relations and regulatory structures of the global system and its local agents largely control the development of the Latin American and Caribbean economies, like all economies in the periphery of the world capitalist system (Amin 2001a). The top officials of the governments of the United States and the other advanced capitalist countries (the Group of 7) use the major intergovernmental institutions, such as the IMF, the World Bank, the IDB, and the WTO, to regulate international finance and trade in the interests of the transnational bloc that dominates both the Group of 7 governments and the intergovernmental institutions. The international financial and trade regimes are global in scope and protect the interests of the advanced capitalist centers of the world system, as well as the transnational corporations based in these centers. Besides the IMF, World Bank, IDB, and WTO, various international political, economic, and military structures are controlled by the governments of the advanced capitalist countries. All of these structures protect and promote the development of the transnational corporations, the advanced capitalist centers, and the world capitalist system in general (Amin 2001a).

U.S. HEGEMONY, THE TRANSNATIONAL ELITES, AND THE IFIS

Since the 1980s, inter-American relations and the political economy of the Latin American and Caribbean states have been shaped by the neoliberal strategic agenda put forward by the U.S. government, U.S.-based transnational corporations, and the three major IFIs that regulate international economic relations in the Latin American and Caribbean region. These IFIs are the IMF, the World Bank, and the IDB. Their policies and practices generally follow the policy and practices of the U.S. government due to the controlling influence that the U.S. government and U.S.-based corporations exercise over the governance and policies of these institutions.

Not surprisingly, Washington's agenda for the Latin American and Caribbean region gives priority to promoting and protecting the interests of the U.S.-based transnational investors and U.S.-based transnational corporations that operate in the region. It also seeks to maintain and strengthen U.S. geopolitical hegemony over the Western Hemisphere. This agenda involves the use of direct means (e.g., diplomacy, foreign assistance, trade agreements, overt and covert forms of political and military intervention) and indirect means (e.g., the conditions imposed by the IFIs for their loans and debt repayments).

This combination of direct and indirect means is used to achieve a number of strategic outcomes (Harris 2000, 9):

- the removal of all restrictions on U.S. investments in the Latin American and Caribbean countries so that their local industries, banks, and natural resources are no longer protected by their governments from being taken over and/or controlled by U.S. companies, banks, and investors

- the orientation of the economies of these countries toward the production of exports so that they can earn the foreign exchange (in hard currencies, preferably U.S. dollars) they need to service their foreign debts and purchase the goods and services produced by U.S.-based transnational corporations
- the reduction of government spending on health, education, and welfare so that these governments can "control inflation" (holding down the wages of the labor force) and ensure that all available funds are channeled into increasing the production of exports and paying the external debts of these countries (one of the main conduits for the transfer of capital from these countries to the centers of the world capitalist system)
- the elimination of tariffs, quotas, and other trade restrictions on U.S. imports so that these economies can buy more imported goods and services from the United States
- the alignment of their local currencies with the U.S. dollar (or the adoption of the U.S. dollar as their currency) and the elimination of restrictions on the exchange of local currencies into U.S. dollars so that U.S. investors and companies operating in these countries can easily transfer their local profits out of these countries and invest them elsewhere
- the privatization of state enterprises and public utilities so that U.S. companies and investors can invest in or buy (out) these entities and make sure they will not be used for the purposes of autonomous national development
- the "deregulation" of the Latin American and Caribbean economies so that the U.S. companies and investors involved in exports, imports, and investments are freed from government strictures that protect the labor force, domestic industries, natural resources, and ecological endowment of these countries

This agenda is supported by what have now become familiar neoliberal arguments about the virtues of "free markets" and "free trade" versus the ills of state intervention in the economy and government-maintained trade barriers designed to protect "uncompetitive" domestic industries and markets from foreign competition. These arguments can be reduced to the United States' fundamental thesis that "open" economies and "free markets" foster rapid economic growth, liberal democracy, and rising standards of living for even the poorest sectors of the population (Reich 2002).

The current statistics on U.S. exports to the region (see table 11.2) reveal the region's economic importance to the United States. The U.S. exports as much to Latin America and the Caribbean as it does to the European Union. And it exports more to Mexico than it exports to Japan and China combined. Moreover, the Latin American and Caribbean region is viewed as the fastest-growing market in the world for U.S. exports. The following excerpt from a speech given in 2002 by U.S. Assistant Secretary for Western Hemisphere Affairs Otto J. Reich reveals how U.S. foreign-policy makers view the economic importance of the region:

> The U.S. sells more to Latin America and the Caribbean than to the European Union; trade with our NAFTA partners [Canada and Mexico] is greater than our trade with the EU and Japan combined; we sell more to the Southern Cone, to Mercosur, than to China; and Latin America and the Caribbean comprise our fastest-growing export market. (Reich 2002)

Because of the economic importance of the region to U.S. interests, the U.S. government is increasingly concerned about the fact that U.S. companies and investors in the region have to compete not only with other producers and investors based in the hemisphere but also with European and Asian companies and investors who have increasingly moved into the region (Schott 1997). A major concern on the part of U.S. policy makers and the powerful corporate interests they protect is securing market access for U.S. products and investments in Latin America and the Caribbean, "as well as preventing the emergence of a major break through in industrialization that would threaten U.S. industry over time as Japan and South Korea have done so successfully" (Onis and Senses 2003, 23) and also, increasingly, China.

Table 11.2. Merchandise Trade of the United States with Selected Regions and Economies, 2004 (in billions of dollars)

Destination of U.S. Exports	Value 2004	Origin of U.S. Imports	Value 2004
World	818.8	World	1,525.5
North America	300.6	North America	417.7
European Union (25 countries)	173.0	European Union (25 countries)	290.9
LAC[a]	175.8	LAC[a]	169.3
Canada	189.1	Canada	259.7
Mexico	110.8	Mexico	157.8
Japan	54.4	Japan	133.3
China	34.7	China	210.5
Brazil	13.9	Brazil	22.7
Venezuela	4.8	Venezuela	26.3

Source: World Trade Organization, *World Trade in 2004*—Overview, p. 51.

[a] LAC (Latin America and the Caribbean), which includes Mexico, the Dominican Republic (exports only), Trinidad and Tobago (imports only), and South and Central America.

In fact, since the end of World War II, the United States' share of world merchandise trade has been declining, while Europe's and Asia's shares of world trade have been increasing (see table 11.3). To promote and protect U.S. economic interests (i.e., exports and essential imports, the expanding operations of U.S.-based transnational corporations and investments), Washington has followed a strategy of maintaining hegemonic control over the economic and political affairs of the entire Western Hemisphere. This political and economic control has hindered the economic, political, and social development of the Latin American and Caribbean countries. Thus, even though these countries have greatly increased the volume and total value of their exports over the last half-century, their share of world trade has steadily declined along with the decline of the United States' share of world trade.

The data in table 11.3 reveal that South and Central America's share of world merchandise trade (in exports) fell from 11.6 percent in 1948 to only 3.1 percent of world trade in 2004. This decline parallels the decline of the United States' share of world merchandise trade (in exports), from 21.7 percent in 1948 to 9.2 percent of world trade in 2004. In fact, the 72.8 percent decline of South and Central America's share of world merchandise trade over this period was greater than the 57.6 percent decline of the United States' share. Indeed, the decline of the region's share of world trade was greater than the 64.3 percent decline of the world's poorest region, Africa, which saw its share of world merchandise trade fall from 7.3 percent in 1948 to 2.6 percent in 2004. Politics, as much as economics, helps to explain the relatively poor economic performance of Latin America, the Caribbean, and Africa in comparison with most of the rest of the world. That is to say, within the capitalist world system, "the hierarchy in economic and political power has been the key determinant of economic outcomes not only between developed and developing countries, but also between the developed countries themselves" (Onis and Senses 2003, 19).

Because of the U.S. government's leadership role in the global power structure and the collaborative, but subordinate, role in this structure played by most of the Latin American and Caribbean governments, the leaders of most of these regimes have pursued the neoliberal policies that are a fundamental component of Washington's hegemonic agenda for the region, often referred to as the Washington Consensus (Williamson 1993). They have implemented these neoliberal policies even though these policies have seriously disadvantaged the popular classes in their countries, prevented the sustainable development of their economies, and provoked increasing popular resistance.

These neoliberal policies were designed by officials in the U.S. government in close association with officials of the three IFIs (the IMF, World Bank, and IDB) that operate in the region and have their headquarters in

Table 11.3.   Percentage of World Merchandise Trade (Exports)

Region or Country	1948 (%)	1963 (%)	1983 (%)	2004 (%)
World	100	100	100	100
South and Central America	11.4	6.3	4.4	3.1
United States of America	21.7	14.9	11.2	9.2
Europe	31.5	41.4	43.5	45.3
China	0.9	1.3	1.2	6.7
Japan	0.4	3.5	8.0	6.4
Six East Asian traders	3.0	2.4	5.8	9.7
Africa	7.3	5.7	4.5	2.6
Middle East	2.0	3.2	6.8	4.4
Others	21.8	13.6	14.6	12.6

Source: World Trade Organization, *World Trade in 2004—Overview,* p. 32.

Washington, D.C. Starting in the 1980s, the officials in these structures of political and economic power insisted that governments in Latin America, the Caribbean, and other parts of the world impose a series of austerity measures on their popular classes designed to guarantee the payment of their countries' debts to the transnational banks and to facilitate the alignment of their economies with the emerging new global circuits of transnational capitalist production, distribution, and capital accumulation. The main policy elements of this so-called consensus, both in its original and more recently augmented, "softer" versions, are as follows:

The Original Washington Consensus:
Fiscal discipline
Reorientation of public spending
Tax reform
Financial liberalization
Unified and competitive exchange rates
Trade liberalization
Openness to foreign direct investment
Privatization
Deregulation
Secure property rights
Labor market flexibility

The Augmented Washington Consensus:
The original list plus:
Legal and political reform
Regulatory institutions

Anticorruption efforts
Financial codes and standards
"Prudent" capital account opening
Nonintermediate exchange rate regimes
Social safety nets
Poverty reduction
World Trade Organization membership
(Malhotra et al. 2003, 67)

The revised, or "Post-Washington Consensus," is softer or more palatable in that it represents a shift in focus from the previous "single-minded concern with growth and efficiency" to a more nuanced approach, which includes an emphasis on policy measures that address "key social problems such as pervasive unemployment, poverty and inequality" (Onis and Senses 2003, 18). However, this new approach has the same fundamental bias that the original version of the consensus had in that it too emphasizes exclusively the need for domestic reforms as opposed to international reforms in the world economy. For example, there is no recognition of the need for reforms in the IFIs themselves to make them more democratic and more representative of the interests of the developing/peripheral countries as opposed to the present subservience of the IFIs to the governments of the Group of 7 advanced capitalist countries, particularly the United States. Moreover, no attention is given to the "establishment of effective international mechanisms for the regulation of transnational corporations with the objective of curbing their monopoly power and for controlling the massive short term capital flows" that have caused severe financial crises throughout the world in recent years in Asia, Russia, Mexico, and Argentina (Onis and Senses 2003, 19).

Moreover, a critical appraisal of the practice as opposed to the rhetoric of the IFIs and the Group of 7 governments reveals that their renewed concern with "poverty alleviation" and more equal income distribution is insincere. By continuing to insist that the peripheral capitalist countries continue to maintain primary budget surpluses, the officials of the IFIs and the Group of 7 restrict government spending on social programs and employment-creation measures in these countries. Thus, the leaders and experts of the system's main centers of political and economic power appear to be using an anticorruption, "good governance," poverty-alleviation, and income-distribution discourse as "a pretext for broadening and deepening the neo-liberal agenda" (Onis and Senses 2003), despite its obvious failures and the increasing popular rejection of this agenda in Latin America and the Caribbean.

It is important to note that the political and economic elites that hold power in this region were (at least until recently) able to pursue the increasingly unpopular and, in the long run, unsustainable policies associated with the Washington Consensus because they have been backed by the U.S. government, the transnational corporations, and the IFIs. They have also been able to pursue these policies because most of the political regimes in the region exclude the popular classes from any meaningful participation in the governance of their countries. These regimes are able to do this because they are based on a system of political domination that Robinson (1996) has aptly described as "capitalist polyarchy." In this type of pseudo-democratic regime, which is also applicable to North America, "a small group actually rules and mass participation in decision-making is confined to leadership choices in elections carefully managed by competing elites" (Robinson 1996, 49). In Latin America and the Caribbean, these arrangements are supported by "political aid" from the U.S. government and, if necessary, military intervention (Robinson 1996, 78).

The region's polyarchical regimes are for the most part dominated by what Robinson and others have identified as the "transnational factions" of the local upper classes (Robinson and Harris 2000). These local elites are the "junior partners" in an emerging planetary transnational capitalist class. Their "senior partners" in this emerging transnational class own and control the major transnational corporations and banks that are based largely in the advanced capitalist countries at the core and in the highest strata of the system. This class has the power of the world capitalist system behind it (i.e., the IFIs, the WTO, the transnational corporations, and the governments of the advanced capitalist countries, led by the United States).

With direct political assistance from the "center" and in some cases military muscle (e.g., Panama, Haiti, Grenada, Nicaragua), these elites gained control over the process of political transition from military to civilian rule that began during the 1980s. The transitional regimes created during this period co-opted and demobilized the popular democratic movements that emerged during the 1980s and 1990s to demand the political democratization of their countries. These movements successfully mobilized the majority of the population in most of these countries to demand the demilitarization and democratization of the U.S.-backed military dictatorships and authoritarian civilian regimes that ruled the region from the mid-1960s through the 1980s. Many of the social movements analyzed by Judith Hellman in chapter 6 emerged during this critical period of transition, as did the indigenous people's movements analyzed by Michael Kearney and Stefano Varese in chapter 8 and the church-sponsored Christian base communities and solidarity movements examined by Wilder Robles in chapter 9.

Despite the mobilization of these movements during this period, the transnational factions of the upper classes and their political allies gained control over the civilian regimes that replaced the military dictatorships, and they have been able through these pseudodemocratic regimes "to reor-

ganize state institutions and create a more favorable institutional framework for a deepening of neoliberal adjustments" and the globalization (i.e.,
denationalization) of the Latin American and Caribbean economies
(Robinson 1998/1999, 121). As we stated in the first edition of this volume,
the sovereignty of Latin American and Caribbean states has been undermined by their overreliance on transnational capital, international financial
institutions, and Washington's "support" (Nef 1995, 102).

Under the pseudodemocratic regimes dominated by the transnational
elites in these countries, the popular classes have suffered political disempowerment and exclusion from the real centers of political decision making. Moreover, the neoliberal "structural adjustments," "financial stabilization," and "austerity programs" carried out by these regimes have forced
most of the middle and working classes to suffer a decline in their real incomes and living standards. They have been forced to pay rising prices for
basic consumer goods and services, and they have frequently been forced
out of permanent and salaried jobs into precarious forms of self-employment, lower paid and temporary employment, and/or unemployment. The
numbers of urban and rural poor in most of these countries have expanded,
and a very large proportion of the population continues to live in poverty
(see chapter 3 by Richard Harris).

In addition, the scope and quality of public services have been reduced as
a result of the neoliberal Structural Adjustment Programs (SAPs) and privatization schemes that have reduced or eliminated many of these services
and/or priced them out of the reach of those who need them the most. The
privatization of municipal water systems in Bolivia is perhaps one of the best
examples of the disastrous outcomes of the neoliberal "reforms" carried out
by most of the Latin American and Caribbean governments (Shultz 2005).
In this case, as in many others, the government's privatization scheme gave
control over the local water systems to a U.S.-based transnational corporation that proceeded to raise the price of water above the ability of the general population to pay for their basic water needs, which provoked massive
popular resistance to the privatization scheme and contributed to the subsequent toppling of the neoliberal government in power.

In carrying out the U.S. government– and IFI-backed strategic agenda for
the region, Washington and the IFIs have pressured the Latin American and
Caribbean governments to undertake SAPs and other "macroeconomic reforms" that have "deregulated," privatized, and "opened" the domestic
markets in these countries to the investments and imports of U.S.-based
transnational corporations. These so-called macroeconomic reforms have
devalued and "dollarized" their currencies, drastically reduced government
expenditures on public services and subsidies, caused the layoff of a large
number of government employees, privatized government-owned enterprises and public services, and diverted revenues from the public sector to

pay the external debt obligations of these countries to the IFIs and the transnational private banks that are their main creditors (Harris 2003). The effects of these measures have been disastrous for most of the population and are responsible for hindering the economic development of most of the Latin American and Caribbean countries (Harris 2005).

Neoliberal ideology has provided the "scientific" justification for the measures that the U.S. government and the IFIs have insisted governments in Latin America and the Caribbean, as well as in other peripheral countries in the world capitalist system, impose on their popular classes (Green 1995, 2–4). In fact, neoliberalism has served as an ideological smoke screen for these largely unpopular and inequitable measures. This ideology has provided the rationale for giving the transnational corporations and transnational investors unrestricted access to the natural resources, cheap labor, local capital, and consumer markets of the region.

The neoliberal agenda shared by the U.S. government, the IFIs, and the polyarchical regimes in the region has negatively affected the balanced and sustainable development of the Latin American and Caribbean countries. The "reforms" have promoted the inequitable, uneven, and environmentally destructive mode of development discussed throughout this book. The human consequences in terms of unemployment, loss of income and personal savings, and poor living standards have been incalculable. Even prominent U.S. economists such as Joseph Stiglitz (2002, 84), former chief economist and senior vice president of the World Bank and the winner of the 2001 Nobel Prize in Economics, have criticized the disastrous effects of such policies and programs.

The above-mentioned policies and programs have redistributed wealth from the poor to the rich and drastically increased the number of people living in poverty within the region. Thus, during the first decade of neoliberal economic restructuring (the 1980s), the number of people living in poverty increased from 120 million in 1980 to 196 million in 1990, a 42 percent increase, or almost double the population growth rate of 22 percent during this period (Vilas 1996, 16). Between 1990 and 2003, the number of people living in poverty increased to 220 million, which resulted in an incredible 44 percent of the region's population living below the poverty line (González 2003).

Consequently, instead of wealth trickling down to the poor as promised by the advocates of neoliberalism and so-called globalization, millions of people have trickled down from the middle and working classes into the impoverished masses. Moreover, the "global competitiveness" of the economies of most of the Latin American and Caribbean countries has not improved as they have been further "integrated" into the global economy. In 2001, according to the IDB, Latin America occupied fifth place among the seven major regions of the world in terms of its global competitiveness, only slightly ahead of the poor countries of Asia and the small group of African countries in the IDB's survey (IDB 2001, 19).

HEMISPHERIC ECONOMIC INTEGRATION
VERSUS REGIONAL INTEGRATION

The IFIs, as well as the U.S. government and the transnational corporations that operate in the region, have pressured the Latin American and Caribbean governments since the 1980s to "open" and "integrate" their economies into the evolving global trade regime that is being created by the transnational bloc of forces mentioned earlier. This global trade regime consists of two levels of regulation: (1) at the global level, there are the WTO and other trade-related regimes, and (2) at the regional level, there are various bilateral and regional "free trade" associations, such as the North American Free Trade Agreement (NAFTA) and the hemispheric Free Trade Area of the Americas (FTAA), which the U.S. government and its neoliberal "free trade" allies within the hemisphere have been trying to create since the 1990s.

In order to secure their privileged position within the Western Hemisphere and thereby strengthen their position in the highly competitive world capitalist system, the U.S.-based transnational corporations and the U.S. government have tried to create a hemispheric "free" trading sphere (encompassing Canada, the United States, Latin America, and the Caribbean). Using this hemispheric trading regime, it is hoped that the U.S.-based transnational corporations and investors will be able to extend their predominance over trade, finance, and transnational production, both within the hemisphere and globally within the entire system. The establishment of NAFTA by the elites of the United States, Canada, and Mexico was the first stage in the institutionalization of this hemispheric trading regime. The second stage has involved the establishment of bilateral free trade associations between the United States and individual countries or groups of countries, such as the United States–Colombia Trade Promotion Agreement, the United States–Central American and Dominican Republic Free Trade Association (CAFTA-DR), and the United States–Chile Free Trade Agreement. According to Robert B. Zoellick, the U.S. trade representative, these bilateral associations are part of the larger U.S. global trade strategy, which is to "pursue multiple market-opening initiatives on a global, regional and bilateral basis" (Zoellick 2004, 4). The U.S. government sees these bilateral agreements as the stepping-stones toward achieving the ambitious goal of creating the FTAA, which would encompass all the countries within the Western Hemisphere, except Socialist Cuba.

This approach to global integration has been characterized by Robinson (1998/1999) as both part of the "logic of global capitalism" and the "logic of regional accumulation" pursued by the transnational capitalist elites throughout the Americas. In the logic of global capitalism, the cheapening of labor and its disenfranchisement by the neoliberal state are considered fundamental conditions for the creation and maintenance of globally integrated production, distribution, and capital accumulation networks. The transnational factions of the capitalist class in Latin America and the Caribbean perceive that their wealth, power, and privileges lie in following this logic of global capitalism and the logic of regional accumulation associated with it. As these elite groups have become integrated into what Robinson calls the emerging "transnational capitalist class," they have created a new pattern of capital-labor relation that is based on this class's contemporary logic of regional accumulation. This logic requires peripheral regions such as Latin America and the Caribbean to provide a docile supply of cheap labor to the emerging global economy, a platform for the assembly of "global products," and the continuing provision of cheap natural resources. In this logic, these factors are the region's "comparative advantage" in the international division of labor that lies at the foundation of the rapidly globalizing world capitalist system.

It is important to note that there is a convergence of interests and consensus about this "logic" of regional accumulation between the transnational corporate elites based in the United States and Canada (as well as in Europe and Asia) and the transnational business elites in most of the Latin American and Caribbean countries.[3] This convergence of interests is based on amalgamating the Latin American economies into the increasingly integrated structure of the emerging global economy that is being created by the world capitalist system. They share mutual interests in "restructuring" (denationalizing) the Latin American and Caribbean economies so that capital-labor relations in these economies facilitate the global integration of production and the accumulation of capital on a transnational rather than national basis.

Since most of the Latin American and Caribbean countries (as well as most countries in the world) are members of the WTO, they are bound by the provisions of their membership in this intergovernmental organization to conform to its neoliberal standards. These standards benefit the transnational corporations and strip the member countries of their economic sovereignty, including their authority to regulate most of the actions of the transnational corporations within their economies.

The WTO is the successor to the General Agreement on Tariffs and Trade and was created as a global intergovernmental regulatory organization capable of overriding national sovereignty and protecting the interests of transnational capital (Kohr 1993). In the case of Latin America and the

Caribbean, this global regime for regulating international trade has institutionalized the already existing subordination of the most important sectors of the Latin American and Caribbean economies to the interests of the transnational corporations. It gives the latter the ability under international law to challenge and potentially overturn domestic laws and regulations that restrict their mobility and access to the markets and resources of the these countries (as well as other economies in the world).

The proposed FTAA is designed to extend and lock in place the subordination of the Latin American and Caribbean countries to transnational capital, particularly U.S.-based transnational corporations. That is to say, this trade regime is designed to maintain the marginal or peripheral position of the Latin American and Caribbean states in the world capitalist system as the source of cheap labor and natural resources, as well as the captive markets for the U.S.-based transnational corporations and their allies in the region. That is to say, it is designed to "integrate" them into a dollarized hemispheric trading block dominated by U.S.-based transnational corporations and the U.S. government (Prevost and Weber 2005).

RESISTANCE TO GLOBALIZATION AND NEOLIBERALISM

However, there is growing resistance among many Latin American and Caribbean governments and from a broad spectrum of civil society organizations in the region to the loss of economic sovereignty associated with the hemispheric trade regime that the U.S. government, the IFIs, and U.S. transnational corporations have been trying to impose on the region (Prevost and Weber 2005). In fact, this opposition represents a serious challenge to U.S. hegemony and is causing a growing conflict over the nature and direction of capitalist development in the region. As a result of this opposition, it seems increasingly possible that counterhegemonic forces within the region and supportive conditions outside the region will lead to a major transformation in the nature of inter-American relations.

Instead of Washington's neoliberal agenda for controlling the capitalist development of the Western Hemisphere under U.S. hegemony, a more progressive alternative agenda for the regional integration of the Latin American and Caribbean countries is being advanced that calls for their autonomous economic development. Consequently, this development poses a fundamental threat to U.S. hegemony and the dominance of transnational capital in the Americas, as well as to the globalization of the world capitalist system in general.

Throughout the region, there is a growing popular backlash against the policies and ideology of neoliberalism, as well as the effects of so-called globalization (i.e., the corporate-dominated privatization and denationalization of the national economies of the Latin American and Caribbean countries). This backlash is coupled with a widespread loss of confidence in the existing political institutions due to their susceptibility to corruption and the fact that they are widely perceived to have been appropriated by the local business elites, transnational corporations, and other privileged sectors of the population. This is having a devastating impact on the very fabric and sustainability of the state.

As we noted in the first edition of this volume, despite the rhetoric of a pretended "democratization" in the 1980s, the dominant political forms in the region are characterized by "low-intensity," restricted, or limited forms of participation. The bulk of civil society is excluded from any meaningful involvement in the governance of these countries. The IMF-imposed structural adjustments and neoliberal reforms have reduced the size and scope of the state, and the existing "receiver states" have allowed a large number of unfulfilled demands to accumulate. As a result, the political process in most of the countries in the region has become a combination of recurring frustrations, unrest, and virtual rebellion, coexisting with authoritarianism and policy deadlock. These may not yet be failed states, as we have seen in Africa, Central Asia, and the Balkans, but the trends so far include acute social disintegration, national fracturing, and institutional decomposition.

Increasing popular opposition and the political mobilization of the most disadvantaged sectors of the population have developed in the region's restricted, low-intensity democracies. These states reflect the region's incomplete transition from authoritarian rule to democratic governance. Since there is in these receiver states little room for substantive democracy, let alone equity-producing policies, popular opposition to neoliberal reforms and the kind of economic globalization these regimes support has developed largely outside the formal structures of the political system. The extent of popular mobilization that has taken place in opposition to neoliberalism and globalization appears to be producing a realignment of political forces and a sea change in the politics of the region (Vanden 2005). There is a definite movement away from the traditional politics and authoritarian political culture that have dominated the political systems of the region to a new politics based on new forms of popular democratic participation and organization.

Civil society, especially the popular sector, is becoming the new locus of political expression and organization throughout the region (Vanden 2005). Traditionally excluded sectors of the population are seeking new forms of political organization that they can call their own, and there is an ongoing search for new structures that can respond to the demands being formulated by the popular sectors of society. In part, this is because common people have become less tolerant of the traditional patterns of politics (i.e., corruption, deceit, patronage, ineffective governance, and vacuous political discourse).

Consequently, when the electorate is presented with what they perceive to be a real choice of political leadership, one that will actually pursue alternative policies that either rectify or prevent most of the economically and socially damaging aspects of neoliberalism and economic globalization, they tend to elect leaders and parties that are opposed to neoliberalism and to unregulated globalization. This explains the shift to the Left in Latin American politics that has occurred in recent years, as witnessed in the anti-neoliberal campaigns of presidents Hugo Chávez in Venezuela, Evo Morales in Bolivia, Luiz Inácio "Lula" da Silva in Brazil, Néstor Kirchner in Argentina, Rafael Correa in Ecuador, Tabaré Vázquez in Uruguay, and Daniel Ortega in Nicaragua.

TRANSCENDING THE CONTEMPORARY ORDER

The urgency of addressing the growing inequality and social injustices in most parts of the world has given rise to increasing calls for replacing the international, as well as the national and subnational, structures that provide the foundations for, reinforce, and/or are responsible for the conditions that give rise to this inequality and injustice. Even some of the erstwhile advocates of the existing system have become its critics and taken up the call for replacing it. For example, Korten (1999) has asked the question that many people in the economic centers, as well as on the periphery, of the contemporary world capitalist system have been asking for at least the last decade:

> Instead of using our power to impose the dark vision of turbo-capitalism on the world, why not bring our wisdom and compassion to bear in creating economic institutions for a world of rich cultural and biological diversity in which everyone is assured access to an adequate and satisfying means of livelihood, individual freedoms are guaranteed, family and community are strengthened, productive work, cooperation, and responsibility are rewarded, and a sustainable relationship is maintained between humanity and the life-support systems of our planet? (76)

Of course, it is not sufficient only to pose such questions. Viable alternatives to the present system are required, as are effective strategies for realizing these alternatives.

To facilitate this alternative course of development, progressive political parties, popular movements, and civil society organizations throughout Latin America, the Caribbean, and the rest of the world are increasingly concentrating their efforts on working together to formulate and propagate viable alternatives that are clearly preferable to the neoliberal project that involves the continued subordination of the peripheral capitalist countries within the world capitalist system.

Political and economic strategies are being developed for moving from the prevailing export-oriented neoliberal model of economic development to new inward-oriented models of sustainable development, tailored to the diverse conditions, economic capacities, political structures, and cultural values of the societies involved. A growing number of international and regional civil society organizations have emerged in recent years to create such alternatives, including the World Social Forum, the Social Forum of the Americas (Foro Social de las Américas), the Forum of São Paulo (Foro de São Paulo), the Hemispheric Social Alliance, the Third World Forum, the World Forum on Alternatives, Focus on the Global South, the International Forum on Globalization, Jubilee 2000, the Bolivarian Congress of Peoples, and the Third World Network. The programs, meetings, and activities of these organizations reveal that new, more equitable forms of international cooperation and regulation can be created that will support inward-oriented and sustainable development, as well as genuine democracy. At the same time, these organizations argue that the present global trading regime being erected under the WTO should and can be replaced by a new global trading system that replaces the present system of "free" but unfair trade with a system that ensures "fair trade."

At the national and subnational level, many of the social movements discussed by Hellman, Robles, Kearney, and Varese in their chapters in this volume are playing an important role in challenging the existing political, economic, and social order in Latin America and the Caribbean and beyond, developing alternatives to this order. As Hellman states, these movements are central to the discussions and hopes for a more humane future in the Americas. Many of these movements are establishing links with independent trade unions and progressive political parties to defend their achievements of the past and to push forward with the project of building social justice. In the case of indigenous peoples' movements, according to Kearney and Varese, they face the challenge of setting up new, decolonized institutional political and cultural relationships among themselves and between them and the nonindigenous peoples of the Americas.

The rapid growth of transnational indigenous political movements indicates that the indigenous peoples have been able to turn their domestic weakness and marginality into a basis for international recognition and support. As Kearney and Varese suggest in their chapter, under the contemporary conditions of "globalization from above," these movements have in many cases been able to respond with a strategy of "globalization from below." They are shifting the target of their activism from national governments to the international level, often with the assistance of international solidarity organizations in the advanced capitalist countries in North America and Europe.

Most of the proposed progressive alternatives to the neoliberal economic policies and globalization strategies of the current regimes in the region give priority to bringing about dramatic economic and social changes in the Latin American and Caribbean societies, while aligning their external relations (what to export, what to import) to the internal needs of the majority of the population in these societies. That is to say, most of the proposed alternatives focus on adjusting external economic relations to internal economic needs and goals. Some of these strategies involve what some refer to as "deglobalization" and involve unlinking the economies of these peripheral societies from the advanced capitalist centers of the world economy and the conditions set by the IFIs, WTO, and other agents of the world capitalist system for their participation in the world economy.[4]

The Chávez government in Venezuela has offered an alternative for achieving a more autonomous path of people-centered development suited to the needs of the majority of the population in Latin America and the Caribbean. It offers a vision of continental development and cooperation based on eliminating the hegemonic control the U.S. government and U.S. economic interests exercise over the Latin American and Caribbean countries. In place of export-oriented development, this alternative involves the pursuit of people-centered economic and social development, combined with South-South economic relations based on "fair" trade as opposed to U.S.-sponsored free trade.

In fact, Venezuela offers an excellent case study of mass popular opposition to neoliberalism and to Washington's project for transforming the hemisphere into a regional "free trade" zone under U.S. hegemony. Popular resistance to the neoliberal globalization of the country's economy gained momentum in Venezuela in the late 1990s. In 1997, the country was wracked by a wave of strikes sparked by the country's public-sector doctors. This situation prompted one of the country's former presidents, Luis Herrera Campins, to publicly warn the country's political leaders that their neoliberal economic policies were provoking "a middle-class rebellion" (*Latin American Weekly Report* 1997a, 35). In fact, public-opinion polls taken during this period revealed that there was almost universal dissatisfaction with the government's IMF-style stabilization program, called the "Agenda Venezuela" (*Latin American Weekly Report* 1997b, 33).

This political situation provided the context for the victory in the December 1998 elections of Hugo Chávez, a charismatic former army colonel who had acquired popular fame when he led an unsuccessful military coup in 1992 against President Carlos Andrés Pérez, unpopular at the time because of his administration's neoliberal policies. The revolutionary nationalist agenda introduced by Chávez after he became president in 1999 represents the most significant departure from Washington's neoliberal agenda in the region and a significant threat to the transnational elite in Venezuela (Coronil 2000).

Within a year of assuming the presidency, Chávez and his supporters succeeded in dissolving both the Congress and the Supreme Court, and in their place, a constituent assembly was elected. The new constitution written by the constituent assembly was submitted to a popular referendum and approved by the voters. Chávez's attempts to bring about what he called a peaceful revolutionary transformation of Venezuelan society polarized the country along class lines and led to an attempted coup and a recall referendum (both backed by the country's upper classes and the U.S. government) that failed to oust him.

In a country where the majority of the people have become poor, Chávez has "garnered loyal support from the nation's lower class through his attempts to redress the socio-economic gap that has left Venezuelan society increasingly polarized" (Scott 2004). Despite his landslide victory in the recall referendum, his opponents in the country's upper and middle classes appear determined to throw him out of power through whatever means necessary, but so far Chávez has kept the support of the popular classes and the country's armed forces (Harnecker 2003).

Chávez has blamed neoliberalism and Washington for many of his country's and Latin America's contemporary ills, and he has called the U.S. backed FTAA "the path to hell" (Palast 2003). In fact, Chávez has made the FTAA an important issue in Venezuelan politics, and the right-wing opposition's unwavering support of the FTAA is one of the factors that has prevented it from gaining any significant degree of support among the country's lower classes (Scott 2004). As an alternative to the U.S.-sponsored FTAA, Chávez has proposed the Alternativa Bolivariana para las Américas (Bolivarian Alternative for the Americas, or ALBA), named after his hero Simón Bolívar, one of the nineteenth-century liberators of South America from Spanish colonial domination.

Chávez's proposed ALBA would require the richer countries in the Americas to contribute to a "compensation fund" that would be used to correct the economic and social inequalities in the region by financing the development of the poorer countries in a manner similar to the way the European Union has financed the development of the poorer countries in the union (e.g., Ireland). The following is an excerpt from the summary of ALBA distributed by Venezuela's Banco de Comercio Exterior (External Commerce Bank):

> The ALBA differs from the FTAA in that it advocates a socially oriented trade block rather than one strictly based on the logic of deregulated capital accumulation. ALBA appeals to the egalitarian principles of justice and equality that are innate in human beings, the well-being of the most dispossessed sectors of society, and a reinvigorated sense of solidarity toward the underdeveloped countries of the Western Hemisphere, so that with the required assistance, they can enter into trade negotiations on more favorable terms than has been the case under the dictates of developed countries. (Arreaza 2004)

ALBA is based on different values and goals than the neoliberal scheme for regional integration proposed by the United States. It provides an alternative model of regional integration based on solidarity and equitable, people-centered development rather than creating the economic conditions that will enable the transnational corporations based in the North to maximize their profits by exploiting the South.

As Rohter notes in his 2005 *New York Times* article on the election of Tabaré Vázquez to the presidency in Uruguay, approximately three-quarters of the region's 355 million people are now governed by left-leaning leaders:

> Uruguay's shift consolidates what has become the new leftist consensus in South America. Three-quarters of the region's 355 million people are now governed by left-leaning leaders, all of whom have emerged in the past six years to redefine what the Left means today. They are not so much a red tide as a pink one. Doctrinaire socialism carries the day far less than pragmatism, an important change in tone and policy that makes this political moment decidedly new. From Brazil to Argentina to Ecuador and Venezuela, while demonstrating important differences in style and substance, these new leaders are united in their conviction that the free market reforms of the 1990s have failed and by a renewed focus on egalitarianism and social welfare, but not to the point where it breaks the bank.

As Rohter and other professional observers of the region have noted, the political shift away from leaders who are avowedly neoliberal to left-of-center leaders who are openly critical of neoliberalism represents more of a shift in the mood of the electorate than a regime change or major shift in the actual policies of the political leadership in these countries. Rohter (2005) points out that the region's elected leftist leaders may be "sympathetic to the symbols and rhetoric of the left's revolutionary past, cozy with Fidel Castro, and frequently anti-American in their talk," but in practice they still tend "to pursue economic policies that are favorable to American interests and sensitive to the perceptions of Wall Street."

Other observers have commented on this gap between the "anti-neoliberal" rhetoric of the new leftist governments and their actual economic policies. For example, Seth DeLong (2005), who is a senior research fellow at the Center on Hemispheric Affairs in Washington, D.C., claims,

> A sober look at these governments—certainly Brazil, Argentina and even Venezuela—reveals a significant gap between their anti-neoliberal rhetoric and their actual economic policies. While bashing the IMF and the World Bank has become the region's polemical norm, no leader—not even Chávez—is seriously contemplating a wholesale rejection of the basic principles of Keynesian economics even if some, like Kirchner, challenge IMF mandates. What this means is that Latin America's new left governments will favor mixed markets modeled on the post–World War II monetarist policies of social democratic European states.

DeLong argues that the new left-of-center governments have introduced "New Deal–style reformist initiatives," while they have left intact "the core free market structures" in their countries.

Some leftist critics go even farther and accuse these left-of-center governments of willingly going along with Washington's neoliberal agenda under a rhetorical smoke screen of leftist and anti-American rhetoric (Chossudovsky 2003; Petras 2004a). These critics claim the brand of politics these governments are practicing is a thinly disguised form of "social liberalism" à la Anthony Giddens or Tony Blair, or "liberalism with a human face" rather than a genuine alternative to the "free market" and "free trade" neoliberalism promoted by Washington and the IFIs. In fact, some of the elected leftist leaders have admitted this fact openly; for example, Senator José Mújica, a former leftist Tupamaro guerrilla and one of the leaders of the Frente Amplio (Broad Front) in the Uruguayan legislature, has stated that "we live in a unipolar world in which attempts at socialism have failed and there are no alternatives [so] we have to take a pragmatic line" (Rohter 2005).

At the very least, the growing popular resistance to neoliberalism and capitalist polyarchy throughout Latin America and the Caribbean appears to have forced most of the political regimes in the region, even those that are not led by leftist leaders, to pursue a "softer" version of neoliberalism in contrast to what Chávez calls the "savage neoliberalism" of the 1990s (Marshall and Parenti 2001). Chile is a good example of this softer version of neoliberalism. Under the leadership of Chile's moderate leftist presidents, Ricardo Lagos and Michelle Bachelet, the Chilean government has pursued a softer version of neoliberalism than preceding governments. Moreover, both of these presidents have claimed that what they have in common with the other left-of-center governments in the region is that they all "favor measures to bring in the segment of the population that has thus far been excluded from the market," and that along with the leftist leaders in Argentina, Bolivia, Brazil, Ecuador, Nicaragua, Uruguay, and Venezuela, they have joined together in "a massive rejection of the IMF and the Washington Consensus" (Rohter 2005). Thus, Ecuador's new president, Rafael Correa, said at his inauguration in January 2007 that "the poisonous neoliberal cycle has now been vanquished," and he promised his government would initiate an "economic revolution" in that country (Xinhua Online 2007).

These leaders also have in common their stated commitment to encouraging greater trade with each other through an independent form of regional economic integration similar to the kind that preceded the formation of the European Union. Lula da Silva's government in Brazil and Chávez's government in Venezuela have taken the lead in this effort, and the Kirchner and Morales governments in Argentina and Bolivia have joined them.

In fact, there appears to be growing interest throughout South America "in revivifying the Pan-American ideal of unity, currently modeled on Chávez's Bolivarian dream of South America as a regional economic hegemon" (DeLong 2005). The governments of Bolivia, Cuba, Ecuador, and Uruguay have indicated they want to join this process. It has been proposed that this coalescing continental alliance should also shift the region's extracontinental trade toward Europe and Asia and away from North America. The prospect of this happening appears to have alarmed Washington more than the increasing number of electoral triumphs of leftist politicians in the region (DeLong 2005).

As a result of the successful blocking role played by Brazil's negotiators in the FTAA negotiations in Miami in November 2003, as well as in the negotiations that took place at the Cancun WTO summit meeting in September 2003, some observers credited Lula with having "made himself the point man for a deep shift underway in the politics of globalization" (Grieder and Rapoza 2003, 6–7). Moreover, they also credited Brazil, Argentina, and Venezuela with having buried the FTAA for good.

For example, the Uruguayan international analyst Zibechi (2004) argues that Brazil was largely responsible for killing the FTAA and for opposing it with an alternative strategy.

> The FTAA is dead in its original version as well as in its "light" version designed to keep this proposal alive. The refusal by Mercosur—led by Brazil—to accept the FTAA, strengthened by the posture assumed by Venezuela and by the reluctance of several countries in the region, made Chile and Mexico the only nations that, as U.S. allies, agreed to this proposal. Meanwhile, Washington has rapidly been signing bilateral free trade agreements with Central America and several Andean countries (Colombia, Ecuador, and Peru), in order to isolate and weaken Brazil, the only country that has opposed the FTAA with an alternative strategy that consists in tightening the bonds with big countries in the Southern Hemisphere (China, South Africa, India).

Whether or not the FTAA is dead for good, it does seem clear that Washington's hegemonic approach to hemispheric economic integration is not likely to succeed so long as it continues to be blocked by Brazil, Venezuela, and Argentina, as well as Bolivia, Ecuador, and a growing number of other countries in the region. Indeed, the planned date for the completion of the FTAA negotiations (January 1, 2005) went by without any agreement being reached between the various parties involved, and Chávez has made it clear on a number of occasions that his government is opposed to the FTAA in any form.

Part of the problem is that Washington has continued to insist on protecting U.S. agriculture, while at the same time insisting that the Latin American and Caribbean countries remove all their barriers to trade, including the tariffs and regulations that protect local ownership and regulation of what is left of their increasingly deregulated economies (Zibechi 2004). The governments of Argentina and Brazil insist that the United States must eliminate its agricultural subsidies (that protect U.S. agriculture from agricultural imports) and antidumping regulations (which further protect the U.S. economy from global competition) if Washington wants the Latin American and Caribbean governments to remove the trade barriers that protect their economies (Dobbin 2005).

It is important to note that the rapid removal of tariffs proposed by Washington in its plans for the FTAA threatens many of the Caribbean governments since they depend on tariffs for most of their revenues. If the U.S. conception of the FTAA were put in place, these governments would have to abolish all their tariffs and introduce new tax systems to replace their lost revenues (Dobbin 2005). Although the pro-FTAA government of Canada has given repeated assurances to the Caribbean countries that they would have an adjustment period to eliminate their tariffs, this issue was not seriously addressed in the FTAA negotiations.

Brazil's foreign policy under Lula has seriously challenged Washington's agenda for the creation of a hemispheric free trade bloc under U.S. hegemony. Thus, even though the prominent Brazilian leftist scholar Emir Sader (2004) has been quite critical of Lula's domestic policies and broken political promises to the popular classes in Brazil, he has acknowledged that in the foreign-policy arena, Lula's government has made an important difference. According to Sader, under Lula's leadership, Brazil has pursued a new agenda in Latin America and the global South in general. In this regard, Sader (2004) notes,

> Prior to the Iraqi war, Lula was one of the most outspoken opponents of the impending U.S. invasion. Then, he helped forge the bloc of 22 nations [led by Brazil and India] that stopped the World Trade Organization in its tracks at Cancun in August 2003. Next at the close of the year he led the charge that forced the Bush administration to back off from its plans to impose the corporate-dominated Free Trade Area of the Americas on the entire Western Hemisphere by 2005.

As of 2007, Argentina, Bolivia, Brazil, Cuba, Ecuador, and Venezuela appear to be pursuing similar foreign policies aimed at unifying the Latin American and Caribbean countries in an unprecedented challenge to U.S. hegemony in the region. One aspect of this strategy involves strengthening the Mercado Común del Sur (the Southern Common Market, or MERCO-SUR) and its links with the members of the Comunidad Andina (the Andean Community, or CAN). Significantly, Chávez's Venezuela is a member of both groupings and has provided an important link between them in promoting this initiative. According to Zibechi:

Mercosur has two objectives: to counteract the free trade agreements yet to be subscribed between the U.S. and Colombia, Peru, and Ecuador; and to tighten the bonds in order to forward the formation of a Community of South American Nations, an endeavor undertaken by Brazil, which has been followed, with different degrees of enthusiasm, by several of its Mercosur partners. All in all, it is a race against the clock to win those that are still hesitant, in which George W. Bush has solid allies like Álvaro Uribe's Colombia, while Mercosur counts on Latin-Americanist Hugo Chávez. (Zibechi 2004)

Brazil and Venezuela are leading this effort to merge MERCOSUR and CAN with the backing of Argentina, Bolivia, Ecuador, and Paraguay. It also is strongly supported by the Cuban government and the Vázquez government in Uruguay.

The opposition to the FTAA presented by these governments has drawn sharp criticism from Washington. For example, at the November 2004 meeting of the Asia Pacific Economic Cooperation Forum in Chile, Robert Zoellick, the chief U.S. trade negotiator for the FTAA, publicly criticized Argentina and Brazil for blocking the creation of the FTAA (Arachín 2004). His criticism drew an equally sharp response from the head representative of MERCOSUR, Eduardo Duhalde (ex-president of Argentina), who stated that in his opinion, the comments of "Mr. FTAA" were a declaration of war on the economic plane. Duhalde said that they reflected "a unipolar vision of the planet, in which countries like our own do not have the right to negotiate, rather only to sign a contract of submission" and emphasized that this unipolar approach was unacceptable (Arachín 2004).

Argentina, Bolivia, Brazil, Ecuador, Venezuela, and Uruguay support the establishment of a South American regional economic union (which Cuba has said it would like to join) as an alternative to the NAFTA-like FTAA advocated by the United States. The formation of the Comunidad Sudamericana de Naciones (South American Community of Nations or CSN) is an important step in this direction. On December 8, 2004, the presidents of the MERCOSUR and CAN countries signed the Cuzco Declaration, which formally established the CSN. This initiative involves the creation of a continental free trade area that will involve "the gradual dovetailing of the Andean Community and MERCOSUR, in such a way that the two integration processes progressively merge on the basis of accumulated strengths and the reciprocal association between their members" (Andean Community 2004).

With regard to the future development of this new economic and political community, it is important to note that MERCOSUR's head representative, Eduardo Duhalde, has said that "our mirror will be the European Union, with all its institutions" (DeLong 2005). Various MERCOSUR and CAN leaders have stated that their intention is to model the new CSN on the European Union, with a common currency, a CSN parliament, and CSN passports. It is worth noting the scale and economic significance of this new economic union: the CSN countries have a combined population of over 350 million people and a combined gross domestic product (GDP) in 2004 of more than US $2.8 trillion (compared with NAFTA's GDP of $15.2 trillion and the European Union's GDP of $12 trillion in 2004).[5] Moreover, the countries that make up the CSN account for 85 percent of interregional trade within South America (ALIA2 2004).

The MERCOSUR and CAN countries have also been involved in negotiating a trade agreement with the European Union. These negotiations, however, have run up against many of the same issues as the negotiations with Washington over the FTAA, including "subsidies to agriculture, and the EU's expectation that the countries of the South [should] open their services, governmental purchases and investments to European multinationals" (Zibechi 2004). On the other hand, it is important to note that Brazil's foreign minister, Celso Amorim, has stated that a trade agreement with the European Union would have considerable political importance because "we want to reinforce a multipolar world context" as distinct from Washington's unipolar approach to trade issues (Zibechi 2004).

Meanwhile, Washington has followed a divide-and-conquer strategy that it calls "competitive liberalization." This approach has involved negotiating separate free trade agreements (FTAs) with the Central American countries (the CAFTA-DR), Panama, some of the Andean countries (Colombia and Peru), and Chile. These "bilateral" FTA treaties have enabled the U.S. government to coerce small countries into accepting its aggressive free trade conditions while giving little in return. For example, a report on this subject by Scott Sinclair and Ken Traynor (2005) states,

> Under its "competitive liberalization" strategy, U.S. priorities have shifted from the stalled FTAA to wrapping up bilateral free trade agreements wherever possible. The U.S. now has free trade deals in place with Mexico, Canada, and Chile; signed (but not ratified) treaties with Costa Rica, El Salvador, Guatemala, Honduras, Nicaragua, and the Dominican Republic; and negotiations underway with Colombia, Ecuador, Peru, and Panama. The U.S. is using these bilateral negotiations to isolate and build pressure on the FTAA holdout countries—clearly a "divide-and-conquer" strategy. (25)

The "piecemeal" nature of this U.S. strategy of negotiating separate free trade agreements was made public in 2002, when U.S. Trade Representative Robert Zoellick (2002) said the United States preferred "to negotiate with all the democracies of the Americas through the FTAA" but that it was prepared to move "step-by-step toward free trade if others turn back or simply are not yet ready" for a hemispheric trade agreement. On several occasions thereafter, he distinguished between the "won't-do" and the "can-do" countries and said the United States was going ahead with its efforts to promote hemispheric free trade by working with the can-do countries (Sinclair and Traynor 2005, 26).

As James Petras (2004b) has noted, even though popular rebellions have forced the resignation of pro-FTAA neoliberal governments, and leftist leaders critical of the U.S. agenda for the hemisphere have been elected in an increasing number of countries, the United States has still gone ahead with its plans to construct the FTAA according to its own agenda. Petras argues that Washington is "less concerned with the past political positions, current 'radical' labels or popular social background of the Latin American presidents" than with their willingness to collaborate with the United States "in pursuing neoliberal socioeconomic policies and pro-empire foreign policies."

Petras has pointed out that Lula's government in Brazil cooperated with the United States on a number of important issues. For example, Lula's government took the lead in trying to negotiate a "light," or compromise, version of the FTAA at the Miami Summit in November 2003, and his government also provided the lead contingent for the United Nations' multinational force sent to maintain order in Haiti after the U.S. government forced democratically elected President Jean-Bertrand Aristide into exile (Petras 2004b). However, another way to look at these moves on the part of Lula's government is that they were designed to dilute Washington's influence. In other words, by taking an active role in shaping these efforts as opposed to standing back, Brazil kept the United States from running the show. This may also explain why Argentina, Chile, and Uruguay decided to send troops to Haiti once Brazil decided to provide the lead contingent for the United Nations' peacekeeping force (Zibechi 2004).

Apart from those already mentioned, there have been other steps taken in the direction of greater regional integration among the Latin American countries as an alternative to the kind of hemispheric integration that Washington seeks to create under its suzerainty. These include the creation of Petrosur by Venezuela and Argentina at the 2004 Iguazú summit meeting between Presidents Chávez and Kirchner. Petrosur is a "multistate oil company" that is supposed to bring the national oil companies of the South American countries together to serve as one of the main engines of regional integration in a manner similar to the role played by the major European coal and steel industries in the early stages of European economic integration (Smith 2004). In addition, there are plans to create a University of the South, a continental Humanitarian Assistance Fund, and a South American Bank. In the case of the latter, this continental financial institution would serve as the depository for the international reserves of the South American nations instead of the U.S., Japanese, and European banks where the reserves have traditionally been deposited.

Also, a new multinational Venezuelan-Argentine-Brazilian-Uruguayan satellite TV network called Televisora del Sur (Television of the South, or

Telesur) has been established (Petrich 2005). Telesur is a public television channel that will compete throughout the region with North American and European networks, such as CNN, Univisión, and the BBC, by providing an alternative source of information and a point of view that is South American, instead of North American or European. According to its director, Telesur is

> a strategic project that was born out of the need to give voice to Latin Americans confronted by an accumulation of thoughts and images transmitted by commercial media and out of the urgency to see ourselves through our own eyes and to discover our own solutions to our problems. If we do not start there, the dream of Latin American integration will be no more than a salute to the flag. (Petrich 2005)

Like the other initiatives mentioned, this Al Jazeera–style South American TV channel is aimed at integrating the South American countries into an economic and political community similar to the European Union.

There has also been considerable talk in the region about creating a single currency for the South American countries that would be modeled on, and perhaps tied to, the euro rather than the U.S. dollar. This discussion is symptomatic of what appears to be an emerging desire to create an integrated economic and political community that is strikingly different from the type of hemispheric integration scheme being pursued by the U.S. government and its allies in the region (DeLong 2005). Moreover, as a further sign of the increasing desire in the region to find alternatives to trading with the United States, several South American nations have been strengthening their economic relations with Asia, particularly with China.

For example, in May 2004, Lula visited China with eighteen ministers and some five hundred representatives from all sectors of Brazilian business and industry (Smith 2004). Shortly afterward, Kirchner visited China with a team of ministers and 270 business people from Argentina. Then, in late December 2004, Chávez visited China, which was followed in January 2005 by the signing of some nineteen different agreements between Venezuela and China. These agreements involve joint ventures in oil, agriculture, and technology and include extensive Chinese investments in oil and gas exploration in Venezuela (Wagner 2005). In a similar effort to strengthen trading relations with Asia, Mexico reached a free trade agreement with Japan in 2004, and Chile entered into negotiations with India for a free trade pact similar to one that it has with South Korea (Smith 2004).

Clearly, the U.S. government is worried about the domino effect of this increasing tendency toward independent economic integration and trade with Asia, coupled with the election of left-leaning governments in South America. It is unlikely that the U.S. government will allow this tendency to move north to engulf Mexico without doing everything it can to prevent it.

As one observer has noted, the U.S. government "would become apoplectic if this movement reaches the U.S.-Mexican border" (DeLong 2005). Thus, the U.S. government opposed the election of left-of-center presidential candidate Andrés Manuel López Obrador in the 2006 presidential elections in Mexico, fearing that the election of a leftist president in Mexico would constitute a grave threat to U.S. hegemony in the hemisphere.

Among other things, the Bush administration was worried that López Obrador might reverse the Mexican government's neoliberal policies, which he promised in his campaign he would do, and also that he might withdraw Mexico's support for the FTAA. In addition, the Bush administration feared that a leftist Mexican president would establish closer relations with Cuba and Chávez's Venezuela, as the governments of Lula, Kirchner, Morales, and Vázquez have done already (DeLong 2005).

The free trade and free market approach promoted by the U.S. government, the IFIs, and the transnational elites in the Americas are not a solution to the poverty and inequality that prevails in the hemisphere because "the rules and practices of liberalized trade are designed primarily to create a stable and profitable environment for corporations and investors" (Prevost and Weber 2005, 25). The U.S. proposal for the FTAA is "like other previous economic integration projects, the primary backers are the business community and the politicians over whom they have the most influence" (Prevost and Weber 2005, 25). The main impetus for regional integration and globalization has come from elite groups in business and government who want to create a free trade area of the Americas as a mechanism to enhance northern economic, military, and political interests over those of the countries of the region and the vast majority of its inhabitants. In this respect, there is a remarkable and unfortunate continuity between what is now called globalization and what has previously been called neocolonialism and "old-fashioned" imperialism. The current U.S. proposal for creating regional economic integration is not aimed at an integration of the peoples of the Americas; rather, it is a plutocratic arrangement to redefine the rules of the game away from domestic democratic controls.

The proponents of the FTAA claim that this international trade agreement will eliminate the remaining barriers to the free flow of money, goods, and services across national borders in the Americas. It would create a single, integrated market within the Western Hemisphere (excluding Socialist Cuba) that would encompass almost seven hundred million people and a combined GDP greater than that of the European Union. This hemispheric economic integration proposal falls within the neoliberal free trade and free market approach promoted by the World Bank, IMF, and U.S. government. The impetus for it "must be placed within the wider context of United States policy toward Latin America and the changing international scene in the wake of the Cold War" (Prevost and Weber 2005, 24), particularly the strategic aim of positioning the United States and U.S.-based transnational corporations so that they can compete in the twenty-first century with their economic rivals in Europe and Asia.

However, even though the U.S. government continues to press for this objective of hemispheric economic integration, there is increasing opposition in Latin America and the Caribbean to this hegemonic project. As Prevost and Weber (2005) have noted, at the base of the Latin American and Caribbean resistance to this project is the failure of the neoliberal policies to deliver consistent economic development and social justice anywhere in the region. The collapse of Argentina's economy in 2001 and 2002 (Latin America Bureau 2002) provides the most dramatic example of the failure of neoliberalism in the region, and the adverse effects of the pursuit of similar neoliberal economic policies in other countries throughout the region have fueled the opposition to the neoliberal economic integration of the region under the hegemony of the United States and U.S.-based transnational corporations.

FINAL CONSIDERATIONS

The foregoing analysis of the global context of inter-American relations at the beginning of the twenty-first century reveals that the neoliberal agenda pursued since the 1980s by the U.S. government, the IFIs, the transnational corporations, and the transnational elites is in serious trouble. Neoliberal policies and corporate-driven "globalization" have engendered growing popular resistance and a counterhegemonic response from both civil society organizations and elected leftist political leaders in the region. In particular, there is growing opposition from a coalition of Latin American and Caribbean governments, as well as from a broad spectrum of civil society organizations, which are particularly opposed to the hemispheric "free trade" regime that the U.S. government, the IFIs, and the U.S.-based transnational corporations have sought to impose on the region.

The expanding popular opposition to neoliberalism and so-called globalization and the shift to the left in the region's politics represent not only a serious challenge to U.S. hegemony but also growing conflict over the nature and direction of capitalist development in the region. Central to Washington's strategy for the hemisphere has been the imposition of a neoliberal model of capitalist development on the Latin American and Caribbean economies and the integration of these economies into a U.S.-dominated hemispheric "free trade" area. This project is itself a vehicle for the domination of the global economy by U.S. transnational corporations and the government that represents them. The restructuring of the economies of the region under the mantra of neoliberalism and the banner of globalization was aimed at giving the U.S.-based transnational corporations and investors free reign within the region and a strong hemispheric base from which to dominate the global economy.

In contrast to the neoliberal, polyarchical, and globalizing model of development imposed by the U.S. government and its allies in the region, a growing movement for an alternative form of development that is genuinely democratic, autonomous, and environmentally sustainable appears to be gaining ground in various parts of Latin America and the Caribbean. This alternative form of development involves the reorganization and realignment of the existing economies in the region, as well as the replacement of the existing political regimes, which serve the interests of the transnational bloc of forces that are behind the integration of the region into the globalized structures of the world capitalist system. New popular democratic regimes are needed to serve the needs and interests of the majority of the people rather than the ruling elites, the transnational corporations, and the transnational capitalist class.

An essential requirement for realigning these economies so that they produce people-centered and environmentally sustainable development is their integration into a regional economic and political union that has the resources, the structures, and the power to operate independently of the U.S. government and the U.S.-based transnational corporations. If this type of regional integration takes place, it will enable the Latin American and Caribbean states to break free of the hegemonic influence of the U.S. government and the U.S. transnational corporations and to stop the denationalization ("globalization") of the Latin American and Caribbean economies.

Instead of the corporate-driven hemispheric integration of the region under U.S. hegemony, a new system of regional economic cooperation and sustainable development has been proposed to improve the lives of the vast majority of the people living in Latin America and the Caribbean. This type of regional, autonomous, and sustainable development can only be successfully carried out by truly democratically elected political leaders with broad-based popular support who are sincerely committed to achieving this alternative rather than the elitist neoliberal model.

Regionalism has been the dream of the democratic Left for some time. The European Union has its origins in the French Socialist dream of ending Franco-German enmity through unifying Europe, and African regionalism was the vision of African Socialists, such as Julius Nyerere of Tanzania, who saw regional integration as the means to progress beyond tribalism and colonialism and create a united Socialist Africa (Faux 2001, 4). Viewed from the perspective of those who want to create a people-centered, democratic, and environmentally sustainable social order in the Americas, the corporate-dominated process of capitalist pseudoglobalization taking place in the region urgently needs to be replaced by what Samir Amin has referred to as a new system of "pluricentric regulated globalization" (Amin 2001a). This alternative form of globalization requires the development of regional economic and political communities in Europe, Africa, Asia, Latin America, the Caribbean, and elsewhere, which collaboratively promote people-centered, democratic, and environmentally sustainable forms of development. According to Amin, these regional unions of states are needed to collaborate as partners in collectively regulating the global restructuring of the world economy for the benefit of the vast majority of humanity rather than the transnational corporations and the centers of the world capitalist system (Amin 2001a).

This type of regional-based regulative order can redirect international economic, social, and political relations so that they serve the interests and needs of the vast majority of the world's population. The present structure of the world capitalist system provides the supporting global context for the transnational, corporate-driven restructuring of the region's economies and societies. The Latin American and Caribbean countries need to "delink," step by step, from this highly unequal and inequitable system. They need to redirect and restructure their economies so that they serve the needs of the majority of their people while also protecting their natural resources and ecosystems. The alternative policies of economic and social development proposed by the new leftist leaders, the progressive civil society organizations and their supporters, and the project of regional integration associated with the new Community of South American Nations are important indications of movement in this direction.

A growing number of civil society organizations and social movements throughout the Americas are pressuring the governments of the region to follow what the Hemispheric Social Alliance (HSA), a network or forum of progressive organizations and movements, calls a regional model of integration that supports the sustainable and democratic development of all the societies in the region (see ASC-HSA 2006). The HSA (which is called Alianza Social Continental, or ASC, in Spanish and Portuguese) also contends that the South American Community of Nations is being threatened by the free trade agreements that Washington has negotiated with Chile, Colombia, Peru, and the Central American countries. According to the HSA, it is fundamental to reverse these agreements and to promote in their place trade agreements that do not compromise sovereignty, medicines, health, water, education, culture, biodiversity, food sovereignty, government purchases, and natural resources but rather promote the sustainable development of these countries. The "Alternatives for the Americas" proposal developed by this inter-American network of progressive organizations and social movements calls on all governments in the region to "subordinate trade and investment to policies that prioritize sustainability and environmental protection" (HSA 2002, 5).

A regional model for sustainable and democratic development requires the incorporation of the principle and objective of sustainability in all the subjects addressed. These issues should be negotiated with the objective of resolving—with the support of national policies—our region's grave social problems, including inequality, unemployment, and environmental degradation. (HSA2002, 5)

The HSA represents what various progressive analysts have predicted since the mid-1990s: the emergence of new social movements capable of challenging the agenda of neoliberal capitalist globalization promoted by the U.S. government, the IFIs, and the transnational corporations. Today, these movements are advocating an alternative agenda that is gaining increasing support from other civil society organizations, political parties, and political leaders throughout the Americas and beyond.

These social movements and civil society organizations, in combination with progressive political parties and trade unions, have in recent years brought about the popular election of left-of-center presidents—Hugo Chávez in Venezuela, Lula da Silva in Brazil, Néstor Kirchner in Argentina, Tabaré Vázquez in Uruguay, Evo Morales in Bolivia, Rafael Correa in Ecuador, and Daniel Ortega in Nicaragua—all critics of neoliberalism, U.S. hegemony, and transnational corporate-driven globalization. These movements and organizations have also organized the popular protests and mobilizations that forced the resignation of neoliberal presidents in Argentina, Ecuador, and Bolivia and created the political conditions for the shift to the Left that has taken place in recent years throughout the region.

They provide unquestionable evidence of the emergence of the social forces and political conditions that Panitch (1996, 89) and others (e.g., Harris 1995, 301–302; Jonas and McCaughan 1994) predicted in the 1990s would arise in opposition to neoliberalism, capitalist globalization, and U.S. hegemony. It seems increasingly possible that these forces and political conditions will transform the nature of inter-American relations, bring about the regional integration of Latin America and the Caribbean, and move the Americas away from "turbo-capitalism" toward a people-centered, genuinely democratic, and environmentally sustainable form of economic, social, and political development.

NOTES

The authors of this chapter have placed some suggested resources that you may wish to consult on the book's website at http://www.rowmanlittlefield.com/isbn/0742555240.

1. For a discussion of the origins and evolution of the world capitalist system, see Wallerstein (1997).

2. For a discussion of this network nature of the global economy, see Castells (1996).

3. This convergence of interests is produced through a network of interactions facilitated by international organizations such as the Association of the American Chambers of Commerce in Latin America, the Council of the Americas, the Canadian Council for the Americas, the Americas Business Forum, the Inter-American Economic Council, and the Inter-American Development Bank.

4. For a discussion of deglobalization, see the book on this subject by Bello (2002).

5. The source for these figures is the CIA's *World Factbook 2005*.

REFERENCES

Agencia Latinoamericana de Información y Análisis–Dos (ALIA2). 2004. "Mercosur and the Andeans in the Final Stretch." August 26. Available at www.alia2.net/article 1942.html?var_recherche=MERCOSUR (accessed March 20, 2005).

Alianza Social Continental–Hemispheric Social Alliance (ASC-HSA). 2006. "Civil Society Organizations on the Road to the Construction of the South American Community of Nations." Presentation to the ministers and vice ministers of the South American Community of Nations in Santiago, Chile, November 22. Available at www.asc-hsa.org/article.php3?id_article=443 (accessed January 27, 2007).

Amin, Samir. 2000. "The Political Economy of the Twentieth Century." *Monthly Review* 52, no. 2 (June). Available at www.monthlyreview.org/600amin.htm (accessed February 2, 2007).

———. 2001a. "Imperialism and Globalization." *Monthly Review* 53, no. 2 (June). Available at www.monthlyreview.org/0601amin.htm (accessed June 12, 2002).

———. 2001b. "Globalism or Apartheid on a Global Scale." Paper presented at the World Conference against Racism, Durban, South Africa, August. Available at http://forum-alternatives.net/eng/index (accessed June 12, 2004).

Andean Community. 2004. "Conclusions of the Andean Presidential Dialogue on Integration, Development and Social Cohesion." Article on the Andean Community Website, December 7. Available at www.comunidadandina.org/ingles/document/act7-12-04.htm (accessed March 23, 2005).

Arachín, R. 2004. "Gran malestar en el Mercosur por criticas de Estados Unidos." *Revista Quantum* (November 30). Available at www.alia2.net/article3050 .html?var_recherche=MERCOSUR (accessed March 21, 2005).

Arreaza, T. 2004. "ALBA: Bolivarian Alternative for Latin America and the Caribbean." Venezuelanalysis.com, January 30. Available at www.venezuelanalysis.com/docs.php?dno=1010 (accessed April 3, 2005).

Bello, Walden. 2002. *De-globalization: Ideas for a New World Economy*. London: Zed Books.

Bulmer-Thomas, V. 1996. "Introduction." In *The New Economic Model in Latin America and Its Impact on Income Distribution and Poverty*, ed. V. Bulmer-Thomas, 7–26. New York: St. Martin's Press.

Burbach, Roger. 2002. "Throw Them All Out: Argentina's Grassroots Rebellion." *NACLA Report on the Americas* 36, no. 1 (July/August): 38–40.

Castells, Manuel. 1996. *The Rise of the Network Society*. Oxford: Blackwell.

Chossudovsky, M. 2003. "Brazil: Neoliberalism with a 'Human Face.'" Centre for Research on Globalization. Available at www.globalresearch.ca/articles/CHO303C .html (accessed October 1, 2007).

Coronil, Fernando. 2000. "Magical Illusions or Revolutionary Magic? Chávez in Historical Context." *NACLA Report on the Americas* 33, no. 6 (May): 34–41.

DeLong, S. 2005. "Venezuela and the Latin American New Left." Council on Hemispheric Affairs Memorandum to the Press No. 05.26, March 8. Available at www.coha.org/NEW_PRESS_RELEASES/New_Press_Releases_2005/05.26%20Ve nezuela%20and%20the%20New%20Left%20the%20one.htm (accessed March 29, 2005).

Dobbin, M. 2005. "Is the FTAA Dead, or Just Resting?" FTAA Resistance Website, January 6. Available at www.ftaaresistance.org/resting.html (accessed March 29, 2005).

Economic Commission for Latin America and the Caribbean (ECLAC). 2005. *Preliminary Overview of the Economies of Latin America and the Caribbean 2005*. Santiago: United Nations Publications.

Economistas de Izquierda. 2004. "Argentina: Program for a Popular Economic Recovery." *Monthly Review* 56, no. 4 (September). Available at www.monthlyreview.org/0904edi.htm (accessed March 18, 2005).

Faux, Jeff. 2001. "The Global Alternative." *American Prospect* 12, no. 12 (July). Available at www.prospsect.org/print-friendly/V12/12/faux-j.html (accessed December 1, 2003).

González, Gustavo. 2003. "Latin America: More Poverty, Fewer Social Services." Terra Viva Online, January 13. Available at www.ipsnews.net/fsm2003/eng/note1 .shtml (accessed March 23, 2003).

Green, David. 1995. *Silent Revolution: The Rise of Market Economics in Latin America*. London: Cassell.

Grieder, William, and Kenneth Rapoza. 2003. "Lula Raises the Stakes." *The Nation*, December 1, 11–17.

Harnecker, Marta. 2003. "Venezuela: A Sui Generis Revolution." Venezuelanalysis.com, September 16. Available at http://venezuelanalysis .com/articles.php?artno=1018 (accessed December 5, 2003).

Harris, Richard. 1995. "The Global Context of Contemporary Latin American Affairs." In *Capital, Power and Inequality in Latin America*, ed. Sandor Halebsky and Richard Harris, 279–304. Boulder, CO: Westview Press.

———. 2000. "The Effects of Globalization and Neoliberalism in Latin America at the Beginning of the Millennium." In *Critical Perspectives on Globalization and Neoliberalism in the Developing Countries*, ed. Richard Harris and Melinda Seid, 139–62. Leiden: Brill.

———. 2002. "Introduction: Globalization and Globalism in Latin America: Contending Perspectives." *Latin American Perspectives* 29, no. 6 (December): 5–23.

———. 2003. "Popular Resistance to Globalization and Neoliberalism in Latin America." *Journal of Developing Societies* 19, nos. 2–3 (June and September): 90–113.

———. 2005. "Globalization and Development in Latin America: Economic Integration, Health, Labor and Popular Mobilization." In *Globalization and Development in Latin America*, ed. Richard Harris, 1–23. Oshawa, Ontario: de Sitter Publications.

Harris, Richard, and Melinda Seid. 2000. "Critical Perspectives on Globalization and Neoliberalism in the Developing Countries." In *Critical Perspectives on Globalization and Neoliberalism in the Developing Countries,* ed. Richard Harris and Melinda Seid, 1–26. Leiden: Brill.

Hemispheric Social Alliance (HSA). 2002. "Alternatives for the Americas." Unpublished document, July. Available at www.asc-hsa.org/pdf/Alternativas% 20ene%202003%20english.pdf (accessed March 20, 2003).

Ikerd, John. 2005. *Sustainable Capitalism: A Matter of Common Sense.* Bloomfield, CT: Kumarian Press.

Inter-American Development Bank. 2001. "Competitiveness: The Business of Growth: Economic and Social Progress in Latin America." Report of the Inter-American Development Bank. Available at www.iadb.org/res/publications/ pubfiles/pubB-2001E_235.pdf (accessed April 4, 2005).

———. 2005. *Annual Report 2004.* "International Scenario" section. Available at www.iadb.org/exr/ar2004/LAC_International.cfm?language=en&parid=4&item1i d=3 (accessed October 1, 2007).

Jonas, Susanne, and Edward McCaughan. 1994. *Latin America Faces the Twenty-first Century: Reconstructing a Social Justice Agenda.* Boulder, CO: Westview Press.

Kohli, Renu. 2003. "The Transition from Official Aid to Private Capital Flows: Implications for a Developing Country." Conference paper, Reserve Bank of India, May. Available at http://62.237.131.18/conference/conference-2003-3/conference-2003-3-papers/Kohli-0508.pdf (accessed January 26, 2007).

Kohr, Martin. 1993. "Free Trade in the Third World." In *The Case against Free Trade,* ed. Ralph Nader, 97–107. San Francisco: Earth Island Institute.

Korten, David. 1999. *When Corporations Rule the World.* Bloomfield, CT: Kumarian Press.

Kregel, J. A. 2004. "Negative Net Resource Transfers as a Minskyian Hedge Profile and the Stability of the International Financial System." International Development Economics Associates Network Paper, November 3. Available at www .networkideas.org/featart/nov2004/fa03_IFS.htm (accessed October 1, 2007).

Kuttner, R. 2002. "U.S. Fueled Argentina's Economic Collapse." *Boston Globe,* January 7, A15.

Latin America Bureau. 2002. "Argentina: Country Files—Introduction." Available at www.lab.org.uk/?lid=83 (accessed June 20, 2004).

Latin American Weekly Report. 1997a. "Venezuela: Strikers Call Seven Day Truce," January 14, 35.

———. 1997b. "Venezuela: Agenda Venezuela Stabilization Program," July 8, 33.

Malhotra, Kemal, et al. 2003. *Making Global Trade Work for People.* London: Earthscan Publications.

Marshall, John, and Christian Parenti. 2001. "New World Order: But Venezuela's 'Revolution' Faces Many Obstacles." *In These Times,* November 9. Available at www.inthesetimes.com/issue/26/01/feature3.shtml (accessed March 29, 2005).

Martin, Matthew. 2004. "Private Capital Flows to Low-Income Countries: Perception and Reality," *Canadian Development Report 2004,* chapter 2. Available at www.dri.org.uk/pdfs/EngPub7b_PCF_CDR_2.pdf (accessed November 3, 2006).

McMichael, A. J., and Robert Beaglehole. 2000. "The Changing Global Context of Public Health." *Lancet* 356:495–99. Available at http://thelancet.com/era/ LLAN.ERA.1060 (accessed June 6, 2002).

Nef, Jorge. 1995. "Demilitarization and Democratic Transition in Latin America." In *Capital, Power and Inequality in Latin America*, ed. Sandor Halebsky and Richard Harris, 81–108. Boulder, CO: Westview Press.

Nuevo Proyecto Historico. 2002. "Las elecciones, nuestra visión." Centro de Medios Independientes, Argentina, August 3. Available at www.argentina.indymedia.org/print.php?id=41445 (accessed March 23, 2003).

Onis, Ziya, and Fikret Senses. 2003. "Rethinking the Emerging Post-Washington Consensus: A Critical Appraisal." Economic Research Center Working Paper, November, subsequently published in *Development and Change* 36, no. 2 (November): 263–90.

Palast, Greg. 2003. "Chávez versus the Free Trade Zombies of the Americas." Working for Change Website. Available at www.workingforchange.com/article.cfm?itemid=16090 (accessed December 21, 2003).

Panitch, Leon. 1996. "Globalization, States and Left Strategies." *Social Justice* 23, nos. 1–2: 79–89.

———. 2002. "Renewing Socialism." *Monthly Review* (February). Available at www.findarticles.com/cf_0/m1132/9_53/82609810/p1/article.jhtml (accessed December 26, 2003).

Petras, James. 2003. "Dependency and World Systems Theory." In *Development in Theory and Practice*, ed. Ronald Chilcote, 166–70. Lanham, MD: Rowman & Littlefield.

———. 2004a. "Argentina: From Popular Rebellion to Normal Capitalism." *Rebellion* (April). Available at www.globalresearch.ca/articles/PET406A.html (accessed September 23, 2004).

———. 2004b. "Latin America: Political Re-alignment and Empire." *Rebellion* (November 22). Available at www.rebellion.org/noticia.php?id=7961 (accessed March 23, 2005).

Petrich, B. 2005. "Telesur: A Counter-Hegemonic Project to Compete with CNN and Univisión." Agencia Latinoamericana de Información y Análisis-Dos (ALIA2), March 2. Available at www.alia2.net/article4055.html (accessed April 3, 2005).

Prevost, Gary, and Robert Weber. 2005. "The Free Trade Area of the Americas in the Context of U.S.-Latin American Relations." In *Globalization and Development in Latin America*, ed. Richard Harris, 24–45. Oshawa, Ontario: de Sitter Publications.

Reel, M. 2005. "Imagine al-Jazeera, South American Style." Agencia Latinoamericana de Información y Análisis-Dos (ALIA2), March 15. Available at www.alia2.net/article4209.html (accessed April 3, 2005).

Reich, Otto. 2002. "U.S. Interests in Latin America." Speech to the Heritage Foundation on October 31. Available at www.usembassy-mexico.gov/st021031Reich.html (accessed April 3, 2005).

Renfrew, David. 2004. "Frente Amplio Wins Elections in Uruguay." World Socialist Website, November. Available at www.wsws.org/articles/2004/nov2004/urug-n04.shtml (accessed March 22, 2005).

Robinson, William. 1996. *Promoting Polyarchy: Globalization, U.S. Intervention, and Hegemony*. New York: Cambridge University Press.

———. 1998/1999. "Latin America and Global Capitalism." *Race and Class* 40, nos. 2–3: 111–30.

———. 2004. "Global Crisis and Latin America." *Bulletin of Latin American Research* 23, no. 2 (June): 135–53.

Robinson, William, and Jerry Harris. 2000. "Towards a Global Ruling Class? Globalization and the Transnational Capitalist Class." *Science and Society* 64, no. 1 (Spring): 11–54.

Rohter, L. 2001. "Consequences for the United States in Argentina's Collapse." *New York Times*, December 25. Available at www.mtholyoke.edu/acad/intrel/globecon/argentina.htm (accessed March 19, 2005).

———. 2005. "With New Chief, Uruguay Veers Left, in a Latin Pattern." Venezuelanalysis.com, March 1. Available at www.venezuelanalysis.com/articles.php?artno=1386 (accessed April 3, 2005).

Rosendo Gonzalez, Pablo. 2003. "In Argentina, a New Optimism: Nestor Kirchner Won the Presidency with Just 22 Percent of the Vote." *New Statesman* 4 (August). Available at www.findarticles.com/p/articles/mi_m0FQP/is_4649_132/ai_106861322 (accessed March 18, 2005).

Sader, Emir. 2004. "The Brazilian Right and the Lula Administration." Americas Program, Interhemispheric Resource Center Website, September 30. Available at www.americaspolicy.org/commentary/2004/0409lula_body.html (accessed March 23, 2004).

Schott, J. 1997. "The Free Trade Area of the Americas: U.S. Interests and Objectives." Testimony before the Subcommittee on Trade, Committee on Ways and Means, United States House of Representatives, Washington, D.C., July 22. Available at www.iie.com/publications/papers/schott0797-1.htm (accessed March 31, 2005).

Schuurman, Frans. 1993. *Beyond the Impasse: New Directions in Development Theory.* London: Zed Books.

Scott, M. 2004. "Venezuela: Referendum Resolves Leadership Crisis, but Fails to Reconcile the Country's Polarized Society." *Spectrezine* (August). Available at www.spectrezine.org/LatinAmerica/Chavez.htm (accessed March 23, 2005).

Shultz, J. 2005. "The Politics of Water in Bolivia." *The Nation*, January 28. Available at www.globalpolicy.org/socecon/gpg/2005/0128bolivia.htm (accessed April 3, 2005).

Sinclair, S., and K. Traynor. 2005. "Divide and Conquer: The FTAA, U.S. Trade Strategy and Public Services in the Americas." Report for Public Services International, November. Bilaterals.org Website. Available at www.bilaterals.org/article.php3?id_article=1211 (accessed April 3, 2005).

Smith, R. 2004. "Venezuela's Geopolitical Chess." Venezuelanalysis.com, July 12. Available at www.venezuelanalysis.com/articles.php?artno=1215 (accessed April 4, 2005).

Stiglitz, Joseph. 2002. *Globalization and Its Discontents.* New York: W. W. Norton.

Unger, R. 2000. "Introduction." In *The Second Way: The Present and Future of Brazil,* trans. Cícero Freitas. Available at www.robertounger.com/secondway.htm (accessed March 21, 2005).

Vanden, Harry. 2005. "Globalization in a Time of Neoliberalism: Politicized Social Movements and the Latin American Response." In *Globalization and Development in Latin America,* ed. Richard Harris, 216–41. Oshawa, Canada: de Sitter Publications.

Vilas, Carlos. 1996. "Neoliberal Social Policy: Managing Poverty (Somehow)." *NA-CLA Report n the Americas* 29, no. 6: 16–25.

Wagner, S. 2005. "Venezuela and China Sign 19 Cooperation Agreements." Venezuelanalysis.com, January 31. Available at www.venezuelanalysis.com/news.php?newsno=1487 (accessed April 3, 2005).

Wallerstein, Immanuel. 1997. *The Modern World System: Capitalist Agriculture and the Origins of the European World Economy in the Sixteenth Century*. New York: Academic Press.

Williamson, John. 1993. "Development and the 'Washington Consensus.'" *World Development* 21:1239–1336.

Xinhua Online. 2007. "Ecuador's New President Promises Economic Revolution." January 16. Available at www.chinaview.cn (accessed January 20, 2007).

Zibechi, R. 2004. "Common Market of the South and Integration, an Endless Obstacle Race." Agencia Latinoamericana de Información y Análisis–Dos (ALIA2), August. Available at www.alia2.net/article1727.html (accessed March 29, 2005).

Zoellick, R. 2002. "Trading in Freedom: The New Endeavor of the Americas." *Economic Perspectives: An Electronic Journal of the U.S. Department of State* 7, no. 3 (October). Available at http://usinfo.state.gov/journals/ites/1002/ijee/toc.htm (accessed April 4 2005).

———. 2004. "Statement of Robert B. Zoellick, U.S. Trade Representative before the Committee on Agriculture of the United States House of Representatives, April 28, 2004." Available at www.ustr.gov/assets/Document_Library/USTR_Testimony/2004/asset_upload_file926_4323.pdf (accessed October 1, 2007).

Index

agriculture: capitalist, 36;
    commercialization of, 17, 35, 276;
    contribution to GDP, 25; and
    exports, 25, 33; and globalization,
    26–30; industrialization of, 276;
    and industry, 25, 68;
    internationalization of, 36; joint
    ventures in, 308; labor productivity
    in, 25; in Latin American
    economies, 257; modernization of,
    25, 200, 262; peasant, 27, 33, 37,
    40; subsistence, 50; subsidies to,
    306; technology in, 258; of U.S.,
    303–4; wage labor in, 37; women
    in, 35. *See also* agrarian reform
agrarian reform: and Alliance for
    Progress, 30–31; and agrarian
    capitalism, 31; implementation of,
    24, 31; and *latifundia*, 31, 258; and
    modernization of *haciendas*, 31; and
    neoliberal policies, 32; peasant-led,
    33; pre-agrarian reform period, 40;
    radical agrarian reforms, 31;
    unfulfilled expectations for, 30–40;
    willing seller/willing buyer reforms,
    33
Aguaruna Huambisa Council, 215
Alborada del Plata, La, 178

Alianza Naciónal Feminista, 185
Allende, Salvador, 86, 215
Alliance for Progress, 7, 30, 127, 186
Almond, Gabriel A., 166
amaranth, 202
Amazon. *See* Amazonia
Amazonia: Amazonian Treaty
    Cooperation, 215–16; Coordinating
    Body of Indigenous Peoples'
    Organizations of the Amazon Basin
    (Coordinadora de las
    Organizaciones Indígenas de la
    Cuenca Amazónica, or COICA),
    215–16; frontier colonization, 27;
    Indian sovereignty in, 214–16;
    indigenous peoples in, 210–11,
    214–17, 219; Chico Mendez, 209;
    the Pan-Amazon Social Forum, 20;
    rubber tappers' union, 209
Americas: economic, social and
    political conditions in, 12–13,
    16–22, 51–55, 118–25, 132–36,
    139–47, 164, 177, 196, 245,
    273–74, 276–88, 298, 309; and
    globalization, 9, 143, 273, 311, 313;
    history of, 5–7, 11–13, 67, 153,
    176–77, 186, 197–98, 202–3, 206,
    212–14, 273; integration of,

About the Contributors

Guido Pascual Galafassi teaches courses on social change and social mobilization processes at the Universidad de Buenos Aires and social theory at the Universidad Nacional de Quilmes. He also works as a researcher at the National Council of Scientific and Technical Research in Argentina. He graduated with a degree in ecology from the Universidad Nacional de La Plata, did postgraduate studies in development at the Universitat de Barcelona, and has a PhD in Anthropology from the Universidad de Buenos Aires. He is the executive editor of *Revista THEOMAI*, published by the Red de Estudios sobre Sociedad, Naturaleza y Desarrollo (The Society, Nature and Development Studies Network). He is also a member of the International Advisory Board of the *International Journal of Inclusive Democracy* (London) and the *Boletín de Educación Superior* (UNAM, México). He has conducted research and published articles and books on ecological issues and social mobilization in Latin America as well as on social theory. He is currently engaged in the critical analysis of Argentina's economic and socioecological development and rural mobilization in Argentina.

Richard L. Harris holds a joint appointment as professor of global studies and world languages and cultures at California State University, Monterey Bay. He has a Ph.D. in Political Science and a Masters of Public Administration from the University of California, Los Angeles, and he has taught, carried out research, and directed programs at various universities in the United States, Latin America, and Africa. Professor Harris is the editor of the *Journal of Developing Societies* and has been one of the coordinating editors of the well-known journal *Latin American Perspectives* since 1977. He has published books, monographs and journal articles on globalization, Latin

American politics, African politics, democracy, revolutionary change, so-
cialism, comparative public administration, and organizational development. Included among his publications are: *Death of a Revolutionary: Che
Guevara's Last Mission* (third edition, 2007); *Globalization and Development in
Latin America* (2005); *Globalization and Post-Apartheid South Africa* (2005);
Globalization and Health (2004); *Media, Identity and the Public Sphere in Post-
Apartheid South Africa* (2003); *Critical Perspectives on Globalization and Neoliberalism in the Developing* Countries (2000); *Capital, Power and Inequality
in Latin America* (1995); *Marxism, Socialism and Democracy in Latin America*
(1992); and *Nicaragua: A Revolution Under Siege* (1986)

Judith Adler Hellman is professor of political and social science at York
University in Toronto. She is the author of *Mexico in Crisis, Mexican Lives,
Journeys Among Women: Feminism in Five Italian Cities,* and, most recently,
The World of Mexican Migrants: The Rock and the Hard Place (2008). She has
been editor of *The Canadian Journal of Latin American and Caribbean Studies*
and writes on immigration, peasant movements, feminism, and social
movements, among other topics.

Cristóbal Kay is professor of development studies and rural development
at the Institute of Social Studies in the Hague, The Netherlands. He is currently doing research on rural poverty in Latin America, principally in Bo-
livia, Honduras and Nicaragua. He also continues to reflect on the Latin
American theories of development, including structuralism and dependency. His most recently coedited books are *Disappearing Peasantries? Rural
Labour in Africa, Asia and Latin America* (2000); *Latin America Transformed:
Globalization and Modernity* (2004); *Land, Poverty and Livelihoods in an Era of
Globalization* (2007); and *Political Economy, Rural Transformation and the
Agrarian Question: Peasants and Globalization* (forthcoming). He is coeditor
of the *European Review of Latin American and Caribbean Studies* and the *Jour-
nal of Agrarian Change*.

Michael Kearney is professor of anthropology at the University of California, Riverside. His main current ethnographic research deals with migration
of indigenous peoples from Oaxaca, Mexico to the United States and the
formation of what he has designated as *transnational communities* that span
the U.S-Mexican border. Relevant recent publications are: *Changing Fields of
American Anthropology: From Local to Global* (selected works of Michael Kearney, including 4 original chapters , 2004); *Reconceptualizing the Peasantry:
Anthropology in Global Perspective* (1996); "La comunidad rural oaxaqueña y
la migración: más allá de las políticas agraria e indígena," *Cuadernos Agrar-
ios* (2000); "Fronteras Fragmentadas, Fronteras Reforzadas," in *Fronteras
Fragmentadas: Genero, Familia e Identitdades en la Migración al Norte*, edited

by Gail Mummert (1999); and "Neither Modern nor Traditional," in *Identities on the Move: Transnational Processes in North America and the Caribbean Basin*, edited by Liliana R. Goldin (1999).

Francesca Miller is the author of the prize-winning *Latin American Women and the Search for Social Justice* (1992) and coauthor of *Women, Culture and Politics in Latin America* (1990). Miller is an independent scholar and writer affiliated with the Department of History (Professor IV) at the University of California, Davis. She has served as consultant to the White House press corps and to First Lady Hillary Rodham Clinton. On March 18, 2006, Miller spoke on "One Hundred Years of Feminism and Internationalism" at a plenary session of the International Conference of the Latin American Studies Association in San Juan, Puerto Rico. In addition to her chapter, "Latin American Women and the Search for Social, Political and Economic Transformation," in the present volume, she has contributed a dozen articles to the forthcoming *Encyclopedia of Women in World History*, including "Mothers of the Plaza de Mayo," "Inter-American Commission of Women," "International League of Iberian and Spanish-American Women," "First Feminine Congress of the Pan-American League," and "Pan-American Conferences on Women." Miller is currently engaged in writing a trilogy that explores issues without borders through the lens of contemporary realist fiction in Costa Rica, Brazil and Cuba.

Jorge Nef (PhD) is professor and director of the Institute for the Study of Latin America and the Caribbean (ISLAC), University of South Florida, and president of the Canadian Association for the Study of International Development (CASID). His areas of interest are Latin America, development studies, human security and comparative public administration. He is the author of over one hundred journal articles and chapters in books, and has written or edited over a dozen books. His most recent are *Managing Development in a Global Context* (coauthored with O. P. Dwivedi and R. Khator, 2007), and *Inter American Relations in an an Era of Globalizations* (coedited with H. Vanden, 2007).

Viviana Patroni is associate professor in the Division of Social Science at York University. Between 2000 and 2007 she was the director of the Centre for Research on Latin America and the Caribbean, also at York. Her work has focused on the experience of development in Latin American, the changing nature of state-labor relations under neoliberalism, and the emergence of new forms of unionism in Argentina. Her most recent work includes an interest on the impact of Canadian investment in the Latin American mining sector. Her articles have appeared in *Capital and Class, Research in Political Economy, LABOUR*, and *Capital and Society,* among other journals, and she is one of the coeditors of *Community Rights and Corporate Responsibility: Canadian Mining and Oil Companies in Latin America* (2006). She is also the codirector of a Canadian-funded project of activities aimed at supporting the development of a Latin American network for human rights education and research.

Wilder Robles is a Peruvian scholar educated at the State University of Campinas (Brazil), Regent College (Canada), Ohio University (United States), and the University of Guelph (Canada). He is assistant professor in the Faculty of Human Ecology at the University of Manitoba, Canada. Dr. Robles is also the current conference chair for the Canadian Association for the Study of International Development (CASID). Dr. Robles's PhD dissertation was on "Peasant Mobilization, Land Reform, and Co-operative Formation in Brazil, 1984–2004." His research and teaching interests are community development, social movements, humanitarian aid, religion and politics, and environmental policy. He has published a number of articles in academic journals in both English and Spanish dealing with the above topics. His "Beyond the Politics of Protest: The Landless Rural Workers Movement of Brazil" in *Canadian Journal of Development Studies* was awarded The Kari Polanyi-Lewit Academic Prize at the CASID Conference held in Edmonton in May 2000. He is finishing a book on the Landless Rural Workers Movement (MST).

Stefano Varese is a Peruvian anthropologist with many years' experience in Peru's Amazonian region, Southeastern Mexico, Central America and the trans-border social and cultural space of Mexico and California. His publications include *Salt of the Mountain* (published in Spanish as *La sal de los cerros*, 1968, 1973, 2006; English edition 2002), *Indígenas y Educación en México* (México, 1983), *Proyectos Etnicos y Proyecto nacionales* (México, 1984), *Pueblos Indios, Soberanía y Globalismo* (ed., Quito, 1996), *La Ruta Mixteca* (co-ed., México, 2004) and *Witness to Sovereignty* (Copenhagen, 2006). Varese is professor in the Department of Native American Studies and director of the Indigenous Research Center of the Americas at the University of California, Davis.